FROM OMAHA TO THE SCHELDT

The Military Cross
Captain John Oldroyd Forfar M.B. (227049)
Royal Army Medical Corps

At Walcheren, on the afternoon of 2nd November, 1944, during the advance along the dunes S.E. of Zouteland, the leading troop of 47 (Royal Marine) Commando came under extremely heavy and sustained fire which killed 15 and wounded 21, including 3 officers. Amidst the bursting mortar bombs and whilst casualties were still being inflicted on those around him, Captain Forfar went forward to attend to the wounded. The troop commander could not be found and Captain Forfar went on another 50 yards in incessant mortar fire, where he found him grievously wounded. Whilst he was dressing his wounds, 5 Germans appeared over a sand dune 250 yards away and opened fire with a machine gun, killing one and wounding another of the stretcher party who had meanwhile crawled forward to join him. Captain Forfar with complete disregard for his personal safety coolly went on giving first aid and he, together with the wounded, were later withdrawn under cover of smoke.

Throughout the whole of the first 3 days of the battle for Walcheren, when 82 ranks were wounded, many of whom were recovered by this officer personally with the greatest heroism, the courage and devotion to duty of this officer were above praise.

FROM OMAHA
TO THE SCHELDT

The Story of 47 Royal Marine Commando

JOHN FORFAR

TUCKWELL PRESS

First published in Great Britain in 2001 by
Tuckwell Press
The Mill House
Phantassie
East Linton
East Lothian EH40 3DG
Scotland

Reprinted 2003

ISBN 1 86232 149 3

British Library Cataloguing-in-Publication Data
A catalogue record for this book is available
on request from the British Library

Typeset by Carnegie Publishing Ltd, Lancaster
Printed and bound by Bookcraft Ltd, Midsomer Norton

To my wife who, during these events,
so patiently and loyally waited, worried and wondered

Contents

Acknowledgements

A CONSPECTUS of even a small piece of military history relies heavily on the records made at the time. I am grateful to the senior officers of 47 Royal Marine Commando who, on the battlefields of Europe in 1944–45 wrote and issued the battle orders, the reports, the war diaries and the appreciations which determined and recorded so many of the Commando's actions.

Other important documentary sources have been the Public Record Office at Kew, the Royal Marine Museum (Commander W. G. Samways and Mr Ed Bartholemew), the Imperial War Museum, the Ministry of Defence (Messrs C. A. Rowsell and D. A. Belson), 'After the Battle' (Mr W. G. Ramsay, Memorial Caen Services des Archives (Mr Franck Marie), Éditions le Goubet (Mr Patrick Le Goubet), the Arromanches D-Day Museum (Col G. Legout), the Westkapelle Museum (Mr Piet Minderhoud), the Middelburg Public Library, and the Defense Intelligence Agency of the United States (Mr Robert P. Richardson). I am likewise grateful to the historians of the European campaigns of World War II who have enabled the Commando's actions to be set in the context of wider campaign strategies.

My grateful thanks are also due to those Frenchmen and Dutchmen whose personal accounts of their experiences as civilians in occupied Europe made it possible to appreciate the setting of oppression into which 47 RM Commando entered in June 1944; and the effect of liberation. In France these chroniclers included particularly (Sir) Phillipe de Bourgoing later Senator of France, those men in the Port-en-Bessin area particularly Mr Antoine Langlois and Mr Raymond Marie who were kindly identified, interviewed and interpreted by Mr Michel Deserable, and Mr Didier Beau. Likewise in Holland contemporary accounts were related by Mr Harry Schat, Mr Hans Tuynman and Mr J. A. Lantsheer.

Post-war, many civil organisations and individuals have contributed generously to an understanding of 47 RM Commando's role and to the preservation of the memory of its achievements. Among such organisations are the Municipal Councils of Port-en-Bessin (Dr Camille Huet, Mayor, with a unique association with 47 Cdo), Sannerville (Mr Lavalley and Mr Christian Pielot, Mayors), Middelburg (the Burgomasters), Groot Valkenisse (Burgomaster Mrs A. C. de Bruyn); the Foundation to Support the Liberators of Walcheren (Dr L. A. deWitte, President, and Mr Hollander, Secretary), the Dutch Maritime Heritage Foundation (Mr Frank Van Gelder, Chairman, and Mr J. J. van Weering, Secretary) which commissioned the Sterkenburg painting and the Peter J. Sterkenburg Maritime Paintings Foundation (Chairman, Mr Ton van der Werf) which allowed the Sterkenburg painting of the landing at Westkapelle to be used on the book jacket, Friends of the Allied War Graves – Waalwijk and Surrounding Districts (Mr Marius Heideveld), and the Royal College of Physicians of Edinburgh (Professor Anthony Busuttil, Dr Reg Passmore and Dr Wilfred Sircus).

Likewise, among individuals are Mr Yann de Chevigny who has done so much at Maison Chevigny and in Sallenelles to keep alive the memories associated with Sallenelles, Dr Thys van der Velden who has freely made available his studies of the German dispositions and fortifications on Walcheren and facilitated other aspects of the book's publication, Mr John Gibson who has allowed me to quote from the private unpublished accounts of 47 RM Commando's actions written by his brother Sergeant Donald Gibson, Mrs Rose Wood for allowing me to peruse the prisoner-of-war diaries of her late husband Marine George Wood, Mr Reg Quick, ex-41 RM Commando, for translating some of the important Dutch documents, Mr Peter Spear for the account of the social effects of the death in action of his father and Mr Frazer Sedcole for special advocacy. Others who have been most helpful in various ways include Mr Jacob van Winkelen of Serooskerke, Lt General Sir Robin Ross, Commandant General of the Royal Marines, Major Mark Bentinck of the RM Historical Records Office and Major General Pat Kay RM.

My wife has conscientiously and critically read the manuscript, Dr Diana Henderson, Research Director of the Scots at War Trust, has kindly commented on the text and Mr David Sneddon has fulfilled a similar role.

The Headquarters of the Royal Marines (Lt Col Andrew Noyes), the Shell Oil Company, Maurits van Kattendijke Stichting in Amsterdam (Dr W. L. Korthals Altes), Familiefonds Hurgronje in Walcheren (Mr Jonkheer Hugo Schorer), Unilever, the Oldham Trust, Mr Philip Livesey (ex-47 RM Commando), Mr Michael O'Connell and Mr Peter Terry (ex-47 RM Commando) have kindly assisted in meeting some of the costs.

The book has benefited greatly from the continuing contact through 47 Royal Marine Commando Association with those who served in the Commando. Not all can be identified individually but I would mention especially Captain Peter Winter (Chairman of the Association), Major 'Nelson' Vincent, Lieutenants John Bennett, Michael O'Brien and Gerry Brent; Sergeant Roy Mansfield; Corporals George Amos, Peter Terry and Eric Thornton; Marines Ted Battley, Roy Bryant, Arthur Delap, Norman Fussell, Ted Hartwell, 'Ginger' Liggins, John Wetjen and Fred Wildman. I also wish to thank Captain Dan Flunder of 48 RM Commando.

Finally my publisher Dr John Tuckwell of Tuckwell Press has made my metamorphosis from medical writing to military history a pleasure.

John Forfar

Prologue

A DISTINGUISHED JOURNALIST recently wrote that the Second World War produced 'the finest generation of Britons who ever lived'. It is very doubtful whether those of that wartime generation who still survive would make any such claim for themselves, but if such is one of the judgements of a later generation, it may not be inappropriate to add to the chronicles of that war-time generation the history of a small group of men, 47 Royal Marine Commando, numbering 420, among the 156,000 troops who landed on the Normandy shore on the morning of D-Day to engage over the next year in the hazardous occupation of war in the front line.

It recounts the actions, the deeds, the triumphs and the tribulations of that commando as it swept across Europe. The commando breached the defences of the Normandy coast on D-Day, marched 12 miles behind the enemy lines and captured Port-en-Bessin, the first port gained by the Allied armies; linked up with the American forces at Omaha; advanced to the Orne bridgehead, defending its north eastern tip, and raiding the enemy lines from it during the consolidation period; broke out from the bridgehead and fought its way northwards as the fleet-of-foot left wing of the Allied armies along nearly 200 miles of the coastal region of France to reach Dunkirk; took part in a successful assault on Hitler's 'Atlantic Wall' in a hazardous sea-borne attack on the heavily defended Dutch island of Walcheren at the mouth of the Scheldt with a view to freeing Antwerp – so necessary for the supply of the Allied forces; attacked a fanatically defended island on the Maas; and invested and finally accepted the surrender of the German forces on the island of Schouwen. General Miles Dempsey, British Second Army Commander, picked out 47 RM Commando's capture of Port-en-Bessin as one of the two D-Day actions which he considered especially outstanding, and General Dwight Eisenhower, Supreme Allied Commander, considered the capture of Walcheren one of the 'most gallant and aggressive actions of the war'.

Among the 420 original members and the 330 replacements required to maintain the commando's strength throughout the European campaign 112 made the supreme sacrifice and 322 were wounded.

The medical officer in such a unit was in a unique position to observe at first hand, and to appreciate, battle actions in the frontline in all their starkness, and was the privileged witness of the deeds, the achievements, the sacrifices, the motivation, the personal qualities and the thoughts of the men who undertook such duties, stressful both to body and mind, as they faced danger and death. It does not appear that any historical account of a commando has been published by its medical officer

War creates an enormous concentration of dramatic events and deeds which cannot all be told, interpreted and analysed at once. It takes time before battle actions can be fitted into the wider stratagems which determined their occurrence; time before they can be related to other often dramatic events about which nothing was then known but which influenced their course and outcome; time before their military and human consequences can be fully appreciated. A longer timescale has also made it possible to obtain and include the experiences and emotions of some of those liberated by 47 RM Commando from hostile alien occupation and at times brutal repression. For many of these, liberation was the outstanding experience of their lives.

In purely military terms the battles in which 47 RM Commando engaged have their counterparts today. Conventional weapons may have become more sophisticated but, mostly, it is still the bullet, shrapnel from the exploding mortar bomb, the aerial bomb, the shell, the mine, the rifle, the gun, the armoured vehicle and the strafing aircraft with which the soldier in the field has to contend.

The importance of the Second World War has diminished little with the passage of time: what does diminish, however, is the number of those who can give first-hand accounts of it. Historical studies will doubtless continue for many years to come but their authors will not be of the generation which took part. That generation, as Sir Ludovic Kennedy has observed, is now 'in the departure lounge' and it won't be too long before the lounge is empty.

While the story of 47 Royal Marine Commando seems worth recording, it is hoped that its telling has also a wider relevance. The actions of the small group of men who served in it, the successes which they achieved and the hardships, stresses and emotional reactions which they endured are no more than a sample, a small sample, and a reminder, of what many thousands of frontline soldiers, and their counterparts in other Services, likewise achieved in enduring and succeeding all over the world during the Second World War. It is in this spirit that the story is told.

Illustrations and Maps

Illustrations

Maps

Chapter One

Soldiers and Sailors Too, But What Rôle?

Early Days

THE ROYAL MARINES, part of the Navy and the sea soldiers of the armed forces, have a long and chequered history. Prior to 1664 detachments of Army soldiers could serve in ships' companies but in that year a regiment of 1200 soldiers known as the Admiral's Regiment was raised, 'to be distributed into His Majesty's Fleets prepared for sea service'. In 1755, by an Order in Council, 5,000 Marines were raised, grouped into 50 companies each assigned to one of three Divisions named Chatham, Plymouth and Portsmouth, the ports on which the Divisions were based. The numerical strength of the Marines, perhaps more so than other parts of the armed forces, has always been related to the exigencies of war.

While the Marines' primary rôle was as seaborne foot soldiers, Marine Companies performing artillery duties were incorporated into the Marine Divisions in 1805. Prior to that artillery services in the Royal Navy had been provided by the Royal Artillery.

In 1802 George III designated the Marines 'Royal'. By 1827 the official motto was *Per Mare Per Terram*, the badge consisting of a laurel encircled globe indicating the worldwide service of the Marines and 'Gibraltar' commemorating one of their greatest achievements, the capture of that Rock in 1704. In 1855 the entire Marine Corps took the name of the Royal Marine Light Infantry (RMLI) but in 1859 the Royal Marine Artillery (RMA) was formed as a distinct Division, the former acquiring the designation 'Red Marines' and the latter 'Blue Marines'. In 1923 'Red' and 'Blue' Marines amalgamated to form a single Corps of Royal Marines. Despite this, however, the Corps of Royal Marines continued to subsume functional differences as between a preponderating military rôle as sea soldiers or amphibious infantry, and a proponderating naval rôle as naval gunners.

After 1918 the Royal Marine wartime battalions were disbanded and the Marines were deployed predominantly in detachments which manned certain designated battleship and cruiser gun turrets. The increasing size of warships now made it less likely that Marines on such would perform amphibious, landing and infantry rôles. The sea soldier rôle was greatly lessened.

Throughout the long history of the Royal Marines their medical officers, in the naval tradition, have been designated 'Surgeon'. The first Marine Surgeon was Simon Bonigni who paraded with the first muster of Marines in 1664. The life must have been too hard for him, however, as he resigned three months later. His successor, Simon Tatham, was of sterner stuff. He served for 25 years and would have served longer had the Corps not suffered one of its disbandments in 1689.

World War II: The Royal Marine Division – dormant, disillusioned and demoralised

In December 1939, following the outbreak of war, a Royal Marine Brigade, 1,500 men strong and consisting of four battalions (1st, 2nd, 3rd and 5th RM Battalions), was raised. True to RM tradition the remit of this Brigade included 'sea borne raiding'. In April 1941 another Brigade (including 7th, 8th, 9th and 10th RM Battalions) was formed. The two Brigades constituted the Royal Marine Division.

From 1940/1941 until 1943 the RM Division was part of Combined Operations and spent nearly three years training for such operations without engaging as such in any. While, aboard warships, the gunner RM detachments were involved in active operations all over the world, a large force of (sea soldier) Royal Marines trained for amphibious warfare seemed to be doomed to inaction, sidelined it seemed in every operation of the type for which it had been trained. The RM Division's 'proprietors' the Navy could not use it, the Army did not want it, and the Chiefs of Staff decreed what it could not do, rather than what it might do. Inevitably there was the frustration, boredom and loss of enthusiasm which prolonged denial of an active rôle brings to trained soldiers ready and waiting for battle. As the Division kicked its heels, one Royal Marine officer complained that the Marines seemed to be doing little more than carrying out fatigues for the Army, another that 'you don't keep a horse too long without giving it a race'.

Perhaps the problem lay with the seventy-year-old Director of Combined Operations, Admiral of the Fleet Sir Roger Keyes, who in 1918 had commanded the historic assault on Zeebrugge in which the Royal Marines had so distinguished themselves. While in charge of Combined Operations, to which he had been appointed in 1940, Keyes desired to mount a large-scale Zeebrugge-type operation in which the RM Division as such would be involved but had reached an impasse with the Chiefs of Staff who did not feel that his plans were feasible or that the substantial resources required for such an operation could be made available at that time. The RM Division was in an operational cul de sac.

The Metamorphosis

It was an Army officer, Lieutenant Colonel Dudley Clarke, who in the dark days of June 1940, when Britain's military fortunes were at their lowest ebb, conceived the idea of 'commandos'. Following the catastrophic reverses at Dunkirk the Army had lost most of its equipment and its morale had suffered. The nation was feeling threatened and defence against a possible German invasion was the preponderant priority. Impressed with the extent to which, in the South African War, Boer Commandos could tie up, harass and disrupt forces much larger than themselves, and well aware of the extent to which the German forces were stretched out along a coastline extending from North Norway to Southern France, Clarke put forward the idea that similar small bodies of determined, specially trained troops armed only with what they could carry should harry the enemy by coastal raids. Such amphibious attacks would keep the enemy guessing, would help to disrupt invasion preparations and raise British morale. Winston Churchill endorsed such a proposal and the idea of British Commandos was born.

Appropriately the Adjutant-General of the Royal Marines, Sir Alan Bourne, was put in charge of the proposed raiding operations (June 12, 1940). Here was the time when the Royal Marines should have assumed that responsibility. Seaborne raiding was part of their remit and their Adjutant-General was in charge; but not for long. Admiral Keyes took over a month later (July 17 1940) as Director of what was now called Combined Operations. Bourne, however, at Keyes' invitation, became Second-in-Command. With the planning of amphibious operations under the command of an Admiral who had such a close association with the Royal Marines and a Royal Marine Adjutant-General, no command situation could have been better designed for the Royal Marines. But it was not to the Marines that the planners turned for commandos but to the Army.

A number of reasons, apart from Keyes' desire for *divisional* operations, have been advanced for this – Clarke was an Army officer, a number of independent Army units were conveniently available, one of the RM Brigades was currently involved in the aborted Dakar expedition. It is difficult not to believe, however, that in the higher ranks of the Royal Marines themselves and among their Royal Navy masters there was irresolution, inflexibility, lack of vision and failure to appreciate how the amphibious sea-soldier troops under their command could best meet the challenges of the time.

Belatedly, it was the imminence of the Second Front more than anything else which concentrated the minds of those who controlled the destiny of the Royal Marines and resulted in more logical, dispassionate thinking about their deployment. The stultifying proprietorial considerations of the Royal Navy and the disregard of the Marines by the Army, which had dogged the RM Division for so long, were abandoned. The Army Commandos and the Marines themselves – in many of the commando-like operations in which small groups had participated throughout the world, although not designated as commandos – had shown what small, highly trained, mobile assault units could do. The training and ethos of such units made them suitable for many of the specific tasks which would arise in the seaborne assault on Fortress Europe. Their flexibility and minimal administrative 'tail' meant that they could be switched about more easily than larger units and cooperate with, and complement more effectively, the activities of the bigger Army battalions. They could, if necessary, serve under control of larger Army formations. From the Naval point of view the Second Front and the operations which would succeed it would demand large numbers of small assault landing craft, and what could be more appropriate than that the weaponry of these should be manned by Marines? As the RM Division died, the RM Commandos and the RM gunners manning flotillas of small assault craft arose, phoenix-like, from its ashes.

The first RM Commando, later called 40 RM Commando, which had originally been formed in February 1942 as a separate Naval Commando, was joined eight months later by 41 RM Commando – newly formed from 8th Battalion RM. These RM Commandos led assault landings in Sicily and Italy, acting within Army-linked, organisational arrangements. It took another 10 months before the conversion of the RM Division was complete, and in August 1943 the 1st, 2nd, 3rd, 5th, 9th and 10th RM Battalions became respectively the 42nd, 43rd, 44th, 45th, 46th and 47th RM Cdos. 48 RM Commando was formed later. After many frustrations and delays, the RM sea soldiers were returning to their true métier. At last they were going to be given the opportunity to serve their country in active warfare by engaging in what traditionally they had always done best.

Chapter Two

The Creation of a Commando

10th Battalion Royal Marines moved to the barracks in Dorchester on 1st August 1943 and on that day 47 Royal Marine Commando (47 RM Cdo) was born. Radical changes were necessary and started with the appointment of a new commanding officer, Lieut. Colonel C.F. Phillips who came with a formidable reputation as an efficient soldier and disciplinarian. One of his first acts was to address the unit, define the qualities of discipline, self-reliance, physical fitness and skill at arm which would be required and indicate the basis of enrolment. Training would become much more intense and purposeful, discipline more strict.

The personnel of the commando would in the first instance be drawn from 10th Battalion which was numerically considerably larger than the 420 men required for a commando. The principle was simple. Any who did not wish to serve could opt out; those who wished to join 47 RM Cdo had to be picked by their officers as suitable and be physically fit. As the training advanced, there would be a further weeding-out process of those who could not match up to the standard required and they would be posted to other units. Col Phillips' address had a dramatic effect: after months of vacillation, frustrations, dispiriting cancellations and endless exercises, there was a new sense of purpose and relevance: morale went up overnight. The 'Second Front' lay ahead and it was clear that 47 RM Cdo would be involved.

Commando fitness standards had been set down, and all those wishing to stay with the commando had to be re-examined to ensure that they met these standards. Minimum standards included height greater than 65 inches, weight greater than 120 lb, chest girth fully expanded at least 34 inches with a 2 in. range of movement, normal vision without spectacles, normal hearing and no organic disease. Finally there was a wonderful let-out clause, namely, 'a deficiency in physique can be compensated for by an over-abundance of spirit'. I employed this where expedient because I knew personally most of the men concerned and what they could do. Also, a troop officer would come along and say, 'You can't fail Marine –, he is one of the best in my troop'. My own knowledge and a troop officer's judgement proved excellent criteria. Given that they met the 'abundance of spirit' criterion, I passed some men with flat feet, vision which did not quite meet the minimum standard, below minimal height or weight and a number of minor disabilities which a more critical eye might have called 'significant'.

Only two of these sub-standard but spiritually (in the above sense) super-standard marines let me down; the others more than justified their inclusion. One of the two was the unit heavy-weight boxing champion. In a boxing match with a static local unit, most of whose members were such because of low medical gradings, our boxing champion was matched against an older, somewhat portly cook who shuffled into the ring in greasy gym shoes and rather grubby fat-stained shorts. The contest seemed likely to be a very one-sided affair which the spectating marines anticipated with ribald comments on the cook's prospects as he climbed through the ropes. The cook, however, proved to be a skilful and resourceful boxer with an excellent defensive jab and he managed to hold off the initial onslaughts of flailing heavyweight fists launched against him. As the shouts of our champion's backers cheered him on, he became frustrated at the irritating unwillingness of the cook to be knocked out. Sitting at the ringside as the attendant doctor, I became aware that our man was beginning to wheeze, and soon he was concentrating more on breathing than on fisticuffs. His wheeze became increasingly audible and his respiratory distress increasingly visible. Finally he could go on no longer and a rather tactful referee declared that he had 'retired hurt', which was certainly true in so far as his feelings were concerned. He had had an earlier undeclared history of asthma, and with the stigma of his defeat he gladly accepted a recommend-ation for a posting elsewhere.

A year earlier I had been seconded from a Royal Army Medical Corps field ambulance to the 10th Battalion Royal Marines, previously staffed like other RM battalions by a Naval doctor. The Naval doctors were being replaced because the field training of Army doctors made them more suitable for – and much more willing to accept – the rigours of an infantry lifestyle with its mud, its trenches, its long marches and its other physical demands. Now, with men I knew so well, I readily accepted the challenge of the even more rigorous Commando lifestyle.

Commando medical officers had to be examined by another doctor for their physical fitness and for this I had to report to the Special Service Brigade Headquarters. Knowing the commando vision standard, I dispensed with my spectacles for the occasion, being well versed in reading the lower lines of the eye-testing chart off by heart. On attending at the HQ I was somewhat alarmed to discover that my examiner was Lieut. Col John Kinnear, a fellow Scot whom I had twice met recently in my bespectacled mode. As I covered one eye and then the other and read down the chart without fault, he made no comment and duly declared me fit for commando service. I did not know whether my act had successfully deceived him or whether he was quietly condoning a deception which he recognised but was dealing with under the 'abundance of spirit' provision. I never had enough abundance of spirit to find out.

Indicative of the new realism, the 20 naval Sick Bay Attendants were replaced by one sergeant and eight lance-corporal Royal Army Medical Corps stretcher-bearers, all volunteers.

Fitness and Training

After the preliminary sorting out of personnel, training began in earnest. The tests which had to be met in full battle order were:

Endurance: March 25 miles
2 miles cross-country in 15 minutes: meet the shooting standard at the end of this
In a forced march cover 10 miles in 100 minutes
Crawl 100 yards in 3½ minutes

Strength: Carry a man of equal weight 200 yards in 75 seconds
Scale a 6 ft wall
Climb a rope: 18 ft vertically, 30 ft horizontally, 18 ft in descent

Agility: Sprint 75 yards with loaded rifle and then meet shooting standard
Vault a 4½ ft beam
Jump a ditch 8½ ft wide landing on both feet
Swimming: Swim 30 yds with rifle and boots
Swim 100 yds (fresh water), 200 yds (salt water), in clothing; remain afloat out of depth for 5 minutes

Speed marches (a certain distance had to be covered in a certain time), physical training, tactical exercises, cliff climbing, dashing round a home-made assault course, etc. took on a new intensity. In accordance with an instruction and guidance document entitled 'The Hardening of Commando Troops for Warfare', training the body to resist fatigue and exposure, correct marching styles, the correct wearing and care of boots and socks, different ways of carrying equipment, had all to be inculcated.

Castle Douglas

Next the commando moved to Scotland, to better training facilities in the Dumfries and Galloway area. Individual troops were located in Castle Douglas, Kirkcudbright, Dalbeattie, New Galloway and Gatehouse of Fleet. The commandos were billeted in private houses with a billeting allowance to enable them to do so – 6 shillings and 8 pence per day for a marine and double that for an officer (approx equivalent to £8.00 and £16.00

today). This billeting arrangement was peculiar to commandos and designed to create self-reliance and self-discipline. Living out of barracks, the commando soldier had to make his own arrangements for many things which barrack-based troops had done for them. He was personally responsible for being on parade at the place and time ordered – he might have to organise his own transport to achieve this; he had to ensure that his equipment was properly maintained and secure; living within a civilian setting, his conduct had to be such that he did not offend civilian sensitivities or break the civil law. Woe betide him if he failed in any of these responsibilities.

I found myself billeted in Castle Douglas with a delightful couple who had previously billeted two 'other ranks' from another commando. This time they had expressed a wish to have an officer. The house was expensively furnished and contained many valuable objects of which the owner was very proud and about which he was very knowledgeable. Shortly after arrival he asked me in a semi-jocular way if I picked locks, and in similar vein, although surprised by the question, I informed him that unfortunately the medical curriculum did not include such training. Later, when I got to know him better, I asked him why he had asked this strange question. He then revealed that his choice of an officer and his concern about lock-picking derived from the previous other-rank billetees. They had arrived one day, were shown their room, deposited their equipment and went out to explore Castle Douglas. They had hardly gone than he realised that he had not given them a key, so he decided to wait up until they returned. He waited and the hours passed. He was a man of regular habits, and as midnight came and went and the early hours of a new day arrived he decided that he could wait no longer and went to bed with his dressing gown hanging nearby for use when the knocks of the absent commandos signalled their return. Waking in the morning, he realised that there had been no knocks and concluded that the mysterious ways of commandos had apparently kept his two billetees out all night. With Scottish caution, however, he thought he should make sure. Opening their bedroom door, he found to his astonishment that they were both there, fast asleep. As the two sleepy figures gained consciousness, he enquired anxiously how they had gained entrance. 'We didn't want to bother you' was the reply, 'so we just picked the locks. It's all part of the commando training, you know'. The two proved entirely trustworthy but my host had never felt too comfortable at such skills coexisting with his valuable objets d'art and next time round expressed a preference for a non-lock-picking officer.

Achnacarry

As the training in the Galloway hills continued, there was always for all one threatening ordeal ahead, the battle which each man was going to have to wage with the course at the Commando Basic Training Centre at Achnacarry. Those who returned from it told tales, no doubt exaggerated in the telling, of a physical environment, physical demands and a harsh regimen which would strain even the fittest to the limit. All had to undergo and pass the course irrespective of rank.

When the Army commandos were set up, it was recognised that there would have to be a central training school which would set a standard of arduous training, and ensure that each commando met that standard. The Scottish Highlands were very suitable and an ideal location was found, one with ready access to all manner of training facilities, mountains, cliffs, rivers, lochs, wide open spaces with little or no habitation, and a castle – the ancestral home beside the River Arkaig of the Chief of Clan Cameron, Sir Donald Cameron of Lochiel, who was willing to vacate the castle 'for the duration'. So the Commando Basic Training Centre was established, its accolade as essential for an aspiring commando as a university qualification for an academic or a qualifying time for an athlete. All who hoped to wear the commando green beret had to pass the ordeal-by-physical-stress which the course represented.

The Commanding Officer of the Centre was Lieut. Colonel Charles Vaughan, a former Regimental Sergeant Major of the Coldstream Guards. His remit was to produce 'tough self-reliant men with initiative, guts, the will to fight and the will to win'. He controlled his Highland fiefdom with strict but fair discipline and was popular and respected. He ensured that trainees were tested to the limit. He treated colonels and privates alike with a possible bias towards the latter.

47 RM Cdo did its Achnacarry training during the month of December 1943. Setting off from Castle Douglas in the evening, it reached Spean Bridge at 4.30 a.m. after a slow journey punctuated with the stops and the periodic shuntings which were so often the pattern of war-time troop train travel. Spean Bridge station was dimly lit. On the platform were one or two khaki-clad figures in green berets who assumed a sinister significance when they identified themselves as course instructors. The unit was already under surveillance. The usual shouting and shuffling when troops form up seemed a rude disturbance of the peace of this quiet Highland village, but doubtless it was accustomed to these incursions into its privacy. Order achieved, nearly 400 officers and men in full equipment marched off across the bridge over the River Spean and into the outer darkness for the seven-mile march – conducted by the instructors at a fast rate – which

The Commando Training Centre during World War II. Achnacarry Castle, the ancestral
home of Cameron of Lochiel, Chief of Clan Cameron.

led to the Castle. As the commando entered the castle portals it passed a
number of mock graves, sardonic indicators erected by previous batches
of 'Achnacarrians' to indicate the possible outcome of the course.

On the course, officers (including the medical officer, relieved of all
medical duties) had to look after themselves and their equipment without
the services of their MOAs (marine officers' attendants or batmen) and
were treated in the same way as the other ranks except that they occupied
Nissen huts while the other ranks lived in tents pitched on frozen, snow-
covered ground. One stormy night many of the tents blew down. In the
morning the cold wet marines, ever ready to meet crisis with humour,
observed that that didn't make much difference as the tents leaked so badly
anyway.

Because of the darkness the first parade was at 0900 hours and the day's
work was scheduled to end at 1930 hours. All too often, when it seemed
that the day's work was over, a night march or a night landing exercise
on Loch Arkaig would be called.

All manner of schemes had been devised to achieve the aims of the
centre. The morning often began with 'log PT'. Each group of four officer
trainees, out on the parade ground on cold December mornings wearing
shorts and stripped to the waist, would be allocated a large tree trunk –
the caber principle of the Scottish Highland games applied – lying on the
ground. Once lifted, the weight of the tree trunk was such that it could

only be held for any length of time by clasping the hands beneath it and holding it against the uncovered body, a manoeuvre which was singularly uncomfortable with a frequently ice-covered log. If any one member of the team failed to pull his weight, the others often could not hold the heavy log and it fell to the ground, meriting a sharp reproof from the instructor and much cursing and mutual recrimination among the members of the team – team discipline was essential. Any dropping of the caber meant that all manoeuvres had to be performed again.

There was also the assault course with various obstructions which had to be climbed over, jumped off or waded through. On a particularly nasty stretch strands of barbed wire were stretched horizontally about a foot off a piece of boggy ground. To avoid being caught on or scratched by barbs the squirming panting trainee, as he wormed his way under the barbed wire, had to press himself into the ground. He invariably emerged at the other side covered from head to foot with cold wet muddy peat.

Crossing the River Arkaig by the catwalk consisted of pulling oneself along a single rope stretched tight 12 feet above the river by lying face down on the rope with one leg hooked back over it and the other hanging down to keep the centre of gravity below the rope. Heavy men were at a disadvantage here. It was more difficult for them to achieve a centre of gravity below the rope so that they were liable to rotate on the rope and fall into the icy waters of the River Arkaig – to the amusement of those standing dry on the other side who had already achieved the crossing and the alarm of the heavy men who had yet to cross.

Abseiling was practised from the roof of Achnacarry Castle and finally down a 100-foot cliff. At Achnacarry the CO of a commando was expected to do most things first. Col Phillips had no great head for heights, however, and did not relish the prospect of the 100-foot abseil. He asked me if I would follow him on this abseil, presumably on the premise that I would be available to deal with any injury he sustained. As he prepared to jump back over the edge he said, 'I hate this, doc' and proceeded to perform a perfect abseil.

Sometimes marksmen fired live ammunition close to troops practising a charge. There was also the 'death ride' which, despite its name, was one of the easier stunts. A rope was tied to a tree 40 feet from the ground on one side of the River Arkaig and led to the bottom of a tree on muddy ground on the other side. Steps of a sort led up to the 40-foot starting point. The 'rider' had to throw one end of a toggle rope over the sloping rope while holding on to the other end, catch the thrown loose end and, with the toggle rope now looped over the sloping rope, jump. The initial speed was alarmingly high and the slider felt that he must crash at speed into the tree at the end of the rope. However, as the bottom was reached the rope sagged so that the final few feet were horizontal or upward sloping, checking the speed. To escape impact with the tree the rider had to throw himself to the side, ending usually, as most things seemed to end in Achnacarry, in a mud bath. In the presence of so much mud, rain, bogs, river and snow at Achnacarry a state of cold and wet was the norm.

Living off the land was another skill which the course sought to impart. To avoid commandos going out and killing the nearest sheep, raiding hen houses, or 'fishing' by exploding slabs of gun cotton in a large pool close to the bridge over the River Spean, 'off the land' consisted of giving the trainee a chunk of uncooked meat, a few potatoes and a Heinz baked bean tin with a few holes punched in the bottom. So equipped, the embryo chef was despatched to the snow-covered hills. He was supposed to collect twigs and fill the tin with them, using the resultant Heinz 'cooking stove' to cook the meat and potatoes in his mess tin. Pre-warned and knowing that there were very few dry sticks in the whole of the west Highlands in December, there was a good deal of stick drying beforehand. From a culinary point of view the end result of this exercise was seldom satisfactory.

These and other short-term activities such as speed marches were interspersed with longer-term activities, mostly marches over the hills. One 30-mile march taking in a 3066-ft snow-covered peak was too much for one of our officers who collapsed near the top. The accompanying instructor foolishly gave him brandy which merely added inebriation to his exhaustion. Lieut O'Brien was detailed to help me get our semi-inebriated colleague down. Linking arms round his, we were able to frogmarch him down the hillside, glissading over suitable snowfields. After we had reached the bottom and marched him a mile or two, we were delighted to see a wisp of smoke rising from a bothy in the distance. Inside was an old gamekeeper making tea. It was no new thing for him to come across collapsed commandos. He was very solicitous, and the tea proved wonderfully restorative to the rescued and the rescuers. While I waited with the casualty, O'Brien walked ten miles back to base and returned with an army truck.

The course at Achnacarry set out to stress men to the limit, both physically and psychologically – one of the Sergeants, Sergeant Gibson, called it 'a ghastly month of privation'. Apart from the physical demands of individual exercises it was their continuity which added an important dimension. There was no let-up, morning till night seven days a week. Rest after a tiring exercise could be terminated with little warning and a call to further exertions. The psychological element consisted in seeking to engender a certain aura of fear regarding the hazards and possible risks surrounding various exercises (e.g. the 'death ride'). Whether official policy or not, casual remarks, almost certainly of doubtful veracity, would be made by instructors before some new exercise, such as 'Some were killed on this last time'. This overlay added to the background of concern – and was presumably meant to – in the mind of the trainee that he might fail the course, with the stigmatisation and loss of self-respect that that would cause. Only on Christmas day during December 1943 was there any respite, and as usual the marines showed their resilience of mind and undaunted attitude by producing an issue of '47', the commando's newsletter. It contained the usual ribaldries, and poetry such as:

> Oh Achnacarry, oh Achnacarry, what won't you do to me?
> You won't break my heart, you'll b—— soon see,
> With torture inflicted by weather and rain
> By Death Rides and mud baths designed to cause pain,
> They'll have no effect (on this side of heaven)
> On one on whose shoulders is sewn '47'.

At the end of the course Col Vaughan reported favourably on the commando's performance. As the final day ended, a column of tired but satisfied green beret 'graduates' marched out again from Achnacarry Castle into the winter darkness. With a white lantern at the front and a red one at the rear, the column took on something of a glowworm aspect as it wound its way across the floor of the Great Glen and over the Caledonian Canal until it reached the site where the Commando Monument now stands. There, as a final goodwill gesture the Depot Pipe Band was paraded to meet it and to accompany it to Spean Bridge station.

There is no doubt that Achnacarry achieved its main objective, the 'sorting out of the men from the boys' as its instructors so often put it. A man who passed the course would be likely to be able to sustain the stresses, the lack of sleep and the exhaustion which could occur in battle. It gave a sense of self-assurance and self-confidence to those who success-fully completed it. They had proved themselves at what was probably the most arduous training course in the British Army.

Less certain were the claims to improve physical fitness. The instructors declared that by the time a man had completed the course he was, and felt, 'fighting fit' in a way that he had not done before. In the euphoria at completing the course successfully, and anxious not to say anything that might be construed as weakness or complaint, many departing commandos doubtless said good bye in these terms to the instructors whom for a month they had tried to please. Questioned afterwards, however, many indicated that they felt exhausted and lacking in energy after the course and had taken some time to recover.

Surgeon Commander Murray-Levick was adviser to Combined Oper-ations on cold acclimatisation and physical fitness. He was a member of Captain Scott's final expedition, not, of course, with him on the last journey to the South Pole, but he had been a participant in an epic survival. In 1912, as part of Scott's Northern Party, Murray-Levick set out with five companions, on a six weeks expedition. Marooned on an Antarctic island because the ice-bound expedition ship the *Terra Nova* was unable to pick them up as planned, they survived an Antarctic winter, living for eight and a half months in a small ice cave which they hacked out of the ice. Their rations soon exhausted, they existed largely on seal meat and penguins, and finally, when the ice froze and they could escape, made a 200-mile sledge journey back to base.

Murray-Levick had a simple formula for cold acclimatisation – 'live constantly just off the shiver and you will get accustomed to lower and lower temperatures'. He knew all about the Achnacarry course and agreed that it tested will power and the ability to stand excessive physical demands, hardship and stress and was valuable from that point of view, but he did not agree that it was the right way to achieve physical fitness. He considered that continuous arduous training without adequate rest and with limited amounts of sleep checked the development of fitness and considered that if a well-trained fit man (most 'Achnacarrians' were such) lost weight as a result of further training, that training was being applied too acutely. Many 'Achnacarrians' did lose weight. Murray-Levick advised that the highest standards of physical fitness could only be achieved by the progressive increase in physical activity over a longer timescale than the duration of the Achnacarry course allowed, and with adequate rest.

Ardnamurchan

Achnacarry over, the commando returned to Castle Douglas at the beginning of January and later that month returned to the Scottish Highlands for 'battle inoculation' with live-firing landing exercises in the Kentra Bay area and field exercises on the Ardnamurchan peninsula. Leaving Glasgow in open LCTs (Landing Craft Tank), the commando ploughed its way northwards in heavy seas to Oban and thence to the various sites around Loch Sunart to which individual troops were dispersed.

The landing exercises were carried out in dhoris (small assault boats) with as much realism as possible. Machine guns rattled ominously, and as the boats moved in they seemed to be entering a hailstorm of bullets which smacked into the water around them with a characteristic 'ppttzz'. Landing involved jumping into the water near the shore edge and dashing up the beach where slabs of gun cotton hidden in the sand were exploded by remote control just in front of the would-be attackers, confusing them with noise and the sand which showered over them. At night tracer bullets provided visual proof that the 'enemy' was active. The tracers seemed as if they were coming straight at you but passed just overhead. It required will power not to duck and trust that the 'defenders' ashore had sighted their machine guns correctly as the point of light flashed past and disappeared into the dark void beyond. One night, during a field exercise using live grenades on a snow-covered moor near the western tip of Ardnamurchan, a marine suffered a penetrating wound of the chest. After a 15-mile journey along narrow, twisting snow-covered roads he had to be transported across the black waters of Loch Linnhe in the early hours of the morning in a rowing boat with an outboard motor, and admitted into Fort William Hospital.

The different troops of the commando lived in different villages, Acharacle, Salen, Glenborrodale and Roshven. The last was on the south side of Loch Sunart and cut off from road transport. Because of this dispersal on both sides of the loch the commando was given a diesel-engined supply boat manned by a merchant seaman boatswain and his mate, and this was used to visit the troops for sick parades. As the highest-ranking officer using the boat I was nominally in charge of it. The weather was good, the scenery was wonderful and the boatswain and his mate most agreeable companions.

The Second Front approaches

Early in 1944 there was confirmation that the commando would take part in the 'Second Front'. Large numbers of troops were being moved towards the south of England, and in March 47 RM Cdo was posted to Herne Bay. Apart from detachments for special exercises it remained there until almost the end of May. The special exercises included courses for selected troops at the Commando Mountain Warfare Training Centre at St Ives, a somewhat ambitious title for the Land's End area, but one which certainly justified itself in respect of the rock climbing which was its main purpose. Paying a brief visit for three days, the 'easy' climbs on which I was taken seemed to indicate that the instructors suffered from some sort of semantic disorder.

The main activity now, however, was rehearsal for the D-Day landings. The parent ship allocated to 47 RM Cdo for its landing was the erstwhile cross-Channel ferry the *Princess Josephine Charlotte*, and the commando trained aboard it. The LCAs (Landing Craft Assault) – holding 36 marines – in which the commando would cover the last few miles to the landing beach were stored on the deck to be lowered from the davits into the sea. Troops could be loaded into the LCAs at deck level before lowering but the usual way was to lower the LCAs empty into the water and for the marines to descend into them down scrambling nets. In calm seas this was easy, in rough seas not so, as, at the critical moment of the necessary jump, it was essential to synchronise the movement of a mobile scrambling net with the wayward heaving of the LCA.

Landing Craft Assault (LCA). (*RM Museum*)

Finally the day came when the commando moved off to its port of embarkation, Southampton. The training was now over, its worth was about to be tested. As the commando paraded in Herne Bay for the last time, it was evident, but hardly surprising, that despite security many of the good citizens of the town were aware of the significance of the parade. Those, mostly elderly, with whom the commandos had been billeted turned out in force, mixing solemnity with cheerfulness. An occasional wife was there and more frequently the girl friends whom many of the marines had acquired: some were clutching handkerchiefs, some were visibly weeping. As the commandos climbed into their transports and the latter moved out from the parade ground on to the road to Southampton, an old man standing by the roadside looked up and solemnly raised his hat. The die was now cast.

Chapter Three

The Shetland Bus

Months after its formation 47 RM Cdo was given its first active service task. It was asked to select a detachment for 'special duties'. Of the officers who volunteered, two were selected, Captain Isherwood and Lt Bennett, and they were asked to nominate their own men, 30 in number.

The title 'Timberforce' was given to the detachment as it would be serving in boats of wooden construction. The force set off on 4th October 1943 for Lerwick in the Shetlands. It was to operate with a flotilla of MTBs (motor torpedo boats) and a flotilla of MLs (motor launches) commanded by Commanders Gemmel and Russell respectively. Operations were under the overall command of the Admiral Commanding the Orkneys and Shetlands (ACOS) who was delighted to have this group of Marines joining his force and anxious to show what the Royal Navy and the Royal Marines could do together. The Navy freely admitted that, in any shooting which might be involved, the Marines were better shots than the naval marksmen.

The operational command of all the activities in which the marines were involved lay with the Navy: the marines were the sea soldiers of the ships involved. They were to accompany the MTBs to Norway, land there – part of the 'Shetland bus' service – and report shipping movements for the benefit of the RAF. Widely dispersed landings also meant that a relatively small force in the Shetlands was tying up German troops and German shipping in Norway. Alongside the British forces, under the command of a Norwegian Admiral, were a Norwegian MTB flotilla and the Norwegian Commando. Timberforce also carried a responsibility for the defence of the Shetland Islands in the event of any attempt by the Germans to disrupt the ship and submarine activities there – MTBs, MLs, Norwegian fishing vessels, midget submarines, visiting submarines and chariots. At times it was the only defence force. Chariots were small, torpedo-shaped vessels manned by two men who rode virtually astride it: the nose was full of high explosive and could be attached magnetically to the side of a ship, timed to explode, while the two men 'swam' away on the main body of the chariot. A year previously two of the chariots had taken part in an unsuccessful attempt to sink the German battleship *Tirpitz* as she lay in Trondheimsfjord. As the escaping charioteers sought to cross the Norwegian border into Sweden one of them, Able Seaman Evans, was wounded and captured. He was interrogated and then shot. The murder of Evans was one of the indictments which was laid against Field-Marshal Keitel at the Nuremberg trials. It was Keitel who promulgated and distributed Hitler's order regarding the execution of commandos.

The wooden MTBs were 30 feet long, powered by four large petrol engines and carried four torpedoes. They were not designed for the North Sea in midwinter, and as they crossed to Norway and patrolled around the Shetlands, their battles were as much against the sea as against the enemy. In addition to accompanying naval personnel in MTBs, members of Timberforce also sailed in MLs.

Shortly after Timberforce arrived, two of its members were in an MTB which crossed to Norway, landed and obtained the information sought. On the return journey the MTB was spotted by an enemy aircraft which swooped down and shot up the MTB. The two marines were wounded – one with a bullet in the chest – and the MTB's engines were damaged. 47 RM Cdo had suffered its first battle casualties.

One of the Bus Journeys

On 4th February 1944 Bennett and Marines Quinney and Tatton were in one of two MTBs, one British (No. 666 commanded by Lieut. Bullen) and one Norwegian, which set out for Norway. MTB 666 was to take a Norwegian pilot 'to see his family' – at least that was the explanation given - to take a second pilot across, and to pick up two Norwegians in plain clothes who would be located and identified by instructions given by the second pilot. On the way, the wind got up and, surprisingly, a radio message was received direct from the Norwegian MTB that it was turning back. The surprise was at the use of radio. The Norwegian boat had taken homing pigeons aboard so that it would not break radio silence at sea but communicate with the British MTB through pigeons to base, and base would radio back to the British MTB. It was not unknown for the Norwegians to eat pigeons, and it was wondered whether this had happened to the homing variety!

MTB 666 continued alone on its long, 250-mile crossing to a fiord north of Bergen. Twelve hours later it was entering the fiord. The night was beautifully clear and a bright moon shone on glistening snow-covered mountains. As the MTB moved up the fiord it met a fleet of Norwegian fishing boats, lit up like Christmas trees, trawling for herring. MTB 666 merely glided through them and found a suitable place to lie up. It had to trust the fishermen to keep the knowledge of the presence of a British MTB to themselves. Bennett and the two marines then went ashore to look out for movement of ships in the fiord and to pick up the spy passenger. The latter failed to appear or make any contact.

On the following day, in what daylight there was, the MTB went on a reconnaissance. It approached an island with a lighthouse on it as a possible objective for a raid but the German occupants did not fire as they were expected to do. It was concluded that rather than the hazard of putting up a fight, if attacked, they would prefer to surrender and spend the rest of the war in a good POW camp in Canada, and it was considered that it was not worth giving them that opportunity. They avoided not only capture but an enemy more implacable than those who had faced them – the sea.

As MTB 666 turned westward to head home, the winds were rising and it was not long before they had reached gale force. The sea was soon a veritable maelstrom. Horizontal sheets of freezing spume were being whipped off the crests of mountainous waves and voices were often blown away unheard in the blasts of the gale. The MTB bucked and reared as it sank low into a trough one minute and perched precariously on a crest the next. Battling through these conditions in the darkness of these northern latitudes, the MTB began to ship water and show signs of strain. The marine party aboard had to man the hand pumps: the mechanical pumps were out of action. One of the marines was so seasick that he could hardly move but had to rise to this emergency. First, one engine – 'there are still three'; then another – 'there are still two'; and then a third – 'we will have to try and last out on one', were swamped by water and ceased functioning. The single engine, coaxed by the naval engineer aboard, kept the boat going, but frustratingly slowly. Lacking forward momentum, the MTB seemed to be crashing up and down and skewing to right and left rather than moving forward. Long hours of darkness were interspersed by a few brief hours of gloomy daylight which revealed only an expanse of heaving water stretching out to a encircling horizon where sea and sky merged imperceptibly in a misty grey. MTB 666 was very much alone in a hostile sea.

Watched anxiously, the one engine still kept going. As sheets of water broke over the boat, the pumps were being worked furiously to keep the water level down. As brief daylight followed long dark night, anxious eyes peering ahead saw only watery gloom, and yet more watery gloom before night again descended. Three days passed. There were unvoiced fears as to whether the MTB was going to make it. Then, on the fourth day, it happened, quite suddenly as a weary crew peered into the penumbra of yet another day. Was that a low line breaking through the gloom? There were a few moments of indecision. Only the engine remained active as sailors and marines tensed to concentrate their gaze. A few minutes of indecision then a definitive answer – land it was.

Lt Bullen and the navigator Lt Wilson managed to find a sheltered inlet into which Wilson guided the MTB. Fortunately the inlet had a sandy bottom on to which the MTB settled. The water was now halfway up to the top of the messroom table. Using a small rubber dinghy, Bennett and Wilson managed to scramble ashore. They climbed a cliff and found a track with a telephone wire running along it. Choosing to follow the wire in a seaward direction, they found that it led them to a Nissen hut which, as they approached, revealed itself as an RAF outpost. Reaching it unchallenged, they had to wake up the sentry on guard duty! Confronted with two wet, bedraggled figures who had apparently emerged from the sea and were demanding to see the CO, currently abed, the sentry at first demurred at accepting any orders from them. Finally he complied and went off to wake his CO. In due course out came a querulous CO who, to his and to Bennett's astonishment, found that he and Bennett were old school friends. The trip was effectively over; the twelve-hour journey back had taken four days.

In the severe winter weather during Timberforce's five-month stay in the Shetlands the number of trips to Norway could only be very limited. The most ambitious trip which would have involved the 47 RM detachment was one in which it was thought that it might be possible for MTBs to attack the *Tirpitz* with torpedoes. The *Tirpitz* was said to be moving north through the fiords. A group of the marines under Capt. Isherwood was first ordered to Aberdeen. There, on further consideration the Navy decided that the operation was not feasible.

Timberforce rejoined the commando on 24th March. Next day the commando received a congratulatory message from ACOS on the work that it had done.

Chapter Four

The Battle for Port-en-Bessin –
and the Life-Blood of an Army

The Commanders Commend

In his book, *Corps Commander*,* General Sir Brian Horrocks described how when he arrived in Normandy to take command of XXX Corps of the British Army eight weeks after the Normandy invasion had begun, General Sir Miles Dempsey, the British Army Commander, in briefing him on the events of that day said, 'When all did so well it is rather invidious to pick out anyone for special mention, but the two outstanding examples of initiative and the value of tough individual training were on my right and left flanks, carried out by 47th Royal Marine Commando and the 6th Airborne Division respectively'. Emphasising the significance of 47 RM Cdo's operation, General Dempsey went on, 'the capture of Port-en-Bessin had been vital for two reasons: firstly it formed a junction point between the British right flank on Gold Beach and the American V Corps landing on Omaha; secondly it was essential as the main terminal of our petrol, petrol being the life blood of a modern mechanised army'.

When the full story was revealed and comprehended, how 47 RM Commando, outnumbered, outgunned and facing so many fearsome difficulties, reached and successfully assaulted and captured Port-en-Bessin, General Horrocks concluded, 'It is doubtful whether, in their long, distinguished history, the Marines have ever acheived anything finer'.

Sir Robert Bruce Lockhart,† historian and Director General of the British Political Warfare Executive during the war, described 47 RM Cdo's performance in the invasion of Europe as 'the most spectacular of all Commando exploits during the actual invasion'.

47 RM Cdo's D-Day objective was Port-en-Bessin, a small cliff-flanked port sited on the 15-mile stretch of rocky coastline, unsuitable for landing, between the right of the British Army landing on Gold Beach (near Asnelles), and the left of the American Army landing on Omaha Beach (near Colleville). The port was 12 miles from Gold Beach and three miles from Omaha Beach. 47 RM Cdo was to be the slender link, the junction point, between two vast armies, British and American.

* Horrocks, Sir Brian, *Corps Commander*. Sidgwick and Jackson, London, 1977.
† Bruce Lockhart, RH, *The Marines Were There*. Putnam, London, 1950.

21

The port represented a breach in a wall of limestone cliffs with the town in a hollow extending inwards from this. Seaward, there was a near-circular outer port 700 yards across. Leading inwards in a south-eastern direction from the outer port, and bisecting the town, were two in-line elongated inner basins with a combined length of 500 yards. The main part of the town lay to the west of these basins. The ends of the 200-foot coastal cliffs rising steeply on each side of the port comprised the Eastern and Western Features. At the base of the Western Feature, forming the rear of the harbour basin was a sea wall and a promenade with behind it a row of one- and two-storey stone houses. The streets of the town were narrow, and in its centre houses were crowded together. On each side of the port was open rolling country. The main landward entrance to the town was the Bayeux road running from the south through Escures from which a one and a half mile long road led to the port. This road, 13–15 feet wide, had a ditch on each side and bordering hedges in places. In 1944 the population of Port-en-Bessin was approximately 1,600.

The Eastern and Western Features were heavily fortified strongpoints with all-round fields of fire covering approaches to the port from the sea and the approaches to the two Features from the town. The nature and extent of the defences were partially understood from the intelligence gained before D-Day but only fully revealed after capture. The Eastern Feature had a flat top extending 400 yards from east to west and 200 yards from north to south. Within this area were an Oerlikon-type gun and another gun, two open emplacements with heavy machine guns, four light machine guns, two three-inch mortars, other smaller mortars, three concrete pill boxes and four deep dugouts 20–30 feet below the surface used for living quarters and stores. A continuous trench ran along the seaward side with mines in front of it. Facing the harbour and the town was a line of slit trenches, at 30–40 yard intervals, from which small arms fire could be delivered. Behind this line of slit trenches were a wire fence and a minefield. The defences commanded the harbour area.

The Western Feature consisted of an area 200 yards wide from east to west and 150 yards deep from north to south within which were eight concrete pillboxes or concrete defensive bunkers, light machine gun and mortar positions and a series of weapon pits and trenches associated with concrete shelters. These commanded the steep slope leading up from the harbour and the harbour itself. From the south and west the position was protected by a thick belt of barbed wire containing several rows of mines. The access road leading up from the harbour on the east side of the feature was blocked with barbed wire although the available intelligence before D-Day was that this road was open. Unknown before D-Day, there were also several seaward-facing fixed flamethrowers. The business end of the

Port-en-Bessin harbour with Western Feature beyond, and top of Eastern Feature and Round Tower in foreground.

Port-en-Bessin: seaward cliffs of Eastern Feature, difficult to assault.

latter consisted of a right-angled nozzle projecting almost imperceptibly from the ground, and anyone confronted with such who saw a sudden glow in front of him was warned to move quickly to the side as the glow was caused by the electric igniter in the mouth of the flamethrower nozzle.

It was also known that 600 yards south-west of the town on the western side of the Escures to Port-en-Bessin road, and commanding the road, were a series of weapon pits with machine-gun emplacements, trenches and concrete shelters protected by barbed wire. The Germans had obviously considered the possibility of an attack from the south along the Escures road.

Port-en-Bessin was defended by the German 352 Infantry Division, the formidable first-class infantry division which was to decimate the American landing at Omaha Beach nearby on D-Day and seemed at one stage to be on the point of driving the Americans back into the sea. This division covered the coast westward from Le Hamel to Omaha and Pointe du Hoc. 47 RM Cdo was the only British unit meeting this Division on D-Day. The rest of the British landing beaches eastward from le Hamel (Gold Beach) to Ouistreham (Sword Beach) were covered by the German 716 Infantry Division. There was also evidence that there was a significant concentration of German troops, including a sniper school, at Fosse Soucy three-quarters of a mile south of Escures and Point 72.

Life in Port-en-Bessin before the invasion had involved restrictions, demands and shortages. Fishing, the main industry, could only be carried out from small boats as the Germans had requisitioned the larger boats and removed them from the port. Such boats as there were could only go on a fishing trip with German permission and usually had a Kriegs-Marine (German sailor) aboard for surveillance. Evening curfews were often imposed when no local citizen could be out after a given hour. Compliance with these was ensured by German patrols which also ensured that no lights were visible with a shout of 'Licht das' and a powerful knock on doors or shutters if any light escaped. Local men had to work for the Todt Organisation in the construction of concrete bunkers and pillboxes or the repair of damaged railways, particularly around Bayeux. There were food shortages and German-imposed rationing.

The Resistance was active in Port-en-Bessin. Arthur Poiteven was the local music teacher and leader of the church choir and was one of the Resistance's most prominent members. As a resistance worker he had one great asset − if it could be called that − he was blind. He also had an important complementary asset, a retentive trained memory. Because of his blindness he was not suspect even if he was seen walking near the fortifications that were being built. He could have an apparently reliable − from the German point of view − innocent-looking guide with him. Didier

Beau, then aged fourteen, remembers walking with him along the harbour and then beyond to the coastal road to the west when the fortifications on the Western Feature were under construction. As they walked, Didier was constantly being plied with questions about the location, the size, the height and the nature of bunkers and other defences. Poiteven passed that information through the local Resistance to England. He was arrested by the Gestapo in 1943 and returned to Port-en-Bessin after the war a sick man, dying early in the 1950s. There were other local Resistance workers. Charles Hommet was arrested in 1942, and also Georges Thomine. Hommet's son René was arrested later and died in Germany. Madame Vauclin was ostensibly a keen knitter, knitting with a pattern book on her knee as she travelled by bus. The row and stitch numbers which she entered in her pattern book were in fact the distances between various defensive positions, buildings, road junctions, etc.

The German controlled French newspapers prior to D-Day were anxious to assure the French population, particularly those living in the coastal areas, that any invasion would be repelled. One of the regional papers read in the Normandy area described how at the time of the Dieppe raid, even although the building of the coastal fortifications was only at an early stage, the raid had been a complete failure. It also indicated that the Germans had learned from the mistakes made by the French in the construction of the Maginot Line and emphasised that the German fortifications would be proof against aerial bombing and impregnable to attack from the sea. Defensive positions in depth would wipe out parachutists dropped beyond the coastal fortifications. The estimate was that by the third day of an attempted invasion the invading force would have lost two-thirds of its strength.

It was recognised that 47 RM Cdo was being asked to undertake a formidable task. Colonel Phillips was given an option as to how to fulfil it – either attack Port-en-Bessin by frontal assault from the sea or land just behind the first troops to go ashore at the extreme western end (right) of the British front. Under the latter plan the commando would have to make its way inland and, moving surreptitiously behind the enemy coastal defences in a twelve-mile march, attack the port from the south (rear). With the experiences of the Dieppe raid in mind, where, attacking directly from the sea, 3367 of the 5000 Canadian troops who took part had been killed, wounded or taken prisoner, Col Phillips chose the latter plan.

For this operation 47 RM Cdo would operate under 231 Brigade (Infantry) of the 50th (Northumberland) Division. With splendid geographical abandon 231 Brigade consisted of the 1st Hampshire, the 1st Dorset and the 2nd Devon Regiments as its infantry regiments.

Embarkation and Cross-Channel Voyage

Prior to D-Day the commando was incarcerated for a week, for security reasons, in a marshalling area at Southampton. As it made its way towards the marshalling area on 25th May, the roads were filled with guns, tanks, armoured cars, strange amphibious six-wheeled vehicles called DUKWs ('ducks') and lorry after lorry, all moving towards the docks in a steady stream. One could not but wonder whether, seen by so many eyes, the evidence of such imminent military activity had not alerted those on the other side of the Channel?

During May the sun had shone and England was at its best, the fields and trees a luxuriant green, and the blossoms flamboyant and variegated. As the gates of the marshalling areas clanged shut along the south coast and the troops were sealed inside, it appeared that Nature had contrived to provide a Spring send-off of special splendour for the 156,000 Allied troops who on the appointed day would land on the beaches and fields of France. Sadly for many that splendid spring would be their last.

For a few days before embarkation those officers (including the medical officer) who, in strict secrecy, were allowed to know the details of the operational plan had the benefit of studying maps and a model of the relevant section of the French coast. Unheard-of places like le Hamel, Meuvaines, le Buhot, la Rosière, Escures and, of course, Port-en-Bessin excited intense curiosity and assumed ominous significance.

Nearby in the marshalling area the American allies who would be our neighbours on D-Day were in evidence and an American medical general visited us. An American Negro battalion caused great interest, and in military terms something of a cultural shock, as it marched up and down, each man smacking his thighs alternately for a few paces then clapping his hands once above his head while uttering a loud 'Hup', all done in an impressive and catching rhythm.

Of more serious interest was the issue to all members of the commando of a green octagonal fibre identity disc embossed with name, number and religion, and two round, similarly embossed, red fibre discs, all to hang on a string round the neck. There were those who, possibly as a sort of psychological defence mechanism, accepted these discs without question as a form of personal talisman; others enquired, 'Why three, and why two colours?', to which they received the answer, 'The green disc will remain with you if you are wounded and if you are killed will be buried with you for the purpose of later identification of your body; the red discs will be attached to your effects'. The realities of war were becoming clearer.

In a seaborne operation of this sort it was important that all weapons should be waterproofed, and condoms were one means of doing this. The

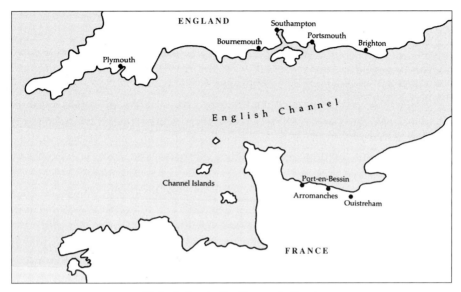

Embarkation to the Normandy Coast.

marines had to submit indents for the number they required: two enter-
preneurial marines in Y Troop submitted indents for two gross each!

There was also the issue of escaping or evading kits which included
magnetised buttons which could be used on uniforms and act as compasses
if cut off and suspended from a thread, or, for the same purpose, little
magnetised bars one centimetre long pointed at both ends which could be
sewn into the uniform. There were also maps of France on silken material
which could likewise be stitched into clothing. 'Liberation' franc notes were
issued to all. Brigadier Hargest, a New Zealander who had escaped from
a prison camp, gave 47 RM Cdo a final lecture on escaping – he was killed
just after visiting the commando shortly after the D-Day landing.

The nearest unit to 47 RM Cdo after it reached Port-en-Bessin was to
be the 16th Regimental Combat Team (RCT) of the 1st U. S. Division
landing on Omaha Beach. I was instructed to visit its Commanding Officer
who indicated to me the medical arrangements planned for Omaha and
said that he would give me any help he could, an offer which in due course
was generously fulfilled despite the difficulties which his own units were
having at Omaha.

Two days before embarking, a marine reported with florid measles.
Bearing in mind the congested accommodation in which the troops were
living, this raised the disturbing prospect that some of them might be
assailed at a particularly inappropriate time by a viral as well as a human
enemy. To avoid any alarm it appeared that the less said the better, and
one case of 'PUO' (pyrexia of unknown origin) to his grave disappointment

was discharged from the marshalling area. Over the next two weeks (the incubation period of measles) I was looking anxiously lest any marine should present with a temperature and a pink morbilliform rash. Fortunately, none did.

47 RM Cdo embarked on the afternoon of Friday 2nd June. That morning an order was issued that as the troops moved through the streets of Southampton they were on no account to comment to the bystanders, as some troops embarking earlier in the day had done, that 'This is it'. The bystanders were looking on with sober interest.

The home of Marine Scott of Q Troop was in Southampton and lay on the route from the marshalling area to the ship. From the back of a truck as he passed by he took a nostalgic last look at his home: it was his last. A few days later a telegram boy appeared there with the dreaded 'We regret to inform you——' telegram. He had been killed as his landing craft was struck by a shell as it closed in on the Normandy coast on the morning of 6th June.

At the last minute there was a redistribution of troops between the two ships on which the commando would sail. Most of the medical personnel were allocated, not to the cross-Channel ferry *Princess Josephine Charlotte*, manned by the Royal Navy, which they knew so well, but to an old and smaller tramp steamer, the *SS Victoria*, manned by merchant seamen. One half of the commando was to go to war under the white ensign, the other under the red. The troops were now 'sealed aboard'. Both ships had been converted to carry Landing Craft Assaults (LCAs), flat-bottomed, shallow-draft craft with a hinged ramp at the front carrying 36 men.

During 3rd June, aboard ship, junior officers and NCOs were issued with bogus maps which depicted the configuration of the beaches and coastal areas where they would land but not place names. Geographers were in demand for this guessing game. One member of the 'I' (intelligence) section showed his competence by making a confident and correct prediction. That evening the *Princess Josephine Charlotte* and the *SS Victoria* sailed out from Southampton docks and anchored in the Solent.

D-Day was to be 5th June but by Sunday the 4th of June the forecasters' gloomy prognostication of a deep depression moving eastward towards southern England were being fulfilled. Gale-force winds were buffeting the ship. Looking up from the watery deck of the *SS Victoria*, dark grey clouds were rushing past above the ship's rigging; looking down, the waters of the Solent were being whipped into angry turbulence. The *SS Victoria* was heaving up and down, swinging at its anchor like a chained animal. The LCAs hanging from the davits looked strangely small and impotent against the broad sea of white-crested waves against which even the big ships seemed to be struggling.

One outcome of this storm seemed inevitable, and so it proved. The biggest amphibious landing in history would have to be delayed, it was announced, for 24 hours. Some of the slower vessels were already underway; ships and men, like tensed-up athletes making a false start off the starting blocks, had to be called back. The ships which still lay at anchor in the Solent bobbed up and down restlessly: thousands of soldiers and sailors steeled up with expectation wondered whether nature was now to confuse and disrupt, even thwart, the months and years of planning, training and effort which they had faced to achieve an end to war, freedom from the threat of tyranny and a return to peace.

That night the troops slept uneasily below deck in a stuffy atmosphere, packed so close together in hammocks that with any movement of the ship one bumped into another. Sleep was a very limited commodity. Sea-sickness in that confined space was very disruptive. Although sleeping on the open deck was not permitted, some sought quiet nooks and crannies there.

Meanwhile the Allied warlords, in whose hands so much of the fate of these young men lay, were meeting at Southwick House near Portsmouth. Their chief 'guest' was the meteorologist Group Captain Stagg. He was leading them through the night with periodic commentaries on weather prospects. The required conditions of moon and tide meant that the landings had to take place on 5th, 6th or 7th of June or else would have to be postponed for a fortnight, an eventuality which could hardly bear contemplation. By the early hours of 5th June there appeared to be some prospect of a limited improvement in the weather. A crisis point had been reached: a decision would have to be taken despite continuing doubt and uncertainty. The airmen Air Chief Marshal Tedder and Air Marshal Leigh Mallory were counselling further postponement, the seaman Admiral Ramsay and the soldier General Montgomery were against further delay. The buck finally stopped at the Supreme Commander-in-Chief, General Dwight Eisenhower. He pondered for a while and then delivered his answer – 'Let's go'.

As Tuesday the 5th of June dawned, anxious eyes, yet unaware of this decision, peered out from the *SS Victoria*: the wind had abated somewhat and the sea was a little calmer. Painful indecision did not last much longer. Soon in sleeping quarters and mess decks, engine rooms and wardrooms the password to a noble adventure was echoing round hundreds of ships – 'It's on'.

As one looked out from the deck of the *SS Victoria* that morning, a strange, slow-moving craft with an enormous drum amidships was setting sail. It was one of the pipe-laying ships engaged in operation PLUTO (Pipe Line Under the Ocean) bound for the planned PLUTO terminal at Port-en-Bessin whose capture would be essential if the direct supply of petrol from England (Ventnor in the Isle of Wight) to the Normandy

Floating drum of 'PLUTO' pipeline ready for laying to Port-en-Bessin. (*Crown Copyright*)

bridgehead was to be achieved. As the commandos waved to it, they could only hope that the confidence of the pipe-laying ship's crew that the harbour at Port-en-Bessin would be in friendly hands by the time they got there would be justified.

Bogus maps were now replaced by operational maps and in any place with a flat surface officers gathered together with their men to translate the erstwhile mythical maps into reality. To the map-reading was then added the officers' interpretation of the military problems ahead and how they planned to meet and overcome them. There was quiet expectancy and relief that the waiting time was over.

The *SS Victoria* set sail in the evening. There was still a swell but the sea had quietened, and as the ship headed southwards through the Solent in the gathering dusk, only the droning of planes overhead and the swish of the ship's movement through the water disturbed the throb of its engines. Below deck the final briefing of the troops and a careful, somewhat anxious, re-examination of weapons and equipment was taking place. There was a great sense of relief and a certain amount of somewhat forced badinage, but there could have been few who did not feel some apprehension, a concern that their courage, their determination, their will would match up to what lay ahead. For those prone to sea-sickness, the heaving of the open sea after the storm was soon taking an increased toll, and for them the Navy's 'bags vomit' were a major preoccupation.

The merchant seamen crew of the *SS Victoria*, mostly older men including some who had survived torpedoing with loss of their ships, displayed a paternal concern for their passengers. Men who had survived for days in open boats at sea had a realistic appreciation of some of the stresses of war. Hardly noted for restrained language, their subdued conversation revealed the sombre realism with which they viewed the prospect facing the group of young men aboard.

Later, as the night wore on and a short period of June darkness preceded an early dawn, the guns of a nearby cruiser, the *Orion*, bombarding the French coast, began to boom out. After a fitful hour or two of disturbed sleep watching eyes from the *Princess Josephine Charlotte* and *SS Victoria* strained ahead: and soon it came in sight – the enemy coast, a low grey line eight miles away. It was 0500 hours.

The Landing

They hove to and waited. Soon the LCAs of the Hampshire Regiment, the first to go ashore in this sector, could be seen leaving their parent ships and heading for the coast, small flat ships, rising and falling in the swell, with only the heads of one or two who were standing for'ard showing above the gunwales. These were the men who would go ahead of us to meet the first fury of Rommel's Atlantic Wall. They were to touch down at 0725. 47 RM Cdo was to land behind them two hours later.

The British landing plan was that the first of the assault troops would land at low tide so that the beach obstacles, many mined, would be visible. It was recognised that as the tide rose many of these obstacles would be covered to a depth that would allow them to rip the bottom out of a craft passing over them, or worse still blow the craft out of the water where a mine was attached. The Germans, on the other hand, had assumed that a landing would be made at high tide so that the width of open beach raked with fire over which the landing troops would have to advance would be narrowed. Both plans had their merits and demerits

By 0730 hours the LCAs of the *SS Victoria* had been swung out on their davits. The loud-speaker system crackled and out came the order, 'To the landing craft'. The commandos, acutely aware that a historic moment had arrived, now went through their well-practised launching routine. Some of the LCAs were filled at deck level and lowered loaded into the water, some by the more usual route of a scrambling net descent down the ship's side into LCAs already lowered. The seamen showed great skill in lowering the LCAs into the troughs of waves – landing on the crest of a wave

LANDING PARTY

Above: LCA with RM landing party aboard.
Left: D-Day: LCA leaving parent ship. (*Crown Copyright*)

D-Day: RM Cdo landing beach near Les Roquettes. View from near Arromanches.

risked capsize. By 0800 hours six LCAs from the *SS Victoria* and eight from the *Princess Josephine Charlotte* were on their way.

The personnel manning the LCAs went about their business, the marines sat, crowded round the periphery of the LCA beneath the protective overhanging gunwales, or on benches amidships, seeing little and saying little. Despite the significance and drama of the occasion there were those whose prime attention was still not so much on the battle ahead as on the 'bags vomit', now particularly meaningful because of the nearness of the man in front. The officers stood, forward, scanning the sea and landscape ahead. Behind, an armada of larger ships stretched back to the horizon, and to the left a swathe of small ships was becoming increasingly visible – LCAs, LCTs (landing craft tank), minesweepers and destroyers. Like a symbolic lifeline to the parent ship, the wake of our LCA stretched back to the ever-diminishing outline of the *SS Victoria*.

As the light improved and the offshore distance shortened, the grey line of the French coast began to transform itself into individual green fields and white-painted houses. A shaft of sunshine focused on a cluster of houses and a church. Who were in them, what were they seeing and what were they thinking and planning? Far to the right, cliffs impregnable to frontal assault stretched away in the direction of Port-en-Bessin. There was as yet little sign of enemy activity. The engines of the LCA purred and the craft rose and fell in the considerable swell: the morning seemed strangely, ominously, peaceful.

The LCAs were now just over a mile from the shore and the scene was changing. Le Hamel and Arromanches were just ahead. An intense naval bombardment was now in progress. For many in 47 RM Cdo the first hostile shots of war were sounding from a battery on the high ground above le Hamel and the battery of 6-inch guns at Longues half-a-mile inland, both now ranging on the approaching assault craft. Spouts of water from ex-ploding shells began to dot the stretch of sea between the LCAs and the coast. Not without reason had Gold Beach with so much high ground just beyond its beaches been seen as a particularly difficult landing section.

First to be hit was an LCA carrying half of Q troop. While still far out from the shore it was suddenly seen to be listing and sinking, hit probably by a shell. Men were jumping into the water: others were not doing so. The Troop Commander Major Feacey and eleven others, including the troop medical orderly L/Cpl Chatfield, had been killed or drowned and fourteen including the adjutant were wounded – 26 out of the LCA's 36 occupants. Sergeant Donald Gibson remembered being in that LCA as it moved in but the next thing that he knew was that he was in a hospital 'somewhere in England'. In the meantime his parents received the ominous news that he was missing believed killed.

One of the guns of the Longues battery which bombarded the ships of the assault landing as they approached 'Gold Beach' and also delayed Lt Bennett's carriers with ammunition for 47 RM Cdo.

The wounded in such sinking LCAs were in a desperate situation. There were to be no rescues by incoming craft – to have stopped would have disrupted the timed landing schedules, made the incoming craft easier targets and obstructed the paths of following craft. Only craft returning to England after landing their occupants were to carry out rescues – and many of the ingoing craft were incapable of returning. The wounded, supported by their Mae Wests, had to float in cold water for one and a half hours, if they could, before anyone came to their aid.

As the remainder of the commando approached 'Jig Green' Beach west of le Hamel, that section of Gold Beach at the rightmost edge of the British front on which it was to land should already have been in the hands of the first wave of troops. The beach, however, was deserted except for two stranded motionless tanks, one with its gun forlornly depressed, the other ablaze. These were tanks of the Royal Marine Armoured Support Regiment. The Regiment had been hastily formed before D-Day and most of its tanks were out-of-date Centaurs. They were to land at H-hour and act as frontal artillery. The landing craft adapted to take them were very unstable: some capsized and others struck mines. Out of 10 tanks allocated to that section of beach, only five got ashore, and within 15 minutes all but one had been hit and knocked out by shell-fire from le Hamel. There were no troop landing craft on the beach. Because of the situation there, the heavy firing from le Hamel and Longues and the tidal current, the Hampshires had had to land well to the east of the beach on which they should have landed and were in process of doing this. The commando would have to follow them: its rôle was not to fight on the beaches but to move inland from a captured beach in as intact a formation as possible. A lateral eastward traverse of one and a half miles was therefore necessary although this would increase the length of the cross-country march to Port-en-Bessin and, more immediately, involve longer exposure to the enemy guns ashore and the danger of a traverse along the band of mine-tipped obstacles running parallel to the coast.

Next the LCA containing half of Y troop struck a mine and the front of the craft was blown off. As a cloud of spray engulfed it, and then settled, this LCA too was seen to be sinking and men were in the water. Eight in the LCA had been killed and others including the troop commander and also the troop medical orderly wounded. Among those in the water was Lt Peter Winter of Y troop. The first he knew of the sinking of his LCA was when, having been knocked unconscious by the blast, he became aware that he was in the water and that one of his sergeants was turning him on to his back from the face down position. He felt very cold, wet and disorientated. He began swimming towards the shore but found that he was making little progress, merely going round in circles. Close by, his sergeant rescuer was unaware of the real reason for this orbital progression, and Winter remembers him shouting to him prescriptively but even somewhat jocularly, 'You won't get very far that way, Sir, I should try something else if I were you'. The real reason that Winter was going round in circles was that the explosion had broken his right leg, his right arm and his nose. In a state of shock and hypothermia, he was unaware of these injuries but as he was propelling himself only with his left leg and his left arm he was constantly going to the right, in circles. He then remembered something about Hiawatha steering a straight course with one paddle and began to make some progress towards the beach. He cannot remember much more of his swim but in due course he found himself lying at the water's edge and began crawling up the beach. It resembled 'a scrap yard of twisted landing craft and broken tanks with many dead and wounded men lying on the sand'. At that point, to his astonishment, he became aware of someone standing beside him holding a white enamel mug and saying nonchalantly, 'I thought you might care for a cup of tea, Sir'. It was his MOA, Marine Woodgate, maintaining, whatever the circumstances, the morning 'gunfire' (cup of tea) with which back home an MOA so often greeted his officer. Woodgate had also been wounded, hit in the face: he too had swum ashore and staggered up the beach where he found his troop officer lying wounded. By means unknown to Winter he had obtained a cup of tea, the best Winter ever tasted.

Marine Burkinshaw of Y Troop recounts that as Winter lay on the beach, he tried to come to his assistance, but not being able to do much for him ran ahead to Winter's fellow troop officer Lt O'Brien who was leading the remainder of the troop off the beach. Using Winter's nickname he said, 'Frosty's down, Sir' but merely got the uncompromising reply, 'Well tell him to get up, there's a war on'. Winter's saddest memory is of lying on the beach wishing the surviving members of his troop 'Good luck' as they formed up and moved off to disappear behind some battered buildings to begin their long march to Port-en-Bessin.

As the remaining LCAs reached the end of their traverse, now opposite a beach on which a landing had clearly been effected, they turned shorewards. On the right another of the 47 RM Cdo LCAs blew up – there seemed to be mines everywhere. Our LCA then passed close to a sunken amphibious DD (duplex drive – 'Donald Duck' to the troops) tank the top of whose turret was just exposed in the trough of each passing wave. Clinging to the exhaust pipe (extended upwards as part of the 'waterproofing' of the tank) was a solitary soldier, still wearing his steel helmet and equipment, shouting for help. Each wave threatened to engulf him and sweep him off the tank. We passed him by. (DD tanks were kept afloat by an upturned canvas 'skirt' fixed around them to form a boat but, bearing a Sherman tank weighing 30 tons, the freeboard between the water and the boat's gunwale was narrow and the boat easily swamped – at nearby Omaha beach only five out of 32 'swimming' DD tanks reached the shore.)

We were now close to a group of incoming LCTs. Because so many of the DD tanks were sinking, the LCTs had been ordered to land them, not offshore, but on it. Ahead the landing beach was revealing itself as a congested jumble of landing craft, some lying beam to the shore obstructing access, disembarking troops, tanks and other vehicles. A naval rating in the prow of our LCA was getting ready to lower the landing ramp. For our LCA that much-desired beginning for all such operations, a dry landing, appeared in prospect. Soon, as we had so often done in training, but this time for real, we would dash through the gap created by lowering the ramp and jump on to the beach. But it was not to be. A hundred yards or so out another of the underwater mine-tipped tetrahedra (four iron bars standing on end but sloping inwards and tied near their top ends) which Rommel had planted as the outmost reach of his Western Wall for just such an eventuality took its toll. 47 RM Cdo was coming in at that critical point of the rising tide when many of the mines tied to obstacles were just below the surface and were catching the LCAs. Too late the dark shape below the water's surface was seen. The avoiding lurch to port was unavailing, the

D-Day: five mined
...edra (mid-distance) with
...ng tank beyond. (*Crown
...ight*)

Above: the flotsam of
war and a crowded
beach. (*Crown
Copyright*)

Left: beach full of men
and equipment and
under fire. (*Crown
Copyright*)

LCA jarred, emitting a low-pitched grinding noise as it scored along the obstruction and tipped to the left nose down, impaled on the tetrahedron. There was a short delay but the thought that the tetrahedron might not be mined was soon banished by an underwater explosion which blew off the stern of the LCA. The stricken remnant of the craft did a slow pirouette, seemed for some minutes that it might float, and then slipped below the surface. Again heavily laden troops were left struggling in the water out of their depth. Fortunately most were still wearing their Mae West lifebelts. In the rear of the craft Marine Kinloch, another of the medical orderly/stretcher bearers, and two others had been killed by the explosion of the mine. The strength of the medical orderly/stretcher bearers had been reduced by 30 per cent even before the commando got ashore. As our LCA sank to the bottom, yet another of our LCAs close by on the left struck a mine. The showering debris from that explosion added to the problems of the swimmers already in the water as it landed on them.

In the water, my concern, apart from survival, was to retain my rucksack of medical equipment. This was heavy but somewhat less than the 40-kilogram loads which so many of the marines carried. Much thought had gone into its contents – field dressings, morphia, simple surgical instruments such as artery forceps and scissors, sutures, antiseptics, Cramer wire splinting, medications for our own troops and for the French population whom we had been told we might have to treat. The rucksack, quickly unshouldered as the LCA foundered, did not immediately sink but floated, iceberg like, with the tip above the surface of the water. It seemed that I would manage to push it ashore as I swam. As I made slow progress to the shore, however, the rucksack became progressively waterlogged and sank lower and lower in the water. It was clear that this was to be a race against time. Breast stroke by an indifferent swimmer wearing a Mae West whose hands alternated between swimming movements and pushing a waterlogged rucksack, whose leg movements were hindered by army boots, whose rate of progress through the water was reduced by the wearing of battledress and webbing to which was attached a .45 handgun was hardly conducive to speedy swimming. The race was lost. Half way to the shore the amount of rucksack projecting from the water was barely breaking the surface and soon a trail of bubbles leading downwards in ever diminishing size marked the course of the rucksack and its contents to the sandy bottom.

At the same time another hazard became evident. The large incoming LCTs (Landing Craft Tank), while ominously visible to those in the water, were unlikely easily to see the bobbing heads of the latter. It appeared that they might overrun some of the swimmers but fortunately they passed just to the left. As they did so, bullets could be heard rattling against their starboard sides. Such logical deduction as was possible under the circumstances indicated that the bullets must be passing over our heads.

At last groping feet touched the bottom and at an individual level the D-Day landing had begun. Waterlogged figures were struggling through the last yards of water, past a row of 'hedgehog' beach obstacles (heavy metal crosses bundled together with their points aiming in all directions) and sloping mine-tipped tree trunks (one end on the sand, the other propped up by a vertical stake) and up the beach. The Normandy beaches were protected by a 400-yard wide band of obstacles of various types extending from the tide mark out to sea. Seen from seaward, the obstacles were only two to three yards apart.

We were near les Roquettes. It was 0920 hours. Five of the 14 LCAs which had set out had been lost in the run in, seven others had been damaged and only two were fit to return to the parent ships. Rommel's alleged statement that 'We'll only have one chance to stop the enemy and that's when he is in the water' didn't seem to be without substance at that moment.

Marine Wildman of Heavy Weapons troop was in one of the sunken LCAs. Unable to undo the buckle of some of his equipment in time, he had great difficulty in swimming and felt that he wasn't going to make it to the shore. He gasped and struggled and, after a while, to his immense relief reached a point where his feet were touching the bottom and he could struggle on to the beach. Looking back, he saw that the rear end of his LCA was still afloat, kept so by the watertight engine compartment. Perched on top of this was one of his friends, now revealed to be a non-swimmer (despite commando qualification instructions to the contrary). Someone found a rope and swam out to the remnant of the stricken craft and Wildman and his colleagues pulled it to the beach. The non-swimmer was the only man in that LCA to land dry!

Marine Greenough, after a long swim in which, carried by the tidal current, he strayed far off course, found himself two miles away among the 3rd Canadian Infantry Division. He had lost all his weapons but helped himself to a Lewis gun (a heavy unwieldy weapon from the First World War) which had been mounted on an LCA and had to be wrenched off. Thus armed, he set off for Port-en-Bessin on his own, too late to catch up with the departed commando. He lay up overnight with some army troops and fortunately, next day, met Lt Bennett in charge of the ammunition carriers and travelled with him to Port-en-Bessin. When asked why he didn't help himself to a lighter weapon than a Lewis gun from the many small arms available from soldiers lying dead on the beach, he replied that 'it would be like robbing the dead' and that 'in any case I rather like the Lewis gun'.

Corporal Terry, an Austrian serving in the British Army and attached to 47 RM Cdo, was one who stepped ashore dry amid the watery chaos of that morning. As his troop waited to establish its exact position, he noted that the tide had reached a row of dead bodies laid out on the beach and that they were bobbing up and down in the swell. Terry was wounded next day but returned to the commando from England three weeks later. In contrast to the first, this second, now peaceful, landing was far from dry. Transported on an American destroyer, he had to wade ashore up to his neck carrying his weapon and kitbag on his head.

My first casualty was at the water's edge, an injured and apparently drowned soldier pulled out of the water by my MOA, Marine (later Corporal) Pymm who had gone back into the sea to rescue him. In my six months' surgical house-officer post between qualifying in medicine and joining the Army I had fortunately agreed to lecture to a railwaymen's first-aid class and to enable me to do this had practised the Schafer method of artificial respiration then in vogue. I had never applied the Schafer method to an actual patient, and to my satisfaction the emergence of water and froth from the drowned soldier's mouth in response to the Schafer manoeuvre was followed by some movement of his apparently lifeless limbs. He began to cough and vomit and to make spontaneous respiratory movements. We carried him up the beach and handed him over to a beach party.

A month later I had the opportunity to return to our landing beach. The human dead had gone but there, washed up and silted with sand, was the shattered forward part of our landing craft identified by '*SS Victoria*' and its serial number. A few yards away lay the severed rear engine section. I felt as if attending a post mortem examination.

The depleted commando was now below the sea wall, but scattered along nearly a mile of beach rather than the 200 yards intended. Five officers, including the CO, and 71 other ranks were missing and some of the marines who had reached the shore had been wounded and had to be left at the Beach Dressing Station. The swimmers were cold and wet some bootless, even trouserless with a view to facilitating their swimming as, under orders as they neared the shore, they had discarded their Mae West's before their LCAs were sunk by mines or gunfire. An inflated Mae West is a restriction and encumbrance to a soldier wearing all his equipment and carrying a rifle who is trying to disembark quickly under fire through the narrow exit of a crowded landing craft: to the same soldier struggling in the water in boots, battledress and equipment the Mae West is a life saver. It was easy to misjudge the critical moment at which the order should be given for Mae Wests to be discarded, and inevitably some officers got it wrong. Some of the men who had been told to discard their Mae

Wests stripped off and removed their boots before setting out to swim to the shore.

Many of the marines had no weapons. Three of the four long-range wireless sets for communication with outside formations such as 231 Brigade had been lost and the remaining set was not working. The only 3-inch mortar rescued had lost its sight. Nearly all the Bangalore torpedoes (6 ft. long 2 in. diameter tubes filled with explosives which are placed under barbed wire or other obstructions with a view to blowing a gap in them) had been lost but Marine Hartwell, although in an LCA which was blown up and sank, managed to hang on to the Bangalore torpedo entrusted to him and struggled ashore with it. It was to prove a vitally important piece of equipment. Hartwell had lost his rifle but re-acquired one by taking it from a dead soldier. It was covered with blood which he cleaned off with a bunch of grass.

The packing of the emergency chocolate ration had proved unequal to the task of protecting it against immersion. The battledress pocket in front of the left thigh in which it was carried had become a sticky gluey mess extruding brown chocolate.

The beach, progressively narrowing and congested because of the in-coming tide, was a mass of ammunition boxes, all kinds of equipment, creaking vehicles, Bren gun carriers, clanking tanks, damaged landing craft, men shouting and churned-up sand. Gunfire, mortar bomb explosions and the rattle of machine guns provided a noisy background and periodically in the foreground demonstrated their reality, although it was often not clear where the fire was coming from or at whom it was aimed. The tide was washing up the material and human flotsam of war. Tanks were coming ashore and manoeuvring towards the beach exits. Nearby the crew of a Bren gun carrier were sitting calmly in their vehicle awaiting orders and listening on their wireless to the BBC announcing the opening of the Second Front – one wondered what families at home, particularly parents and wives, would be thinking. Shepherded by a solitary soldier, a few prisoners, their field-grey arms held high, were being hustled unceremoniously to the beach.

Rank and purpose were difficult to identify. A brigadier, lying on the sand beside the sea wall, was giving orders into his wireless set. Years later he was revealed to have been the commander of 231 Brigade, Sir Alexander Stanier, a distinguished soldier of noble birth who had served in the First World War. France erected a Memorial to him at Arromanches but when he first returned to France after the war he was not so honoured. Nostalgically he called at a chateau which he had occupied during the war. The maid who answered the door announced to her mistress, a French countess, that a brigadier wished to see her. The countess, assuming that

D-Day: dead soldiers, LCA and stern of Landing Craft Tank visible. (*Crown Copyright*)

AU GENERAL

Sir Alexander STANIER Bt

231e BRIGADE – 50e DIVISION

LIBERATEUR D'ARROMANCHES

LE 6 JUIN 1944

1899 – 1995

D-Day: the first German prisoners. (*Crown Copyright*)
Inset: Memorial to Sir Alexander Stanier – the 'Brigadier on the beach'.

'brigadier' meant corporal – as it does in the French Army – ordered that he be sent to the back door.

Apart from the few prisoners, the enemy's presence was largely unseen, but it was increasingly felt. Mortar bombs were now falling just short of the beach on to the road on the other side of the sea wall: a machine gun was firing along the road. In a field beyond was a warning sign displaying a skull and crossbones with 'Achtung Minen' below it. We had been told that many of these signs were bogus, designed to delay advancing troops, but the presence of two bloated cow carcasses just beyond the sign cast doubt on such an assumption. A flail tank promptly confirmed the doubt. As the tank, its rotating flails outrigged in front, rumbled landward across the field, one of its flails exploded an anti-tank mine. The chain flail was blown high in the air and landed nearby: the tank rumbled on. (It was not very long before the Germans 'rumbled' the flail tank and placed the anti-tank mine detonator a few yards in front of the mine so that the mine went off under the tank.) Troops were moving off along the road by the sea wall and were suffering casualties who were collecting at or being transported to a beach dressing station.

Slowly a motley collection of bedraggled marines assembled below the sea wall, under the command of the Second-in-Command, Major Donnell, as the CO was missing. Of the 76 missing, 28 had been killed or drowned and 21 wounded. The 27 uninjured marines missing at that stage had mostly been widely scattered at the landing but rejoined the commando by various means later. Some, landing without boots, made their way across country in makeshift footwear which they 'acquired' or constructed on the way. The training in individual responsibility was paying off.

Spirits were raised by two developments. The padre, the Reverend Reginald Haw, arrived looking very spruce. Chaffed at being one of the few to land dry, he explained that one baptism a day was enough for any chaplain and that as he had started the day with a baptism of fire there had been no need for him to engage in any further baptismal rites. He described his untroubled run-in. As he had no duties to perform, he sat low down in the LCA and could see nothing. As the boat moved in he heard all manner of crashes and bangs and felt reassured by this intensity of covering fire. His LCA passed clear through the coastal minefield and he stepped ashore dryshod and in the best of spirits to see, suddenly, so many sinking damaged craft, and men swimming in the water, and realised that most of the encouraging noise and explosions which he had heard were missiles coming in the opposite direction from what he had supposed.

Secondly, Lt Bennett arrived. He was in charge of four Bren carriers which for the Channel crossing had travelled in an LCT. The Bren carriers were carrying extra ammunition and weaponry. The LCTs had landed

The 12-mile march begins. D-Day: a flail tank explodes an anti-tank mine ... (*Crown Copyright*)

... and the result where flailing was 'rumbled'. (*Crown Copyright*)

D-Day: bloated cow carcasses in a minefield ... 'Achtung Minen' was genuine. (*Crown Copyright*)

Bennett east of the commando, and as he proceeded westward along the coastal road he suddenly espied some marines in green berets who proved to be members of 47 RM Cdo. Among them was Major Donnell, relieved to see the arrival of the carriers. While the commando would move on foot across country, the carriers would have to travel independently as, heavily laden, they could only travel on roads or cart tracks. The commando and its carriers then parted company. In view of the loss of so much weaponry and ammunition, Bennett's ability to join up with the commando would be critical.

The Approach March

Time was passing – it was just after noon – and with a long march ahead Major Donnell now decided that he could wait no longer for scattered remnants of the commando to appear. He led the commando off. Very little seemed to be going right. The planned commando rendezvous, which should already have been captured, was the church at le Hamel and the commando proceeded along the road leading to it. The road was being mortared and the ditches at the roadside which could have provided cover were found to be mined. The only evasive action against an approaching mortar bomb was to flatten ourselves on the roadway. At one point we passed a German officer sitting, lifelike, cap and all, outside a bunker. He was dead.

Marine Archie Daulby was a casualty there, wounded in the legs by multiple pieces of shrapnel from a mortar bomb. I removed some of the pieces there and then but not all, and as Archie, back in England, recovered it was decided that the remaining pieces were doing no harm and should be left. Archie died 54 years later and at his request, and with the permission of the Mayor, his ashes were scattered on the beach at Arromanches. Among them were the remaining pieces of shrapnel, and these were removed and presented to the D-Day Museum at Arromanches. The curator there told me that Archie, with a slightly macabre sense of humour, had wanted them to be given to the Museum, 'with compliments to 'doc' Forfar.'

As the commando sought to advance along the coastal road it was clear that le Hamel, on its planned route, was still in enemy hands and that the leading army troops were heavily involved in attempting to clear it. At this stage concealment, not confrontation with the enemy, was 47 RM Cdo's rôle, its orders being to reach Port-en-Bessin, twelve miles away, in as full fighting order as possible. Under continuing fire it therefore turned inland, moving through two coastal minefields behind some tanks and then a mile beyond, through the village of les Roquettes which had been captured by the 1st Dorsets. The commando was now on its own well behind the enemy front line and clear of the fire concentrated on the coastal belt.

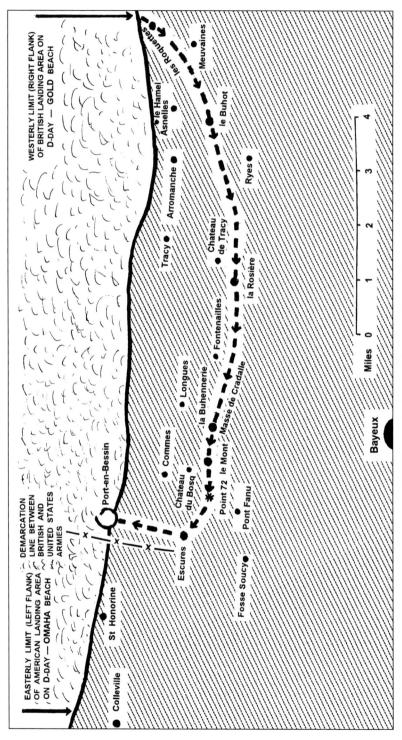

47 RM Commando Approach Route to Port-en-Bessin.

D-Day: alert by the roadside. (*Crown Copyright*)

There was quite a sense of peace exemplified by a man unconcernedly ploughing a field with two horses and apparently paying little attention to the historical events unfolding around him.

Proceeding as unobtrusively as possible, the commando reached the Meauvines–Buhot road. It had taken two hours to get clear of the le Hamel road and through the coastal minefields. Shortly thereafter, Colonel Phillips rejoined the commando. Having advanced towards le Hamel on the ammunition sledge behind an SP (self-propelled) gun, he had lost touch with the commando and had to find his way back again.

The early progress of the depleted force along side roads and farm tracks was encouraging. Moving in enemy-occupied territory is a strange experience. It engenders intense concentration and vigilance. Every tree or animal that moves, every fold in the ground or bend in the road, every copse or culvert, every shadow, every sound assumes significance. Early in the journey a shot rang out and Marine Lumsden fell, killed by a sniper, but the first direct encounter with the enemy was close to where the HQ medical section was moving with B Troop.

As the commando proceeded in file along a sunken road, three German soldiers, one carrying a sub-machine gun, the others rifles, appeared over the brow of a field sloping down to the road. The marines 'froze' and lined the road. The Germans walked on, weapons still slung, unaware of the danger ahead. The man carrying the machine gun suddenly sensed danger. He stopped and began to unsling his sub-machine gun. Several shots rang out and he fell, his sub-machine gun dropping with him. His companions, hopelessly exposed, promptly dropped their weapons and put their hands up. The seriously injured machine gunner staggered down to the road and collapsed at the roadside. He had been hit several times in the stomach. As I examined him he kept muttering 'Kaput, Kaput' and, apparently seeking sympathy, or possibly fearful of what his captors might do, fumblingly produced from his tunic his field pocket book showing me within it a photograph of his wife and two children. There was little I could do for him other that try to refute, without any inner conviction, his own fatalistic prognosis. Soon, the commando was on the move again. I looked back at a pathetic figure slouched at the roadside, alone and clutching the photograph of the wife and children he would probably never see again.

Our two prisoners had to be taken with us and one was offered to me for non-combatant duties. He was more than willing to oblige. It was surprising how many (light airborne) stretchers this frightened but surprisingly jolly man, relieved that he had escaped the fate of his companion, was anxious to carry and how ready the erstwhile bearers of these stretchers were to accommodate his enthusiasm!

At one point, a little further ahead, a German soldier, probably an officer, was seen riding a horse. He appeared to be approaching the column then turned away. Had he seen us? The risk that he had done so could not be ignored and his fate was sealed. A single shot rang out and he fell from the saddle. The horse stopped, apparently mystified by the unusual behaviour of its rider, hesitated, scraped its hoof several times on the ground, looked at the motionless form of its erstwhile master and turned aimlessly away.

Further along the road the column halted. A German jeep-like vehicle was approaching round a bend ahead. The vehicle suddenly slewed round at right angles to the road and stopped ... The driver jumped out, taking up position in a ditch at the roadside with a MG–34 machine gun. Cpl Terry ordered a marine with a rifle which could fire a 36 grenade to fire. Going forward, Terry found the German, a corporal, lying with 'a terrible wound in his groin' and gave him some morphia tablets. As the corporal lay dying, he was asking for his mother. He carried a pass enabling him to travel to his unit near Caen. On his way there he had seen the British troops ahead and had decided to face them alone rather than put his hands up and surrender.

As the column continued to move ahead, periodic bursts of firing meant that the leading troops had met with resistance. The most serious encounter was near la Rosière, less than halfway to Port-en-Bessin. The D-Day plan had been that the army, advancing from the coast, would already have captured la Rosière before 47 RM Cdo reached it and that the commando would be on its own beyond that. But la Rosière was still occupied by the enemy and had to be captured if the commando was to proceed. Under fire, 'A' troop shot up a machine-gun post on the flank and took prisoners but X Troop had to meet the main opposition. It came under accurate machine-gun fire. Quickly sizing up the position Captain Walton recognised that the commando would need to make speed to the port and that any delay would prejudice the chance of surprise. He led his troop straight into attack and quickly overcame the opposition. In this engagement L/Cpl Kendrick, the X Troop medical orderly, showed conspicuous courage in rescuing wounded under fire. As B then Q troops followed up, a German machine gun firing from the left-hand side of the road near the rear of the commando column caught Q troop as it crossed a gap in a hedge in single file. The RAP (Regimental Aid Post) group was just behind. Two corporals and six marines were wounded, two seriously. Seven of the wounded marines moved quickly out of the gap but one of them, Marine Fussell, lay where he had fallen. Examining him where he lay – with the uncomfortable feeling that some unseen marksman had you in his sights – it was obvious that he had been hit in the spine and that his legs were paralysed. There was no nearby accommodation and he had to be left with some of his wounded companions with instructions regarding handling. Fussell was later rescued by the 2nd Devonshire Regiment which, moving in from the coast at right angles to 47 RM Cdo's line of march, was now advancing towards la Rosière. Years later, Fussell remembered that he fell to the ground but felt no pain. He realised that he should lie still as he was still being shot at. He remembered his colleague Marine Barnard coming back to him and telling him that he too had been wounded, in the foot. Fussell's next recollection was finding himself aboard an LCT where someone was cutting his trousers off and causing him severe pain: his next was finding himself in hospital at Ascot.

About the same time, Cpl. Terry, from the rear of the column, saw some Germans running along a crest on the left of the road. One of them was screaming 'Lauft 'runter, das sind Indische Truppen' (Run down there, these are Indian troops). These were probably the same troops who fired on Fussell, and because some of the commandos had blackened faces, the Germans thought that they were Indians. None ran down.

In a column moving surreptitiously across country one sees little of one's companions except the few in front and the few behind. If troops sustain casualties, the troop medical orderly is likely to be on the scene. The 'doc' has to catch up with the wounded, alerted by a process of passing word along. His dilemma is that he must not lose touch with a column on the march yet has to spend time treating and trying to make some sort of arrangement for the care and evacuation of wounded. For such, field dressings and the nearest house, reached by stretcher if necessary, with the hope that the house was in French occupancy, were usually the best that could be done. Walking wounded, after being treated, had to make their own way back to the beachhead as best they could. Despite the risks that French civilians took in helping our troops the farmhouses or cottages approached invariably and readily admitted wounded marines. In these diversions which were necessary during the march the unplanned absence of a heavy pack did have its advantages – in a breathless catching up with the column.

In these encounters with the enemy a number of German weapons were captured which, in view of the commando's own depleted weaponry, were put to good use. The commando had been trained for such a contingency. The possession of German weapons also provided excellent auditory camouflage because the characteristic sound of the German Schmeisser or Spandau being fired by our own men created confusion in the minds of the enemy. The Spandau's rate of fire was more than twice that of its British counterpart, the Bren gun.

The commando halted at la Rosière. It was 1530 hours. Since leaving the beachhead, one marine had been killed by an unseen sniper and 11 wounded. Snipers were a problem, with officers as the main target. As anyone carrying a handgun rather than a rifle or Tommy gun was likely to identified as an officer, most of the officers were carrying rifles or Tommy guns – scant solace for the medical officer who was prevented from carrying such offensive weapons but carried an automatic handgun for self-defence.

The commando, now numbering 360 – a few stragglers had already caught up with it – regrouped and redeployed. Col Phillips held an 'O' (officer) group under a tree. The remainder of the commando lay quietly under hedges or in ditches, ever alert. The sun was going down, and in contrast to the recent rattle of automatic weapons birds were singing and the countryside was pleasant and peaceful. Twenty prisoners had been taken on the approach to and occupation of la Rosière. They, including our 'volunteer' stretcher bearer, were handed over to the forward elements of the 2nd Devonshires who had now reached la Rosière.

The commando moved off from la Rosière at 1945 hours, routed across country rather than roads to preserve concealment. The objective was Point 72 (Mont Cavalier), the highest point on an east-west ridge close to Escures and one and a half miles south of Port-en-Bessin.

Just after restarting, the commando encountered a German regimental

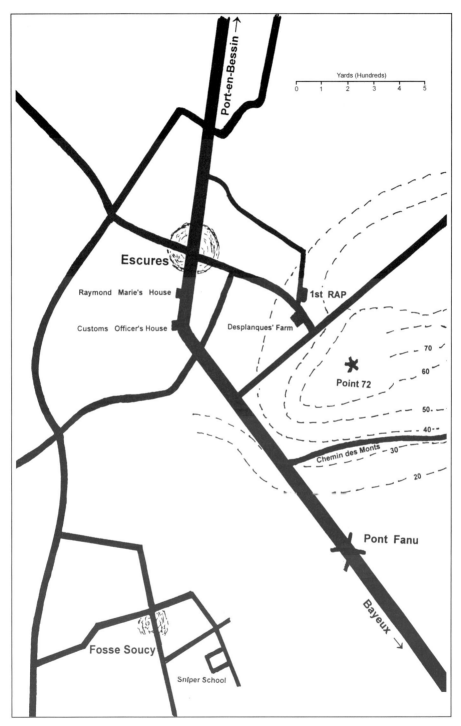

The Escures and Point 72 (Mont Cavalier) Areas.

sergeant-major cycling unarmed along a side road. He seemed strangely unconcerned at being captured, declaring in a tone of injured innocence that he was only on his way to see his girlfriend who was to be found in a brothel in Ouistreham (12 miles away). Closer questioning revealed that this was to be his final visit to his girlfriend and that he planned then to give himself up as he had had enough of war. Sadly, 47 RM Cdo deprived him of fulfilment of his first objective – but not his second. When Corporal Terry, who had captured and interrogated the German RSM, was wounded and evacuated next day to the beachhead, he saw again his erstwhile captive, now complaining bitterly, not about the interference with his sex life, but about such mundane matters as sanitary facilities and food.

The journey from la Rosière was over the Masse de Cradalle, across the road running south from Fontenailles, past la Buhennerie, then le Mont and into the Chemin des Montes leading to Point 72. During this part of the journey there were exchanges of shots on two occasions. On one of these the rear of the column under command of Lt O'Brien was fired on and responded: the enemy fire ceased, and on going forward to investigate O'Brien found two dead Germans. Such episodes tended to reveal the commando's position.

Much of this part of the journey was over fields, in single file, and by the time le Mont was reached it was almost dark. For most, darkness in these circumstances provides comforting cover although some feel darkness oppressive and dangerous and prefer daylight whatever the circumstances. The very limited vision in the dark does create navigational difficulties for a column moving in single file. Concentration on the silhouette and sound of the man in front becomes intense. If you lose him, you find yourself the inadvertent, probably ill-qualified, and almost certainly unappreciated leader of the remainder of the column.

Near to the commando's route to Point 72 was the Chateau du Bosq which was thought to be the German Signals HQ and was supposed to be linked by cable to the German HQ south of Caen. A small party under Sergeant Fuller and including Corporal Terry was detached to find the Chateau and cut or tap into the cable. The Chateau turned out to be mainly a camp for Spanish refugees who had escaped from the Spanish Civil War and were kept under guard by French Milice (militia). There was also a small signals unit there but the troops manning it had themselves cut the cable and fled along with the Milice.

The Point 72 ridge proved to be unoccupied although there were signs of considerable defence works in progress. The north-west-facing slope of the ridge led down to the village of Escures from which the main road ran north to Port-en-Bessin one and a half miles away. The troops, although tired, had to dig in along the ridge to provide defence and a base from

Château du Bosq.

which Port-en-Bessin would be attacked next day. They had little chance to rest and were allowed only two hours' sleep. At the base of Point 72 near Escures was a large concrete bunker. As Sergeant Mansfield approached it, two Germans in uniform, one an officer who proved to be a naval medical officer, and another who was an army medical officer, were standing outside the bunker door smoking. Turning round as Sergeant Mansfield approached, they were astonished to find themselves facing the muzzles of the Tommy guns of a group of British soldiers advancing from the landward side. Putting them under guard, Mansfield entered what he now recognised was a medical bunker. As he entered the dark interior of the bunker, he saw two soldiers in bed. One made a movement under the bedclothes. In a split second Mansfield had to decide whether or not the man was going to shoot and whether he should shoot him there and then before that happened. Instead he grabbed the bedclothes and pulled them off the bed. The man had not been trying to shoot. At considerable risk to himself a British sergeant had been unwilling to shoot a German who might be defenceless – hardly Hitler's depiction of a British commando. The German naval medical officer was in charge and with other personnel was incarcerated under guard in the rear section of the bunker as it was important that they should not escape to give away the commando's whereabouts. The RAP was established in the front section of the bunker. The naval medical officer revealed himself as an ardent Nazi. He objected to confinement in the rear of the bunker with 'other ranks', complaining that he was not being accorded the 'privileges of an officer'. He assured me – not without some justification, as it transpired – that there were strong German forces nearby (they were at Fosse Soucy half-a-mile away) and that shortly the position would be reversed and we would be the prisoners. The German army medical officer seemed much more amenable to instructions and expressed some dissatisfaction at being involved in a war at all. With a guard on the outer door I allowed him to continue treating the German wounded in the bunker. When Cpl. Terry interrogated the naval medical officer later that night, he found that he like Terry came from Vienna, and he was much more forthcoming. He gave Terry some information including the name of the German Naval Commander in the port. During what remained of the night a seriously wounded German soldier with a bullet wound of the abdomen was brought in but died shortly thereafter.

As the morning of 7th June broke on Point 72, 47 RM Cdo was getting ready to attack Port-en-Bessin. The marines had had little sleep. The medical bunker at the bottom of the hill had a strange early-morning call. The marines in one of the defensive trenches nearby were surprised to see a group of German soldiers being marched along unconcernedly towards the bunker under command of a German NCO. Apprehended without any resistance, but a bit astonished, they had not been aware that Point 72 and the Escures bunker had been captured and they were attending, as they thought, the German morning sick parade. Adding these 'patients' to those already incarcerated in the bunker, the German military doctor was deputed to see them – and get them fit for captivity. The RAP medical staff and the medical orderly/stretcher bearers in the individual troops had their hands full preparing for the day ahead.

The troops had breakfast as best they could. On the previous night Cpl. Terry, returning from the Chateau du Bosq, arrived at Point 72 in the dark, later than the main party. He found himself on such stony ground that the entrenching tool, one of the pieces of equipment with which the marines were draped, could make little impression. He had slept in the open. Walking down the hill in the early morning, he came upon an unoccupied dug-out and on entering it found a whole loaf of German dark bread, a sausage and a copy of a German newspaper reporting the fall of Rome (4th June). For him D+1 began in style with breakfast and the latest paper.

No counter-attack had occurred during the night although there had been some desultory shooting. Patrols had been sent out to attempt to locate enemy positions. The reserves of ammunition in the four Bren gun carriers under Lt Bennett had not yet arrived. Only the ammunition and weapons carried by the marines were available.

Col Phillips despatched the German naval medical officer with a speculative note – translated into German by Cpl. Terry – to the Port-en-Bessin Commander demanding the surrender of the port. The medical officer was not seen again nor was any answer to the note forthcoming, but the defenders in the port would now be fully on the alert.

Lack of adequate wireless communication was a serious drawback creating delay. The attack on Port-en-Bessin was to have been supported by American artillery but no contact with the Americans was possible and, in any case, the American units concerned were themselves in difficulty at Omaha beach just over two miles away. Later, at 1530 hours, an American LCT-based rocket-firing group offered support but this was declined in case it endangered the commandos. The Cdo's British FOO (Forward Observation Officer linking with the artillery) had been lost on the run-in on the previous day, and a replacement FOO from 147 Field Regiment of 231 Brigade in a hectic journey due to bomb craters had made his own way forward in a Bren carrier. Fortunately, by mid-morning the one remaining wireless set was repaired to the extent that contact could now be made with 231 Brigade which through its FOB (Forward Observation Bombardier linking with the Navy) could call for support from the cruiser HMS *Emerald* lying midway between Arromanches and Port-en-Bessin at a range of about 5000 yards.

At Point 72 two young Frenchmen appeared and eagerly joined the commando, providing valuable information about the defences of the port and the deployment of troops in and around it. As later events tragically proved, however, they were not fully informed of all the enemy dispositions.

Col Phillips held an 'O' group at 1350 hours. The axis of the attack would be along the Escures to Port-en-Bessin road. X, A, and B troops, which had lost fewest of their personnel and equipment on the landing, were to lead the attack with forward HQ behind them. X troop's first task was to assault the Weapon Pits to the left of the Escures to Port-en-Bessin road as it approached the port. A and B troops were to move through the town, clearing any opposition there, A attacking the Western feature and B the Eastern feature. These attacks were timed for 1600 hours. With the establishment of communication with 231 Brigade and the Navy it was arranged that prior to that the port would be bombarded from the sea by the cruiser HMS *Emerald*, followed by an attack by RAF rocket-firing Typhoons, then smoke laid down on the Eastern and Western Features by the 231 Brigade artillery. Q Troop, half of which had been lost in the landing, was to be held in reserve in the Escures area. Y Troop, also seriously depleted in the landing, was to be left to defend that area, deployed against a likely counter-attack from Fosse Soucy. Rear HQ was to remain on the Point 72 ridge with responsibility for its own defence. The RAP, currently in the Escures bunker, was to operate at the discretion of the medical officer.

'The Liberators are here!'

As 47 RM Cdo passed by, the local population were experiencing emotions ranging from fear and apprehension to euphoria. The 'memory of my life, a sea full of boats' is how Philippe de Bourgoing, then aged 22 and living in Tracy – close to la Rosière and the coast – feels even more than half a century after the day on 6th June 1944 when as 47 RM Cdo was approaching La Rosiére he jumped up on to the top of a wall beside a minefield close to the cliff edge by the sea a short distance away from la Rosière and looked seaward. Young Philippe was the son of the Mayor of Tracy whose home was the Chateau de Tracy about half-a-mile from la Rosière, and la Rosière was within the mayoralty.

Tracy, near the coast, was a 'forbidden zone' during the German occupation. Civilians were subject to restrictions and orders of all kinds. Requisitioning was rife – of houses, agricultural products, horses, cattle, foodstuffs, etc. As Mayor, Philippe's father had to be involved in the implementation of the German edicts including the organisation of the working parties which the Germans demanded. All fit men were compelled under threat of severe penalties to work for the Germans in tasks such as placing obstacles (Rommel's 'asparagus') on the beaches, cutting down trees to construct casemates, building defences – but in doing these tasks they sought to do as little as possible. In the afternoon they could do agricultural work on their own farms, which were very difficult to run because they were deprived of much of the agricultural equipment and materials they needed. Things like fertilisers, bicycle tyres and petrol were almost unobtainable. Travel was severely restricted, a special pass was needed to travel to other communes, and the road to Bayeux, the nearest large town, was barred with guarded gates. Despite wireless sets being confiscated, the French, listening secretly, found one of the most sustaining influences throughout the war was the BBC French broadcast, 'France speaks to France'.

One day an order came from the Prefecture that the identity of any Jews must be declared. Putting himself at considerable risk, Mayor de Bourgoing replied that there were none in his area; but he was well aware that there was a Jewish family in Tracy. He continued to provide this assurance, and the Jewish family remained in Tracy, unmolested throughout the occupation.

When the Germans arrived in 1940, the coastal villas were at first most

Château de Tracy. (*Courtesy Éditions le Goubey, Caen*)

popular, but early in 1944 as houses were sacrificed in the building of the Atlantic Wall, more and more of the villas were destroyed or damaged and houses further inland requisitioned. Part of the Chateau de Tracy was taken over as the artillery headquarters carrying responsibility for nine miles of coastline including the major battery at Longues which proved so active on D-Day. An officers' mess was established in the Chateau but the Bourgoings continued to live there. The German officers did not make too many demands.

In April 1944 an RAF plane was shot down over Tracy. The pilot, a Belgian, bailed out and landed by parachute, uninjured, in a field where Monsieur and Madame Henriette were working. Approaching the Henriettes, the pilot said, 'If you deliver me to the Germans I will be a prisoner, if you hide me you will be taking a great risk'. Without hesitation the Henriettes hid him. The Germans were doubtless aware that a pilot was being harboured somewhere and issued a decree warning inhabitants that if they did this they risked being shot. Because his father's health had deteriorated, Philippe had taken on some mayoral duties, including making a round of the houses to inform people about the decree. As he passed the house of the Henriettes, he was always conscious of their dangerous secret. In due course the Resistance was able to organise the pilot's escape and ultimate return to England. Later a message was received, 'Lulu has returned to England'.After the liberation the Henriettes were decorated by the French General Koenig.

On the morning of 5th June 1944 Philippe de Bourgoing was at work for the Germans when a liaison officer arrived and told him that there would have to be an alteration in the Frenchmen's working routine that day as there would be an afternoon open-air concert for the German soldiers at the Chateau. In due course the soldiers arrived and the concert was held with the soldiers sitting under the apple trees. In the evening it was the officers' turn, and they arrived from near and far. For them, dinner in the Chateau preceded the concert. As the officers enjoyed their meal, sipped their French wine, listened to the concert music, they were blissfully ignorant that an armada of ships loaded with British troops and every conceivable type of military equipment and gunnery was moving towards the Normandy coast less than a mile away from where they sat. Towards midnight, after their convivial evening, the officers departed. Indicative of the shortages which the Germans were experiencing at that time, many of them left the Chateau de Tracy on horseback: the HQ could muster only one motor car.

The party over, quiet had descended on the house when, little more than an hour later its peace was disrupted by a sudden outbreak of noise and commotion in the military quarters. Information had been received that there appeared to have been parachute landings at Pegasus Bridge 25 miles to the east and St. Mère Eglise 40 miles to the west. German soldiers were being despatched to the various gun positions round about. As the night advanced, aeroplanes flying high were dropping bombs; later, low-flying hedge-hopping aircraft began to make direct attacks on the German defensive positions. Towards 0700 hours the Commandant appeared and Philippe's sister heard him say, 'This is very serious, I have come to look for my maps'. That was the last that was heard or seen of the Commandant.

About the same time, because the bombing had been intense, Philippe decided to tour the village accompanied by M. Lamoureux, the local warden. No one had been killed or injured but the Allied bombing was still continuing and a cluster fell 800 yards away towards the Longues battery, which seemed to be the particular target of the bombers – 2,800 bombs had fallen on it during the night. (Yet until it was silenced late on 7th June as a result of combined aerial and naval bombardment, it remained very active and a serious threat to the invading forces.) Finally Philippe's tour of duty brought him to the coast. There he climbed on to the coastal wall to look out to sea. As he straightened up, he was utterly astonished at the sight which lay before him. No longer was there the expanse of rolling open sea to which he was accustomed; the sea was full of ships as far as the eye could see. He could hardly believe that after all these years, while he had dreamt of liberation, the liberation was actually taking place, virtually on his own doorstep and in front of his own eyes. As he watched, he was fascinated with what seemed to him an odd feature: 'They have even brought sailing boats', he said to himself – but he later discovered that the 'sailing boats' were DD (duplex drive) tanks 'swimming' ashore with their canvas skirting looking like some sort of sail.

Aware now of the dramatic event unfolding before him, Philippe returned to his house, announcing, 'It is the liberation, we have not long to wait'. He was joined by his neighbours M. and Mme Gibert and they waited. By midday they were still watching and waiting, looking out through the kitchen window. Suddenly a tank came down the road. Aware of their dispositions, Philippe knew that there were no German tanks in Tracy/la Rosière. 'It must be British', he said. Soon the identity was established as the tank, named 'Angela', and now seen to be heading a group of tanks, came nearer. Philippe went out to the road and stood in front of the tank. It was a DD tank which had landed at Asnelles and was making for various gun positions which were controlled from the German artillery HQ at Chateau de Tracy. Philippe was astonished that the tank commander had a map so accurate that the lawn of Chateau de Tracy was identified on it. Riding on the third tank in a very agitated state was a Pole who had been previously been forcibly enrolled in the Wehrmacht and employed at the Chateau HQ. He had sometimes listened to English radio and now he cried, 'Tell everybody that all goes well: I am a prisoner'. Following the tank came the foot soldiers, their faces blackened.

Meanwhile 47 RM Cdo was at la Rosière, a short distance ahead of, and moving at right angles to, the troops of the 2nd Battalion of the Devonshire Regiment who were making for Ryes. The Devons, having penetrated the front line, like 47 RM Cdo were encountering pockets of Germans putting up resistance from ditches and thickets. Following up behind the Devons, Philippe remembers the place where he saw several dead British soldiers. When he reached la Rosière cross-roads a further 400 yards ahead there were a number of wounded British soldiers at the house of Monsieur and Madame Camille. They may well have been those from 47 RM Cdo who had been wounded near la Rosière

In the public service tradition of his family Philippe de Bourgoing followed his father as Mayor of Tracy and at a national level became a distinguished Member of the French Senate. In the Senate he was President of the Group of Senators concerned with promoting friendship between France and Great Britain. When, in more recent years, he accompanied the French President, Monsieur Chirac, on a State Visit to Britain, Queen Elizabeth made Philippe de Bourgoing a Knight Commander of the British Empire in recognition of his services to Franco-British friendship and he returned to France as (Honorary) 'Sir Philippe de Bourgoing'.

At Escures

Further along the road towards Post-en-Bessin, in Escures, Raymond Marie lived with his parents and two sisters in a house 200 yards south of the Escures cross-roads on the road leading south to Pont Fanu. On 5th June Raymond's mother moved to the house of the Customs Officer, M. Germain, 300 yards along the road to the south because the Germain family had an air-raid shelter. The shelter was built to accommodate four but that night it had nine or ten occupants. Feeling that he had 'only enough floor space to stand on one foot', Raymond and young Edouard Germain decamped in the early hours (6th June) to a nearby farm. As they ran across a field, they heard a great deal of firing and bombs dropping: the battery at Longues seemed to be a particular target. Later in the morning they met people fleeing from the coastal area because of the bombing and were told that the 'landings had begun' and that 'English soldiers' had been seen. From the bend in the main road near Escures they could now see the invasion shipping out at sea, particularly the sausage-shaped barrage balloons flying above them. That day an RAF Spitfire made a crash landing nearby. The airman had apparently got out (was he the airman whom we later tried to rescue at Commes?)

Next day (7th June) Raymond and a few of his friends met Albert Blaie who earlier that day had visited the Point 72 area and claimed that near the Escures bunker (the RAP position at the base of the Point 72 ridge) he had met 'English commandos' and that one of them gave him a written message to take to the Germans in the Port asking them to surrender. Blaie thought that if he took this message to the Germans he would run the risk of 'being gunned down' and therefore had not taken it. Raymond's group were doubtful about this story but decided to investigate Point 72. They had not gone very far when, near to the RAP bunker, they too came upon marines of 47 RM Cdo and as a precautionary measure felt it wiser to put their hands up. They gathered that an attack was to be launched on the Port that afternoon: obvious preparations were being made for this. They also noticed some German prisoners. Returning to Escures via the road from Longues they passed the Deplanques farm close to the RAP bunker and about 300 yards from the Escures cross-roads and learned that the Deplanques' son had been fired at by a sniper, had been hit in the head and was dying. There were apparently snipers in the trees round about – not surprising in view of the German sniper school at Fosse Soucy. One of the commandos at the cross-roads indicated to Raymond's party that when he had revealed his position by lifting a bag above his head he had promptly been shot at.

It was now also revealed that a wounded commando had been taken in to 'Les Joyeux Compagnons' and cared for there by old M. Leherisser. When a German soldier entered the inn and found Mr Leherisser in the cellar looking after a British soldier, he shot the old man. What with bombing, sniping and marauding German soldiers Escures was a dangerous place.

At Port-en-Bessin – 'Ils arrivent! Ils arrivent!'

As 47 RM Commando closed in on Point 72, the people in Port-en-Bessin were tense, experiencing both expectation and apprehension, but were ill informed on how the landings were progressing. Two days previously, on Sunday 4th June, young Didier Beau was with his father when two rows of sailors came marching along Rue Nationale taking up the whole width of the road and singing as they marched. In the middle of a song they would cry, 'Krieg finish' (War finish). They seemed to be drunk. Did they signify the arrival of the two flak ships which two days later caused such havoc with 47 RM Cdo? What did their refrain signify?

Early on the morning of Tuesday 6th June, Didier and his family were awakened by flashes and the sound of gunfire, not a particularly unusual situation, but now much more intense. It was thought prudent that the family should go down to the ground floor of their house until the worst was over. Later, plucking up courage, Didier went out to investigate. Leaving his house situated on Rue Michel le Fournier at the point where it forms an extension of Rue Nationale towards the harbour, he ran down the 150 yards of Rue Michel le Fournier until he reached the harbour wall and the narrow rubble-littered passage through it leading to the harbour itself. Emerging on to the quayside, he could see the harbour and the sea beyond. What he saw left him transfixed. He could only raise his arms above his head and shout at the top of his voice, 'Ils arrivent, Ils arrivent'. Before him, stretching back to the horizon from a line half-a-mile offshore, was an armada of ships seemingly occupying the whole sea. Many of the ships were flying silvery balloons at different heights.

Didier turned to run back to his home with the news. On the way he passed a lady, a near neighbour, lying dead on the pavement. Planes were still flying overhead. He reached his house and gave the news. A little later, when a naval shell hit a storage shed attached to his house, the family moved to the house of a neighbour fifty yards away in Rue Traversière which ran at right angles to Rue Michel le Fournier and led to la Rue du Phare, the access road to the Western Feature. Didier and his family spent the day and the following night with their neighbour; in their state of tense expectations it seemed a very long night. Reconnaissance planes flew over; others seemed to be firing cannon shells. There was much splintering of roofs. As the morning of 7th June dawned, Didier and his

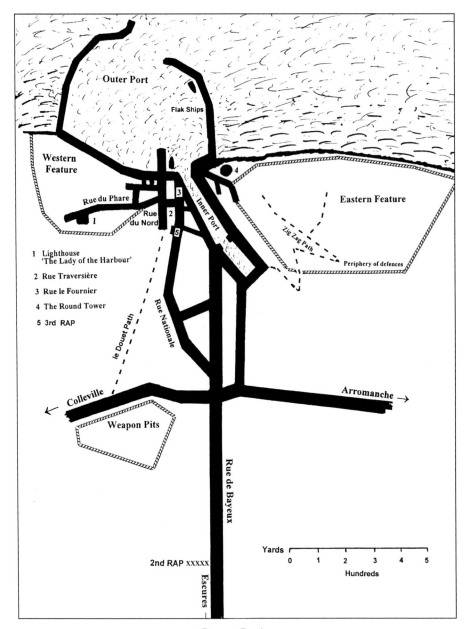

Port-en-Bessin.

family and neighbours looked out, waiting and watching, unsure of what might happen.

Nearby Young Antione Langlois lived with his family at a house in the Rue du Nord at the point where the Rue Traversière joins it and leads into la Rue du Phare. There had been a good deal of bombing of the coastal area round Port-en-Bessin, but on the night of 5th June this was much more intense and Antoine opened his bedroom window to watch. The intensive bombing lasted for several hours and as it died down there was an even more dramatic occurrence. The Todt organisation working on the sea-front defences was manned by Poles. Round about 0400 hours on the 6th a number of Poles came running from the harbour shouting, 'It's the landing, It's the landing'. At the same time Antoine could see people walking away from the harbour along 'the Douet', a path leading from the end of the Rue du Nord into the fields. Charles Jeanne, a sailor living across the road, came out and said, 'Let's go to the sea front and see what's going on'. Down at the harbour he and Antoine climbed up to a vantage point and were astounded at what they saw – 'thousands of ships' as they described it. As they watched, they saw that the Longues battery was firing on the ships, the fire including tracer shells. When they saw what the battleships were sending back, they took to their heels and returned home. By this time the Langlois family, afraid of the bombardment, thought that, like so many others, they should escape to the fields along the Douet. Then Antoine's father said, 'No, we'll all stay here in the cellar, it will be worse to be shelled on the roads'. The cellar was a good one and as neighbours round about appeared Antoine's mother would say, 'Do come in, don't stay outside'. Soon there were 15 in the cellar.

They had been there for one or two hours when a neighbour, Paul, arrived half-dragging, half-carrying on his back Madame Roussel who had been killed at the sea front. With them was Mr Roussel and his daughter, very shocked. Paul, a sailor, was as white 'as if he had come out of a sack of cement'. The body was covered with blood. It was laid at the door and the Roussels and Paul went away. The body lay for three days; there was no way it could be buried so Antoine's mother wrapped it in a sheet.

The bombardment continued throughout the forenoon but the firing was being directed further and further inland. The shells passing over sounded like trains rushing past. A large piece of shrapnel struck the house next door. The night the Langlois family stayed in the cellar, more than one of them was praying.

The Attack on the Port

On Point 72 ridge on 7th June the forward elements of 47 RM Cdo were waiting to move off. At 1400 hours two LCG(L)s (Landing Craft Gun, Large – but small craft in artillery terms) had engaged houses along the port promenade, and at 1500 hours HMS *Emerald* began to bombard the port defences with its 6-inch guns, continuing for an hour. At 1550 the RAF Typhoons engaged the defences with rocket and cannon fire and repeated this five minutes later. At 1600 hours the 231 Field Battery began to smoke the port and the ground on either side, a procedure augmented by a grass fire on the Eastern Feature.

As A, B and X troops moved away from the base of the Point 72 ridge about 1500 hours, they came under fire from the Fosse Soucy direction and returned the fire. Y troop in the Escures bunker area was also fired on twice over the next half-hour.

Closing in

X troop, commanded by Captain Walton, now proceeded first along the Escures to Port-en-Bessin road, halting 200 yards from the Weapon Pits in cover to the left of the road until the agreed start time for their attack. A and B troops, led by a French gendarme Henri George Gouget (who was wounded later in the day), followed. Gouget led them along ditches at the side of the road, bypassing the Weapon Pits unseen and entering the outskirts of Port-en-Bessin. They came under mortar fire on the way which killed one marine and wounded an NCO. At one point the troops had to dash across a gateway covered by enemy machine-gun fire. Four hundred yards from their objectives, while the naval and artillery guns fired and the Typhoons swooped in, they waited. They then moved on, A under command of Captain Cousins with Gouget leading, to the left along the Rue Nationale and into Rue Traversière with the Western Feature as its objective, and B under Captain Isherwood, onward to the harbour with a view to clearing that area and proceeding to the Eastern Feature.

While A troop was moving in, Didier Beau and his parents were still (7th June) close by with their neighbour in the latter's house in Rue Traversière. The atmosphere was tense. Action was expected but no one knew what to expect. The house overlooked the road junction between Rue Nationale and Rue Traversière. Sometime after 1500 hours Didier noticed that the street door of the house was unlocked and told his father. Father and neighbour then double-locked the door. About an hour later there was an alarming turn of events: a German officer and three German sailors were on the road outside. The officer had a revolver in his hand, the sailors carried rifles. All were grim-faced. They looked about them, right and left and upwards. After trying the door, the officer gave an order to one of the sailors who began to strike the door with the butt end of his rifle. This was repeated several times, the door shuddering as each blow was delivered with a noise inside the house which was almost palpable: but the lock and the door held. The Germans hesitated, then shouldered their weapons and, to the relief of those standing anxiously inside the house, departed. Didier's father and his neighbour were surprised that the Germans had given up so easily. It seemed that they were looking for a good vantage point covering the approach to the Western Feature and had found one because a window on one floor of the house had a commanding view along Rue Traversière to the Rue Nationale/ Rue Traversière junction.

Didier and those with him still waited and watched, silent or speaking with bated breath. Half an hour or so passed and then another turn of events raised their excitement to fever pitch – coming round Rue National/Rue Traversière corner in single file were armed khaki-clad troops (A Troop) led by gendarme Gouget. The watchers, transfixed with excitement, saw the troops pass below the house along Rue Traversiére and at its end turn right into the Rue du Nord. Had the German officer and sailors been more persistent and taken up position in the house, they could have brought down devastating fire on the commandos from very close range.

Further along the street, 50 yards away, the Langlois family were still in the cellar of their house on the far side of the Rue du Nord at its junction with Rue Traversière, and Antoine's father was keeping watch by the cellar entrance. Suddenly, he said, 'I can see soldiers coming: I can't see who they are, be quiet'. Then he cautiously opened the door and shouted, 'They're English!' The occupants of the cellar came out and met gendarme Gouget who was leading the commandos. His first words were, 'Are there any 'Boche' around?' He was told that there did not appear to be any there but that there were many at the top of the cliff (Western Feature). The commandos gave Antoine's father a packet of cigarettes and Antoine's mother gave individual soldiers flowers. Then the commandos departed, turning left into the Rue du Phare which led up the hill to the Western Feature. It was not very long before there was a great deal of firing and many explosions coming from the hill.

The attack on the Weapon Pits

While the bunker near Escures provided excellent accommodation for an RAP, it was too far from the port. Leaving the Q and Y troop medical orderlies (L/Cpls Thornton and Hancock) to serve the Point 72 and Escures areas, the RAP (medical officer RAMC, sergeant RAMC, one medical orderly/ stretcher bearer, one marine and one MOA, together with the padre and his MOA) moved off down the Escures to Port-en-Bessin road after A, B and X troops. By 1600 hours the RAP was established about a mile from the Escures bunker and less than half a mile from the port, in a sunken lane on the left of and at right angles to the road just short of the Weapon Pits ahead but shielded from them by a bank of earth and a line of trees.

The main battle, however, would be in the port itself so, a little later, leaving Sergeant Leaman, RAMC, in charge of the RAP, I went forward

The RAP (2nd) by the Escures road (Rue de Bayeux), which passes at right angles to the now overgrown trench. The bank and row of trees on the left shielded the RAP from the Weapon Pits.

The road leading from the RAP beside the Escures road to Port-en-Bessin – at night.

Port-en-Bessin: inner harbour, bridge at the entrance withdrawn. The Escures road leads into the port past the church on the right. (*Courtesy Éditions le Goubet, Caen*)

alone to reconnoitre, as the only way that I could communicate with the commando and judge the medical needs of the battle situation was by direct contact. Unaware that A and B troops had bypassed the weapon pits by concealing themselves in ditches, I walked openly along the main road. I had not gone very far when, looking to the left, I found to my astonishment that I was looking straight into the Weapon Pits and that they were still manned by soldiers in field-grey uniforms. Fortunately their attention was directed elsewhere as almost simultaneously there was concerted shouting and shooting from the left and behind. Looking round, I saw two sections of X Troop, bayonets fixed and led by the troop commander, Captain Walton, charging across the open ground in front of the weapon pits. The attack which I had assumed would be over was just beginning. It was an old-fashioned charge accompanied by much shooting and shouting from the assailants. Standing on the wrong side of it, as it were, I hoped that my commando colleagues would shoot straight. There was in fact very little response from the Weapon Pits. The defenders occupied a dug-out and a group of trenches but despite the advantage of their defensive position the menace of the commandos bearing down on them proved too much for them. One after another they filed out of the dug-out or climbed out of the trenches arms held aloft. The first phase of the battle for Port-en-Bessin was over.

The attack on the Western Feature

Moving into the port and following the route taken by A Troop, I made for the Western Feature where the main action appeared to be taking place. At one point a shot from an unseen sniper was uncomfortably close as it smacked into the wall beside me – my immediate reaction did not accord too closely with that of Winston Churchill when he said, 'There is nothing more exhilarating than being shot at and not being hit'. I was blissfully unaware at this time that there was at least one German patrol roaming the streets close by and fortunately I saw nothing of them. Reaching la Rue du Phare, the access road which led between houses on to the Western Feature, I met Captain Cousins, the A Troop commander. He was clearly very anxious. His troop had attacked the Western Feature and had been repulsed with heavy losses.

Moving up the Rue du Phare access road, A troop had found that where it emerged between the last of the houses on to the open slope of the Western feature it was blocked by coils of barbed wire (not unobstructed as intelligence had stated). Using Marine Hartwell's Bangalore torpedo, Lt Goldstein, a South African, went forward with Cpl. Amos and Marine Wood, covered by two Bren guns, and blew a gap in the wire using a three-second fuse, Goldstein being blown back by the explosion.

Marine Ted Hartwell (left) entering Rue Traversière from Rue Nationale as he had done with A Troop 55 years previously. A Troop, as they rounded this corner, were the first liberation troops seen (by Didier Beau and Antoine Langlois).

At the end of the Rue Traversière where it runs into Rue de Nord and then up to Rue du Phare. Mne Hartwell is in front of the house from which Antoine Langlois emerged to meet the commandos.

The Rue du Phare, the approach road to the Western Feature. Barbed wire obstructed the road just beyond the house on the left.

The assault route up the Western Feature. A preserved bunker is visible at the top. Leaving the Rue du Phare, the right-hand group advanced up this steep slope and found that they were in full view of the flak ships in the harbour as well as the defences above.

Advancing on to and up the face of the Western Feature, A troop now deployed in two halves, one group under Lt Wilson going right and another under Goldstein going left. By this time the artillery smoke which might have covered their advance had dispersed.

As the right-hand group moved upwards, the marines were in view of the outer harbour but it was not thought that this exposure constituted any serious danger, the latest intelligence reports having indicated that there were no armed vessels in the port. Unfortunately the reality was different. Two armoured flak ships had moved into the harbour just before D-Day (their crews were probably those seen by Didier Beau on 4th June) and had been unaffected by the naval and aerial bombardment which had preceded our attack. Unlike an aerial photograph taken a few days before D-Day, which showed the harbour empty, an aerial photograph taken on 6th June, the day before 47 RM Cdo attacked Port-en-Bessin, clearly showed the two flak ships in the harbour. Had the evidence from this second aerial photograph been available to the commando, the plan of attack and its outcome would probably have been very different. Flak ships with their anti-aircraft armament are capable of intense fire. The right-hand group of about 30 men advancing up the face of the hill, unaware of the flak ships behind them, were in full view of the latter. As soon as they were exposed, they came under fire from the harbour and flak shells were bursting among them. From the defences above, rifle and machine-gun fire, and stick grenades (the 'potato masher' type used by the Germans with a foot-long wooden handle which enabled them to be thrown further

Aerial photograph taken a few days before D-Day, showing the port empty of ships. The zig-zag path up the Eastern Feature found by Captain Cousins is visible. (*Crown Copyright*)

than the British grenade) were raining down on them. The commandos responded with small arms fire and threw grenades but, trapped by fire from both front and rear, they were in a hopeless position and suffering casualties. Cousins had to order a withdrawal. While some were able to withdraw to the right, down to the east end of the harbour wall, Marines Delap and Webb were detailed to provide covering fire for those who had to withdraw through the original barbed-wire obstruction in the access

Aerial photograph taken on 6 June 1944. Unknown to 47 Cdo two flak ships (arrowed) had arrived in Port-en-Bessin harbour. (*Crown Copyright, Ministry of Defence*)

road. Among them, seriously wounded were Marine Walters with shrapnel wounds of eye and face, Marine Walker with a neck wound and Marine Nicholson with multiple wounds of arm and shoulder. Having completed their task, Delap and Webb moved back down the hill and through the town towards the harbour. They were held up when they had to engage a German machine gun at a road block. They thought that they might have hit one of the German gunners and the Germans withdrew. They

Above: The firing slit of the bunker at the top of the Western Feature.

The view through the firing slit from inside the bunker – it was not obstructed by grass in 1944.

The entrance to the bunker.

also came under fire from the Eastern Feature. As they moved towards the harbour, they were delayed at a house from which Major Donnell was directing fire. Major Donnell took possession of Delap's Bren gun. Delap was then told to rejoin the remainder of his troop in the harbour area. On his way he passed a dead Marine lying half on the pavement, half in the gutter, with a Bren gun by his side. He took possession of the Bren gun and rejoined other members of the troop who, thinking that the Germans had 'got' Delap, gave a cheer when they saw him.

Simultaneously with the advance on the right, the left-hand group, led by Goldstein, also advanced. They were less exposed to the fire from the flak ships. As they advanced, they came under fire from the positions above. Marine Hartwell lobbed a grenade into an enemy pill box. The group then heard a loudspeaker from one of the ships outside the harbour announcing, 'Commandos, there are German soldiers coming towards you from your left'. They continued to advance and squeezed through another barbed wire obstruction. When they had almost reached the defensive positions above them, a German machine gun opened fire on them from a half-demolished pillbox. Goldstein threw a grenade at it but in so doing revealed his position. This brought a shower of hand grenades down on the group which flattened itself to the ground to avoid flying shrapnel. Goldstein then saw a grenade thrown from a communication trench in front coming straight at him; blacking out, he knew no more about it until he found that bullets were cracking above him. Marine Hartwell, close by, had seen the grenade exploding against Goldstein's tin hat as Goldstein lay flattened to the ground. Goldstein's head was covered with blood and Hartwell thought that he was dead until Goldstein began to move. Recovering, while in this position near a concrete emplacement above him, Goldstein tried to lift his Tommy gun but found that his left arm was useless and that his right arm was numb. He crawled back through the barbed wire, joining up with five other marines including Marine Hartwell. Among them were Marine McAllister, seriously wounded in the neck, and other wounded. The order had already been given to withdraw from the hill and the party continued its withdrawal. Marine McAllister, who had lost a lot of blood, collapsed. They had reached some buildings by this time and they moved McAllister into an outside toilet where they sat him down and left him. Reaching the town, the group saw a German patrol ahead of them which in their wounded state they wanted to avoid. They saw an open shed door with a large key in the lock and went in, finding themselves among some large wine vats. They positioned themselves behind these with their feet against the rims and their backs against the wall so that they could not be seen. As they waited, they heard the German patrol approaching. They stopped, came in, had a quick look round, did not see the marines and went out, closing the door behind them. Thirty minutes later as the group waited, the door opened again but this time it was a Frenchman who came in. He explained that he had seen the marines going in and that it was now safe to come out as the Germans had gone. He took the marines to a house where, assisted by the owner, Goldstein was carried up some steps into a room and laid on a bed. As the rest of the group moved down towards the harbour, they passed a house containing a number of their A troop colleagues wounded, some lying, some sitting and all seemingly in a bad way with bandages on their heads, arms and legs.

In the meantime the Langlois family were still waiting in their cellar. They had heard much firing and many explosions from the hill, and then it had died down. Antoine's father along with Charles Jeanne was smoking a cigarette when suddenly there was a knock on the door. Antoine's father said, 'Don't move. Let me see'. He gently opened the door. Outside were two commandos covered in blood. Both had field dressings on their wounds. One was holding his arm which had been hit by a bullet and his mouth and head were bleeding. Both said 'Water' in English but no one in the cellar knew what that word meant. Making gestures, the marines then said 'Drinking'. To the Langlois family 'drinking' meant alcohol, usually cider, so Antoine's mother then offered them a precious bottle of wine which she had been saving. The marines would not have that and it was finally understood that it was plain water which they wanted. Given water, they put some tablets into it and drank. (It seems a little bizarre that under these circumstances the marines were taking trouble to put sterilising tablets into the drinking water but at least the medical officer's instructions about the possible dangers of local water supplies were being heeded!) The other marine then rolled his shirt up and trousers down and revealed shrapnel wounds of his abdomen. There were still pieces of shrapnel sticking in the wounds. He then, by miming, indicated to Antoine that he would like him to pick some of the shrapnel out of the wounds. Antoine, possessing no knowledge of such things, felt unable to undertake such a task. The marine then undertook his own surgery. He took a puff at a cigarette and with a knife proceeded to dig out the most prominent pieces of shrapnel. Antoine then re-applied the dressings. The two marines by this stage seemed completely collapsed. They rested and then took some more water. Then, suddenly, Antoine's father, still standing at the door, said, 'Quiet, there are Germans coming'. A patrol was approaching. It stopped and took up position in the middle of the road at the junction of Rue Nationale and Rue Traversière. The two commandos could see all that was taking place. The Germans waited, looking about them, then all of a sudden it seemed that they had seen something, and they moved off. The commandos now asked that certain papers, probably maps, should be burned. They also wanted to hide their ammunition. This was placed in a large copper pot. After a while, although apparently very exhausted, they said that they wanted to leave. Antoine and his father led them down some steps at the back of the house and across the small garden. The commandos had to be helped to climb over the garden wall.

Returning to the cellar, Antoine and his father were worried about the copper pot with the ammunition in it so they took it out and buried it in the garden. Half an hour later a Kriegsmarine officer came to the door. He had been wounded in the leg which was bleeding and his boot was open. He had a revolver in his hand and said that he was looking for commandos. He then proceeded along the Douet Path. Antione and his father did not see him again but learned that he had been killed not many yards from their home. He might have been an officer from one of the flak ships.

When I reached the Western Feature, the problem was to ascertain if any wounded marines had been left lying on the hill. Cousins, who had waited behind while the others withdrew, did not think that any had and told how the A Troop medical orderly, L/Cpl. Jesney, had gone out repeatedly under fire to bring in those who had been wounded. From a vantage point at the top of the access road it was possible to see most of the approach route taken by the marines. A number of them were lying dead, there was no sign of movement and shouting produced no response. Cousins now departed into the town and took up position with what remained of the two sections of his troop in a house on the west side of the inner harbour towards its landward end.

As the others were withdrawing from the Western Feature, Corporal Amos delayed to apply a field dressing to his troop sergeant, Sergeant Fletcher, who was lying mortally wounded. As Amos finished doing this, he suddenly saw a German above him. The German threw a grenade which exploded beside him, miraculously without seriously injuring him although it tore off part of his trouser leg and left him dazed. As he lay he felt himself being pushed by a foot and turned to find the German standing over him. The German had thought that he was dead. Amos was taken prisoner and, outside one of the strongpoints, was put in charge of a guard who kept his rifle pushed against Amos's temple. Taken later into the strong-point, he was marched along a trench and into another strongpoint where he was interrogated in front of a notice which said that all captured commandos were to be shot. In October 1942 Hitler had issued an order that captured commando soldiers, even those who gave themselves up, were not to be treated according to the Geneva Convention but were to be interrogated and then shot ('slaughtered to the last man'). The order stated that commandos were ruthless killers who shackled their prisoners and killed them on the spot if they were a hindrance. Commandos were stated to be partially recruited from 'freed criminals in enemy countries' (doubtless to justify the execution of those who escaped from occupied countries to fight in the Allied forces). All commanders and officers who neglected to instruct their troops about this order or themselves neglected it would be held responsible under Military Law. The order did exclude 'enemy soldiers who in the course of normal hostilities were captured in open battle or gave themselves up', so there was something of a loophole for commanders like Rommel who did not implement the order.

I gave first-aid to only two of the commandos who had been wounded and had withdrawn from the Western Feature. In withdrawing by various routes the troop had become very dispersed, and most of the wounded had found their way into or had been carried into French homes, often into cellars. Out of A troop's strength of about 65, 11 had been killed and 17 wounded. Amos was known to be missing. One or two of the wounded were able to make their own way back to the RAP by the Escures road.

The position at the Harbour

Moving then to the harbour area to ascertain the situation of B troop, I found that the troop had reached the western side of the inner harbour close to its landward (southern end) without encountering much resistance. There was, however, a prominent pillbox near the top of the Eastern Feature which could command many of the streets in Port-en-Bessin including the Rue du Phare, the Rue de Bayeux and the area round the church. Seeing ten Germans on the other side of the inner harbour, and two coming down from the Eastern Feature, Sergeant Fuller (an Austrian, real name Kagerer-Stein, who was a member of the 10th Inter Allied Commando and attached to 47 RM Cdo – he was killed a few weeks later) said, ' I'll go forward and they'll give in'. He walked forward twenty yards and with a voice of great power shouted to the Germans to surrender. The ten came forward with their hands up and were followed shortly by the other two. Sergeant Fuller collected them at the landward end of the inner basin and was searching and interrogating them when a machine gun opened up from a building on the far side of the harbour and another from a position on the Eastern Feature. Marine Breach fell dead and 11 others were wounded. The marines had to withdraw into houses on the west of the inner harbour, taking the wounded with them. Again some of the severely wounded were taken into French-occupied houses, and those capable of walking were bandaged up and directed back to the RAP. Other marines had also been wounded by mortar fire from the Eastern Feature, which was a continuing threat.

The fate of the Rear Headquarters on Hill 72, and the troops manning Escures

It was now clear that the RAP must move into the port itself. While I had been able to attend briefly to some of the wounded in the town, many of the more serious casualties were still widely scattered and needed to be concentrated into a central RAP.

Return to the RAP in the lane about 1900 hours revealed that a crisis was threatening there. Earlier, intermittent firing had been heard from the Point 72 area, which seemed to indicate that a counter-attack was developing. After my arrival back at the RAP Quartermaster Sergeant Fletcher and one of his staff came down the road from Escures, passing by the RAP. They had two prisoners, who apparently thought, quite wrongly, that they were going to be held captive in the RAP and became quite excited, shaking their heads, pointing to our red-cross armbands and saying 'Rotes Kreus', 'Rotes Kreus'. I was surprised that they should think that imprisonment by a group of medicos would be such a bad thing but a prod from Sergeant Fletcher's rifle clarified their thinking as they were marched down the road to Port-en-Bessin. Two marines then followed. The important information that we gathered from Fletcher and the two marines was that counter-attacks against Point 72 were in progress and, more relevant to the immediate future of the RAP, that the road between Y troop in Escures and the RAP was now under fire. The enemy appeared to be closing in towards it. The RAP was under threat but some wounded marines from the port were still reaching it.

Before this Lt Bennett with the carriers had arrived at the Escures area at 1700 hours. The carriers could not move across country in the same way as the troops on foot. Compelled to keep to roads and lanes, they early ran into pockets of Germans. After exchanging fire, Bennett usually had to disengage as his primary task was to get to Port-en-Bessin, not to engage the enemy or to run unnecessary risks of being captured. Delayed by these encounters and deviations, he had not got much further than la Rosière by the end of D-Day, and in falling light returned there for the night. At dawn on the next day, having been told (wrongly) that Bayeux had been captured, Bennett set off hoping to reach Port-en-Bessin quickly by the inland Bayeux-Port-en-Bessin road. Entering the outskirts of Bayeux, he found that it was still in German hands. He reckons that, among the invading forces, he was the first man into Bayeux – and the first man out of it! Returning to la Rosière, he sought to reach Port-en-Bessin via the coastal road but was held up while Flying Fortresses bombed the German battery at Longues which was still very active. The bombing destroyed the road ahead, and in trying to negotiate bomb craters some of the carriers lost their tracks. Fortunately, Lt Col Cosmo Nevill, commanding officer of the 2nd Devonshire Regiment which had reached this area, was willing to lend Bennett some of his carriers and Bennett set off again. On the way he captured a number of prisoners; this threatened to cause further delay but fortunately he met three 47 RM Cdo marines who had been sent to rescue a wounded British airman at Commes and handed over his prisoners to them. At 1700 hours Bennett unloaded his carriers at the Escures bunker as ordered. At Escures Lt Col Phillips took one of the unloaded carriers and proceeded in it to Port-en-Bessin.

Meanwhile counter-attacks on Point 72 were continuing. The enemy small-arms fire from the Fosse Soucy direction which had been directed against Point 72 area as A, B and X set off was resumed at 1815 hours, directed against the small Rear HQ. Mortars falling on the position were also being fired from the eastern end of the Eastern Feature. At this stage, at Point 72, Lt Hughes, the Signals Officer, estimated that about 60 Germans were moving towards the Point 72 position. At 1900 hours the bunker area in Escures was also being mortared and Capt Spencer, the Adjutant, who was on Point 72, went down the 500 yards to Escures and ordered Bennett to reload half the ammunition into the carriers and proceed with it to Port-en-Bessin. Spencer then returned to the Rear HQ on Point 72.

Most of the members of Rear HQ on Point 72, numbering fewer than 20, occupied two of the hastily dug trenches near the centre of the ridge. Because of the loss of arms during the landing, only eight of the party possessed arms. To concentrate fire power, all of the party joined in one trench. At 2030 hours more accurate rifle fire and mortar fire were directed at the trench and a little later 15 of the enemy advanced towards it. At first it was thought that they might be Americans from the way they were beckoning, but as they advanced and the occupants of the trench held their fire they were revealed to be enemy. The foremost German was shot dead, as was another who shouted to the occupants of the trench to surrender. The rest of the enemy then withdrew. During this period Marine Gadsden was moving about outside the trench bringing fire to bear from different positions, deceiving the enemy as to the actual strength of the position. Later a further attack was made on the trench while two enemy machine guns gave enfilade fire. This attack was also repulsed.

Towards 2100 hours Bennett in his carriers set off from the Escures bunker for the port. As he turned into the Escures-Port-en-Bessin road, he came under machine gun, rifle and mortar fire. Cpl. Hucklebridge, in charge of one of the carriers, was wounded, the bullet passing through the side of the carrier and entering his chest. Escures was in process of being cut off from Port-en-Bessin. As Bennett's carriers approached the RAP, less than half-a-mile from the port, we could hear but could not see them and thought that they might be the enemy. While we were relieved that they were not, it was evident from what Bennett told us that the enemy was just behind. Bennett departed in his carriers, leaving Hucklebridge behind. From the RAP we now observed German soldiers moving a field's length away, apparently closing in on the Escures–Port-en-Bessin road. Movement in the part of the RAP lane adjoining the road was apparently visible to the enemy as the RAP now came under small-arms fire. It was therefore necessary to crowd the casualties into a part of the RAP which was hidden from view and protected by a bank. It appeared that we were about to be overrun. There was no prospect of evacuating the RAP. To have done so would have meant exposing to enemy fire those who could be sent out as walking wounded, and for those who could not walk there were not enough stretchers to carry them or fit personnel to undertake this task, quite apart from the fact that they would be shot at. We put up a small Red Cross flag at the entrance of the RAP facing the Escures–Port-en-Bessin road and waited for the field-grey uniforms to appear. Time passed, there was a period of ominous silence as we waited and watched, all eyes concentrating on the short section of the Escures road which we could see from the RAP a few yards away: but no grey uniforms appeared. Half an hour passed and it was getting dark. I made a cautious reconnaissance of the road: there was no evidence of the enemy as far as I could see.

Around 2200 hours, back at Point 72, the Germans mounted yet another attack on the Rear HQ. By this time the occupants of the trench had destroyed all documents. Illuminating the position by firing star shells, 30 to 40 Germans, closing in from the semi-darkness beyond the star shells, attacked. They got within ten yards of the trench when they were temporarily held up by two grenades and two smoke bombs thrown by Capt O'Connell. An attached corporal from the artillery regiment, Cpl. Jenkins, was killed and the FOB, Lt Irwin, and his sergeant wounded. In the confusion some of the HQ personnel managed to escape from the trench. Others, including Regimental Sergeant Major Dollery and Marine George Wood, together with the wounded officer and sergeant and Marine Bryant (also wounded), were captured. The intelligence officer, who had been observing from a post outside the trench, was cut off without being noticed and escaped in the darkness later.

At the base of the Point 72 ridge in the Escures bunker area Q troop, in reserve, had already been called forward. The depleted Y troop there was also in difficulty. It had put out a 13-man covering party under Sgt. Tomlinson south of Escures at the junction of the roads leading to Fosse Soucy and Pont Fanu. For a while heavy small-arms and mortar fire was heard from that area, then suddenly stopped, and contact with the covering party was lost. Three of the party had been wounded. At about 2130 the position was about to be overrun and the remainder had had to withdraw, leaving the wounded in a ditch. About this time, unaware of the serious situation developing around Point 72 and Escures, Col Phillips ordered Y troop to make its way to Port-en-Bessin, but due to wireless failure Y troop could not communicate back and explain its position. It was coming increasingly under fire, and with the enemy closing in from north and south, Escures was largely cut off. At 2230–2300 Lt O'Brien, commanding Y Troop, sought to make contact with the group on the Point 72 ridge from where a great deal of firing and explosions had been heard intermittently. His men had grenades but not all had rifles. Reaching the hill, he came under fire and realised that the hill had been overrun and was now fully occupied by the enemy. Cut off and incommunicado, Y Troop was also in danger of being overrun in Escures. O'Brien therefore mustered his depleted ill-armed troop and decided to report for instructions to 231 Brigade (near Longues) which had some responsibility for the commando. In the dark, that involved a cross-country compass march south-east through possibly enemy-held territory. Brigade was reached at 0400 hrs and O'Brien was given a Jeep mounted with a Vickers machine gun and a 15 cwt truck so that he could if necessary fight his way through the as yet uncleared area between Brigade and Port-en-Bessin. In due course he reached the port but too late to be involved in the actions which had taken place there on the night of the 7th. Escures was not fully cleared of the enemy until the evening of 8th June.

Meantime, since Bennett had passed by the RAP some time after 2100 hours, we had waited and watched. There was still no sign of the enemy approaching although they were close by. About 2200 hours with darkness falling I decided to go back into Port-en-Bessin to try and raise a carrying party with a view to establishing the RAP in the port. Return to Port-en-Bessin in the dark was not without its anxieties as we knew that it would be assumed there that the RAP had been captured. Expecting a counter-attack down the Escures to Port-en-Bessin road, the commando had put up a defensive screen across the road. Any movement beyond the screen was likely to be considered to be enemy, and in that trigger-happy environment shooting first at anything that moved on the Escures road was likely to be the order of the day. As always, my MOA Marine Pymm came with me. A Rotherham steel worker in civilian life and at 37 years ten years my senior, he was one of the oldest men in the commando. He tended to look on young men in their twenties, including medical officers of that age, as slightly irresponsible and requiring some protection from youthful follies. He made sure that vocal communication in a Yorkshire accent preceded any visible presence. A barrier which appeared to be deserted, but which we felt sure would be covered by guns in the hands of those for whose shooting abilities we had some respect, was approached without any demonstration of hostility. Identity confirmed, shadowy figures emerged from the darkness. Rightly or wrongly, troops in action and in danger of being wounded look on their medical officer as someone of some importance. Thinking that I had been captured, they gave me a warm reception.

We returned to the RAP in the lane with a carrying party. The seriously wounded were carried and the walking wounded assisted into the Port, about a dozen in all. As so many of our airborne stretchers had been lost in the landing, or were already in use elsewhere, carriage of the wounded who could not walk had to be by pick-a-back. At the port I established an RAP in a stable-like building where some of the wounded were already located. It was after 2300 hours.

The Commando at a nadir

I then learned the course of events since I had left the port. After capturing the Weapon Pits, X troop under Walton had moved with his troop to assist in the attack on the Western Feature. Working his way through the west side of the town, he saw that A troop were withdrawing from the Western Feature and at first thought that this indicated it had been captured. Meeting a group of these A troop marines, however, he took charge of them and learned of the danger from the flak ships and turned his attention to them. He actually saw one of them firing. As the flak ships were armour-plated, small arms fire would be ineffective and he realised that they would have to be boarded. Arranging covering fire from four Bren guns, a captured German machine gun and a 2-inch mortar, Walton, with about 25 men, then engaged in a flanking movement through the harbour installations, then east across the bridge at the seaward end of the inner harbour with a view to attacking one of the flak ships lying against the harbour wall in the north-east corner of the harbour. He was then informed, falsely, that the flak ships were already in marine hands. He therefore retraced his steps westward, concentrating his troop, and began to move through the town to the inner harbour area.

Earlier in the day Q troop, withdrawn from reserve at the Escures area, had arrived at the west side of the inner harbour with a view to assisting B troop in an attack on the Eastern Feature. Captain Vincent led a section to the south-east end of the innermost basin and there contacted B troop.

At the same time, Lt Stickings of Q Troop led a five-man patrol along the west side of the inner harbour where snipers were operating from houses. Reaching the main harbour, Stickings could see the flak ships and also the destroyer HMS *Ursa* lying outside the harbour. He signalled to *Ursa* and received the reply, 'Attention Royal Marines, there are enemy on the cliff path behind you'. Attempting to climb up the cliff using a rope, Stickings' men were shot at by a sniper. They could make little progress, found that they were entering the line of fire of the X troop Brens covering Walton's planned attack on the flak ships, and had difficulty in withdrawing. When Walton's attack was aborted, the X Troop Brens covered Stickings' withdrawal and he and Walton were then ordered to rejoin Q troop which was preparing for an attack on the Eastern Feature.

Thus, a few hours before the RAP was established in the port around 2300 hours, the commando was in a parlous position. It was isolated and threatened by the counter-attack from the south which had already overrun rear HQ. Y troop in Escures was under attack and unable to assist with the action in the Port. Ammunition among the troops in the Port was running low, and Lt Bennett at that time had not yet arrived with the extra ammunition and weapons. Only the weapon pits had been captured; the Western Feature attack had been repulsed with heavy losses; it had not yet been possible to attack the Eastern Feature as none of the strong-points and concealed snipers in the inner harbour area from which the attack would have to be mounted had yet been overcome; the two highly armed flak ships were still in a position to threaten most of the moves which the commando might make and if the flak ships moved away from the quayside they would be virtually unassailable as the commando had no boats or artillery; the troops were scattered and inadequate communi-cation made control very difficult; the toll of killed and wounded was rising with a corresponding depletion of the commando's strength; the remaining troops were tired having had little more than two hours of sleep since leaving England 48 hours earlier; it was feared that the RAP had been captured.

The assault on the flak ships

Despite these predicaments two further moves were now initiated. Knowing of 47 RM Cdo's task – the capture of Port-en-Bessin – two ships, the destroyer HMS *Ursa* and another (Polish) ship the *Krakowiak*, had moved towards the Port and at 1650 hours were positioned 700 yards from the harbour's eastern breakwater. Observing the attack on the Western Feature and other marine movements, they could not give any supporting fire for fear of hitting the marines. At 2100 hours at high tide, with the top of the flak ship's bridge just visible above the harbour wall, they came under fire from the bridge of the flak ship in the north eastern corner of the harbour. *Ursa* and *Krakowiak* opened fire with Oerlikon guns at the flak ship's bridge. It was not known what damage, if any, they had done and they were now asked if they could neutralise the flak ships. They decided to use armed motor boats, one from each ship, and at 2235, in half dark, the two boats entered the harbour, passing over the top of the net defence. They discovered two flak ships, not one as they had supposed. The Polish boat went for one flak ship and the British boat for the other, both firing rifles, Lewis guns and Lanchester guns. They came under rifle, machine gun and mortar fire from the shore but not from the flak ships, and when they approached the latter they found that one had been partially sunk by the earlier naval fire. Three Germans lay dead; the survivors had fled: a dog was the only living occupant. The other ship had been abandoned. The only naval casualty was a member of the gun's crew of the *Ursa*, hit in the leg. During this action the commandos ashore were aware that at least one British naval assault party was in action from the amount of English swearing echoing across the water.

The final throw and climax; the Eastern Feature captured; the battle turned

The second move, begun earlier, was to try and maintain the momentum of attack by sending a small party from B troop under Lt Lloyd to make an armed reconnaissance of the Eastern Feature and attack it if possible. So far B troop had been held up dealing with defences round the inner harbour. Because the bridge at the mouth of the inner harbour had now been withdrawn, this party had to detour round the southern (landward) end of the inner harbour to reach the Eastern Feature. It immediately ran into heavy mortar fire as it moved through the buildings at the base of the Eastern Feature. Nine marines were wounded, and by the time the party had cleared the buildings only a few remained. In the meantime Capt. Cousins had also gone out with some of the remnant of A troop to reconnoitre the Eastern Feature. He met Lloyd's group and the two parties, three officers and about ten other ranks in all, combined under Cousin's command. Near the landward end of the inner harbour they now found a zigzag path leading up the Feature. The path was not apparently mined and except at the bends and near the top was not easily visible from above. The party moved up this path but twenty yards from the summit plateau came under heavy machine-gun fire. Grenades were thrown down on them, fortunately falling short. Further progress was not possible and Cousins and his party withdrew under smoke cover. Returning from this first attempt on the Eastern Feature, Cousins told Col Phillips that if he could give him 24 or 25 men, he was certain he could get to the top. He planned a two-pronged attack up the zigzag path.

As the Bren carriers under Lt Bennett had now arrived, it was possible from a position close to a cemetery 400 yards south of the innermost end of the inner harbour to give covering fire from the carriers and for the Heavy Weapons troop to lay a smoke screen across the zigzag path using

The harbour wall over which HMS *Ursa* and *Krakowiak* fired followed by the despatch of two armed motor boats into the harbour. The arrow indicates the position of one of the flak ships.

The end of the other flak ship. (*Crown Copyright*)

Part of the zig-zag path. Captain Cousins advanced up the path protected from the fire from above the bank on the right. He was killed as he rushed the blockhouse ahead.

mortars. When the Brens started firing, Germans on the skyline could be seen and began counter-firing with machine guns.

Towards 2200 hours, in semi-darkness, Cousins led his men up the zigzag path. To begin with, the marines were not visible to the enemy above but the latter were aware of their presence. Cousins had arranged that when he got to the exposed upper reaches, he would fire a red Verey light and that half the attackers would then assault to the left (west) and half to the right (east). At 2220 both groups were well up the zigzag path. The Verey light was now fired, the groups moving left and right. The left-hand group with Cousins leading moved through several wire fences, breaking up into small parties to suppress harassing fire from pillboxes by firing at the slits and lobbing grenades. Nearing the west end of the hill, the group came under heavy fire from a concrete blockhouse at close range. Cousins halted his men and told them to get into some unoccupied trenches. Taking his Bren gunner, Marine Delap, and Marines Howe, Madden and Tomlinson with him, Cousins led this group through a gap in a wire fence ahead and rushed the blockhouse. All were shooting as they went. As they charged the blockhouse, grenades were thrown at them, and as one exploded in front of him Cousins fell forward, killed outright. Madden received a severe head wound and Delap was concussed. The waiting group under Lt Wilson heard bursts of fire, exploding grenades and a lot of shouting including 'Kamerad'. Wilson's group then ran forward as planned. Forty yards ahead Cousins was lying dead with Marine Madden beside him. Delap had recovered quickly and was continuing to fire his Bren gun; Tomlinson and Howe were firing and throwing grenades. Wilson by this time had a German prisoner with him who was ordered to shout to the men in the blockhouse to surrender: a white flag appeared and they did so. Cousins had been killed but his sacrifice was not in vain. The blockhouse had not only been captured but its capture and the manner in which this was achieved had weakened enemy morale.

Captain Vincent leading the right-hand group now advanced up to the summit and traversed a further 100 yards to the right (eastward), the group firing from the hip as they went. In the dark possible mines and trip wires had to be ignored. Determined attackers scarcely visible in the dark, unidentified explosions, gunfire, the shouts of excited men engaged in battle and the possibility of fixed bayonets had doubtless further weakened the will of the defenders. As Vincent's men turned to close with them, an officer and seven Germans surrendered. Sending two prisoners ahead of him so that he would avoid mines, Vincent then moved 100 yards westward along the ridge. An Oberleutnant now surrendered. As Vincent continued to move along the ridge, more shadowy figures emerged from the darkness in surrender. Having traversed the ridge to its west end, Lt Stickings of Vincent's party met the remainder of Cousin's left hand party. They were in a position in which the enemy could see them on the skyline but they could not see the enemy. Reinforced by Stickings, the left-hand group charged the position and overcame this last resistance. Another four officers and 34 other ranks surrendered.

The assault party of four officers and 24 other ranks, outnumbered four to one, without artillery or air support and attacking up a steep slope an enemy familiar with the terrain and enjoying much greater fire power and the benefit of concreted, entrenched, barbed-wire and mine-protected positions which looked down on their assailants, had succeeded against all the odds. The critical point in the battle for Port-en-Bessin had been reached and the determined, courageous action and superior will power of a few dedicated men had turned the tide of battle in the commando's favour. On such, so often, does the outcome of battle depend.

The Final RAP

The RAP had now completed its move into the port. It was nearly midnight. In the RAP lay 30 British and three German soldiers, now enemies in name only and in contrast strangely united in their common battle for survival. There were also two injured French civilians. As the night wore on ten more commandos were brought in, mostly from houses whose

Outbuilding near Port-en-Bessin used as the final RAP.

French occupants had taken them in despite the risk of reprisals should the Germans retake the port. Only a single Tilley lamp provided the lighting. There were gaping abdominal wounds with ruptured intestines, chest wounds exuding bloody froth with each breath, genitals lacerated by shrapnel, bullet and shrapnel wounds of the head and face, and all manner of limb wounds. There was no hope of evacuating casualties as Port-en-Bessin was effectively cut off. Clearing wounds of debris, control of bleeding, field dressings and bandaging, morphia, splinting, oral fluid where indicated and such sustenance as was possible were as much as could be provided in a physical sense, encouragement and optimistic explanations in a psychological sense. Despite so much pain and suffering there was little noise but rather an absence of talk, a stillness as men previously so active and committed lay prostrate, uncomplaining, without self-pity or recrimination, turned in on themselves and fearful not of the enemy but of the fallibility of their own bodies. Most were now relieved of the anxiety of the conscientious soldier that in the face of danger and hardship he should maintain his self-respect and the respect of his 'mates'. Some of the casualties, including Corporal Robertson, a distinguished Scottish athlete, were mortally wounded.

On the morning of the 8th, with the Western Feature still unconquered and the prospect of yet another bloody battle ahead, medical supplies in the RAP were almost exhausted. With the commando still cut off from the British Army, a call was relayed to the Americans nearby at Omaha. Despite the difficulties which they were having, it was not long before an American aircraft was overhead and a parachute fluttered down. It carried generous supplies of dressings and sulphonamides and more than made up for the instruments lost when my medical rucksack sank, so tantalisingly, off the Normandy shore.

The enemy morale broken

Near to the RAP a mass of prisoners were herded together in a courtyard. Turning from any consideration of the part they had played or failed to play in the recent battles, they were busying themselves with personal effects, comfortable sitting positions, cigarettes, appropriate toilet opportunities and contemplation of their uncertain future. A few remained arrogant and defiant, most sought to assume an outward attitude of indifference, a few seemed more concerned with demonstrating obsequiousness to their captors than resolution to their colleagues. Concern about the future seemed to be relieved by the knowledge that at least for them the war was probably over and they had survived.

During the night the news of the capture of the Weapon Pits, the defences in the harbour area, the destruction of the flak ships and, most of all, the rout of the Eastern Feature garrison despite the advantages it held, doubtless reached those defending the Western Feature. From a military point of view all the advantages still lay with the Western defenders – they would be looking down on their attackers, they had more guns and a wider range of weaponry, they were protected in trenches, concrete pill boxes and bunkers. The commando on the other hand would once again have to attack up an open, steep, mined slope providing virtually no cover. As it turned out, however, the final round was to be a battle of wills rather than of weapons and it was the will-power and determination of the marine commandos, tired, exhausted and at a disadvantage although they were, which prevailed. Faced with the threat which now confronted them, the morale of the German defenders cracked. Corporal Amos in one of the dug-outs at the top of the Western Feature saw this. He had been aggressively interrogated shortly after capture by an officer in riding breeches in the presence of a corporal who seemed to have some political function and was urging that, in accordance with the notice on the wall, Amos should be shot. As the Germans now guarding him spoke little English and Amos no German, there was not a great deal of understanding. Amos was covered in blood – the blood of his dead troop commander, Sergeant Fletcher, whom he had tried to help – but was unwounded. Seeing this, the Germans came to the conclusion that he must be a medical corporal. He was therefore told to treat a number of German wounded including one with a serious chest wound and another with a compound fracture of the forearm. Amos thought it wise not to disabuse them and resourcefully played the part.

Exhausted, in time he fell asleep and when he wakened at 4 o'clock in the morning it was clear that he was to take part in some German plan. The German corporal who had wanted him shot appeared to be given some message and, to quote Amos, 'equipped with a Schmeisser and haversack disappeared into the dawn'. A German officer gave Amos a cigar and, displaying a very different attitude from that of the night before, said 'Kamerad prisoner'. A number of Germans collected and showed him a large flag with a red cross on one side, white on the other. (I later took possession of this flag and used it in an incident some weeks later.) The Germans indicated their intention to leave the strongpoint. Amos motioned to the front door leading to the direct route to the harbour below but the Germans directed him to the back door, indicating that the direct route (up which the marines had attacked) was mined. Leaving the dug-out, each of the Germans surrounding him shook Amos by the hand and saluted. Duly impressed by this display of soldiery subservience, Amos descended by the circuitous route indicated to him. He finally ran into a defensive outpost of the commando and handed over his 'prisoners'.

The arrival of Amos and the 23 Germans who accompanied him was greeted with some astonishment, relief and a sense of anti-climax by those preparing for a further assault on the Western Feature. Captain Spencer, the new adjutant and a fluent German speaker, led a party up the feature to accept the surrender of the other occupants. All the positions were unoccupied: the other Germans had fled.

On the Western Feature the 11 marines who had been killed lay where they had fallen, cold, pale and stiff, their wounds now congealed with blood, a sad testimony to what they had endured. A short distance from one lay his rifle with the wooden butt slightly charred. Just above it the nozzle of a flame thrower projected from the ground. The absence of the seal at the end of the nozzle indicated that it had been fired.

Throughout the night of 7/8 June Antoine Langlois and his family did not know what was going on in Port-en-Bessin. There was a lot of firing but they did not know whether the commando had captured Port-en-Bessin or not. Looking out in the morning, however, they saw a Bren carrier at a house previously German-occupied, and only British marines in the street. From a commando who spoke French they learned that the battle for the port was virtually over. They asked about the two commandos whom they had sheltered and were told that they would be evacuated back to England. They then revealed their buried copper pot full of ammunition, and the marines took this away.

Later that day, 8th June, Antoine Langlois endured what he described as 'an awful sight' when he assisted the 47 RM Cdo medical orderlies in bringing down the bodies of commandos killed on the Western Feature, laying them on a small plateau in front of 'The Lady of the Harbour' at the lighthouse. He could hardly come to terms with the thought that these pale, rigidly stiff, lifeless corpses with their closed eyes and expressionless faces were the same intent but jaunty young men, twenty or so years old, whom, the previous day, he had seen advancing along the Rue du Phare and disappearing up past the lighthouse at the base of the Western Feature to be mown down before an hour was out in a torment of shrapnel and bullets. He had seen few coming back, and many of these were severely injured. He himself had looked after two of them, another had been looked after at François Thomine's house, Mme. Thin, the grocer had looked after another, and yet another had been sheltered in the house of M. Mauger, the slater.

As Antoine and his father walked among the bricks, slates and dust which littered the streets everywhere, they remembered also what they had seen of the nuns, the Sisters of St Vincent and St Paul, whom they had invited into the shelter of their cellar on the previous day. The nuns had turned down the offer and had spent the day, out in the open, looking for and tending any, soldier or civilian, who had been wounded.

Escures and Mont Cavalier reoccupied

Early on 8th June, in Escures now re-occupied by the Germans, Raymond Marie was looking through the slats of the closed shutters of the Customs Officer's house. He saw a British tank approaching the bend of the road from the south. It passed by his house which was just past the bend in the road. Suddenly, from a field beside the road Raymond saw a German soldier rush out. The tank fired but missed. At that point the tank stopped and began to retreat, stopping again almost under the windows of the house. Raymond could see a group of German soldiers hiding in the ditch beside the road and tried to draw the attention of the tank commander to them. The tank switched off its engine, did not seem to understand what Raymond was trying to indicate, restarted its engine and moved away. Raymond was afraid that the Germans might have seen what happened and come after him, so he and all the others in the house escaped to a nearby farmhouse and hid there.

About the same time two 47 RM Cdo Bren carriers under Transport Sergeant Ellis entered Escures from the north. The three marines from the Y Troop covering party who had been wounded on the previous day were missing and were thought still to be in the ditch south of Escures, having lain there all night in an area still controlled by the Germans. Ellis drove a Bren gun carrier through Escures to their expected position and found them but came under fire. He manoeuvred the carrier close to them then jumped out, still under fire, succeeded in getting all three into the carrier, and brought them back.

Meanwhile Raymond, in the farm house, had been joined by Cliquet, the son of the Mayor. Cliquet had a hand gun, and with a measure of bravado he and Raymond returned to the Custom Officer's house and found it occupied by several Germans. The Germans promptly surrendered. He and Cliquet then realised what a foolhardy thing they had done as the Germans could quite easily have shot them.

On Mont Cavalier those seriously wounded when the final defensive trench was overrun were still there, left behind by the Germans when they withdrew. They were rescued.

By the evening all resistance in Escures had ceased.

The British and United States Armies united

On the evening of 8th June an officer patrol of Capt. Isherwood and Lt Bennett was sent sent out along the road leading westward towards the American sector to establish a link with the Americans at Omaha. Isherwood and Bennett were near to Omaha and it was getting dark when, in a relaxed mood, they decided to have a quiet smoke behind a hedge. As they did so they heard a vehicle approaching from the west. Bennett suggested that Isherwood might jump out and challenge the vehicle while he (Bennett) kept him covered. Isherwood rejoined that as he was senior Bennett should do the jumping out while he, Isherwood, kept him covered. Shouting 'Hande Hoch', Bennett jumped out to be met by a voice from the darkness, 'Say, are you British?' 'Yes, are you Americans?' 'No, we're not Americans', came the voice, 'We're Texans – do you need any help?' Thus did the British Army join up with our American Allies, all two of them! 47 RM Cdo now linked the British and United States armies as they embarked on a unique joint enterprise.

Next day, with the battle for Port-en-Bessin effectively over, and communication with the United States Army established, 47 RM Cdo's wounded could now be evacuated from Omaha, transported there in considerable discomfort in the only transport which 47 Cdo had, Bennett's carriers. En route the cavalcade met another American patrol. The Germans had left snipers behind and a member of the American patrol had been hit. During the meeting another sniper shot was fired. The Americans left, intent on getting the sniper while Bennett's carriers handed over the wounded to an American medical unit for transport back to England. Bennett was impressed with the American medical arrangements and also with their priorities – in what seemed a rather dirty pool of water they already had a water purification plant working.

POSTSCRIPTS

PLUTO arrives at Port-en-Bessin

On 9th June an Army Port Company entered Port-en-Bessin to take over its administration. Already the arrangements for bringing in the vital supplies of petrol for the 21st Army Group were under way and one of the pipe-laying ships last seen in the Solent was in sight. Soon large petrol pipes were snaking round the streets of Port-en-Bessin. When a heavy truck succeeded in severing one of the pipes, the street flowed deep with petrol, a commodity which for the local population had long been virtually unobtainable. But vital petrol supplies for the 21st Army Group were now secure and 'the petrol port', the first to be captured, was in Allied hands.

There was some amusement among the marines when seven members of the newly arrived port company, unblooded in battle, proudly brought in a solitary miserable-looking German soldier whom they had found hiding in a building. All seven were menacingly pointing their loaded rifles, fingers

Petrol was coming ashore on D-Day + 2. (*Crown Copyright*)

on the trigger, at their understandingly apprehensive captive. One marine relieved them of their prisoner.

An abortive mission of mercy

Also, on 9th June, the medical orderlies left behind with Q and Y Troops at Escures who had gone missing, presumed captured, reappeared. On 7th June, before the counter-attack on the Escures area had developed, the Mayor of the nearby village of Commes arrived to say that a wounded British airman was being cared for in the village. He had been there for a few days and needed medical help. The Q troop medical orderly, Lance-Corporal Thornton RAMC, was despatched to attend to him. Thornton was a man of great determination and initiative. Young in years, he was already a veteran of many battles including Dunkirk in 1940 and then as an Army commando the Lofoten Islands raid, the Dieppe raid, the North African campaign and the invasion of Sicily. He was accompanied by Cpl. Terry and Marine Greenough with his Lewis gun. They had not gone far, near the Chateau du Bosq, when they met a group of Germans, including a Naval Lieutenant, who wanted to surrender. Terry told them to wait in a barn in a farm nearby until he returned.

When the rescue group reached the Mayor's house in Commes, they found the airman comfortably ensconced in bed wearing the Mayor's pyjamas: in the fluid military situation he preferred to stay where he was! Rejected, the rescuers then set off to return to Escures, intending to pick up their waiting prisoners. On the way they learned that they could not return to the Escures/Point 72 area with prisoners as it was under counter attack. They were walking down a field just above the lane leading to the farm where they had left their prisoners when they saw Sergeant Fuller and a few of 47 RM Cdo running along the lane. About 70 yards behind them were several dozen Germans on bicycles. Terry called to Fuller to look out but it was too late: Fuller was soon surrounded by hostile Germans and had his hands in the air. For Fuller, had his origins been discovered, capture was likely to be followed by execution but he escaped next day and rejoined the commando. Terry and his two colleagues, in the open, watched this scene from above. They had no cover whatever and were astonished that they had not been seen and that Terry had not apparently been heard as he called out. After the group of Germans had disappeared round a bend in the lane and Terry and his two colleagues were continuing on their way down to the farm where the prisoners were waiting, a single shot rang out and Terry was hit in the leg. Greenough went to get help. Thornton bandaged Terry up and then went after Greenough. Terry waited and then decided to hobble down to the farm. At that point a solitary German soldier appeared on the crest of the hill shouting something. With that there was the distinctive sound of a Lewis Gun firing and the German disappeared – Greenough was still around somewhere!

Terry reached the lane. Some children came running to him but were called back by their mother. The woman's husband and son came out and helped Terry to the farm where the family were just starting a meal. Also there was a German Feldwebel (sergeant) with his gun leaning against the table. The farmer poured out some Calvados and they all drank, whereupon the German got up, took his gun, walked out to the farmyard and proceeded on his way. Such are the oddities of warfare. In the meantime Terry's prisoners in the barn including the Naval Lieutenant were getting restive and now came out asking for food. While Terry had been away, a number of German stragglers had come through the farmyard but the prisoners had kept themselves concealed in case they were ordered to accompany them. Terry in his turn was rescued and evacuated by British troops entering Commes.

Thornton succeeded in making his way back to the Escures RAP and joined L/Cpl. Hancock, the Y troop medical orderly manning the concrete bunker there. In the late evening the bunker came under mortar fire. When the mortaring stopped and darkness fell, the exhausted occupants fell asleep in the rear section of the RAP bunker. They awoke a few hours later to find that as they slept Y Troop had gone and the RAP area had been overrun by the Germans and ransacked with the exception of the rear section of the bunker which had not been entered. The whole area was now deserted. Thornton and Hancock with another marine then set out for Port-en-Bessin on captured bicycles seeking to follow a circular route. Shortly they ran into a German cyclist patrol and were made prisoners. Their captors took them to a nearby chateau, passing on the way 250–300 Germans, all with bicycles, a self-propelled gun and several staff cars. At the chateau the medical orderlies were set to attend to German wounded of whom there were many. Next day the wounded were evacuated and the marines were marched six miles, halting in the evening at a farm where they were imprisoned in a barn. Sounds of battle were heard and a report of tanks in the vicinity appeared to create some panic among the Germans. Recognising that their guard did not seem very anxious to maintain his enemy status, Thornton and Hancock and another marine made their escape into the farmyard to be joined a little later, as a colleague in hiding, by their erstwhile guard. In due course American troops appeared in the farmyard and Thornton and Hancock found their way back to the Commando. Rejoining his troop, Thornton reported to his troop commander, Captain Vincent, to be met by the troop commander's comment, 'You haven't shaved, Thornton'.

Captured on Point 72

Among those captured at Point 72 was Marine Bryant. He had been wounded in the German attack on Point 72 but could walk and was marched off from village to village until he reached Bayeux. There he saw hundreds of German infantry, and Tiger tanks being fuelled and reloaded with ammunition. He was taken to a German Military Hospital in the Chateau Balleroi where there were many wounded British and American as well as Germans soldiers. After seven days, with the Allies drawing near, an SS officer arrived to order the evacuation of the hospital. He eyed Bryant's commando flash and ominously drew his hand across his throat. The walking wounded prisoners were ordered to help load ambulances with wounded, and lorries with stretchers and other equipment. In the commotion Bryant and an American paratrooper, Bill Smith from Texas, were able to escape together into a nearby wood where they remained all night. In the morning, making their way towards the Allied lines, they saw an American patrol approaching. Jumping out and waving their arms, they were almost shot. Duly identified, they were taken back to Omaha beach and were evacuated from there.

Another of those captured at Point 72 was not so lucky. Marine George Wood who, during his 24 hours on Point 72, had been involved in the capture of five prisoners, was himself captured when the HQ trench was overrun. He was marched off for interrogation. While this was taking place, the village where he was being interrogated was bombed by Allied planes, killing one of the British prisoners. For two days, in a group of 800 prisoners, he was marched without food. This included being paraded through Bayeux so that the prisoners might be humiliated in front of the French people. For Wood, however, there was a redeeming feature: a French girl handed him a flower which he kept throughout his captivity, and it is still, over fifty years later, well preserved in dried form in the prisoner-of-war logbook which he kept and his widow proudly retains. Reaching a dilapidated and filthy monastery, the group were kept in grossly unhygienic conditions, without food until the guards killed a cow. Proceeding now by transport, they reached Alençon. There they were told that for every prisoner who escaped, 10 would be shot. On 21st June they were moved to Chartres where 680 men were crowded into an old washhouse 60 feet square. For a week none was able to sleep properly or wash and they had one loaf per eight men per day. At the end of this some collapsed. On July 4th, for reasons which he could not understand, Wood was given five days' solitary confinement. For a while the British prisoners were put into a camp with Russian prisoners. The conditions there were very bad. On 1st August Wood reached a permanent Naval prison camp

Point 72 (Mont Cavalier) pointed out by Marine George Wood of 47 RM Cdo. He had been captured here 51 years earlier.

Above: Gendarme Gouget (nearest camera), who guided 47 RM Cdo through Port-en-Bessin, at the parade where he was decorated with the Croix de Guerre.

Left: Marine Roy Bryant, wounded and captured at Point 72, at the below-ground passage in Château Balleroi through which, threatened with execution, he escaped, aged 19, 55 years previously.

near Bremen. Only some time after that did one of his friends at home hear his name read out on German radio by Lord Haw Haw (William Joyce), the British traitor of American antecedents, who, by occasionally releasing the names of men missing, attracted listeners in Britain to his mocking speeches. Until then all Wood's mother had was a telegram and then a confirmatory letter that her son was 'missing while on War Service' and that 'there is insufficient evidence at present to show whether your son may be alive or not'. She received a confirmatory telegram on 30th August that he was a prisoner.

At the prison camp Wood was given a leaflet inviting him to join the German-promoted British Free Corps – one of his camp acquaintances disappeared at that point and Wood suspected that he had joined that organisation.

When the Allies were about to reach his prison camp in May 1945, the prisoners were to be marched eastward in a forced march to Lübeck but Wood and many of his companions, at the risk of tracker dogs and bayonet jabs into suspected hiding places, went 'underground' by hiding – under floorboards, in attics, in preconstructed tunnels etc – until the camp was relieved. One six-foot Marine who had crammed himself into a tea chest had inscribed on it, 'This side up for God's sake'.

The Casualties

Of the 420 commandos who had left the *Princess Josephine Charlotte* and SS *Victoria*, 276 could be mustered on 9th June. Of the 144 casualties, 46 had been killed or drowned, 65 wounded, six captured (at Point 72, one wounded) and 28 missing. In addition one of the attached artillery personnel had been killed and three wounded ... The missing were nearly all marines whose LCAs had been sunk and who had been picked up by returning craft and taken back to England as orders demanded: by the end of June, most had rejoined. During the two-day battle for the port 52 commando officers and other ranks and a number of Army soldiers had been dealt with at the RAP as well as seven Germans and two Frenchmen.

The Generals visit Port-en-Bessin

On 9th June the 21st Army Group Commander General Montgomery, along with General Graham, visited the commando to congratulate it on its achievement, and next day the Army Commander General Dempsey did the same. 47 Commando had conducted a typical commando operation, virtually on its own, lightly armed and deprived of many of its men and much of its weaponry and ammunition by losses sustained at its landing. It had marched 12 miles through hostile territory, overcoming opposition on the way, and had had to launch its attack after a 48-hour period when

Fellow-Countrymen!

We of the British Free Corps are fighting for YOU!
We are fighting with the best of Europe's youth to preserve our European civilisation and our common cultural heritage from the menace of Jewish Communism,

MAKE NO MISTAKE ABOUT IT! Europe includes England. Should Soviet Russia ever overcome Germany and the other European countries fighting with her, nothing on this earth would save the Continent from Communism, and our own country would inevitably sooner or later succumb.

We are British. We love England and all it stands for. Most of us have fought on the battlefields of France, of Lybia, Greece, or Italy, and many of our best comrades in arms are lying there— sacrificed in this war of Jewish revenge. We felt then we were being lied to and betrayed. Now we know it for certain.

This conflict between England and Germany is racial SUICIDE. We must UNITE and take up arms against the common enemy. We ask you to join with us in our struggle. We ask you to come into our ranks and fight shoulder to shoulder with us for Europe and for England.

Published by the British Free Corps.

- -

Application Form

I . . . . , ... being a British subject consider it my duty to offer my services in the common European struggle against Communism. and hereby apply to enlist in the British Free Corps.

Signature . . . .

The Germans tried to persuade British prisoners-of-war to join a traitorous organisation, the so-called British Free Corps.

General Montgomery arrives at Port-en-Bessin (left), and talks to the fishermen (below). (*Crown Copyright*)

He inspects the damage (left) and then confers (below) with General Dempsey, Commander of the 2nd British Army, and General Bradley, Commander of the US First Army Group. (*Crown Copyright*)

At this meeting, with maps on the bonnet of a jeep, the three Army Commanders planned the assault on Caen.

Left: The 47 RM Commando Memorial Plaque on the harbour wall.
Right: The Monument in the town erected by the Municipality.

the marines were tired and had had little or no sleep. Despite the severe early setbacks which it had sustained, it had achieved all its objectives. It had paid a high price in casualties.

The Germans on their side had more soldiers, reputed to be of high calibre, more powerful guns, more mines and more grenades than the marines who were attacking them. They occupied ground whose topography gave defenders all the advantages and they were in concrete bunkers, concrete pillboxes and trenches, protected by defensive minefields and barbed-wire fences. Faced with an increasing threat to their homeland, they might have been expected to be more highly motivated than their attackers. The marines who had languished so long in the 10th Battalion RM had shown that when given the chance, particularly when operating in the traditional Royal Marine rôle as amphibious infantry, there were few who could equal them.

After the Port-en-Bessin battle was over, Col Phillips recommended Cousins for the Victoria Cross but the recommendation did not succeed, with the result that Cousins was awarded the only other distinction which could be given to someone killed in action, a posthumous mention in despatches. Many who served in the commando feel that the initiative, the leadership and act of outstanding courage with which Cousins turned the tide of a battle of such importance was not adequately recognised.

An 'Inescapable Reality' in question

In his book, *Overlord*, Max Hastings said, 'The inescapable reality of the battle for Normandy was that when Allied troops met Germans on anything like equal terms the Germans almost always prevailed'. At Port-en-Bessin the terms were not equal: there they were heavily loaded in favour of the Germans, not the British, but despite that it was not the Germans who prevailed; it was the superior will power, courage and fighting skill of the Royal Marines which prevailed. Those best qualified to make objective assessments of that battle recognise its unique contribution to the success of D-Day, but Hastings mentions it in only 3½ lines. His statement that five LCAs brought 47 RM Cdo ashore, whereas the number was 14, provoked one of those who took part in the Port-en-Bessin battle to comment with some cynicism, 'I suppose he thought that the LCAs sank because they were overloaded with 100 men when they could only carry 36'.

Another Assignment

Already, on 10th June, the main body of the commando was on its way to its next assignment, a move from the extreme right to the extreme left of the British front to support that other formation picked out by General Dempsey for special mention, the 6th Airborne Division.

Chapter Five

'... But Our Patrols Are Out': Battles and Brinkmanship at the Border of the Bridgehead

Outside Right to Outside Left

ON 10th June the commando bumped a dusty way eastward in three-ton lorries, through Ryes and Colombiers to Douvres where it spent the night. Next day, with orders to join the 6th Airborne Division, which beyond the Orne was under severe pressure and vulnerable, the commando proceeded towards the Benouville (Pegasus) and Ranville Bridges.

The Scene beyond the Orne

The need for a bridgehead east of the Orne lay in the vulnerability of the left (eastern) flank of the British assault forces to the powerful German forces of the 15th Army, including the 21st Panzer Division, which could attack it from the east. In addition the Sallenelles-Troarn ridge just east of the Orne would provide vantage points from which enemy artillery could command the eastern flank of the British invasion force. With a view to establishing and consolidating the bridgehead the objectives given to the 6th Airborne Division were: the capture of the bridges over the Orne (Ranville Bridge) and the Canal de Caen parallel to it (Benouville or 'Pegasus' Bridge); the 7-mile-long Sallenelles-Troarn ridge; the five bridges over the Dives between Dives-sur-Mer and Troarn; and the high ground in the five-mile-wide flooded area towards the Dives. The destruction of the large gun battery at Merville which could fire along the 5 mile stretch of Sword beach, the most easterly of the British landing beaches, was vital. This battery would need to be silenced before daylight when the sea-borne landings would begin.

On D-Day, shortly after midnight, the Benouville and Ranville bridges were captured by glider-borne troops of the Oxfordshire and Buckingham-shire Light Infantry and 249 Field Company of the Royal Engineers. The task of destroying the Merville battery fell to the 9th Parachute Battalion, reduced to only 150 men because so many of its members had been dropped wide of the dropping zones – only 60% of the 6th Airborne troops were in a position to take part in the early days of the Orne Bridgehead battles.

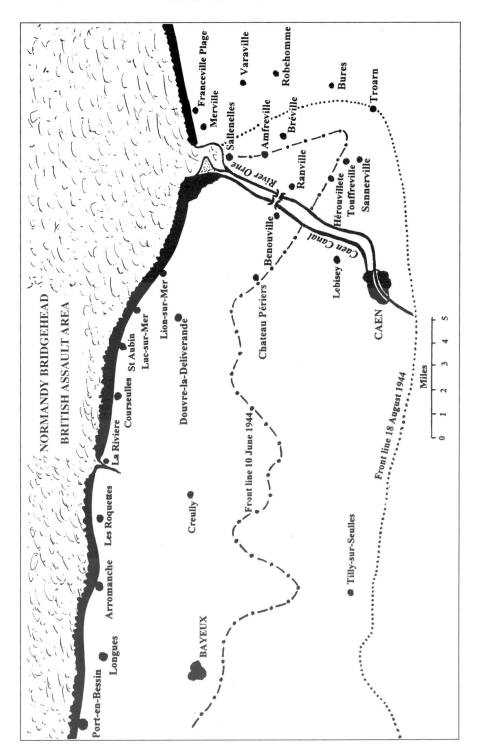

NORMANDY BRIDGEHEAD
BRITISH ASSAULT AREA

Port-en-Bessin
Longues
Arromanche
Les Roquettes
La Riviere
Courseulles
St Aubin
Luc-sur-Mer
Lion-sur-Mer
Douvre-la-Deliverande
Creully
BAYEUX
Tilly-sur-Seulles

Franceville Plage
Merville
Varaville
Robehomme
Bures
Troarn
Sallenelles
Amfreville
Bréville
River Orne
Ranville
Hérouvillete
Touffreville
Sannerville
Benouville
Caen Canal
Chateau Périers
Lebisey
CAEN

Front line 10 June 1944
Front line 18 August 1944

Miles
0 1 2 3 4 5

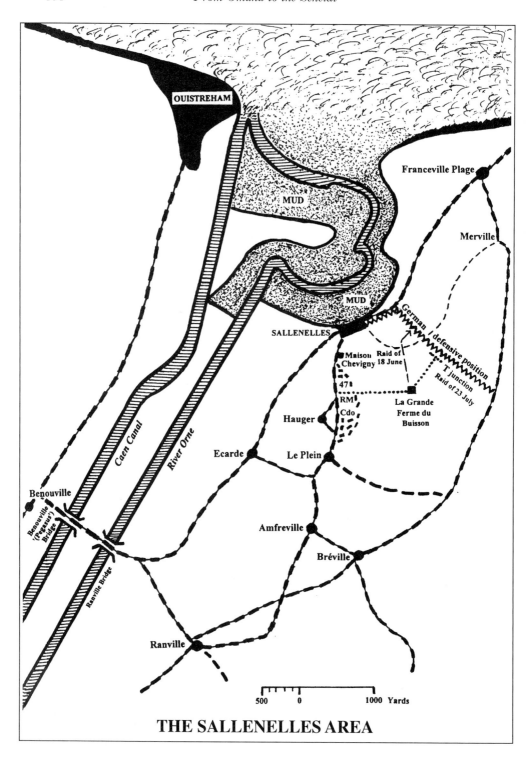

THE SALLENELLES AREA

Despite this, by 0445 hours, the 9th Parachute regiment had captured the heavily defended Merville battery destroying its guns, but suffering 65 casualties. The attackers then withdrew. A major threat to the troops landing on Sword beach had been aborted.

Although the airborne landing between the Orne and the Dives, at Varaville 3 miles short of the River Dives and the same distance from the coast, and at Touffreville to the south, 4 miles short of the Dives and 6 miles from the coast, had had mixed fortunes, there had been success in cutting the bridges over the Dives at Varaville, Robehomme, Bures and Troarn, mostly by rapid forays made from the landing positions. Although a group of airborne sappers in a dash by jeep damaged the Troarn bridge it would appear that the Germans themselves played some part in blowing it up, possibly to obstruct pursuit. The wide scattering of so many airborne troops prevented the holding of the high ground towards the Dives.

The biggest task was to gain a firm lodgement on the Sallenelles-Troarn ridge. During D-Day the initial limited airborne occupation of the ridge had been extended by further airborne reinforcements and by the 1st Special Service (Commando) Brigade (3, 4, 6 Army commandos and 45 RM Commando) which landed on Sword beach during the afternoon. After crossing the bridges 6 (Army) Commando and 45 RM Commando were ordered to move to the ridge and then north to secure Merville, now reoccupied by the Germans, and Franceville Plage. No. 3 Commando was ordered to assist the airborne troops under attack at Ranville, No. 4 to advance to Amfreville and le Plein. 45 RM Commando advanced briefly to the outskirts of Franceville Plage but was not strong enough to go further and fell back to re-occupy Merville. Surrounded there it had to fight its way out and next day was ordered to withdraw to le Plein. Airborne troops and elements of 1st Commando Brigade occupied the southern section of the ridge for 2–3 miles as it ran south east from Amfreville.

Over the next few days the Orne bridgehead was attacked incessantly. On 10th June, 6 and 45 Cdos on the northern section of the ridge were attacked. The enemy recaptured Amfreville but were then driven out. Further south, equally severe attacks were launched against the air-borne troops south of Amfreville and still further south against Ranville. On the 11th the 5th Black Watch of the 51st Division was brought from across the Orne with a view to capturing Breville but did not succeed. Next day (while 47 RM Cdo was advancing along the Sallenelles-Troarn ridge towards Sallenelles) the Germans launched a major attack from Breville. The para-chutists and the Black Watch joined by the 13th/18th Hussars (Queen Mary's Own, to whom for a short time I had been medical officer) bore the brunt of this attack. The battle raged back and forth throughout the day, the enemy advancing as far as Le Plein and Amfreville. Next day the British forces, now further strengthened by the under strength 12th Parachute Battalion, counter-attacked and in a fierce battle advanced beyond le Plein and Amfreville and captured Breville. Of the 160 men of the 12th Battalion 141 became casualties during that day's battle: over the three day period 418 of the 564 men of the German 858th Regiment were casualties. General Gale, commander of the 6th Airborne Division, considered the Battle of Breville to be the turning point in the fight for the Orne Bridgehead.

During the early fighting at the Orne bridgehead some of the airborne troops were captured at Herouvillete and bayoneted after capture. As a parachutist, wounded in the neck, lay in a Jeep his head was beaten in with the butt of a revolver. A perverted German corporal by the name of Carl and his assistant, called Willy, told some prisoners to run away and then used them for pistol target practice as they ran. The two also took pot shots at a group of wounded parachutists leaning against a wall, firing at them from strange 'music hall' positions, such as bending down and firing between their legs. One of the murderers was killed later, the other captured.

Gliders involved in the initial landing at the Orne Bridgehead on the early morning of D-Day. (*Crown Copyright*)

Sallenelles

Concluding its journey on 11th June 47 RM Commando crossed the Canal de Caen over Pegasus Bridge and then the Orne at the Ranville Bridge, the sites a few days previously of that historic first action of the Normandy campaign. Like a flock of birds resting during migration the ground was covered with the gliders of the airborne forces. The night was spent at Ecarde which, reminiscent of the static warfare of the First World War, would intermittently over the next seven weeks provide a rest area when the commando was withdrawn from the line. The RAP was established for the night in the Café Tabac. The owner was fulsome in his welcome, and promptly removed all his stock!

On 12th June the route was by march, eastward up the road from Ecarde to le Plein and then northwards along the top of the Amfreville-Sallenelles section of the ridge, already the scene of so much fighting on the previous two days and still under threat. Close by, there was much sound of battle – the battle for Breville was raging. The commando was to move to the

A crash landing among the enemy. (*Crown Copyright*)

German soldiers – dead by the roadside.

extreme north end of the ridge close to the German-occupied village of Sallenelles. As it advanced along the ridge the road on its crest was littered with dead Germans, casualties of the previous days' fighting. Near the road, by a tree, a British officer (Lieut Dillon) from 6 Cdo was found lying, still alive. He had been shot in the chest, was unconscious and profoundly hypothermic. It appeared that he had lain for a day or more and had survived as a result of the life-preserving effect which, under certain circumstances, hypothermia can have. Sadly he died later. At the base of the tree lay a dead German, also shot, apparently a sniper who had come off second best in a sharp-shooting contest with Lieut Dillon and had fallen out of the tree. During the march four Free French members of 10 Inter-Allied (I.A.) Cdo, incapacitated by shrapnel wounds to their legs, were also rescued.

The sides of the ridge road were mined and as the commando advanced it came under fire which intensified as it approached a prominent house on the Western outskirts of Sallenelles which were now the extreme leftward limit of the British beachhead. The house was later called 'Maison Chevigny' after the present owner Monsieur Yann de Chevigny who became Mayor of Sallenelles and after the war organised the erection of a Commando Memorial outside the house: house and Memorial have become a place of pilgrimage for many of the commandos who served in that area.

Maison Chevigny.

The house has also a Royal link with Britain – Mr Chevigny's son-in-law, Sir Robin Janvrin, is Secretary to the Queen.

On entering the garden of Maison Chevigny the commando was subject to intense mortar fire which killed one of the accompanying Royal Engineers and seriously wounded two others. The engineer who died was almost completely decapitated by a large mortar fragment. As he fell his head rolled to the side and blood was squirting from the severed blood vessels of his neck: he lay convulsing.

The commando, with orders to hold the Sallenelles end of the ridge, then deployed short of Maison Chevigny establishing a defensive position from the outskirts of Sallenelles to Hauger. Sallenelles itself was occupied by the Germans. A camouflage net was hung across the Sallenelles road where it dipped down towards the village. 47 RM Cdo's position consisted of slit trenches and any natural defences. Eastwards of the commando's position was an area of which a large farm, la Grande Ferme du Buisson 800 yards away, was the centre. The enemy line extended for half-a-mile from Sallenelles north-east along the Franceville-Plage road, then at right angles to that in a south-easterly direction.

The Regimental Aid Post (RAP)

The Second Front was now entering a period of consolidation; there was a need to find as suitable a place as possible for the care of the sick and wounded on a more established basis. The options were slit trenches in a field, or Maison Chevigny, the latter much more suitable and arguably safer. The snag was Maison Chevigny's position; it was in front of the commando's forward defensive position. Because of the house's exposed position Col Phillips did not wish to use it in his defensive dispositions. It was, however, the only sheltered accommodation available and I decided to use it as the RAP. The CO did not demur. He nearly always trusted my decisions and even when I proposed something about which he probably had reservations he would respond with a quizzical expression and somewhat ambivalent remark such as, 'Doc, you are a prescriptive fellow'.

As Maison Chevigny was in front of the front line there were no British troops between it and the Germans. Protective barbed wire rolls were therefore placed round it on the enemy side and across the Sallenelles road, and mines laid beyond the barbed wire.

When we entered the house it was evident that it had been used as a brothel and evacuated in haste. It was filthy and littered with women's clothing of all kinds, soldiers' uniforms, boots, helmets, webbing, leather belts, knives, forks, crockery, army and home-made beds, half-eaten food. Women's names were written all over the walls. Considering the amount and nature of the clothing left behind the imagination boggled at the possible state of dress or undress of those who had so obviously fled in panic from the quasi-military activities in Maison Chevigny as face-blackened parachutists dropped from the heavens in the middle of the night and began emerging from the bocage like killers from outer space.

To make the house suitable large amounts of rubbish were cleared out. Sandbags were placed over the windows at ground level excluding natural light from the basement which, partly below ground level and with thick walls, was safe from mortaring and rifle fire. Four RAP medical orderly/ stretcher bearers, two MOAs (Marine Officers' Attendants) and our new acquisitions, two medical Jeep drivers with Jeeps, slept on stretchers in the large basement room; the padre and medical officer in a smaller basement room.

The house was infested with rats. Although a determined assault on these with anything which could act as a truncheon resulted in a number of rat casualties, the rodent reserves were clearly adequate to replace any deficiencies in front line marauders. The rats scurried about in the darkness when the occupants of the basement lay down to sleep: their characteristic squeals were particularly unpleasant. The large basement room contained an unused stove with overhead pipes leading to it and at night the room's occupants often lay watching with a torch the antics of the rats as they sat on or ran along the pipes. Marine Pymm and Driver Tarbin constructed a rat trap, a box with a heavily weighted portcullis which was actuated by a pad inside the box. Tested by touching the pad with a stick the trap seemed highly efficient but it appeared that Army rations, as bait, were no more attractive to the rats than they were to the soldiers and the former could look elsewhere. No rat ever ventured into the trap although they would look at it, walk round it, even rub against it, but no more.

The Army with its understanding of the realities of war had foreseen the rat scenario. Some months earlier one of the more flamboyant lecturers at the Army School of Hygiene and Tropical medicine had given advice, said to be based on personal experience, on 'how to get a rat out of your sleeping bag before it does unmentionable damage to masculinity'. The story did not now seem so apocryphal as it had at the time. It was time for discretion, not valour; fighting with a trapped angry rat inside a sleeping bag was unwise and attempts at manual extraction risky, the balance of tactical advantage lay with the rat. An attempt should be made to encourage the unwelcome bed-fellow to leave quietly by creating an easy escape route through the mouth of the sleeping bag. This scenario was avoided by a nightly ritual of inspecting beds for 'cuckoo rats' before occupancy. At Sallenelles the plague of the rat at night was replaced by the scourge of the mosquito, the 'mossie' by day.

Inevitably, too, at Maison Chevigny, with nothing between us and the enemy but rolls of barbed wire and some mines, there was lurking concern that, despite our defences, we might be captured. One night as the padre and I slept on our stretchers in the smaller basement room we heard a knocking, scraping noise at the small ground-level window above us. With the prospect that our defences had been breached and that the usual method of entering a defended house might be employed – a grenade or a burst of automatic fire through the window – we dare not show a light or reveal any other evidence of occupancy. I could not escape the thought that I might have been foolhardy in preferring the amenity of Maison Chevigny to the austerity of a muddy hole in the ground. We lay, not daring to move and not a little apprehensive in the dark. After a while the sound stopped: we cautiously shone a torch at the window. A large rat in a stage of exhaustion was trapped between the sandbags outside and the intact glass of the window. It had been hurling itself at the glass in an attempt to escape.

To begin with I thought that I would use the large front room above ground level as my 'surgery' but had to abandon that as movement there could result in a fusillade of shots coming through the glassless windows. The 'surgery', with its 'operating table', a stretcher laid on two trestles, was in the large basement room. The house was frequently mortared and anyone in the garden was at risk at such times. We particularly disliked

Multiple mortar firing *Nebelwerfer* of the type which frequently mortared the 47 RM Cdo position at Sallenelles and Hauger. The bombs which it fired travelled with a peculiar moaning sound – 'moaning Minnies' – and were sometimes filled with an incendiary fluid instead of explosives. (*Crown Copyright*)

the attention of a *nebelwerfer* which could fire six mortar bombs simultaneously. The basement was safe. We were frequently shelled and on one occasion a shell went through the roof leaving a large hole. Lacking electricity we relied on paraffin lamps. We were told that after we had departed a booby trap wired to one of the switches exploded when the electricity was turned on.

Now, unlike the position at Port-en-Bessin where, lacking motorised transport, casualties had to be manhandled, we were able to use jeeps fitted with stretchers. The jeep with its four-wheel drive and cross-country capability was the army's universal utility vehicle. Initially the stretcher was placed transversely across the bonnet but as the army stretcher was longer than the width of a jeep and projected on either side there was a serious risk that the stretcher would be knocked off with disastrous results. The next adaptation was a raised steel frame in line with the vehicle. This was more satisfactory but patient and stretcher had to be strapped down tightly because the height of the frame accentuated any tilting movement over rough ground. The discomfort of wounded men could be significantly aggravated by such travel and they were also exposed to the weather. Conscious of these drawbacks our Jeep drivers, Stow and Tarbin, evolved a method whereby the rear seats were removed and a steel frame made by REME (Royal Electrical and Mechanical Engineers) was bolted behind the front seats. The stretcher extended beyond the rear of the vehicle but a canopy was made which extended to the rearward end of the stretcher frame. With this arrangement the patient was much less shaken, was sheltered from the elements and found travel less painful. Sadly, the 'Sallenelles Jeep' did not find its way into the book on *World War Two Military Vehicles!*

During the first four days at Sallenelles 23 casualties were treated at the RAP for shrapnel or bullet wounds. One of these, Marine Tatton, died, another marine, Marine Maud, missing on patrol, had been killed.

On 16th June the commando's position was mistakenly bombed by the RAF or the American Airforce, we were not quite sure which. Each member had a bright yellow square of silk to put out on the ground as identification in such an eventuality but these did not seem to have any deterrent effect. As the aerial bombs dropped with the high-pitched screech and then tearing explosion which identified them from the German mortar bombs to which we were so accustomed, we flattened on the ground, but Sergeant Fuller was killed. On the same day Marine Ron Tullett was killed while on patrol.

That day, too, a mine caused another casualty who was rescued in circumstances which elevated warfare above the disregard for human suffering which so often characterise it.

Civilians had been warned of the danger from the mines protecting the commando's position but an old Frenchman, ignoring or unaware of these warnings and wishing to gain access through a mined area, trod on a mine and was severely injured. As he lay his plight was seen by one of our officers, Lt O'Brien. Although unaware of the positions of the mines, which had been laid by the Royal Engineers, O'Brien immediately entered the minefield and rescued the old man, who was brought to the RAP with multiple severe injuries.

On another occasion 5 Messerschmitts flew over at about 100 feet blazing away, their machine guns and engines creating a deafening cacophony of noise. Everyone felt that shots were landing all around him. It seemed that there would be casualties but not one person was hit.

One day a Sergeant Major of the German Medical Corps was picked up by one of our patrols as he crossed into our lines. He spoke almost flawless English explaining that he wished to 'establish himself' in England or America, apparently entertaining no doubt that this would be possible.

When I explained that there would be a preliminary period of probation in a prisoner of war camp he seemed quite offended!

On another occasion when we were 'out of the line' two youths were seen outside the RAP eyeing an army bicycle, part of our equipment. Bicycles were highly prized by the civilian population. Confronted by the Padre and myself the elder of the two youths indicated by sign that they would like to take the bicycle away. An indication that they could not do so, even on payment, was meant to close the matter but the Padre, perhaps a little sorry to be so uncompromising, thought that he should engage the youths in a little friendly Christian conversation. He asked the elder one where he lived; and did he have any brothers or sisters. To the latter question the youth replied 'deux soeurs'. 'Quelles âges?' said the Padre innocently. 'Dix-neuf et vingt-et-un' replied the youth and then his face lit up with understanding, 'Ah, Jig-a-Jig – trente francs'.

Patrolling

The main activity of the commando, and of the enemy, at this time was patrolling in no man's land, a form of sparring between two protagonists scowling at each other across a large 'ring'. Patrols would go out from our positions towards Sallenelles or to and beyond la Grande Ferme du Buisson. The patrols could be of four types. A *standing patrol*, often one or two men crawling if necessary, approached a position close to the enemy lines from which they could observe the enemy and report what was going on. At night such patrols were often *listening patrols* and would take up position 50 yards or less from the enemy lines. The patrol members were usually placed some distance apart so that one could cover the other or escape should his colleague be captured. A *mobile or reconnoitring patrol*, usually of five or ten men, traversed a predetermined route seeking information on enemy positions, minefields, trip wires etc. A *fighting patrol* went out with the object of engaging the enemy in battle in a planned way. The rescue of marines wounded on patrol could be difficult as they could be in a minefield or in a position close to the enemy.

The reporting of static warfare by the media where no major battles are occurring tends to create the impression that nothing much is happening, that 'all [is] quiet on the Western Front'. Lacking dramatic events, communiqués and media reports often ended, as it seemed to the troops engaged in patrolling, on a somewhat apologetic note, '– but our patrols are out'. Patrolling, however, is a stressful form of soldiering in a psychological sense and carries considerable risk. Those involved are operating in small groups, isolated from the main body of their colleagues and devoid of the sense of mutual support which working within the latter gives. They are frequently operating in the dark. The bocage country was excellent for concealment but that applied to both sides. The hidden mine was the silent, deadly enemy causing wounds which were often permanently disabling, the ambush the unseen foe which could strike before there was a chance to reply. A rustle nearby could presage the arrival of a hand-thrown grenade. It was not unknown for patrols to be creeping along and suddenly come face-to-face with an enemy patrol. The shadowy figure suddenly looming up in the dark might be the enemy at close quarters or, tragically, might be assumed to be such and prove too late to be a British patrol – unfortunately, on one occasion, a member of one of our patrols was killed in this way.

A corporal leading a patrol carried total responsibility, not the limited responsibility which would be his on other occasions when his troop officer was present. Patrolling did not usually give the sense of achievement which assault and capture of an enemy position gives. Although patrolling was not a popular duty there were exceptions, often individualists, human nocturnal predators, who preferred stalking at night to the open fight.

Patrolling was often a battle of wits. Deceptions were used by both sides. German tricks included turning signposts to face in the wrong direction. Boards with 'Achtung minen' and a death's head would be placed in a fenced-off unmined area and a path made round the area, the path being mined. Noise-making devices in the vicinity of dummies were designed to induce our patrols to fire and so give away their position. A German patrol which had been seen and fired at would leave one or two in cover, firing blanks to continue attracting attention, while the rest would creep round to attack the British patrol from the rear. Decoys would create an activity, drawing one of our patrols towards it, but meanwhile an ambush had been laid on the route to the decoy. If one of our telephone cables was found at night it could be cut and one end led into an ambush so that the investigating linesman could be killed as he traced the line to the break. Trip wires could be attached to explosive devices. One morning on patrol Marine Delap was ordered to move forward through a gap in a hedge and take up a better position with his Bren gun. When he apparently refused, he was threatened with being 'put on a charge' to which he replied, 'if I go through that gap in the hedge you will never put me or anyone else on a charge'. A wire across the gap was fastened to the withdrawal pins of two grenades. Had it not been raining Delap would not have seen tell-tale raindrops hanging from the wire. On retreat, the Germans could put a notice on a bridge that the weight on it must not exceed so many tons whereas the maximum weight which it could sustain was far less than that. The hope was that a pursuing vehicle, particularly a tank, would fall through the bridge. The possibility of these devices threatened all those on patrol but static mines caused most casualties. These could kill, could blow off limbs, or if 'umbrella mines', could jump up and explode at face level

La Grande Ferme was the focal point of many standing patrols. Sergeant Gibson as the 'I' (Intelligence) Sergeant often took part in these. He has amplified a typical cryptic HQ record of a patrol of 2 officers and 15 men: 'Standing Patrol relieved patrol 'X' at Grand Ferme du Buisson 263472, +2130 hrs, cas nil, NTR' (map reference, time, casualties nil, nothing to report).

Clad lightly with nothing to shine or rattle we set off. Sandalled feet scythed through the grass in a single file of silence, past the orchard at whose further end lay the enemy, across the plank bridge, gingerly through the white tapes which marked the cleared path through the minefields, past a decaying cow lying in the farmyard and on to the two-storied building from which the outgoing patrol was just departing. The tide of battle had become static on either side of this farm.

On arrival the troops fanned out into positions on each side of the farm along hedgerows and into a small wood: the 'I' section took up position in the farm loft. Somewhere out there were the enemy in slit trenches. Darkness came quickly: we spoke only in whispers and then only a little, but it was a relief each hour to lift the receiver of the wireless set and call up Brigade, 'Hello, Easy Love, Victor – DOG Op here – no activity to report'.

The hours moved slowly and uneventfully past and then the peace was shattered – flash, flash – beaming 142° – and we saw two shells fall about FOX OP. Lifting the receiver quietly, 'Hello E. L. V. two shells falling approximately on FOX, bearing from DOG 142°'. But before the receiver could be replaced a deafening crash shook the back of the building and another straight after that. Flat on the floor we listened to the brittle fall of stonework.

At 0216 hrs two green flares went up from the enemy FDLs (forward defence locations). We froze to the spot as the eerie light dropped low, flickered and died out, followed by two others. At 0355 hrs one of the gunners, presumably seeing something, let off a burst of Bren fire. Back came the response, tracer bullets flashing past the window.

But now light was coming, the outline of the trees, then the hedges and the dewpond: soon the sun glistened on the shimmering garb of the field. The book of the night was closed: daybreak had come and we had to move carefully again; but that was relief compared with the silent blackness of the night.

Towards 0800 hrs the 'Stand to' was given. We clambered down the debris covered stairs into the warm daylight of the courtyard. The night patrol was complete – very little to report.

In his book of poems, *Now the Bell Rings* Gibson wrote of patrolling:

> Each patrol,
> Moving across the silent plain by night
> Was very death when one was left behind;
> Morning was hope, rebirth to the glad world.

Patrolling was not without its amusing incidents. Night reconnaissance patrols were active at Sallenelles and our patrols and enemy patrols frequently stalked each other. On one occasion two members of one of our night patrols positioned themselves up a tree close to one of the routes which enemy patrols were likely follow. In due course they heard an enemy patrol approaching: as it reached a point where a well placed grenade would put an end to its activities a grenade was hurled from above. Unfortunately, aim and timing were poor: the force of the blast dislodged the grenade throwers from the tree but the enemy, apparently unable to interpret these events, beat a hasty retreat.

On one occasion, in daylight, a patrol led by Sergeant Mansfield saw the back of a board ahead. When they reached it and looked at the other side it said 'Achtung Minen'. They were in the middle of a minefield! As they looked around to see how they would get out of the minefield one of the patrol declared loyally, 'We will follow in your footsteps Serg'.

On another occasion on a dark night a member of a patrol turned when he thought he heard the whispered word 'Muller' from one of two 'comrades' walking behind him. The 'comrades' promptly disappeared. A quick check revealed that none of the patrol was missing. Two Germans had been following to find out the safe routes through the minefields.

Another possible danger to patrolling was the occasional arrival of a ration of whisky at the officers' mess after long periods when there was none available. On one occasion the ration had arrived just before a very sober minded officer, given more to caution than to foolhardiness, was ordered to lead out a six hour nocturnal standing patrol to la Grande Ferme. As the patrol moved out its members thought that their officer was a little more talkative, less cautious, than usual. They reached the farm without incident and were settling down for the night when their officer announced with apocalyptic rhetoric that the patrol would 'defend the farm to the last round and the last man!' As the function of the patrol was to observe and report not to engage in uncalled-for heroics there was considerable relief that there was no sign of the enemy that night!

Because la Grande Ferme du Buisson had been abandoned the animals there were uncared for. The cows must have been very uncomfortable and it was not unknown for a patrol to bring back a can of milk. Nor was it unknown for the yield to prove surprisingly low – the Germans had been there first. Another farmer had for years been putting his cows out in an orchard near our position and was not going to let a war upset his routine even although his cows were repeatedly running into our trip flares.

On one occasion a patrol captured and brought back a goose, tying it by the leg to a sapling pending further 'processing'. Unfortunately the goose escaped and ran into an adjacent minefield. Everyone was wondering how to stop it before it set off a mine when the troop commander, Captain Isherwood, appeared and ordered his troop marksman, a qualified sniper enjoying the title of 'Silver Spoon' as a mark of his prowess, to 'shoot the b***** goose'. At a range of approximately 25 yards 'Silver Spoon' took aim at the jerky fluttering target but through excitement or compassion he missed it completely. As he prepared to fire again the field telephone rang, 'Spencer (the Adjutant) here; who fired that shot at the Colonel?' The erring shot had just missed the CO standing at his HQ and he was on his way to investigate such a disorderly deed of arms. Lt Bennett, the observer of the incident, merely on a social visit to Isherwood, felt it better to beat a retreat rather than wait to become involved, even by association, in the wrath which was about to be unleashed.

On 24th June a detachment of 14 men under Lt Wilson was detailed for duty to act as personal protection for General Montgomery in the caravan in which he lived and did much of his planning. Captain Hunter (later Lord Hunter of Newington) the General's personal medical officer recounted that on one occasion, contrary to blackout rules, the General opened his caravan door at night without putting out the light. A marine shouted aggressively, 'Shut that door' at which the General immediately retreated into his caravan and put out the light before re-emerging, without further comment, to be recognised by the marine. When the marine re-covered from his involuntary temerity in shouting at the Commander-in-Chief of the 21st Army Group he was heard to declare proudly that he was glad to observe, with the pride of a loyal member of the Corps of Royal Marines, with what alacrity and subservience Army Commanders obeyed the orders of even the lowest ranking Marine.

The Sallenelles Routine

* We lived in there with our own kind, and smells, in holes in the ground, and 'standing to' at dawn and dusk and always, always being

* After David C. Simpson's account of 'The Little World of Infantry' in *Interesting Times. A Foot Soldier's Verses*. The Ramsey Head Press, Edinburgh, 2001.

alert and checking each small thing we did. You could be in for days or weeks without a break but all that time you knew those others facing you would try to kill you if they could so you must kill them if you can.

There were some periods of very wet weather at Sallenelles. At times the marines were perpetually wet, living and sleeping in trenches with an inch or two of water and mud in the bottom: ammunition boxes were in demand so that they could sleep on them above the water level. Any marine who was using a slit-trench latrine felt that there was something unsporting about the Germans if they mortared, shelled or machine gunned the position at that time. Whatever the activity at Sallenelles much of the time was boring and revolved round a day and night routine. Sergeant Gibson wrote:

One's chief impression of those weeks at the Normandy front was of the passage of time, days and nights during which each hour seemed a poised and slow development from one to the next. Meal times were the only times of definite activity and the monotonous round of tinned feeding and hard biscuits – no bread – tended to stereotype even these. Days were long and mostly sunny but there was little enough to do but wait and watch. We moved around ever keeping a weather eye open for approaching shells which generally gave about two seconds warning. Unfortunately the enemy had our HQ just taped and the presence of our mortar batteries beside us was a constant invitation to trouble. Many shells, mostly 75 mm would fall on the commando area, but it was surprising how few casualties there were.

After dark, however, everyone tended to lose that veneer of sangfroid, reverting to darker and more primitive apprehensions. By day most of the commando was awake, by night only a few in each troop. Then it was that imagination began to people the lower orchards with movement; then it was that every flash and bang in the night sent us flying face down on the ground waiting for the inevitable whiz, bang and the stench of cordite that hung about the trees for minutes afterwards. Two hours patrolling was a kind of sepulchral horror. Sentries would challenge each other, talk hoarsely about the quietness of the night, go in now and then to where the signal (wireless) set crackled in the darkness to look at the luminous hands of the watch, and all the time, listening, listening, listening.

At one half hour before dawn, roughly 0430 hours the whole would 'Stand to' for half an hour in expectation of an attack, but this was never achieved without much grumbling and dripping: fellows stood around in steel helmets and rifles, bleary eyed, thinking only of the command 'Stand down' which would be whispered from group to group. Reveille came about 0700 hours and the day's round of fatigues, washing, cooking and the like began anew.

The Fighting Patrol (Raid) of 18th June

In the somewhat static warfare at this time the need was to defend and build up the Normandy bridgehead as a base from which further advance would be made. Intelligence regarding the enemy's intentions was important. Valuable as patrolling is, interrogation of captured enemy provides a more definitive source of information. With this objective and the further objective of weakening the enemy's morale by demonstrating his vulnerability to attack, a daylight fighting patrol, or raid in force, covered by machine gun fire and mortar fire, and involving four troops and the heavy weapons troop was made on the enemy lines north-east from la Grande Ferme on 18th June, zero hour 2115 hrs. This was an 'in and out' raid made over a 400 yard front and it was hoped to penetrate up to 500 yards.

As the raiding party attacked they were subject to the ultimate test of the front-line soldier's discipline, courage and fieldcraft, his willingness to advance in daylight over an uncharted area likely to contain mines against an enemy deliberately firing at him if he exposed himself, or showering mortar bombs or shell salvos on him if they sensed where he was. He was likely to see some of his comrades being wounded or might be wounded himself.

As prisoners were to be taken, language skills and intelligence expertise might be required and the Intelligence Sergeant, Gibson with three members of his 'I' section took part.

This was the first raid of this sort which we had done. At 2000 hrs we were off to la Grande Ferme. The "mossies' were out biting and sucking till we writhed in agony. The evening was warm and still, threatening perhaps a little rain. On occasions like this I always wondered whom the night might claim. Bob was my nearest companion on this occasion.

An hour later we were at the farm draped in camouflage netting, faces black and green with grease paint. The fighting troops concerned had gone to ground ahead, slithering silently in a sunken ditch behind a hedge. Then we too went ahead. The silence was audible; the air hung heavy; and in Varraville woods birds startled from their nests rose up in angry complaint. A dark figure crept up silently and touched me. 'From the CO; if we send up two reds and a green withdraw at once'. 'Right'. Now we waited. I looked at my watch whose hands were widening remorselessly. There was no sign of the enemy.

Then, suddenly along our lines to the rear the whole air seemed filled with the 'phut', 'phut', phut' of mortars firing. Seconds later we were burying ourselves in the earth as our bombardment of mortars on the enemy positions came screaming down just in front. There seemed no end to it. The ground trembled and the silence was further stubbed with the staccato of machine guns. Now and then shrapnel whined viciously over us. Still it went on, the curtain of bombs shrieking its way to the target. Then, just as suddenly, there was silence.

At once we were up, moving quickly down a hedgerow now and through a gap. A loud bang and a flash brought the column to a halt – 'Some poor sod on a mine' whispered my companion. 'That'll give the show away'. We had to move on slowly in grass which literally bristled with S-mines. Suddenly on the right a Bren opened up and the crack of rifles followed. Somebody had run into trouble. On our front and to our left all was quiet. Were they waiting for us? Were the eyes watching? Two Spandaus had added to the opposition to the party on the right where things seemed pretty lively.

Suddenly we were on them, the enemy positions: a dozen grenades were thrown and crashed down. Next minute the whole air was alive with bullets. An MG 42 (German) had opened up on the other side of our hedgerow, all too close. The enemy had realised at last that something was afoot: but we had reached the first objective, a plain line of slit trenches interspersed with barbed wire. Our left flank had now contacted the enemy and for a few moments there was a vicious exchange of MG fire. Bob and I moved on over rough scrubby land through a little apple orchard. A second vicious exchange of shots on the left drove us to ground as the strays ripped dangerously over us. It was getting dark and ahead someone was lying there in the grass – ugh, it was a dead Jerry. We got going again, half running half walking. Flares were now creating an unreal illumination. The fellow in front of me rolled over, looking sick; he sighed and gave a little short cry. The way ahead was under a hail of MG fire so we deployed to the left and through a hedgerow. We were now at the second objective – the enemy had apparently withdrawn in great haste, probably to our third objective. On our right the fighting was now well to our rear. Was X Troop held up? If so we were dangerously outflanked. The cracking of small arms fire filled the air on our left, but the going was easier in this little wooded strip. In the gloom ahead I saw two horse-carts and timber stacked up. Two figures staggered towards us, wounded were they? – no, prisoners! 'Shiess nicht!, schiess nicht!' (don't shoot!) they shouted for they probably knew no English. 'Wir ergeben usis' (we give ourselves up): I ordered them into a trench until we were ready for them. We then reached the third objective; it was as deserted as the others had been.

Here the troop section to whom we were attached halted and fanned out to right and left to take up defensive positions awaiting the consolidation of the other troops. I looked around. We were on the edge of a little wood by a small stream. I waited for another flare to go up. 'Ready Bob and set your compass'. It came, a white flare rising silently in a parabola of light. 'Bearing 54°' he grunted. We crept forward through the soaking grass, probably only about 120 yards dead reckoning but it seemed to take many minutes. 'Someone moving over there' said Bob, pulling my sleeve. We lay still but he was wrong. Then 'Look' I said: two mortar barrels reared up above the ground, 'Go easy' I said, 'Let me have a look first'. Ever so slowly I crept to the edge of the pit and looked in: there was no movement. Four mortars of the 8 cm variety had been abandoned in all haste. Breathlessly Bob gulped, 'When we make a break for it sling a grenade at the mortars, we might as well do some damage'. We jumped up and – one, two, three – in they went, deafening us with their roar. We dashed back down the hedgerow then, 'Get down Dave' Bob shouted. We fell in a heap, just in time too. Mercifully there was a small ditch to give protection for three 88 shells crashed down not more than 20 yards away churning up great clods of earth which rained down on us. We now bumped into the 2 i/c. 'Anything wrong, Sir?' 'It's a bit sticky on the right: left has reached its objective: we're outflanked. CO has just told us to withdraw'. 'Found anything out there?' he asked. 'Four mortars, Sir' – we were interrupted by another salvo of 88s one of which rent the air not 10 yards away.

Our withdrawal was rapid, almost a run. On the way we picked up the two Jerry prisoners who were shivering in the trench. They wanted to talk but a jab with a rifle butt and a curt 'Halt's maul!' (shut up!) silenced them. In the darkness figures were tumbling backwards, scrambling through bushes. Another 88 landed and the Troop signaller's set went 'dis'. We had lost communication. A sharp instruction was given and we tumbled into empty Jerry trenches. Now we were on the move again, 'Withdraw to the farm' was on everyone's lips. A flare went up – red, then another red, then a green. We didn't wait. Everyone stumbled along the hedge at top speed. The wretched prisoners whimpered as we drove them on: one seemed to be wounded the other just plain scared. Once we had to go to ground when another salvo landed close but we were now relatively safe despite the continued shelling. As we cleared the enemy lines our own mortars again opened up to silence the enemy batteries, filling the west with gaudy flickerings. How endless that scramble had seemed. Darkness now filled the night and at last the wall of la Grande Ferme lay before us. No one was loitering because it would be just a matter of time before la Grande Ferme would be shelled to blazes.

The overall result of the raid was that along most of its front it overran the forward enemy positions as planned and captured eight prisoners. But this achievement exacted a high price in those fronting the attack. Marine W. N. Davies was killed and 26 others were wounded. One of the latter, Marine Zammit, suffered severe chest and spinal injuries from which he died five months later. In a flanking machine gun position Cpl Bryce, in command of No. 1 machine gun detachment, stood on a mine and sustained a compound fracture of his left foot and was in great pain. Despite this he remained in charge of his section, and got his gun into position to fire on an enemy post of 3 machine guns. Throughout the raid he maintained covering fire against this post although he himself was under fire. L/Cpl McGuire, one of the medical orderly/stretcher-bearers, had his left leg below mid-thigh virtually blown off when he stood on a mine. He had entered the minefield to rescue a wounded marine who had himself trodden on a mine. As McGuire lay bleeding he tied a tourniquet round the bleeding stump of his own leg and then dragged himself out of the minefield. Marine Didd suffered a penetrating sucking wound of the chest. Marine Dixon was hit in the face by a piece of shrapnel which ruptured his left eye. Marine Viner lost his left foot. Shrapnel lacerated Cpl Mold's neck and fractured his jaw. The remainder suffered mostly from lacerations or penetrating wounds of the lower limbs or pelvis and bullet wounds.

Marine Ray Tullett of B Troop was on the raid. Two days previously his brother Ron in the same Troop had been killed in a minefield. At one point Tullett jumped up and in what appeared to be a spirit of retaliation for the death of his brother ran forward 'hose-piping' the enemy trenches with his Tommy gun. He returned uninjured. It is probably unwise to have two brothers in the same troop.

The task of rescuing the wounded was difficult because of the extent to which the enemy lines had been penetrated and because of the number who had suffered minefield injuries of feet and legs and could not walk. All were rescued and brought back to the RAP. Confidence in rescue, the feeling that when they have done their bit they will not be allowed to lie wounded without help, plays an important part in creating and sustaining morale in fighting troops.

Excision of destroyed tissue, patching of the sucking chest wound, bandaging, dressing, splinting and morphia were the order of the day. In the RAP some of the seriously wounded were grey and shocked, little aware of their surroundings, others lay on stretchers waiting their turn to be dealt with, quiet despite their pain and suffering. They were assisted in many ways by the padre, the Rev. Reginald Haw, whom they trusted because he shared their risks, understood their feelings and gave great practical help. He recognised that understandably soldiers have little specific medical knowledge and, while well aware of the risks of wounding, tend to suppress contemplation of it. When wounded, a theoretical possibility becomes a reality which often engenders undeclared apprehension as to outcome, best met by an understanding voice and such reassurance as is possible. The severity of the wounds on this occasion was such that all but one of those wounded had to be evacuated. Our medical jeeps had a busy night.

Sergeant Mansfield, on the raid, describes what he calls 'limbering down' after such a raid. He and his fellow occupant of his slit trench just sat for an hour not speaking. Neither of them wanted to do so. Then they were all right again.

Even amid bloodshed the British soldier's capacity for humour, no matter the circumstances, was not lacking. In the RAP L/Cpl McGuire, medical orderly in battle but Liverpool butcher in civilian life, managed to mutter to me, as I removed dead tissue from the stump of his left leg, that he had not thought that he himself would be the subject of such butchery!

Out of the line

Next day, 19th June, 46 RM Cdo relieved 47 RM Cdo which was withdrawn to the region of Hauger and Ecarde, the medical section renewing the occupation of Café Tabac. Of these days out of the line Sergeant Gibson wrote:

> And there were these slow summer days behind the line, 500 yards behind, but what a difference that made. Here there was no 'Stand to' at dawn, no dash past areas exposed to enemy fire, none of that uncanny feeling of being incessantly watched and ranged upon. But we were always aware that behind us lay those accursed orchards, the Grande Ferme and all these thousand eyes watching and waiting.
>
> At night we could stand gazing eastwards looking now at the coast, now at the sky where the stars lay luminous in deepest blue. Far from home, we talked of the future, of the chance of survival, of death.

One night, out of the line, the sleeping medical occupants of Café Tabac were awakened by a loud bang outside. Bangs were so much a way of life that no one thought of exchanging welcome sleep, while in reserve, with nocturnal investigation of bangs. Inspection in the morning, however, revealed a large hole in the road. We also learnt that during the night there had been casualties among some of the 6th Airborne Division camped in a field nearby. The artillerymen who investigated concluded that a shell had hit the road outside Café Tabac without exploding and then re-emerged to explode in the field.

The medical officer of 46 RM Cdo did not initially use Maison Chevigny as his RAP when 46 RM Cdo was in line. He considered its position too dangerous and preferred to use slit trenches. One day while I was visiting him an officer and a marine in his unit, close to where I was standing, were killed while taking cover in a slit trench near his RAP. The mortar bomb hit the side of the trench burying the occupants who were dead although we dug them out within a few minutes.

On 24th June the commando moved back to the front line and was then rested again between 3rd and 10th July.

Caen

The capture of Caen was a virtually all-British battle, the last such to be fought in Europe. On 7th July the 450 bomber daylight raid which heralded the attack on Caen took place. From a vantage point close by we watched in awe as, for an hour and a half, the earth shook as wave after wave of Lancaster and Halifax bombers lumbered low overhead in a sinister procession dropping 2500 tons of explosive. As two bombers plunged earthwards we counted parachutes emerging from them, unsure what the total complement should be and whether the airmen dangling from them would land among friend or foe. Two other bombers, returning, had large holes in their wings.

Close by, Madame Marie-Louise Osmont,* a World War I nurse and widow of a distinguished French surgeon, lived in the Chateau Périers, now on the British front line. She kept a diary ...

July 7, 1944

Never, never will I forget that Caen offensive of July 7! For several hours we felt it coming; six hundred men arrived in the morning. At the farm the Red Cross arranged everything in the barns and made room. At the house the non-commissioned officers bustled about near the offices with papers in their hands. And among the men the murmur began to spread: 'Offensive for tonight.'

The evening consummated the annihilation of Caen. The bombardment on the first day of the landing on Tuesday 6th June had already caused enormous damage; entire streets had been

* *The Normandy Diary of Marie-Louise Osmont 1940–1944.* Translated by G. L. Newman, Random House Inc., New York N.Y. 10022. Reproduced with the permission of the copyright holder, *Memorial, Caen, Normandie, Services des Archives, Caen.*

The destruction of Caen. Some of the ruins. (*Crown Copyright*)

The railway station. (*Crown Copyright*)

destroyed, La Miséricorde (Mercy Hospital) destroyed with so many nurses, so many nuns and patients. Every day after that bombs fell but nothing approached the disaster of July 7. The entire city was annihilated in an apocalyptic chaos. Thousands killed, people horribly wounded, the remaining survivors destitute. There are similar examples in the course of history, but few as tragic.

We were finishing dinner at eight o'clock. The batteries began barrage fire, an intense pounding; then, above their familiar clamour we suddenly heard the long mewing sound that had already passed our heads on the day of the landing. It was the battleships joining in. Endlessly, endlessly, their long unmistakable hiss slid over us, just above our heads, it seemed.

And suddenly a heavy, powerful roaring reached us. All the men massed around us at the gate; all those grouped in the drive turned and greeted it with a clamour. The squadrons of bombers came in at an angle, close together, steady, massive, one following another continuously, endlessly, without a gap. It was crushing in its strength and terrifying in what one imagined of the potential death hidden in their flanks. They passed over continuously; perhaps a thousand of them passed, greeted by furious ack ack fire. They slid with their heavy and confident flight among the fireballs of the shells; red streaks rose toward them and exploded in luminous sprays, in black plumes, but they passed without pause and the ground beneath our feet shook with the terrible weight of their bombs; the houses trembled, the doors opened the noise of the window panes rattling could be heard in spite of the terrifying roar. Firing by the batteries, hisses of the naval shells, crushing falls of tons of bombs: and coming towards us among the trees, then at ground level, enveloping us in an opaque, acrid vapour, the artificial clouds released to protect the tanks and infantry drowned everything in a sinister shroud. Chests tight, nerves tense, we were lost, drowned in this fog and this noise. Horrible vision of war! We were part of this sinister thing; it was in us and we were part of it, a hell of fire and noise in which we would perhaps disappear with so many others, so many innocent children, women, and men distraught with horror, so many animals mad with terror.

And in this suffocation the voices of the men in khaki, men ready for the sacrifice, were a blessing to us. Edgy, excited by 'great battle,' proud also of these powerful English arms, their youth rose above the storm and made us pull away a little from its grip. Yet some were sad to have lost comrades killed during the day; one of them, melancholy, thinking of the English women told me, 'Mama cry'; but all were vibrant with that terrible excitement of combat. The cook

spoke to me of the German bombardments of England: 'Comrade lost
eight people in his family, he all alone now. Comrade over there lost
four children, no more children now'. And this avenged the other! As
for our sergeant, he exulted, 'Boches much afraid now.'

We left to lie down, still in our stair hole of course, where fortunately
the noise was slightly reduced; in my room, with the batteries opposite
and not a pane in the windows it would have been unbearable! We
chatted for a long time without sleeping. It was just an uninterrupted
rumbling of cannons and the endless hisses of the naval long-range
shells. What a night!! Disturbed sleep, interrupted a hundred times.
Officers restless, talking, opening and closing the doors of the parlour
and hall. Hellish roaring. We talk, we doze, when suddenly – – –
rran – – – a shell! To me it seemed so close that it must have hit
the house! Window panes flew in shards, everything banged
everywhere! It was seven o'clock in the morning.

July 8, 1944

From the noon report: few details yet on the progress of the (Army)
offensive, certainly it will continue for several days. They announce,
nevertheless that 2,300 tons of shells have been fired during the night
– five villages taken back: Hérouville, Lébisey, Epron, Authie, and one
other (all heavily defended villages forming a line round the north of
Caen) – they're 2 km from Caen. In Manche: St-Jean-de-Daye.

I spent the afternoon at the farm. Since this morning the ambulances
have been on alert and have had to ask for additional vehicles. It's
just an incessant coming and going between the front line and us.
The vehicles leave rapidly and return more slowly, carefully, loaded
with wounded men in khaki. What a procession; what sights! Some
slightly wounded, smoking the inevitable consolation cigarette; others,
whom they unload with the greatest possible gentleness, and who are
white as sheets, their nostrils tight, their eyes rolled back. Wide,
bleeding lacerations, shattered limbs, internal injuries, faces in shreds
– – – – an entire poor youth martyred. Some are simply shell-shocked
and it's moving to see them sob, hiccup, supported by comrades who
walk them round in a tender maternal way, talk to them, try to
reassure them. Their hands are shaking with convulsive tremors; a
cannon shot – one of theirs – that's too loud, makes them jump and
crouch down like hunted animals. What visions of horror have their
haggard eyes recorded?

The captured Germans are placed apart, in a stable, but are examined
in their turn, carried with the same careful precautions. Many are
very seriously wounded. All are dirty, their hair long, faces unshaven,

they who were so well groomed not long ago. Their long hands, their thinness speak of the privations of this month-long siege in the Lébisey Blockhauses under the incessant shelling. Perhaps their status as prisoners seems sweet to them after this nightmarish night. Some throw themselves in rapture on the tea, the jam, and the biscuits offered them. Twelve hours ago these men were enemies; now we support them with kind gestures.

A visit to Caen two days later (riding my motor cycle with the padre on the pillion) showed the result of the raid. The approach roads, tortuous as they re-routed round bomb craters, were littered with shattered vehicles, tanks, abandoned equipment. We were dismayed at the immense destruction which had been wrought. Caen had been almost obliterated, its streets and buildings merging in piles of rubble from which here and there smoke was still rising. Occasional knots of civilians were digging in the rubble – what were they searching for, relatives or possessions? An ancient, historic Norman city had been destroyed and two thousand of its citizens had been killed.

Although at this stage of the campaign the front was relatively static casualties continued, mostly from patrolling. On 24th June Lt Whittaker joined his brother (an RAF pilot) on the roll of those killed in action. L/Cpl Young and Marine Smith were killed and 22 marines injured.

The Fighting Patrol (Raid) of 23rd July

On 22nd July the commando was ordered to send out a night-fighting patrol to breach the enemy line beyond la Grande Ferme du Bouisson and take prisoners. The patrol was to be led by Lt O'Brien accompanied by a South African, Lt Collett, who had just joined the unit and 14 volunteers including Marine John Wetjen and Corporal Peter Terry. The latter, as a German speaker, was an invaluable member of any patrol.

The patrol would set out from la Grande Ferme, moving from there to a starting point midway between the farm and the German forward defence locations (FDLs). From the starting point a hedge led 300 yds to another hedge at right angles to it. This was the so called 'T' junction, 100 yards from the enemy defensive positions.

Two members of the raiding party were armed with Bren guns, the remainder had Tommy guns and all carried three grenades. A support group, a firm base for the patrol, consisted of seven Bren guns, four 3 inch mortars and four 2 inch mortars sited along a 200 yard band parallel with the enemy FDLs and approximately 350 yards from them. Beyond the outer extremities of the 200 yard band there were two light machine guns. The support group Brens would neutralise the enemy FDLs on each side

In No Man's Land: La Grande Ferme du Buisson.

of the raiding party and mortar fire would be brought down on the enemy trenches just ahead of the patrol. Light artillery fire from the Royal artillery would also straddle the enemy positions in some depth just before the raiding party moved in. An advance RAP would be at la Grande Ferme.

Prior to the departure of the fighting patrol a standing patrol had been established 150 yards lateral to, and to the right of, the T junction. At 0100 this patrol saw flares being fired from the enemy lines at the point at which the fighting patrol would enter them. From the same area a number of single shots were heard. Such activity at the precise point where the fighting patrol would attack seemed ominous. As the standing patrol lay and watched it heard whispering and saw two figures about 30 yards away, too far for the patrol to challenge for fear of giving its position away. The figures scrambled through the hedgerow and ran down a field towards la Grande Ferme. Another standing patrol in position at the farm apprehended them and established that they were deserters. The flares and the shots were interpreted as likely to have been an attempt by the Germans to bring down the fleeing deserters. On interrogation the deserters provided some disturbing information. That night they had been laying mines beside the hedge along which the fighting patrol was to approach the enemy position but, oddly, they said that the path adjacent to the hedge was not mined. They said that there was a single strand of trip (warning) wire 10 yards in front of the FDLs. Sentries armed with machine guns were posted at 30–40 yard intervals along the whole enemy front. The area selected for the raid was not heavily manned. This information was communicated to Col Phillips and Brigadier Leicester who, bolstered by the information about an unmined path decided that the raid should go on. Marine Wetjen and Cpl Terry, with detail added by Lt O'Brien, have described the raid.

John Wetjen, having volunteered, was ordered in the evening of 22nd July to muster for a dummy run. The thick hedges offered concealed routes but the deep ditches in their centre or at the sides created difficulties particularly where they were filled with water. The dummy run – exploring the early part of the route and determining tactics – went off without incident and the raid proper was 'on' for later that night.

At 0330 hours on the 23rd the members of the patrol set out from la Grande Ferme. They proceeded cautiously and silently and all went well as they moved down the reputedly unmined path by the hedge until, past the 'T' junction, they were 30 yds from the enemy lines. Suddenly, up front, an explosion rent the night air: Lt Collett had trodden on a mine. This was followed shortly by a further explosion as Sgt Gutteridge did the same. Other members of the patrol were also wounded. They would have to be left to be picked up later. Alerted by the exploding mines the enemy opened fire with machine guns. The Germans as yet could not see the patrol: their Spandaus (machine guns) were firing on fixed lines trained on the higher ground occupied by the main body of the commando and therefore aiming too high. As the tracer bullets passed just above his head Wetjen reflected with a certain grim satisfaction that they were probably shaking up those who were relaxing back at base!

As the enemy defences burst into action O'Brien ordered everyone to lie flat but he recognised that surprise had now been lost. He knew that, according to plan, the patrol's supporting fire would be coming down just ahead and lift as, according to plan, the marines moved forward; and so it did. Delay would negate the beneficial effect of this supporting fire so without further delay O'Brien ordered the patrol forward. As Collett had activated a mine it was clear that the final advance to the enemy position was through a minefield. O'Brien first threw a grenade and a smoke bomb into a gap in a hedge ahead and through this he and Sgt Horsfield, the remaining sergeant, led the patrol, now reduced to about seven men. O'Brien led a group to the right, Horsfield a group to the left. As the marines dashed in firing automatic weapons and throwing explosive and smoke grenades they encountered no retaliatory response from the outer trenches – it appeared that the enemy had withdrawn from them. In the face of enemy fire and with some of the commando's own supportive mortar fire falling dangerously close the patrol advanced. Because of their dispersal the enemy trenches were difficult to find in the smoky semi-darkness but the patrol reached the rearward enemy trenches. Three of the enemy were killed and one so severely wounded that he had to be left. Two figures then rose up from a trench, one of them an officer. As they were about to be taken prisoner one of the marines, thinking that they were acting hostilely, fired and wounded both of them. O'Brien was furious but the officer could walk and Sergeant Horsfield took possession of him. O'Brien now fired the withdrawal signal and ordered Wetjen and Marine Lloyd to act as a covering party for two minutes as the patrol withdrew taking the officer prisoner with them.

When the others seemed away Wetjen and Lloyd too withdrew. By this time the Germans were reacting more accurately and bringing down a heavy concentration of fire on the patrol's retreat, extending back to and including la Grande Ferme. The two marines had not gone far when they came upon Collett, lying on the ground wounded in both legs. They half lifted him so that his legs were clear of the ground and began dragging him back but they had not gone very far when a mortar bomb landed close to Wetjen seriously wounding him in the left leg. Collett who couldn't walk at all had to be left and Lloyd helped Wetjen along. After about 50 yards they met two of the commando medical orderly/stretcher bearers who had been following up behind the patrol and knew that there were wounded ahead to be rescued – the temporary RAP at la Grande Ferme had established a further out-post, manned by the two stretcher bearers, close to the T junction. One of the stretcher-bearers carried Wetjen (weight 90kg) by a fireman's lift, the other went back with Lloyd to where Collett was lying and carried him back.

About the same time at la Grande Ferme I received a message that two other members of the raiding party, Sergeant Gutteridge and Marine Warren, were seriously wounded and required medical help before being brought back. They were lying by the hedge close to the T junction. The mine on which Sgt Gutteridge had trodden had virtually blown his foot off. Warren, lying close by, had a compound fracture of his leg. The mortaring was continuing but falling wide. We bandaged them up, gave them morphia, and brought them back on stretchers to a point which the medical jeep had been able to reach, and thence to the main RAP at Maison Chevigny. In the meantime Lt O'Brien, who had himself been wounded, together with Sgt Horsfield and Cpl Esther (also wounded) had returned to assist others who had also been wounded.

At the main RAP in Maison Chevigny there were 15 wounded men. Thirteen of the 15 patrol members and one of the support group had been wounded plus the German officer. Corporal Terry was missing – he was brought in later, seriously wounded. Collett, Gutteridge, Warren, Wetjen,

Corporal Ostle (although suffering from multiple wounds Ostle had tried to help Collett when the latter fell), Marine Julian (multiple shrapnel wounds) and the German Officer were seriously wounded. As I prodded wounds to remove shrapnel, bandaged, splinted, injected, advised and talked to the wounded, Brigadier Leicester and Col Phillips visited the RAP. With the impotence which laymen exhibit when confronted with such a scene these two figures of military authority were uncharacteristically silent in a setting where their orders could play no part. The day was well advanced before the last of the wounded were carried up the narrow spiral stair which led from the basement of Maison Chevigny.

Twenty-five years later, attending a meeting at the Wellcome Institute in London, the commissionaire, checking the identity of those attending from a list, looked up when I gave him my name, 'I'm right' he said. 'You are Doc Forfar of 47 Commando aren't you?' It was Sergeant Gutteridge.

Peter Terry's story does not begin with the wounds he suffered at Sallenelles or at Port-en-Bessin. He was an Austrian who had escaped from that country after it had been occupied by the Germans. Just before D-Day Terry presented himself along with Sergeant Fuller and three other Germans – all refugees from the Third Reich and members of 10 Inter Allied Commando – for attachment to 47 RM Cdo. It could be recognised that Terry was a very cultured man, well educated, fluent in French, English and German. His involvement in patrolling, however, carried a sinister risk. With Jewish antecedents, capture, had his origins been discovered, would have meant for him the likelihood of very different treatment from that accorded to British prisoners of war. Two of his 10 I.A. colleagues who had been captured had been interrogated and then shot. Yet Terry had participated frequently, at times almost daily, in patrols either alone or with X Troop. The patrols in which he was involved would usually go out to la Grande Ferme du Buisson from where the route beyond was usually along the hedge to the T junction. No patrol other than that of 18th June had been beyond that point. On one occasion, hidden by a hedge near the T junction Terry observed two Germans, one cleaning his boots. He recognised them as Austrians because of their, to him, unmistakable accents. Taking a risk he called to them from his hiding place. They seemed scared to death to hear his Viennese voice telling them that if they came with him they would be sent to a camp in Canada. Canada, he knew, was a magic word among German soldiers. After further discussion and perhaps cognisant of the safe conduct leaflets – dropped by our aircraft on enemy lines – which they had with them they walked unarmed towards Terry's hiding place. Terry's slit trench was a very unsatisfactory affair so, arriving back at base in the dark, Terry set his prisoners digging a new slit trench for himself. He was most impressed with the skill with which they did

PASSIERSCHEIN

An die alliierten Vorposten:

Der deutsche Soldat, der diesen Passierschein vorzeigt, benutzt ihn als Zeichen seines ehrlichen Willens, sich zu ergeben. Er ist zu entwaffnen. Er muss gut behandelt werden. Er hat Anspruch auf Verpflegung und, wenn nötig, ärztliche Behandlung. Er wird so bald wie möglich aus der Gefahrenzone entfernt.

SAFE CONDUCT

To Allied sentries:

The German soldier who carries this safe-conduct is using it as sign of his genuine wish to give himself up. He is to be disarmed, to be well looked after, to receive food and medical attention as required, and is to be removed from the danger zone as soon as possible.

Safe conduct pass proffered by two of the prisoners who deserted to 47 RM Cdo lines on 23 July 1944.
On the back, in German, was:
'A message to each German Soldier – The War is almost over. After five years you are still alive. Why die in the last week? The prisoners of 1944 will see their families soon again.'

this, complete with entrance steps and an earthen shelf for his belongings. In the morning he fulfilled his part of the bargain, handing them over for onward transmission to Canada.

On the morning of 22nd July Captain Walton of X Troop gave Terry a lift to Amfreville nearby. There was a rumour that the commando was returning to England and Terry, not too enthusiastic about the standard of laundry which could be achieved in a slit trench, had identified a French lady who would do his laundry expertly for a few bars of 'real' soap. A nearby farm had stocks of Camembert cheese and Terry's father, also an escapee and now in London, had said that one of the things he missed most was Camembert cheese. With the prospect of remedying this Terry acquired several Camemberts and returned with Walton in time for the afternoon 'stand to' in his slit trench. In the late afternoon the CO sent for Terry and informed him of the patrol that night, indicating that it was hoped to take prisoners for interrogation. At the briefing the adjutant (Captain Spencer) suggested that because of his knowledge of the terrain Terry should lead the patrol up to the T junction. The CO agreed. Terry was introduced to a new officer, Lt Collett. In view of the careful briefing for this patrol Terry felt that it must have a special significance.

In preparation for the patrol Terry then returned to his trench for a few hours sleep. Towards 2300 hours he was wakened to be informed that two deserters (those referred to above) had appeared at the Grande Ferme and he was needed to interrogate them. They proved to be Poles who spoke little German and brandished their British 'safe conduct' leaflets. One had cut off the embroidered German eagle with swastika worn above the right breast pocket on his uniform and was holding this up repeating over and over again 'Polski, Polski – nix Nazi'. They informed Terry that they belonged to the 716th infantry division and gave the information about mine laying close to the very route which the patrol was to follow. Armed with this information, Terry secretly thought it might result in the cancellation of the patrol and sought out Lt O'Brien who was to lead the patrol. The latter passed the information to Col Phillips who, in conjunction with Brigade Headquarters decided that the patrol should go on. Terry's apprehension was hardly allayed when he was told that he could write an uncensored letter and hand it to the post corporal who would post it if he did not return. His account of the further events of the night are best told in his own words.

> We met outside the sandbagged HQ building at 0200 hours. There we applied black camouflage cream to our faces, drew 200 rounds of ammunition for our Tommy guns, grenades, flares and all the usual paraphernalia of war, and fifteen minutes later moved down the little path past our forward lines to the Grande Ferme in no-man's-land which an advance group had secured for the night. Apart from encountering the two Poles earlier they had not seen or heard any enemy activity. I now saw, leaning against the farm sheds, several stretchers. I had never seen stretchers there before and, while this did not exactly help to build up my morale, I felt that at least someone had made sure we were prepared.
>
> We moved off at 0330 hours with me leading the way for the first ten minutes or so along the first hedge leading to the T Junction.

There we lay on the ground for a while and, not hearing anything, silently moved off along the continuation of the hedge, on its right, Collett leading. I was about in the middle, behind Lt O'Brien. Some minutes later there was a bright flash and an explosion at the head of the column. We all threw ourselves down on the ground and Lt O'Brien crept forward to investigate. Then word was passed back that Collett had stepped on a mine and I soon heard him crying out for help. Otherwise there was eerie silence for a couple of minutes after which all hell broke loose. Tracer bullets came at us from the right and front. In the darkness of the night these appeared to come directly towards one and only veer off at the last second. Then a flare went up and in its light I saw, some 50 yards ahead, some of our men still lying on the ground and two Germans running along the hedge away from us: one of them stopped, turned round and made a movement which I took to be the throwing of a stick grenade. I just had time to call for everyone to make for the cover of the hedge to our left when the mortar fire began – possibly our support fire as well as that of the Germans. Whoever was responsible it all seemed to land on us and just as I got up to run for cover I felt something hitting my back and was thrown forward. I remember calling out, 'I'm hit' and realised that I was unable to get up to run to the hedge. Someone pulled me there and I came to rest on an incline inside it. I felt no pain but was fighting for breath. The wet trickle I felt on the left side of my back made me believe that something had pierced my heart and I lay there on my stomach thinking that I would die. I don't think I passed out but cannot remember anything until it was daylight. Looking over the edge of the incline I heard and saw some motorised vehicles moving along what must have been a branch of the Sallenelles-Merville road. I remember calling out for help in German, 'Ich bin verwundeter englischer Soldat. Brauche Hilfe' (I am a wounded English soldier. Need help). Luckily as it turned out they did not hear me and I decided to somehow make my way back to our lines. It seemed to me that all our chaps had disappeared or possibly were lying dead in the hedge. My main problem was breathing, and making my way along the overgrown water-logged ditch inside the hedge. I knew I was making a lot of noise. After what seemed a long time, the hedge became impenetrable and I decided to risk making my way alongside it by the open field. I climbed up the incline and just then I heard small arms fire and felt something hitting me below the left shoulder, which caused me to let myself fall back into the hedge and come to rest in the water. It was at that point that I gave up. (After the war Terry learnt that the probable explanation for this wounding was that someone from 46 RM Commando, who were also in that area, had seen him emerging from the hedge but as he was coming from the wrong direction thought he was the enemy and fired a burst at him. A bullet had lodged in his left arm. It was removed later at the field hospital at Douvres-la-Délivrande). I do not know how long I lay there in the water, but at last I heard a friendly English voice calling out, 'Is there anyone down there?' It turned out to be the Commando Brigade Major from Amfreville, Major Wood, who alone had gone along the hedge hoping to find survivors from the patrol and had heard rasping breathing coming from the ditch. He tried to extricate me from the hedge and called for help which came in the form of my friend Ian Harris of 10 I.A. Cdo attached to 46 RM Cdo in the same capacity as I was at 47. The Brigade Major and Harris dragged me out of the ditch and to Captain Forfar's RAP.

I remember a cellar with quite a lot of wounded men from the patrol, me on my stomach with the Padre Rev Haw holding my hand while Captain Forfar probed around in my back. I was in a bad shape and required all my energy and concentration to keep breathing. When Captain Forfar prepared to give me an injection I feared that it would send me to sleep, preventing me from breathing. When I said this Captain Forfar replied, 'Don't worry. You won't go to sleep unless it is good for you'. It was the single most important sentence said to me and the first to really calm me down. Later I found that Captain Forfar had removed all the shrapnel pieces he could but quite a few others are still safely embedded in my back and chest after fifty years. I remember being carried out of the cellar on a stretcher, up the hill past our forward dug-outs, from which our chaps called out encouraging words, sentences like, 'Lucky you – for you the war is over', and then being strapped in on the top of a jeep. In the stretcher below me was Lt Collett, who was in great pain and thought to have lost his left foot. Someone came up to me and asked if there was anything I needed from my slit trench.

I could not speak properly but just managed to whisper 'Cheese ... Cheese'. Thus a few minutes later my haversack, containing the Camembert for my father, was placed below my head in lieu of a pillow. It was to remain there with some embarrassing consequences for the best part of a week.

The jeep took us to the big square at Douvres la Délivrande where, in front of the Gothic Cathedral, the RAMC had erected large tents for the wounded. I saw the first female nurses, a reassurance that this place must be reasonably safe. It was, in fact, less than five miles from the front line south of Caen. I was told that my left lung had collapsed, which had caused the breathing difficulty and the following day was shown a 9 mm bullet extracted from my arm above the elbow. It had entered below the shoulder luckily causing little harm.

Two or three days later I was taken to the beachhead, where several dozen men on stretchers were lined up on the sand waiting for transfer to a hospital ship offshore. I was covered with an army issue blanket and within minutes it began to pour with rain, soaking me from head to foot, a condition I had to endure for several hours. Finally, we were taken off on a small craft and, in quite heavy seas, transferred to a hospital ship where I soon found myself in the comfort of a real bed and real sheets. I had not seen sheets for many weeks. Because of my condition breathing was easier sitting up, and the cheese-filled haversack under my head served me well. In Southampton I spent a night at a hospital where I was X-Rayed just as the first German 'doodle-bugs', or V-1 rockets, began to appear over the coast. All wounded were to be evacuated to the north of England.

The following day we were shoved into a converted cattle train inside which stretchers were attached to the sides in layers of three. Mine was at the top, close to the roof so that sitting up was virtually impossible without my head hitting the ceiling. The nurses must have noticed my discomfort and tried their best to help but I noticed that each time one came near she grimaced and turned her head away: the Camembert was getting somewhat overripe though I must have become used to it. Then one nurse called the sister who asked when my wounds were last dressed, believing that the odour emanated from the holes in my back.

Fearful that my cheese trophies would be confiscated I lied saying that no one had attended to my wounds since leaving Normandy, knowing that the nurses on the train were unlikely to perform this function while we were moving. We were on that train for two and a half days, being shunted around to avoid bomb damage and circumventing London which was now under constant attack from V-1 rockets. Finally one evening we arrived in Manchester from where an ambulance took me to (Withington) hospital. By this time the poor soldiers and nurses in the train must have been overwhelmed by the malodorous cheese and I must admit that I too began to have misgivings. As soon as I was in my assigned bed in the hospital ward I called the night nurse, told her the truth and asked her to store the Camembert in the ward kitchen's fridge. Breathing real air, in spite of having only one lung to do it with, was a relief.

A week or so later my parents were to arrive from London and I was looking forward to presenting them with the spoils of war. Shortly

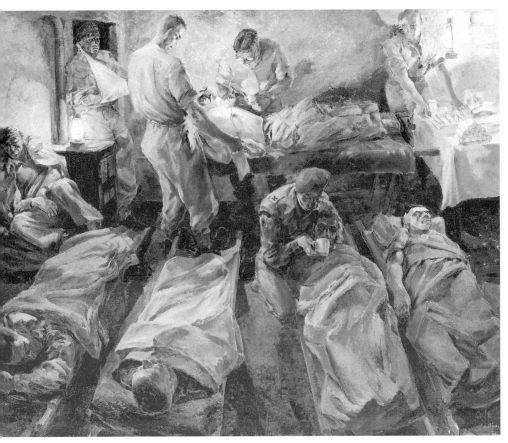

Painting by war artist Leslie Cole, entitled *Scene in a Regimental Aid Post in a Filthy Cellar at Sallenelles after Action*. Cpl Terry is being operated on; the German officer is second from the left of the four stretcher cases on the floor. (*Crown Copyright*)

before their arrival the ward patients were served afternoon tea and I heard someone at the far end who had been served first comment on the 'smelly cheese' given out with our biscuits – and before I realised what was happening I found that my Camemberts had been cut up into 40 pieces. Most left it on their plates. I actually ate the little piece lying limply on my plate though I felt that I had let my father down. Ever since, whenever I eat Camembert, I think of July 23, 1944.

The Sallenelles Painting

When Brigadier 'Jumbo' Leicester and Col Phillips visited the RAP on the early hours of 24 July the scene in the basement must have impressed them because later Col Phillips had it painted by one of the official war

Casualty jeep crossing Benouville (Pegasus) Bridge over the River Orne. The stretcher
mounted transversely across the bonnet and projecting beyond the sides of the jeep is in
danger of being knocked off. In the background are the gliders which led the D-Day
invasion. Landing in the first few minutes of 6 June, the troops whom they carried rushed
and captured the bridge. (*Crown Copyright*)

artists. The painting was entitled *Scene in a Regimental Aid Post in a Filthy
Cellar at Sallenelles after Action.* It was not painted that night nor during
the period when the commando was at Sallenelles. When we were half
way across France, an official War Artist, Leslie Cole, visited the commando
to paint one of the commando's actions and Col Phillips directed him to
me. I was able to explain to him exactly how the wounded had been lying
in the RAP basement and how they were being dealt with. Various soldiers
had to re-enact the positions of the wounded but Padre Haw, Hoskins
(medical orderly), Tarbin (Jeep driver), and myself were painted as we had
been on that night. The artist then went back to Maison Chevigny and
completed his initial drawings in the old RAP basement. In the painting
Corporal Terry is on the 'operating table' and I am leaning over him
probing the shrapnel wound in the back of his chest – he had a pneumo-
thorax and haemothorax – with Private Hoskins (RAMC) beside me and
Driver Tarbin holding a torch to illuminate the wound area. The padre is

Casualty care and casualty evacuation. Jeeps with raised in-line framework for stretchers. (*Crown Copyright*)

The Sallenelles Jeep.

kneeling beside Sergeant Gutteridge; the German is in the forefront, supine with his head towards the viewer. There is a paraffin lamp on the stove in the corner. The painting is now in the Imperial War Museum in London.

The Local GP

Before D-Day the Germans banned doctors from the coastal areas of France or severely restricted their movements because of the ease with which, on their rounds, they could observe defence preparations. In these areas medical officers of the invasion forces had to give such civilian help as they could. At Sallenelles I had a small, entirely gratuitous, civilian practice. The medicaments available to a field medical officer hardly met the needs of civilian practice although there was an ample supply of the Army's panacea for all 'complaints medical' in the soldier, the 'number 9' tablet designed to cure by activating the most recalcitrant of bowels. To improve our range of prescriptions Sergeant Leaman RAMC set about extending our pharmacopoeia. The Germans had left behind in Maison Chevigny large quantities of white sodium bicarbonate tablets − presumably their debaucheries there had resulted in frequent indigestion − and with these as a substrate and a few colouring materials, mostly blue and red ink plus water, Sergeant Leaman soon had a range of coloured tablets and 'mixtures' in the 'dispensary'.

He averred that the prescription of the bicarbonate, red, white or blue, often led to benefit being attributed specifically to a bicarbonate pill or potion of a particular colour. I dismissed this as scientifically unsustainable. How satisfied Sergeant Leaman would have been with the results of a serious research study published in the British Medical Journal 52 years later which concluded − 'Colours affect the perceived action of a drug and seem to influence the effectiveness of a drug'. Perhaps in his honour this should now be called the 'Leaman effect'.

The padre, the more accomplished linguist, frequently accompanied me on civilian visits without exhibiting any of the trappings of his office. With his semi-bald head he looked and was older than me and was often assumed to be the 'senior doctor'. He took great pleasure in such vicarious recognition, always explaining however in grave but halting French that he felt he should pass the case over to 'my junior colleague who happens to have a special knowledge of your particular problem'.

The Last of the Bridgehead

On 24th July the commando moved to le Plein/Amfreville and on 8th August to Sannerville/Troarn close to the German positions which were on higher ground. Sannerville/Troarn had been and continued to be the subject of heavy shelling and mortar fire. It was a desolate shambles of shattered buildings, enormous bomb craters – confluent due to their numbers – dust and the smell of decaying bodies. The scene was reminiscent of pictures of front line positions in World War I. Among this desolation the medical section conducted a revealing but macabre experiment. Arriving at night we had established the RAP in the remains of a house and in the morning saw that almost opposite was a large crater resulting from a bomb which must have fallen a few days previously. At the heaped up earthy edge of the bomb crater were two blackened German corpses side by side, the top halves of each sticking up vertically above the ground one with his helmet still in position. Several shots were fired at the helmet with a rifle and all ricocheted off. A British helmet was then placed on the head of the other corpse and the experiment repeated from the same distance. The shots penetrated the British helmet. We felt that the commando preference for green berets rather than steel helmets, unless ordered to wear the latter, now at least had some experimental justification.

At Maison Chevigny: '4 Special Service Brigade. From June to August 1944 the Brigade held positions in this area. This memorial honours the men of the Brigade HQ, 41, 46, 47 RM Commandos who gave their lives.'

Monsieur Chevigny unveils the Fourth Special Service (Commando) Memorial. Beside him as interpreter is his son-in-law, Sir Robin Janvrin KCVO, CB, Secretary to Her Majesty Queen Elizabeth II.

While at Troarn there was a short rest period in a wooded area which had been so heavily shelled that there were more tree roots than trees showing. One day when the sun was shining Captain Isherwood and Sergeant Mansfield of B Troop thought that their marines should 'get some sun on their bodies', so the troop stripped off completely. Isherwood and Mansfield retained their berets and still had their binoculars slung round their necks. As they walked around quite happily in the nude severe shelling started and everyone darted to his trench. Unfortunately Isherwood had strayed too far from home and jumped into the nearest hole. It was a latrine trench.

Aggressive patrolling was demanded and during this 10 day period Lt Borne and Marines Griffiths and Rowlinson were killed and 34 wounded.

The outward pressure on the border of the bridgehead was now progressively increasing and on 18th August the border was finally broken. Marching men, motorised transport and clanking tanks began fanning out into the French countryside after a retreating Wehrmacht. 47 RM Cdo was on a bearing to the French coast and Fécamp, 100 miles away. The stage of brinkmanship was over and the long chase had begun.

The 'Last Post' at the Fourth Commando Brigade Memorial at Sannerville.

Casualties

From 12th June until it left the Sannerville area on 18th August 47 RM Cdo suffered 117 casualties out of a total strength of 370. Fourteen of its members (2 officers and 12 other ranks) were killed and 103 wounded. In addition, 23 wounded servicemen from other units were treated at the RAP and four German soldiers ... Such was the toll of 'static' warfare. Due to losses since D-Day the medical staff had been reduced by fifty per cent, so far without replacements

Chapter Six

A Royal Rescue and a Despot's Demise

Armageddon

CORPORAL Peter Terry's experiences with 47 Cdo were not the first life-threatening events in his life. As a schoolboy in Vienna he had been the innocent ostracised victim of Nazi hatred, and the impotent observer of Nazi brutality. He had seen the subjugation of right by a cruel tyranny and, perhaps to him the most disturbing of all, the abandonment by so many of the standards of humanity and decency which, without question, he had previously taken for granted in the society in which he lived. In a wide cross-section of acquaintances whom he considered friends, be they family friends, playmates, fellow pupils, teachers, spiritual advisers, servants, tradesmen, he had discovered that for personal advantage, or personal fear of failing to conform to diktats which they knew were evil, there were some who would abandon the loyalty and the mutual support which he had always considered as inherent in friendship and discount these on the basis of expedient new-found convictions. Equally, there were others who were not prepared to compromise the standards of justice and kinship to which they had always subscribed and which at personal risk they would continue to uphold.

A Royal Patient's Concern

Before the Anchlüss in Austria the Tischler family had moved in high social circles. Peter Terry's father was a Viennese physician who had also qualified in dentistry and belonged to an élite within which he held a high professional position. Vienna for a hundred years or more had held a leading place in the world of medicine. Dr Tischler had an engineering bent which had led him to switch from medicine to dental and oro-facial surgery. He was an international leader in orthodontics and as such attracted a wide range of illustrious patients including statesmen, aristocrats, authors, actors, musicians and royalty. In the culture of Vienna he also had a significant position in the world of music and the arts. Peter's mother came from a Jewish patrician family. Her father had been awarded the title Hofrat (Court Counsellor) by the Hapsburgs for distinguished Government Service.

Among Dr Tischler's royal patients there was one notable Briton, ex-King Edward the Eighth, now the Duke of Windsor. When in Vienna the

Duke usually invited Dr Tischler and his wife to have dinner with him at the Hotel Bristol where he usually stayed. At one of these dinners, just after the Duke's abdication (1936), Mrs Simpson was present. Peter was introduced to the Duke and Mrs Simpson and his mother mentioned that this was his 12th birthday: next day there arrived for Peter a present from the Duke and Duchess, an expensive bicycle.

Terry's father had fought in the German army on the Russian front in the First World War. At the time, compared with Czarist Russia, he saw Austria as a paragon of liberty, an Empire where Jews could be integrated into urban society without the fear of pogroms or lesser manifestations of anti-semitism. Both Dr Tischler and his wife, however, were anglophile and young Peter was sent to a boarding school in England (Frensham) at the age of 12. He returned to Vienna for the Easter holidays in March 1938 just in time to hear the Austrian Chancellor Kurt von Schuschnigg announce the German invasion of Austria over the radio. 'I yield to brute force' he said, his voice breaking with emotion. Two days later from the balcony of his house Peter Terry watched the German Army enter Vienna. He did not return to England as his father felt that the family should stay together.

Not long after that Dr Tischler had a dramatic telephone call from the South of France. It was the Duke of Windsor asking if he could be of help and urging Dr Tischler to leave the country. Dr Tischler thought over this 'kind and generous offer' but declined it as he thought that the worst of the Nazi excesses would pass.

There now followed the period when Peter had to endure what he described as 'the daily life of an outcast'. The 'excesses' did not diminish but increased. He was ostracised, easily identified as Jewish because he did not wear the swastika badge and without that, in the street, always felt at risk and was at times subject to abuse. He was discriminated against in many ways and subject to the segregation rules imposed on schools. Immediately after the German occupation he was confronted by a national epidemic of 'brown shirts', local thugs glorying in anti-Jewish malevolence. They included some of his school-mates who had joined, and prided in, the Hitler Youth. He had to engage, with his father, in a surreptitious burning of many of the latter's books of Jewish origin. The discovery of such could be an excuse for looting a house and subjecting the occupants to physical or verbal abuse, or arrest. Dr Tischler's new car was confiscated when two men came to the door demanding the keys, but he had to continue paying for its maintenance and petrol. Peter saw violence to Jews in the streets and at times had to tread very warily to avoid being caught up in such violence himself. He saw premises with 'Juden' scrawled over them being ransacked. He lived under a constant feeling of threat, and at

The Royal Rescuer and the Despots. King Edward VIII making his first broadcast to the nation on 1st March 1936. Later that year he broadcast his decision to abdicate the throne. (*PA*)

The despots in the dock at the Nuremberg Trial.
Front row (left to right): Goering, Hess, Ribbentrop, Keitel, Rosenberg, Frank, Frick, Streicher, Funk.
Back row: Raeder, Shirach, Sauckel, Jodl, Papen, Seyss-Inquart (holding microphone to left ear), Speer. (*PA*)

times fear. Because of suspect Nazi sympathies in one of the Tischler's servants, conversation in the home had to be conducted very carefully and often in whispers.

Another Patient

About the same time another patient of Dr Tischler's, an ambitious 46 year old Viennese attorney, sprang to prominence. His name was Seyss-Inquart. His forebears had come from Germany and he had served in the First World War in the Emperor's Riflemen Regiment and had been severely wounded. In 1937 von Schuschnigg, impressed with Seyss-Inquart's ability and respectability – he was a diligent churchgoer – had appointed him a State Counsellor. For years, however, Seyss-Inquart had hidden a fanatical belief in a greater Germany and Anschlüss – union of Austria with Germany – as the way to achieve this. He did not join the Nazi party but became a front man for its activities. In 1938 his active involvement with Nazi Germany became evident when, under threats from Hitler, von Schuschnigg was forced to appoint him as Minister for the Interior. When von Schuschnigg resigned in 1938, Seyss-Inquart used his Ministerial position to abrogate the Treaty of St Germain-en-Laye which proclaimed that Austrian independence was inalienable. After the Anschlüss he was appointed Reich Governor of Austria within the Nazi hegemony.

Hitler described Seyss-Inquart as an 'extraordinarily clever man, as supple as an eel, amiable and at the same time thick skinned and tough'. When his IQ (intelligence quotient) was tested prior to the Nuremberg trials it was found to be high at 141. When Poland was overrun in 1939 Seyss-Inquart was made second-in-command of that country and when, later, Holland was likewise overrun he was made its all-powerful State Commissioner. As such he presided over a system in which 120,000 Dutch Jews were dragged away to extermination camps (104,000 dying there), 5000 other Dutch men and women died in prisons and concentration camps, 2,800 Dutch citizens, including a few women, were executed and 550,000 Dutch men were forced to work in the Third Reich or for the Nazis in Holland, 30,000 never returning. He implemented a policy which deprived Holland of food and resulted in the Dutch Hunger Winter of 1944–45 in which 18,000 died of starvation. At the end, however, he disobeyed Hitler's final vindictive order to destroy Holland.

At the Nuremberg trials although he himself was a barrister Seyss-Inquart surprised the Court by showing a remarkable lack of will to defend himself and unlike so many of the major war criminals who were his co-defendants he did not seek to blame them and others. His manner was mild and his speech quiet: in striking contrast he admitted the fearful excesses of the Nazi régime and agreed that he must, in part, take responsibility for what happened. He had anticipated a death sentence when he commented, 'Whatever I say, my rope is being woven in Dutch hemp'. He was condemned to death. Just after sentence was pronounced upon him he learnt that his son, missing on the Eastern Front, was alive in Russia.

In his final testimony Seyss-Inquart remained loyal to Hitler, saying, 'To me he remains a man who made greater Germany a fact in German history. I served this man. And now? I cannot today cry 'Crucify him,' since yesterday I cried 'Hosanna'. His final message as he took his place last in the queue of the major war criminals waiting to mount the gallows, was, 'I hope this execution is the last act of the tragedy of the 2nd World War, and that a lesson will be learnt so that peace and understanding will be realised among nations. I believe in Germany'. His ashes like those of other leading Nazi war criminals were dumped in an obscure stream so that 'no grave, no urn, no relic could become a shrine to Nazism'.

An Enabling Certificate, Brownshirt Thugs and Arrest by the Gestapo

To begin with Dr Tischsler continued with his practice and one day Seyss-Inquart came to see him as a patient. Seyss-Inquart noticed that someone had painted the word 'Jude' over the brass plaque outside Dr Tischler's surgery. He said that he would see to it that certain Jewish doctors could practice without hindrance. Dr Tischler doubted whether this would happen but several days later received a certificate dated 28 April 1938 headed, 'National Socialist German Workers Party: Hitler Movement' which, translated, stated:

> By order of the official authority the bearer of this document is authorised to continue his work as a member of the medical profession. He is not to be disturbed even at night, for purposes of street scrubbing, etc. It is also ordered that the plaque outside his medical practice must not be over-printed or defaced in any manner.

The signature on the certificate was too illegible to be recognised. In the light of what happened subsequently Dr Tischler later concluded that Seyss-Inquart's real motive was to ensure that he did not lose the benefit of his own treatment from Dr Tischler.

As time passed the anti-Jewish malevolence of which there was so much evidence seemed to be closing in on the Tischler family. Soon Peter's parents left their house only when it was absolutely necessary but a few weeks later on a beautiful spring morning Peter's father decided to risk taking a walk with him in wooded Prater Park. Within the park there was a football stadium. After they had walked some distance dozens of brown-shirted S. A. Troopers (Sturm Abteilung – the political para-military organisation of the Nazi party) appeared from among the trees and advanced towards them. Hoping to avoid a threatened confrontation Peter and his father turned and walked away but were soon surrounded. They were not wearing the aluminium swastikas worn by almost all non-Jewish Viennese. The Storm Troopers were a thuggish looking bunch, all Austrians. Admitting on questioning that he was Jewish Dr Tischler produced the certificate from Seyss-Inquart. This appeared to make some impression and he and Peter were led off to an open car, with two large Nazi flags in front of it, in which sat a very fat red-faced officer in the uniform of 'Political Leader' of the Nazi Party. He looked at the certificate and declared it invalid. At a command from him the Brownshirts then made Peter and his father jog to the adjacent stadium. There, there was already a crowd which must have numbered several thousand and it transpired that they had all been rounded up that morning from all over Vienna. After a long wait the crowd was formed into a long line, six abreast, families sometimes being separated. They were then marched to a down-town part of the city known for its high crime rate. One of the guards told Peter and his father to remove their ties and to dishevel their hair, 'to look more Jewish'. A civil policeman who tried to interfere with the proceedings was arrested by the Brownshirts.

As they approached the down-town heartland it was clear that a large crowd had been organised there to engage in vilification of the Jews. Already whipped into a frenzy of hostility the crowd shouted and screamed abuse and threats. Finally the column came to a halt at the Danube Canal. An order through a megaphone then told the Jews, still in a line, to face the canal, warning them not to turn round. Afraid that they might be about to be thrown into the canal Peter's father told him to remove his shoes as soon as he hit the water and swim down-stream. They waited and then, after a while, everything seemed to go silent. Surreptitiously someone turned round and suddenly all were facing the other way – the Brownshirts had gone and the street was empty: but no one wanted to move lest the Nazis and their followers might pounce on them in side streets as they dispersed. Then they heard the sound of approaching motors and a long line of taxis appeared. The ever alert Viennese taxi drivers knew when they could enjoy a fare bonanza among those whose one aim was to disappear as quickly as possible!

That night Peter's father's appreciation of the situation had changed. The brooding fear of arrest and what might follow that hung over him. His son heard him say, 'Now we have to leave'. For Jews, however, it was virtually impossible to obtain the necessary visa without help. The only chance was that the Duke of Windsor might still be willing to provide that help and Dr Tischler hoped that he might be able to contact him.

Hardly had this hope been expressed than its fulfilment was denied. One day, Dr Tischler failed to return from work: he had been arrested by the Gestapo and taken to their headquarters in the Hotel Metropole. During interrogations he discovered that a man whom he had employed a few years previously as a servant, and dismissed because he was a member of the Nazi party, had denounced him to the Gestapo.

Dr Tischler's wife, aware of her husband's plan to try and reactivate the Duke's earlier offer and of the serious danger of the family's position decided that night to take action. She knew that, just after the Anchlüss, Baron Louis Rothschild, head of the Rothschild financial empire in Austria and a friend of the Duke of Windsor had been arrested and was incarcerated in the Gestapo headquarters – along with Kurt Schuschnigg the deposed Austrian Chancellor. Baron Louis's brothers in France had earlier urged him to leave Austria but he had been unwilling to do so. The 55 year old Baron was a man of impressive appearance and authority and when arrested he had treated the armed, helmeted men who came to arrest him with a dignified aristocratic nonchalance which led them to await his convenience subserviently as he responded that he must dine before going with them. In captivity, in direct confrontation with the feared SS and Gestapo Chief Heinrich Himmler who came to see him, and despite the weakness of his position, he argued the conditions under which he would surrender the Rothschild financial and business interests, obtaining guarantees of compensation from a reluctant Himmler by exploiting the international pressures which the Rothschilds could exert. When, post-war, Germany paid that compensation Baron Rothschild donated it to the Austrian Government on condition that former employees of the Rothschilds in Austria were paid pensions comparable to those received by retired civil servants.

Frau Tischler also knew that the Duke of Windsor at that time was staying in the south of France with relatives of Baron Rothschild. She therefore despatched a cryptic message through the Rothschilds to the Duke to the effect that her husband was 'staying with Louis' and that 'it would be nice to hear from' the Duke. The Duke of Windsor clearly understood the meaning of Frau Tischler's coded message and set in motion, in the British Embassy in Vienna, the procedures necessary for facilitating the Tischlers' escape.

In his Gestapo cell with six occupants Dr Tischler was filled with foreboding: his future and that of his family were under grave threat. At every interrogation his Gestapo interrogator, Sektionschef Dr Schmitz began, 'Are you the Jew Tischler' and then proceeded with his questioning. Then one morning Schmitz bluntly suggested that for 'a consideration' he could facilitate Dr Tischler's release. Dr Tischler was taken to his bank by two guards and on return the guards handed over 'the consideration' to Schmitz, sitting at his desk. To Schmitz Dr Tischler was now no longer 'the Jew Tischler' but 'Herr Doktor Tischler' and that afternoon he was released. Schmitz gave him some further assistance with documents but warned Dr Tischler that he might well be arrested again by some other agency and should not stay at home at night.

Escape to Britain

The influence of the Duke and the British Embassy in Vienna was now evident. The Tischlers were able to complete the formalities necessary to leave the country, greatly assisted by being able to travel about Vienna in a car flying the Union Jack which afforded them protection from the molestations of roving bands of uniformed Nazis and their opportunistic camp followers. The Duke sponsored the affidavit required by the British Immigration Authorities. On July 2nd, 1938 the Tischler family escaped into Switzerland and from there through France to England. When they finally reached London they were met at Victoria Station by Sir Geoffrey Thomas, the Duke's Secretary. They felt that they had reached London as honoured guests.

Peter Terry considers that the Duke has been much maligned and that his efforts in helping some of those who would otherwise have suffered Nazi persecution have not been adequately recognised. Nine of Peter's mother's relatives perished in Nazi gas chambers and Peter believes that but for the Duke, assisted by the Rothschilds, the Tischler family might well have been one more to perish in Auschwitz.

After reaching Britain, Dr Tischler joined McIndoe's plastic surgery unit for wounded servicemen at East Grinstead where his skill in oral surgery, particularly the repair of fractured jaws, was put to good use. When he died in 1962 there were many moving tributes to the work which he had done in Britain.

Life in London and the British Army

Financially Terry's family had lost nearly everything. In London they lived in a drab house in Maida Vale. They were safe but they had exchanged prosperous lives in their own country for impoverished refugee status in a strange land. Just into his teens Peter was astonished to see there neatly dressed children romping around, turning cart-wheels and playing 'tig'. In Vienna after the Anschlüss he could never dare venture out because to him so many things were 'verboten'. The inhibitions of living under the Nazis still hung heavily over him. One night from his house he heard to his horror someone coming down the street whistling the Horst Wessel song, the party hymn of the Nazis. A leather coated man wearing jack boots strutted past. This sent a shiver down Terry's spine as if he had been followed all the way from Vienna. It took him days to recover from that British Fascist passer-by.

Terry returned for a short time to Frensham as a refugee whose parents undertook to pay the fees as soon as they could afford it. He then went to Cambridge but as soon as he reached the age when he could join the British Army (1943) he did so. As a refugee he was originally assigned to a unit of the unarmed Pioneer Corps consisting largely of refugees who undertook supervised labouring duties such as rolling barrels of tar and stacking parts of Bailey Bridges as an alternative to internment – hardly the fulfilment of his ambition to join a fighting unit.

In due course, however, after many frustrations he realised that ambition, being accepted for commando service as a member of 10 Inter Allied Commando. He undertook one short cloak-and-dagger overnight landing on the French coast and just before D-Day was seconded to 47 Cdo. As an escapee from the Nazis he had been given a cover story and a new name lest he was captured. His cover story was that he had an Austrian mother and that his father had been with the British Consulate in Vienna and subsequently in Geneva where he (Peter) picked up his fluent French and German. Asked on the spur of the moment to suggest a name for himself he suggested 'Terry' as he had just been reading a book about Ellen Terry.

Before joining up, still with the name of Tischler, he had attended the Architectural Association in London where a fellow student was one Brian Stickings. To his consternation one of the first people he saw on joining 47 Cdo was Stickings, now a Lieutenant in the Commando. Stickings recognised him so he told Stickings the truth, begging him never to use the name 'Tischler' from which, literally on pain of death, he had to dissociate himself.

There was another sequel to Terry's escape. When he sought, in Britain, to apply to leave the Pioneer Corps to join a fighting unit he found himself being interviewed along with one Peter Arany. What Terry and Arany did not know at that meeting was that Arany had previously seen Terry in Vienna. In 1938 the sixteen-year-old Arany, of an Austrian family threatened in the same way as the Tischler family, was walking, anxious and rather desperate, along the Alserstrasse in Vienna when, parked at the sidewalk, he came upon a luxurious car flying the Union Jack. Inside he saw what he took to be a British family including a boy. For a moment he considered approaching the protected foreigners to beg for help for himself and his family. Shyness made him hesitate and as he did so the car took off and disappeared into the traffic. The car on that day contained the Tischler family. Happily, Arany, his mother and sister did finally escape to Britain and Terry and Arany reconstructed their earlier meeting.

The war over, Peter Terry was told that there would be career opportunities if he had knowledge of Arabic and Persian. With this in mind he returned to Cambridge University and graduated. The opportunities did not materialise, however, and he became a successful business man first in Britain and then in the USA where he is now retired.

I saw Terry only once again, in circumstances reminiscent of the Arany sighting. Just after the war, as a London bus in which I was travelling on the upper deck pulled away from a bus stop, I saw him walking past on the pavement. I knocked on the bus window but he did not hear and he disappeared from sight.

Nearly fifty years later in Bridgehampton, New York State, Terry heard of an article in *the Proceedings of the Royal College of Physicians of Edinburgh* which dealt with Port-en-Bessin where he had been during the War. Pursuing this further, he found to his astonishment that the author was none other than the doctor whose syringe in the basement of Maison Chevigny had filled him with such apprehension.

Chapter Seven

The Great Chase: From the Dives to Dozulé, Duclair and Dunkirk

The Dives to Dozulé

THE long eastward march really began on 16th August when a fighting patrol from 47 RM Cdo entered Troarn to investigate a report that the enemy was withdrawing. It encountered little resistance but Captain Wood, who was leading, and a marine were wounded by a booby trap. Next day a fighting patrol of three troops explored south to the River Muances on a 48 hour sojourn and found that two bridges over the river had been blown by the retreating Germans. Six prisoners were taken.

At 0500 hrs on 19th August moving in column under command of the 6th Airborne Division as part of the 4th Commando Brigade 47 RM Cdo advanced to the Dives and continued three miles beyond that to la Collerie (nr. Goustrainville) where it took up a defensive position centred on le Manoir. The exact whereabouts of the retreating Germans was not known but their rearguard was shelling the British positions and as the commando advanced two officers, including the Intelligence Officer, Lt Gower, and three marines were wounded.

Cross Purposes with the Red Cross

On 20th August the commando set off for Putot-en-Auge a few miles away. Marching along a country road with fields on either side it was necessary to watch the flanks. At one point Sergeant Morley and a corporal were out on the left of the column as 'flank men' when two shots rang out followed by others. 'Down' was the unuttered order which each man in the column gave himself and the commando immediately took up a defensive position along the road. Momentarily some Germans were seen taking cover among a line of trees about a hundred yards to the left, parallel to the road on the far side of the adjacent field. At that the corporal came dashing back to the column. As he and Morley, with Morley leading, had approached the line of trees a single German emerged who had not apparently seen them. Morley and the German had been equally surprised to meet each other and simultaneously both had fired hitting each other. Both had fallen. Exposed in the open the corporal beat a hasty retreat and

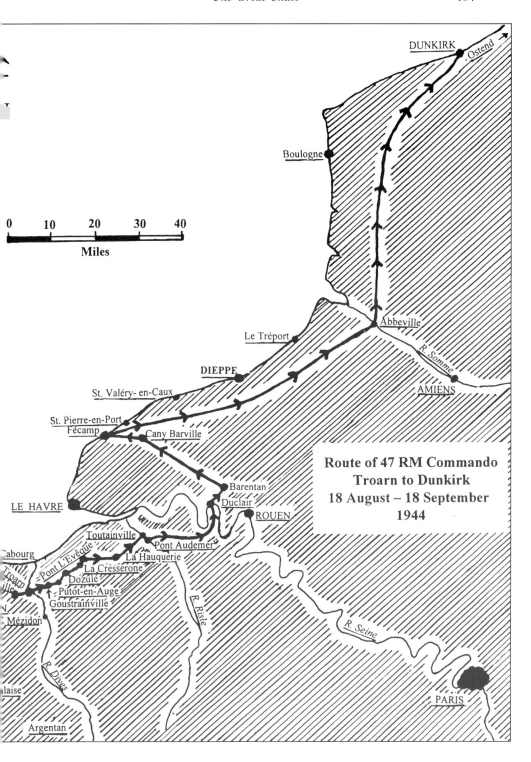

Route of 47 RM Commando
Troarn to Dunkirk
18 August – 18 September
1944

as he ran back was fired on from the line of trees where the Germans had been seen. He did not know whether or not Morley and the German were only wounded or had killed each other. From the road they could not be seen in a dip in the ground.

The large pole-less red cross flag which we had taken possession of from the Germans who had surrendered on the Western feature at Port-en-Bessin was now brought into use. It was large enough to cover most of my body frontage so I wrapped it round me, red cross to the front. Tentatively, I stood up and walked down the side of a wooden-slatted barn, which projected from the road into the field, and then walked out into the open field towards where Morley was lying. There was no response from the Germans. They could not but have seen me and I considered that they were going to respect the red cross and allow me to examine Morley and their colleague. I reached about forty yards away from the barn and could see Morley and the German lying ahead: neither showed any sign of movement. At that point, to my consternation, a shot rang out and then another not from the Germans but from the left of the commando column lining the road behind me. The shots were being fired, not by but at the Germans by my own unit. Now the Germans did respond. A shot was fired at me and missed. As I turned and dashed for the barn using the weaving run appropriate for such occasions another erring shot was fired but I reached and entered the barn. The barn gave a false sense of protection. Wooden slats are little protection from rifle shots and bullets began to smash through the woodwork. The barn had a brick base extending about two feet up from the floor so I flattened myself against the floor, protected by the bricks. As I lay there shot after shot from the Germans splintered the woodwork above my head. In time the shooting died down and I returned to the road not a little incensed at the foolish action of my own unit in opening fire with what I saw as its apparently mindless flouting of the Geneva Convention and, considerably more important to me at the time, the stupidity which had put their own medical officer at risk. The explanation was that a troop corporal at the rear of the column seeing the 'doc' in the open decided that he should 'give him covering fire to try and keep the Germans' heads down'!

Brought to a halt, the commando now sent out a patrol to try and capture the Germans by getting round behind them. They had gone. I was sorry as I had hoped to find out what they had had in mind ... I believe that they had respected the red cross flag but when they were fired at thought that this was some sort of trick and responded accordingly.

While the patrol went out the mortar platoon laid down a smoke screen to cover the area where Morley lay. Both he and the German were found dead where they had fallen.

Sergeant Serendipity and the Capture of Dozulé

The commando now moved on, through the hamlet of Putot-en-Auge south of Dozulé. It had reached a point where it was advancing up a hill when it had to halt as it came under sniper and mortar fire. Three marines and another medical orderly/stretcher bearer were wounded.

Dozulé was now the immediate objective of the Brigade. It was a small town about three miles away known to be occupied by the Germans in some force and we were now on its outward defences. As the evening advanced word was received by the various COs of the commandos that the Brigadier had decided that Dozulé would be attacked by 41, 47 and 48 Cdos at dawn. The commandos were to move off from their present positions at midnight. Yet unaware of this next move 47 RM Cdo waited on the hill.

As Lieut Gower the 'I' officer had been wounded on the previous day the 'I' sergeant, Sergeant Gibson, was now in charge of the 'I' Section. He had the unique distinction of capturing Dozulé single-handed and has written an account of his achievement from the time that the commando was halted on the hill:

> The sun was nearing the end of its westward course inflaming trees and hedgerows, casting long shadows among the rank grass. The situation was impasse; at least there was tacit understanding that we would dig in for the night and only attempt the crest ahead with the return of light in the morning. Little groups of fellows stood around talking, or prowled in the hedgerows as though they thought they should find something lurking there.
>
> Headquarters had been set up in a cottage on the reverse side of the hill. The building, deserted and neglected, had obviously seen no occupants but the enemy for a week or more; the garden, once trim and functional as these French gardens are, lay trampled and overgrown with the weeds of a week's rain and sun. As the evening grew perceptibly cooler the rank smell of damp vegetation hung in the air. But suddenly I noticed something else: smoke was descending, first tenuous, then wreathing and thick, blotting out the paling blue sky. Soon we were shrouded and the wisps of smoke were feeling their way down the hill and beyond, to far below us. Everyone stopped digging and foraging to watch in silence and speculate what it might be, and then, quietly resuming, carried on preparing shallow trenches for the night. Dew would be heavy, the early morning cold; there might even be rain – better to make it as comfortable as possible. I started to scrape a hole for Frenchie, the Colonel's driver and myself,

but with little enthusiasm. I felt vaguely insecure in this eyrie, felt that the night might not prove quite so pacific as it seemed at that moment.

An orderly told me to report to the Colonel; and I smiled to think that the IO (Intelligence Officer) had caught a packet yesterday, just a bit of shrapnel, leaving me, all unwittingly, to carry on with his job. I pushed into the office and saluted. 'I'll need you at an O Group in 20 minutes time' the Colonel said; 'Inform Heavy Weapons troop personally: take a signal for the other troops'. He dictated it and I took it to Gadsden to pass across. Thain was standing by a half dug trench waiting. 'Moving?' he asked. 'Don't know yet' I said, 'wouldn't be surprised. See take this over to Jeep O'Connell (Capt O'Connell was in charge of Heavy Weapons) – first gate along there on the right'. 'Know where the smoke's coming from Don?' he asked. 'Not the faintest' I said. Frank Garner was pulling his rifle through. 'What do you think?' 'There's no word yet'.

Heavy hung the night, as though all nature were engaged in healthful respiration after a long day of sunshine. Strange elf-like things moved in the grass, the hedge-rows rustled. Then I saw the stars again. The smoke was clearing and at that moment I guessed what was what. The enemy was withdrawing in the darkness, presumably to Dozulé down in the valley beyond the hill, covering his retreat in smoke. But not a sound broke the silence of the night.

Back in the 'O' group at headquarters by the light of a Tilley lamp we learned the worst. The Brigade Commander had ordered a dawn attack on the enemy stronghold at Dozulé, preceded by a three-fold pincer movement. Deadline 1 a.m. Of all the unholy hours to choose, I thought – I scanned my map. The contours lay like the grain of an oak log, knotted into spurs and steep valleys. Dense woodland covered the hills, intersected by countless mazy tracks, and there some three miles away was the market town of Dozulé at the intersection of roads. The directions were explicit: X troop, followed by others to lead, moving on compass bearings by a circuitous five mile route to take up positions on the south east of the town on the main road. Attack to commence at 5.30 a.m. Intelligence Sergeant to take up position at cross tracks (he indicated on the map) and gave the initial compass bearing 112° Magnetic. All very easy, I thought, but I wonder? I looked at the Colonel, that arrogant juggernaut of a man, with his fixed sneer: but I knew there was strength in his command, in his plan.

Outside, my eyes were blinded by the darkness. All the fellows, sensing what was in the wind were standing about waiting. I saw young Rollins the Jeep driver and told him how he was to pick me up at the tail of B troop as the cavalcade passed through the forest. I saw the section (the 'I' section), detailed them off, one with X, one with B, the rest with HQ. In an outhouse someone was brewing up tea, and what better else at midnight on the brow of a hill. High above us the wind sighed in the trees, and I could now see great masses of opaque darkness coming across the face of the stars: rain-clouds.

Now it was well past midnight. A and Y troops had been withdrawn from their insecure hold on the perimeter in the fields above us. Jeeps spluttered and shuffled along without lights on the rutting roads. B and HW closed in from along the field road. Everywhere black figures were lurching and stumbling in the darkness cursing the obstacles and ditches under their breath.

I shouldered my rifle and went forward. The soft crunch and tread of the feet of marching troops halted; they were now lying back against the high grassy banks, resting. I went on ahead stubbing my heels into deep ruts as the track turned uphill between spectral gorse bushes. Funny I thought: an act of faith, only 2 hours ago the enemy were here for certain. Theoretically they were now gone and in that faith I was going on.

Half a mile, and the cross tracks were reached, right in the heart of a beech forest. It was six minutes to one. Soon the first dark figures came tumbling up towards me. 'X troop there'? 'Troop Commander here'. I indicated the first bearing 112° Mag. As they halted everyone had automatically gone to ground until, at a word, they were up and moving forward 1 a.m. exactly. The other troops followed hard on. I checked them off, A, Q, HQ, Y, B and then Heavy Weapons. Strange, I thought, as the last of the troops disappeared into the darkness, how all that Cdo is moving in single file through this labyrinth of a forest and only X troop commander knows the way – but now for the transport which was to pick me up and take me by a circuitous route a jump ahead to a point where I could rejoin the column.

Time was passing yet no sign of my transport. Suppose my transport didn't come, – – – how long should I wait – – –, where did devotion to duty end and individual initiative begin. I put my ear to the ground and heard nothing. I stood up and only heard the sighing of the wind in the tree tops and the uneasy stir of the lower branches. Time, one twenty five, a full quarter hour since the last troops passed.

Supposing I did go on and try to catch up, would I ever find the others; might not the transport be lost. It was a perplexity. But I referred the matter to God and decided to know the answer at 1.30

exactly. Until then I idly recited the stations from Glasgow to London, London to Penzance and Bristol to Derby (Sgt Gibson had a remarkable knowledge of trains and their timings) and knew I was just there – when I knew I was to go forward. So I strode out through the forest on bearing 112° Mag.

Clutching the large situation map whose talc gleamed wanly in the faint light I crossed tracks, met another, took the right fork as my memory or my power of auto-suggestion told me. Everything seemed all right except for the contours; and I could not convince myself that the land should slope as it did. You're on the wrong path said Intelligence, the wrong path, the wrong path; where is it leading? Will answered. Rubbish, its just that in reality there are more woodland tracks than are shown on the map. I paused in a clearing to peer at the map but there was little to be seen. Suddenly I saw two figures lurching unsteadily towards me. Lit by the wan light of a clearing their dark silhouettes were unmistakably human. Instantly I dropped on one knee and froze. They had not seen me. Across the clearing they came dimly lit by the starlight of the warm summer's night. My breath came short, my heart raced – 100 yds, now 80, 60 – still they didn't see me, – I'll beat them to it, – 40 now, and then 'Halt, who goes there' – the spell was broken. I noticed the dark silhouette of my rifle – the two figures stopped in front. After an eternity one said 'Friend'. It was soon solved. An officer and a marine of 48 Cdo on their way back to Brigade had become lost in this wilderness and only knew their general direction. They had seen nothing, had heard nothing, could tell me nothing. We passed on, on opposite courses: but for quite a little way I noticed my heart pounding fast.

It is impossible to stop in the middle of a maze. Desperation drives a man forward. But slowly, imperceptibly I resigned myself to the realisation that I was completely lost. With no aid whatever from memory or map I pushed on and hoped for the best. I was suddenly aware that the track had become a lane, flanked with steep earthen banks crowned with beech trees that sighed drearily in the wind. But perplexity was deepened by the first faint flush of dawn, which by all reasoning was in the North West. However, dawn in the North West at 2 a.m. would be something of a phenomenon, so I reserved my judgement. There was a sickening moment as I approached the silent gable of a house which abutted on the road. I thought of mines, sentries, ambush, of the miles which lay between our fellows and myself.

The road widened, the ruts became deeper. A long low building on the right gave me an anxious moment, but no – there was no movement. Ahead the streamers of dawn were too good to be true at this hour: I decided there must be a barn on fire somewhere: by the Pole star I was going due North. Then it came to me suddenly. I was near the top of a little steep hill, when I took to the ditch to avoid the tell-tale skyline. Still in the ditch I reached the crest of the hill and there it was, a whole valley dotted with fires. Buildings roared and crackled as beams gave way; flame spurted from gable windows. The whole air was filled with the crackling and hissing. It took about 5 seconds to decide that this was Dozulé and another ten to locate myself on the map now faintly glowing in the light of the flames.

If then this was Dozulé – and it seemed pretty certain – I must turn away, avoid it, go on bearing about 140° to meet the others; it would be cross-country but, avoiding the town, ought to be reasonably safe. Yes the sooner the better; black figures appeared to be moving in the town; what a grand piece of information to take back anyway.

Then it came as it had sometimes come before, the clear call and command, not from conscience or courage – I had little enough of that. I said to myself 'Good God, no, I couldn't do that'. I argued with myself but it came on me again like a chill shadow. 'Forward (into Dozulé); you can trust that it is all right'. I asked for resolution, parked the map, now dangerously glinting in the light, and went forward.

It was only half a mile, but that deadly glare lit me up all the way. I scarcely noticed what was around me for watching the rapid destruction, the flame that visibly devoured about eight or more buildings in the town. When I reached the first house I stopped on the shadowy side to fix my bayonet and ease forward the safety catch of my rifle. One must take no chances. The small side street was dark and silent: doors stood open and shop windows were shuttered. I paused at the corner of the main street and called myself a coward. But damn it all the main street was bright as day: one could not avoid being seen. God this strain is awful. But no, forward, I am to go forward. It is dead safe.

Then cautiously I entered the High Street creeping from doorway to doorway wondering how far I might get with it. Ahead, 2 two-storey buildings were afire and burning down rapidly. One of these forced me out into the middle of the street. I felt as though thousands of eyes were gazing at me as I crept gingerly down the street in a blaze of glory. And then the cross roads, Mezidon 25 km I read – to the right, Pont l'Evêque 18 km forward. So this was it. Dozulé on fire and not a living soul in it. I looked at my watch. It was 2.29.

A great loneliness came upon me as the utter wonder of my

surroundings intensified. The night was an enormous silence with one solitary figure in all the world, and right at the centre of it — a silence in which the deep roar of flame, the helpless crumple of timber and masonry were foreign and unreal noises. Only the light was real, too terribly illuminating for safety. I took counsel; our troops lay some 4 miles down the Mezidon road; but to walk down it towards them must mean walking into a couple of their Bren guns. To try any other road round must lead to the risk of losing my way again. It is necessary above all to get back to the Brigade Commander with information: besides the enemy may have left ambushes. A thousand ifs and buts raced through my head, but in a moment of quiet I knew that I must hedgehop through the back gardens of houses, keeping close to the Mezidon road, close enough to spy out any ambushes that might be laid. I remember laughing a little at Dozulé cross-roads as I thought of the novelty of walking about like this behind the enemy's lines.

As I made my way back along the High Street with a view to getting to a side street which would lead me into the back gardens of the houses along the Mezidon Road one of the fires was dying out but another building with a thatched roof had caught the spark: with a sudden puff and roar the flames leapt to high heaven. Then, arriving at the side street I entered a back garden, dark and shadowy, and crossed a fence. An extensive orchard on a sloping terrain led me to a muddy stream which defied my efforts to jump it and I cursed the thing as the mud went over my ankles. Crossing hedges and high barbed wire fences was little pleasure when there was fighting order, rifle, full carry of . 303 ammunition and grenades as well. The barbed wire tore me and called forth a stream of imprecations. After about a mile I had crept down to the road again. A strange movement had attracted my attention. Ahead was a large house with a deeply shrubbed front garden. No doubt I was becoming jumpy, losing nerve gradually. But almost certainly there was movement across the road. For a minute or two I just crouched there panting, then decided to make a long detour round the back garden of the house — a detour which involved a scramble over a high wall and that dreaded silhouette against the glare of the fire. The garden was overgrown with large-leafed plants of some kind. There was a tool-shed in the middle by which I crouched listening. Did I hear a grunt from within? I listened, just lying there in silence. There was no sound except the first few drops of rain falling on the large leaves. It was a heavy wetting rain dropping out of a night which was now starless. Then the rain stopped; but all the leaves were wet.

Subconsciously in the great room of the night I heard a faint pop,

pop-pop: a few seconds later a salvo of three shells with a soaring scream swerved to earth about 100 yards away. I buried myself in the wet plants. Had I been observed? One could believe anything of a cunning enemy. There was no one else in all this territory. Surely an enemy would not allow himself the grim irony of releasing a salvo at one mortal. For some 3 minutes I lay there while another heavy shower fell out of the blackness. There was no sound in the garden. I had been wrong about the noises in the tool shed. Having resolved to move again I had just got to my feet when, – pop, – pop-pop once more – I didn't wait and was down before the scream and 3 deafening crashes 300 yards to the south. The sense of being pinned down grew stronger. I felt hopeless, terribly lonely, stripped to my naked cowardice. I lay there until my watch had registered three more minutes, then sure enough – pop, pop pop once more, but this time the shots fell far to the north.

Cheered by the discovery of the enemy's firing plan I got up and slithered through the large rhubarb leaves to where the house, a large villa stood dark and silent. With one eye on my watch and one ear open to the east I skulked among the laurel bushes till 12 minutes exactly then – off went the pop, pop-pop. Like a flash I was down and over they came, three heavy shells on the first target: they went off with a fearful crash and flash in the night: and the shrapnel went singing over my head. Then up and watching again. I decided I had been wrong about the ambush; it was only a low branch swinging in the night wind. Then with only 15 seconds to go I was down waiting for it and over they came again 3 shells which cracked down on the Mezidon road only 150 yards away: with any luck I would now have 15 clear minutes.

In that time I raced along a hedge peering into the dark recesses of a barn and the musty gloom of a cider press. It was tiring work wading through the long grass, now heavy with moisture. The 15 minutes up I was down waiting for it and sure enough that terrible shriek like a tube train and a flash which I could see although my eyes were closed. And then, horrors, a great ragged lump of shrapnel thudded into the bank hardly a foot above my head. In 3 minutes time the second load came over to thunder down with a deafening crash on the very buildings behind which I was lying. Listening to the splintering woodwork and tiles, feeling the choking fumes of cordite, I felt an instantaneous sickness. Then summoning up my reserves I beat a hasty retreat to a ditch by the roadside. I felt as a caged animal must feel. But that was the last of the shells. The first light of dawn was breaking and men would soon be afoot: they could only be half a mile or so ahead. Then, as usual, I suddenly knew what to do.

About 5.10 a soft pad of feet in the undergrowth brought me to my feet: my heart was beating wildly: this was the worst moment of all; would they fire first? but I must get the news to the Brigade: must take the risk. The seconds passed; a moment more as they drew level I summoned everything I had and said aloud, 'Blister, Blister (the pass word), 47 here'. That instant I found myself facing more rifle barrels than I ever hope to see again. It was 41 Cdo. I crawled over the hedge and found the section officer, explaining to him the situation. Brigade, he said, was just behind: would I dash back to the Brigadier and tell him.

It was a momentary mixture of pride and relief to find the Brigadier in the darkness, and say in as nonchalant a tone as was possible, 'Sir, I think there is little need to attack: I have already occupied Dozulé'. He listened to my account, then bursting out laughing he turned to the Brigade Major saying, 'I say, do you know, this damned Sergeant has spoiled my attack'.

So there was no attack on Dozulé. Next day I re-explored the scene of my wanderings and had a peep at Dozulé. It seemed strange, vaguely unreal when I recalled the terrors of the night. The High Street, then lurid with flames and seemingly endless, now bore only the debris of the night's conflagration. One by one the few inhabitants who had not been deported crept back from the woods. I spoke to one, an old man, very well spoken. He stood at his door, 'Oui' he said, 'le Boche a franchi a deux heures vingt'. I asked him to repeat the time.

'Deux heures vingt' he said; he had seen them from the forest. So the Germans left at 2.20 in the morning did they: and I had stood at the cross roads – was it at 2.29?'

Close to where Sergeant Gibson met 41 Cdo, 47 was waiting ready to go into the attack on Dozulé. We had wended our way though a maze of forest tracks and settled down to wait, very wet from the night rain. Then suddenly a message was received that the attack was off. First thoughts were that this would only be a postponement, a battle merely deferred. We waited for further clarification: then came the glad news. The Germans had withdrawn from Dozulé. We would enter it in full daylight. There would be shelling and probably mortaring but not the dangerous house-to-house battle that had been expected.

But the night was not without its casualties and not all were as fortunate as Sergeant Gibson. In the darkness of the approach march amid the densities of the forests and the wanderings of the forest tracks elements of 47 Commando and 41 Commando unfortunately overlapped. Each saw 'enemy' ahead and fired. One marine in 47 Cdo was killed and one wounded: 41 Cdo suffered similarly. In war in that environment and under these conditions there are complexities, imprecisions, necessary improvisations and dilemmas of decision which render such 'friendly fire' almost inevitable from time to time – although latter day armchair warriors of the virtual variety may seek to deny this. Neither undue caution nor bold action can provide guarantees. In human stalking in the dark the finger is never far from the trigger. That night the medical Jeep driver was also wounded by enemy fire as was the Signals Officer. The Dozulé area remained the focus of much enemy fire.

By morning Dozulé was occupied with 47 Cdo ensconced in a brick factory.

Dozulé to Dunkirk

Next day (22nd) the commando moved by 10 mile march to la Cresserone near Pont l'Evêque and went into a reserve position. The first week of pursuit of the Germans, marching and with little sleep, had been very exhausting: given the opportunity men were sleeping from morning till night on an open field without waking. Twice within the next few days the military situation was such that the commando was ordered to prepare for action but on both occasions the orders were cancelled at the last minute. Very few of those who sought to 'get into action' in the war did not, from time to time, wonder why they had done so when they got into action of a front line nature. Whatever the long-term thinking, cancellations usually gave a feeling of relief.

Up till now the great chase had been conducted on foot. Now the Germans were retreating more quickly and motor transport was becoming the order of the day. There were plenty of signs of a rushed and ragged German retreat with abandoned vehicles lying at the roadside and stacked up at river crossings. The RAF had done its work .

Toutainville

On 25th August the Commando moved by motor transport to la Hauquerie near Beauzeville but having arrived there was ordered at 0100 hrs on 26th to undertake a 9 mile night march to Toutainville, near Pont Audemer, to cut off German troops apparently moving towards the Seine. Reaching Toutainville the commando liberated it and took a number of prisoners, most of whom appeared disillusioned and ready to surrender. One of them was wounded and as he was brought in on our medical jeep an old lady stepped out from the roadside, screamed something at him then spat on

The Chase. Liberation and acclamation. (*Crown Copyright*)

Stragglers are brought in and the tables are turned as the *quondam* oppressors avoid any eye
contact with the local population. (*Crown Copyright*)

him. For the next five days there was a pleasant halt at Toutainville with the RAP housed in a country mansion.

The British Liberation Army (BLA) was now living up to its new name. British troops in trucks, tanks or other vehicles, the first of the liberators, were sweeping into town after town, village after village, to be met with the uncontrolled joy of cheering crowds who for so long had endured the excesses of a hostile occupation, personal fear, oppressive laws and regulations, and vicious punishment or death if oppressors were opposed. The cheerers were usually the elderly or the children. Many husbands, fathers, sons were not there, but languishing as slave labourers in the third Reich, often with their location, or their existence, unknown. Many town or village halls could produce lists of those who had been summarily executed during the last few years.

Duclair

Leaving Toutainville on 31st August the Cdo moved in motor transport to the Seine ferry crossing point at Duclair. There was a sense of historic symbolism in crossing France's premier river, even in small infantry assault boats. It was evident that there had been a considerable build up of motorised German columns as these sought to get across the Seine, and the RAF had taken advantage of this. Piles of smashed German vehicles littered the roads approaching the south bank of the river. In places dead bodies of German soldiers were piled up.

Barentan

Next stop was close to Barentan ten miles further north. Very evident at Barentan were the steps which local populations in France were taking to deal with those whom they accused of collaboration with the Germans. The latter had just gone and retribution was beginning. Driving into the city I encountered a large crowd in the city square. In its centre stood a group of disconsolate frightened girls, some weeping and clutching themselves, others putting a brave face on it as they waited their turn. In front of them was a chair and on it a girl who was having all her hair cut off. The barber, a young man, seemed to be anxious to demonstrate a gloating, flamboyant revenge as the locks which were presumed to have captivated the Germans were crudely slashed with scissors and thrown to the ground. One could not help feeling that the barber's enthusiasm for his task might be related to a desire to cover possible, yet unrevealed, collaborative activities of his own by demonstrating that he was a 'good Frenchman'. Sitting on the ground beside the chair, amid the fallen locks, were the alopecic victims of this ritual, sunburnt faces contrasting starkly with pallid scalps. As each girl received her 'treatment' and took her place on the

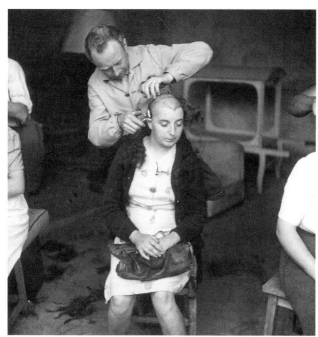

Retribution. For collaborators. (*Crown Copyright*)

... for traitors. (*Crown Copyright*)

ground the crowd jeered. There was clearly much hate: it was not a pleasant sight. These were girls who had fraternised with the Germans: but no men were being cropped. Why? I asked a bystander. Men who had collaborated would be treated elsewhere, and differently, he informed me!

At Barentan I was taken by a civic official to a German military hospital which had been captured along with its patients and its German staff. I got the impression that the civic official wished to introduce a British doctor who would take command and give orders to German staff. I had no intention of doing quite that but accepted the senior medical officer's invitation to conduct a ward round with him. He spoke some English and tried to explain what was going on, but all seemed embarrassed at my presence. Two things impressed me most. One was the sight of bedridden German soldiers springing to attention when the medical officers reached their beds. Even men with legs in plaster, arms in splints or heads in bandages managed to go through some motion which gave the semblance of being at 'attention'. The second thing was that the doctors paid hardly any personal attention to the patients. At each bed case sheets were produced and long charts unrolled. These were carefully studied and commented on among the staff who then moved on, often without exchanging word or glance with the patient involved. There were a few Russians in one ward. They looked very depressed but did not show any overt signs of maltreatment.

Le Havre on the coast was in German hands and showed every evidence of defending itself against attack but some of the other coastal defences were being evacuated and troops from them were escaping eastwards. The Cdo was now ordered to cut this escape route. It moved 20 miles north to Cany Barville and from there X troop was sent to reconnoitre the road to Fécamp which was still German occupied.

Fécamp

Next day the Cdo advanced to Fécamp. As it entered at one end the last of the Germans were moving out from the other. The reception which the Cdo received on entering Fécamp must, I fear, have assisted the last of the departing Germans to escape in that it made it very difficult for 47 RM Cdo to pursue them. It looked as if every inhabitant in Fécamp had turned out into the street and a large crowd blocked the City Square, la Place Thiers. The enthusiasm of the crowd knew no bounds. Cheers greeted every vehicle which appeared, girls threw kisses or achieved them in a more natural way, flowers were thrown, bottles of wine appeared, children climbed all over the trucks and Jeeps as soon as they stopped. Every bell in the town was ringing.

Amidst these celebrations I was informed that a French lady had been

47 RM Commando enters Fécamp.

asking for the 'British doctor' and in due course she was brought to me. Would I come and see her daughter? I took her to her house in my Jeep: her husband as far as she knew was in Germany as a forced labourer. At her home I was confronted by a distressed weeping 15 year old. On the previous day she had been raped by a departing German soldier who had preferred her to her mother who had 'volunteered' to save her daughter. The situation was one in which the most that I could do was to console the girl and her mother and advise them to see a French doctor. In coastal areas, of course, the latter were scarce as so many had been evacuated by the Germans for security reasons. At that time it was remarkable, and at times embarrassing how, with no more justification than that they came with the liberation forces, the status of British doctors was enhanced in the eyes of many French civilians.

On the Sunday after arrival the commando, passing between serried ranks of happy yet solemn civilians standing on the pavements, held a ceremonial parade in Fécamp and attended a church service where Col Phillips laid a wreath on the French War memorial.

The formal task of blocking any further escaping was light but one of 47 Cdo's most distinguished officers, Major Walton, was killed when, on reconnaissance, his Jeep ran over a mine. His companion Captain Stickings was wounded. Few of the fighting troop officers who had left Herne Bay now remained.

At Fécamp the hunt for 'collaborators' was also soon in full swing and such cars as there were available were being used to extend the hunt into the countryside. Unlike the public retribution in the town square in Barentan collaborators were taken into the town hall passing between lines of civilians hissing at them. I did not investigate what went on inside.

While the Cdo was at Fécamp le Havre nearby was captured (12/9/44). I accompanied Col Phillips when he visited it next day. There was a great deal of destruction. The local population seemed to be emerging from heaped-up ruins like ants creeping from ant-hills. As we passed, two civilian women were fighting in the street hitting each other and pulling each other's hair. It did not seem that there was much joy in le Havre at the reality or the manner of their release.

The famous Bénédictine factory in Fécamp had apparently been well used by the Germans and was now anxious to establish its bona fide with the British overlords. Somehow one of the medical boxes seemed to have been designed for the shape of Bénédictine bottles!

St Pierre-en-Port

While we were at Fécamp a young woman appeared at the RAP seeking to speak to an officer. At the RAP only the padre and I answered to that appellation. She announced herself as Miss Harrison, the daughter of a British soldier of World War I who had stayed on in France after the war and married a French girl. Miss Harrison and her family lived in St Pierre-en-Port six miles away. She told us that there was great concern and disappointment in the village because it had been heard that the commando would be moving on and would by-pass the village so that it would not be 'liberated'. Would it be possible for someone to come and formally 'liberate' the village?. The padre and I, ever keen for new experiences, politely offered to undertake this honourable and onerous duty provided it took place that evening as the Cdo would be moving off in the morning. A few hours later, with the padre on my motor-cycle pillion, I drove the six miles to St Pierre-en-Port. The symbol of liberation in that phase of the war was often a leather-jacketted, binocular-decked, peak-capped tank commander standing up imperiously and high in the turret of his Sherman tank as he swept into a city square or village centre exuding the awesome power and authority conferred by the heavily gunned steely monster which he controlled. I didn't feel that two non-combatants on a low powered motor-cycle would be likely to make quite the same impression! To the good citizens of St Pierre-en-Port, however, liberation was liberation no matter how it was expressed and it was much easier to get at a motor cyclist than a tank commander. When we arrived we did not dismount from our motor cycle, we were pulled off by hand-shaking men and screaming women who were only silent when they were kissing us. In a small hall there were speeches in French – and in broken French – speeches in broken English, platters heaped with vol au vent, wines of all sorts and much drinking of toasts. Then, with these jollifications over and without any previous warning, the 'parade' was announced – to be led down the main street by the two 'liberators'. It was a very rag-tag affair with a man in front attempting to play 'God save the King' on a concertina. As the triumphal march moved along flags were waving, children were running alongside and acclamation was unbounded; then suddenly the atmosphere changed. A group of men looking out from the window of a house which the parade was passing were scowling in an aggressive, joyless manner at the procession and the objects of its adulation. Curious about this striking change in mood we enquired who these men were. In a somewhat embar-rassed sotto voce voice we were told that they were members of the local communist cell. They apparently opposed the group who had invited us and did not appreciate our presence, seeing British officers as of the Right. We were beginning to learn something about post-war French politics.

As we returned on our Matchless motor cycle, however, French wine and French perfume prevented us from thinking too deeply about weighty political issues.

Dunkirk

On 15th September the commando was ordered to move to Dunkirk some 150 miles away. Setting off the next day the night was spent at St Pierre-en-Val and on the following day we arrived at the outskirts of Dunkirk. On the way we had crossed a peaceful, moderately-sized river, the Somme, and remembered the thousands of soldiers who had been killed in that battle 28 years previously, 20,000 on the first day.

Dunkirk was still in the hands of the Germans but they were trapped there, surrounded by the British Army. Over four years the wheel of history had turned full circle. The military plan was to invest it, not attempt to assault it. Useful as the port might have been, a much larger and better equipped port, namely Antwerp, was already in British hands although, because of access problems, it could not yet be used. We did not then know that we would soon be called upon to assist in solving these 'access' problems.

Next day the commando moved into its investing position at Ghyvelde. Life at Ghyvelde was unexciting. Patrolling was limited by the extent of the surrounding minefields laid by the Germans. Occasionally there was a certain amount of shooting in both directions. On one occasion a group of German soldiers raided the headquarters of the army unit adjacent to 47 RM Cdo. Its CO had to make a rapid retreat by jumping from a window at the back of the house to avoid being captured. Five Marines were wounded during the period at Dunkirk.

Around Dunkirk it was possible to examine some of the impressive coastal fortifications facing the Channel. One could not but commend the judgement of those who chose the Normandy coast for D-Day.

Of most concern to the German troops and the civilian inhabitants in Dunkirk at that time was the shortage of food and water. Wells were being used for the latter and German forays beyond the defensive perimeter of the port were more often for the purpose of bringing in farm animals for slaughter that for hostile action against their enemies. At one stage there was an agreed release of civilians who wanted to leave.

At Dunkirk, excluding le Havre which required a much bigger force, 47 RM Cdo had completed its rôle as the fleet of foot 'left winger' of the British Army, and indeed the Allied forces, as it advanced 250 miles northward. As September drew to a close there were rumours of a major operation ahead which received tacit confirmation when 47 Cdo was ordered to Wenduine on the Belgian coast for 'operational training'.

Chapter Eight

The Battle for Walcheren –
Five Miles of the 'Atlantic Wall'

Maps for the Marines

A T Wenduine the commando's new task was revealed – participation in the capture of the heavily defended Dutch Island of Walcheren lying at the mouth of the Scheldt. Its guns were preventing any Allied shipping from entering the Scheldt, thus depriving the Allies use of Antwerp.

In *The Eighty-five Days, the Story of the Battle of the Scheldt*, R. W. Thomson commented that the higher a soldier's rank the smaller is the scale of the maps he uses as he ponders large areas of a battlefield and the broad tactical and strategic considerations which are his responsibility. At divisional level 1:100,000 maps are likely, at battalion level 1:25,000 maps. But the even larger scale map required by the individual front-line soldier is more likely to be little more than the ground around him, a house, a hedge, a ditch, a fold in the ground, a few yards of river or stream, a copse, a cross-roads: and in human terms the comrades with him – his mates. In the final analysis the important features on his map are likely to be the suspect minefield ahead of him, an enemy rifle or gun muzzle pointed at him, an enemy rifleman, enemy soldiers manning a machine gun, unseen mortarmen or artillerymen, strafing or bombing aircraft.

A Royal Marine commando contemplating the battle for Walcheren knew little more than that he was to participate in an attack against powerful coastal defences on the Dutch coastline, part of the vaunted 'Atlantic Wall', and that his task was to put into practice his training for such an assault. He knew, too, that earlier opposed sea landings of the type planned for Walcheren had proved very hazardous. His 'maps' on this occasion would be the inside of a Landing Craft Tank (LCT) or Landing Vehicle Tracked (LVT) and the sea around them; beach obstacles possibly tipped with explosives; pools of mud; wet, sliding and seemingly endless sand dunes; hostile enemy pill boxes; trenches and gun casemates; ground to be fought over, a heavily armed and well protected enemy. He had to put his trust in many matters of which he knew little, trust the officers who led him and trust that if wounded others, especially the commando medical staff, would make every effort to rescue him. The officers' appreciation and understanding of their role, although wider, was also inevitably limited, defined from above in terms of the specific tasks allocated to them.

Time, an understanding of many of the features of the Walcheren operation unknown to the men involved when they participated in it, and a wider appreciation of its strategic and historical background, has put the operation into a more ordered, comprehensive and comprehended perspective and revealed more of its significance and consequences.

PRELUDE TO WALCHEREN

The Germans consolidate and the Generals argue

Three months after the D-Day landings on the Normandy beaches on 6th June 1944 the Allied Armies had almost reached the Dutch border. During the advance across France and Belgium the supply lines from the dispersed Channel ports had progressively lengthened. The port of Cherbourg, laid waste by the Germans before they surrendered it, and still limited by this damage, was now over 300 miles away. The 'mulberry' port of Arromanches was almost as far; le Havre, recently captured along with Boulogne and Calais, was 200 miles away: these were minor ports and all had suffered considerable damage. Dunkirk, which 47 RM Cdo had just left, was isolated, still in German hands. Dieppe and Ostend had been captured, the former almost intact but they too had only limited capacity. The key to the increasingly critical supply problems of the Allied armies – now approaching two million men – was Antwerp, the second largest port in Europe, boasting 20 miles of docks and a capacity to cope with 60,000 tons of supplies per day.

On 4th September 1944 the British 11th Armoured Division with a dash which took the defenders by surprise captured Antwerp virtually undamaged. The port, however, is 50 miles from the sea at the head of the tortuous Scheldt estuary, 5 miles wide at its widest part.

Surprisingly, the powerful German 15th Army, 80,000 strong, made no attempt to retake Antwerp. Instead the Germans sought to deny the Allies the use of the port by closing the mouth of the Scheldt estuary with the powerful defences which they had created on both sides of it. The land to the south of the estuary, the so-called 'Breskens Pocket', and to the north, South Beveland and Walcheren, remained firmly in German hands. The Allies would require to clear the Breskens pocket and South Beveland and then overcome the powerful coastal defences on West Walcheren before Antwerp could be used. The waters of the Scheldt were also heavily mined. Admiral Ramsay, Eisenhower's (British) Naval Chief of Staff considered that the Allies' first priority must now be the opening of Antwerp.

At this time, however, General Montgomery was intent on a direct strike on a very narrow front into Holland with the objective of reaching Arnhem and capturing in one incisive operation the bridges over the Maas, the Waal and the Rhine. The operation, designated 'Market Garden' was to split the German army and open up the way for a thrust into the Ruhr and the heart of Germany. There was, however, an inherent contradiction between Montgomery's views and those of the Supreme Commander. General Eisenhower endorsed a 'broad front' policy – 'bulling ahead on all fronts' as Montgomery rather disparagingly described it. This meant that Antwerp had to be opened if the supplies necessary for the implementation of such a policy were to be available. Montgomery's view was a reversal of this – if supplies were limited such supplies, equipment and manpower as were available should be concentrated on a single strike on a narrow front. Essentially, such a narrow front operation would be a British initiative but to implement it Montgomery would require a large contribution of American airborne troops. Although Eisenhower's priority was Antwerp he was not prepared to veto Montgomery's plan and saw some attractions in it. His (British) Deputy Supreme Commander Air Chief Marshal Tedder was more forthright in discounting as unrealistic the idea of driving towards Berlin with an Allied Army which was still relying so heavily on being supplied far too far away 'from the beaches north of Bayeux'.

While the 'Antwerp question' raised serious dilemmas for both Eisenhower and Montgomery the latter's priority, whatever the contrary arguments, remained 'Market Garden' or the Arnhem operation as it is better known. 'Market Garden' required a very large concentration of men, materials and transport. It meant that the pursuit of the powerful 15th German Army retreating from the Pas de Calais would have to be halted. It meant that any attempt to open the mouth of the Scheldt by attacks on the Breskens pocket, South Beveland and Walcheren would have to wait, and this would give the Germans the opportunity to reorganise their forces on both sides of the Scheldt – 3,000 German troops now escaped from South Beveland to Walcheren to strengthen the 9,000 already there. It meant that other military activity over the rest of the Allied front would be strictly limited.

'Market Garden' began on 17th September. By 25th September it was clear that, valiant as was the attempt, it had failed to achieve its main objective and that substantial resources of men and materials had been lost, compounding the problem of freeing the Scheldt estuary by reducing the size of the forces now available – the Allied forces had lost over 7,000 men killed, wounded or captured. At the same time the importance of freeing Antwerp had increased because the failure of the hoped for rapid advance into Germany meant that the war would now be prolonged and even larger amounts of supplies would be required for a broad-front attack over an extended period. For an advance, for instance, each of the four Allied armies (2nd British, 1st Canadian, 1st and 3rd U. S.) would require one million gallons of petrol per day. Further, the liberation of a semi-starving Paris at the end of August meant that the Allies now had an additional requirement of 4,000 tons of food, fuel, medicines, etc. per day; and the liberation of Brussels on 3rd September had also further compounded the supply problem.

This supply problem was particularly acute for the Americans with their main port of Cherbourg so far away. Their troops were now representing a larger and larger proportion of the Allied Armies and the inherent structure of their armies created high supply demands. General Patton, halted outside Metz, was restlessly awaiting assurance of supplies before beginning his planned thrust into Germany. With the explosive vehemence with which he could conduct conversation, even with his superiors, he was exclaiming to General Bradley, 'My men can eat their belts but my tanks have gotta have gas'.

Increasingly concerned about the need to free Antwerp and fearful that preoccupation with Arnhem would blunt appreciation of that paramount need the Supreme Commander, General Eisenhower, in the middle of the Arnhem operation (September 22nd), was urging that Antwerp must be opened as a matter of urgency and as an essential prerequisite for the final drive into Germany adding, almost certainly for the benefit of Montgomery, 'this must be accepted by all'.

Even after Arnhem was over, however, it appeared that Montgomery was still dragging his feet regarding Antwerp and was reluctant to delay his advance to the Rhine and into the Ruhr. On 4th October Sir Alan Brooke the British Chief of the Imperial General Staff, after a meeting with Eisenhower and Army, Naval and Air Force Commanders at which Montgomery was, of course, present wrote: 'I feel that for once Monty's strategy is at fault. Instead of carrying out the advance on Arnhem he ought to have made certain of Antwerp in the first place'.

On 9th October Eisenhower sent Montgomery a further message:

I must repeat, we are now squarely up against the situation which we have anticipated for months; our intake into the Continent will not support our battle. All operations will come to a standstill unless Antwerp is producing by the middle of November. I must emphasis that I consider Antwerp of first importance for all our endeavours on the entire front from Switzerland to the Channel. I believe your personal attention is required in the operation designed to clear entrance.

By 16th October Montgomery had clearly got the message and issued the following to his Commanders:

> I must impress on Army Commanders that the early use of Antwerp is absolutely vital: the operations ordered by me must be begun at the earliest possible moment; they must be pressed with the greatest energy and determination; and we must accept heavy casualties to get quick success.

Admiral Ramsay subsequently wrote:

> I told the Field Marshall before Arnhem that he ought first to open Antwerp but he would not do so. Now he realises that I was right and that we must open Antwerp before we can advance into Germany.

Montgomery later admitted this:

> I must admit a bad mistake on my part – I underestimated the difficulties of opening up the approaches to Antwerp so that we could get the free use of the port. I reckoned that the Canadian Army could do it while we were going for the Ruhr. I was wrong.

When it came to carrying out the Walcheren operation Montgomery had some cause for feeling that he was denied some of the support he had expected. Even before the Arnhem operation he had indicated that he would wish to include airborne troops in the forces needed to attack Walcheren. Eisenhower was sympathetic but General Brereton commanding the First Allied Airborne Army (which would have had to supply the airborne troops) turned down the request on the basis that Walcheren was unsuitable for airborne landings – this was said in advance of any plan to flood the island.

Paradoxically, Eisenhower's Deputy, Tedder, whose top priority had been Antwerp not Arnhem and who had scoffed at Mongomery's desire to strike towards the Rhur before Antwerp had been captured, was now party to a decision which reduced the chance of effecting that capture and of correcting the very position regarding supply which he considered so critical. Although there had been some bombing of the coastal defences of Walcheren during October, Tedder, on 24th October, ordered that this should cease. Thus one week before the sea-borne assault on Walcheren would take place, a week in which 'softening up' bombing of the Walcheren defences before an attack on them would be important, Tedder issued an order which prevented this from being carried out. All he would agree to was that very much lighter, continental based, air support in the from of rocket firing Typhoons of 84 Group RAF, 2nd Tactical Air Force could be used. It was known, however, that these were not very effective against concreted emplacements. Tedder and his fellow air chiefs had apparently come to the conclusion that their first priority must remain the bombing of targets in Germany itself and were not prepared to continue heavy bombing of Walcheren, even for a further week, a strange decision considering the importance which all had attached to the freeing of Antwerp and the very limited period for which the bombers would be required. It was also a decision contrary to an earlier agreement made by Air Chief Leigh-Mallory with Montgomery, with Eisenhower's approval. The agreement was that while bombing of the Walcheren defences could be run down throughout most of October, for the critical three days before the final assault the heavy bombers would return in force. The assault forces did not know it, but they had been deprived beforehand of the outer assault shield of aerial armour which had been considered so necessary on D-Day in Normandy.

For their part the Germans considered the denial of the Scheldt to the Allied armies as vital to their interests. Hitler had ordered that the Breskens pocket, South Beveland and Walcheren be designated as 'fortresses' and that as such they must be held to the last. General van Zangen, Commander of the German 15th Army, issued an order on 7th October:

> The defence of the approaches to Antwerp represents a task which is decisive for the future conduct of the war. Every man in the fortifications is to know why he must devote himself to the last in this task. After overrunning the Scheldt fortifications the British would finally be in a position to land great masses of material in a large and completely protected harbour. With this material they might deliver a death blow at the North German Plateau and at Berlin before the onset of winter. These fortifications occupy a rôle which is decisive for the future of our people. Each additional day that you deny the port of Antwerp and all its resources to the enemy will be vital. In this hour the eyes of the German people are upon you.

Appealing less to patriotism and relying more on threats of personal sanctions against any contemplating surrender, General Eberding, the German Commander of the 64th Division defending the Breskens pocket, issued a more decisive order:

> Any man who surrenders, no matter the circumstances, will be regarded as a deserter. His name will be made known to the civilian population at home and his next of kin will be looked upon as enemies of the German people.

In the end the General, as he himself surrendered, was not equal to the standard of conduct which he had laid on his troops.

The Troops Involved

The task of freeing the Scheldt estuary was allocated to the First Canadian Army's 2nd Corps including the 2nd and 3rd Canadian Infantry Divisions and the 4th Canadian Armoured Division, the British 52nd (Lowland) Division (essentially Scottish and trained paradoxically for mountain warfare and the invasion of Norway but now asked to operate, according to its title but not its training, at or below sea level), the British 30th Armoured Brigade, the First Assault Regiment of the Royal Engineers, two Groups of Royal Artillery and the 4th Special Service (Commando) Brigade. The latter consisted of 41, 47 and 48 Royal Marine Commandos and No. 4 Army Commando. The Royal Navy would have a very important part to play in any sea-borne attack with a two-fold rôle – to mount a naval attack from the sea at close range on the western defences of Walcheren, and to transport and land the attacking sea-borne troops. In Southampton a naval 'T Force' was being assembled for this purpose. In addition the battleship *Warspite* and the monitors *Erebus* and *Roberts*, all with 15 inch guns, would support the operation with long range fire.

The Breskens Pocket and South Beveland

The first of the three Scheldt 'fortress areas' to be attacked was the 'Breskens Pocket' on the south bank (operation 'Switchback'). This task was allocated to the 3rd Canadian Infantry Division and part of the British 52nd Division. Early assumptions that this would take three days grossly underestimated the difficulty. The Germans were no longer in headlong retreat, they had reorganised and had turned to fight. This difficult task given to the Canadians took over three weeks of bloody fighting over flat, cold, water-logged polders against a determined well armed enemy who now perceived an increasing threat to their homeland. The attack began on 6th October: Breskens, including General Eberding, was captured by 25th October, and the whole of the 'Pocket' was in Allied hands by 31st Oct.

The clearing of the South Beveland peninsula on the north bank of the Scheldt was allocated primarily to the 2nd Canadian Infantry Division. Among the troops defending the peninsula were German paratroops. By 23rd October the neck of the South Beveland Peninsula had been closed with the capture of Bergen-op-Zoom by the 4th Canadian Armoured Division. Next day the Canadian 2nd Division turned west into the peninsula ('Vitality I'). By 31st October the Canadians, assisted by elements of the 52nd Division who on 25th October had made a landing on South Beveland from across the Scheldt, had reached the causeway linking South Beveland with Walcheren and established a precarious hold on the causeway's western

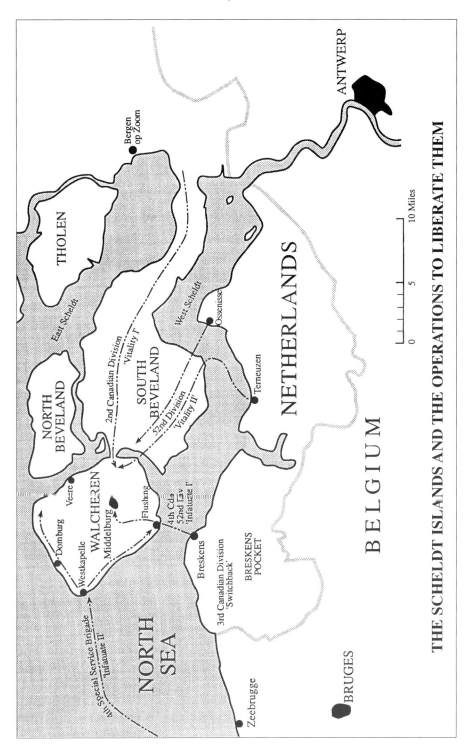

THE SCHELDT ISLANDS AND THE OPERATIONS TO LIBERATE THEM

end. This was only achieved after heavy fighting often in darkness, over exposed mud flats, ditches and a narrow causeway giving every advantage to the defenders. The bridgehead at the Walcheren end of the causeway was lost and then retaken and the hold there then strengthened when the 52nd Division in a daring amphibious crossing of the Scheldt from Terneuzen ('Vitality II') landed on Walcheren south of the causeway on 28th October and turned north to join up with the Canadians at the causeway bridgehead. Further progress into and across Walcheren was not possible. By controlled blocking of the Sloedam on the east side of the island, allowing water to overflow and seep into the ground, the Germans had created a barrier of soft saturated ground, mired polders sown with mines, defensive emplacements and other obstructions stretching across Walcheren from north to south. In addition, further west, the island had now been deeply flooded and rendered impassable by the breaking of the dykes by British bombing. Thus, while German resistance on the east side of Walcheren was rapidly crumbling, by 1st November there was no way by which the Allied forces on the east side of the island could advance further to the west. From the German point of view the defences on the west side of Walcheren were vital to their national survival and from the Allied point of view the destruction of these defences was vital to the Allies' ability to continue the successful prosecution of the war.

On the night that the Breskens defences (31/10/44) crumbled, an armada of small gun ships ('T' Force) together with 4th Special Service (Commando) Brigade was setting sail from Ostend ('Infatuate II'), and a combined force of amphibious vehicles and small ships together with 4 (Army) Commando, and the 52nd Division ('Infatuate I') was setting sail from Breskens. Both were on their way to the western coast of Walcheren. At dawn on the following day, with the British forces on the east coast of Walcheren halted, these forces from Breskens and Ostend were closing in on the island's formidable west coast defences.

Approach from the West

In 1944 the disaster of Dieppe two years previously and the risks of sea-borne frontal assault which it had revealed had not been forgotten. The Walcheren coastal defences were assessed by Combined Operations Headquarters as 'some of the strongest in the world'. There were those, including General Crerar commanding the First Canadian Army, who considered that a sea-borne attack against these defences would be impossible. General Simonds, aged 42, commanding the Second Canadian Corps, did not share this view. On 26th September, due to the illness of Crerar, Simonds, a man with something of a reputation for ruthlessness, but determined and assured, had been promoted to command the 1st

Canadian Army. He was also an innovator and considered that Walcheren could be captured by a sea-borne assault; but that if the plan was to be successful it would need to have a surprise element which would discount some of the extensive German defence preparations. Much of Walcheren is below sea level and, as the surprise element, Simonds conceived the idea of flooding the western and northern sides of the island by blowing gaps in the dykes at Westkapelle primarily and also at Flushing (Vlissingen) and Veere, allowing the sea to flow in. Most of Walcheren's western coastal defences were sited above sea level on the dunes and on the dyke (i.e. on the edge of this saucer-like island) and would not be flooded but inland the island would become a sea. Some of the inland defences would be flooded and while some of the roads, and some of the defences on canal banks, would be above the water level the German supply problem would be aggravated. Simonds also entertained the notion that if the attacking forces could sail through the gaps in assault boats they might attack the coastal defences from the rear. Most of the big guns were on the seaward slope of the dunes and few of them could be turned round but there were small-arms defensive positions which could fire to the landward. Also there were known to be extensive minefields on the landward side of the dunes. The idea of attack from the land-ward side was finally abandoned.

There was considerable resistance to Simonds' plan to flood the island, even by his own planners. When first studied the Canadian Army's Chief Engineer considered it impracticable. The Royal Air Force (RAF) Bomber Command doubted whether it would be possible to breach the strongly built dykes – 120 yards wide at the base, rising 30 feet above sea level at low tide and 16 feet at high tide, and constructed from large blocks of unmortared basalt and enormous wooden piles. Simonds persisted, however, and gradually his planners accepted that the plan might work. The RAF agreed to 'have a try' with bombs which would penetrate to the base of the dyke before exploding.

The western defences of Walcheren consisted of about 30 batteries mounting approximately 60 major 3.0 to 8.6 inch coastal guns, many housed in concrete casemates up to 14 ft. thick; anti-aircraft guns, concrete 'pill-boxes' and sand-bagged emplacements from which machine gun and rifle fire could be directed; mortar positions; concrete bunkers; trenches and weapon pits; mines; barbed wire; flame throwers (in the event none of them worked as they were clogged by the sand which was frequently blown along the dunes), concrete 'dragons' teeth' anti-tank obstacles; vertical steel girders concreted into the dykes; and off-shore, mined under-water obstacles. The dunes were almost a continuous line of fortifications, thickest round the large gun batteries and mostly concentrated on the critical (from a defence point of view) 10 miles of coast from Westkapelle

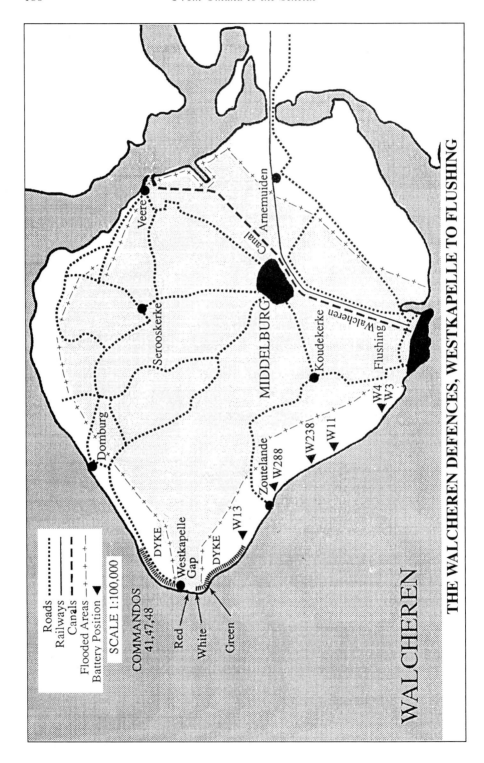

THE WALCHEREN DEFENCES, WESTKAPELLE TO FLUSHING

WALCHEREN

Roads ··········
Railways ————
Canals ———————
Flooded Areas —+—+—+—
Battery Position ▼

SCALE 1:100,000

COMMANDOS
41,47,48

Red
White
Green

DYKE
Westkapelle
Gap
DYKE

W13

Zoutelande
W288
W238
W11
Koudekerke
W4
W3
Flushing
Walcheren Canal

Domburg
Serooskerke
Veere
Arnemuiden
MIDDELBURG

to Flushing. It was the batteries in this stretch of coast which, above all, were preventing access to Antwerp. It was also known that a strong tidal current swept along the western coast of Walcheren and could make the deployment of landing craft difficult and that there were off-shore sandbanks. The total estimated strength of the enemy on Walcheren was 9,000.

Simonds' plan to flood Walcheren required the final approval of General Eisenhower and this was given on 1st October. There is considerable debate as to whether the Dutch Government in Exile in Britain was informed of this decision. Queen Wilhelmina, also exiled in Britain, was informed and was not in favour.

The inhabitants of Walcheren, who at one time had hoped that the route of any liberating armies would be such as would pass them by, now knew that they were in the front line and that there were likely to be battles ahead. They waited and watched. One day (2nd October, 1944) Radio Oranje twice broadcast a message from Supreme Allied Headquarters and the RAF dropped leaflets from the sky. Only a limited number of the Walcheren inhabitants heard the messages (radios were banned by the Germans) or found the leaflets. If they did they were warned that heavy bombing was to be expected and advised to avoid low ground, to keep away from roads and railways and if possible to leave the island – which for most could not be contemplated and if it was contemplated, was virtually impossible. Few who knew of them recognised the significance of these cryptic messages. The inhabitants of Walcheren recognised the strength of the formidable German defences on the 'Atlantic Wall' and the likelihood that the Allies would bomb them, but very few contemplated a destructive attack on the dykes themselves or entertained the thought that the huge dykes which defended their island from the sea could be breached by bombing.

Next day they knew better. Walcheren citizens were well accustomed to RAF bombers flying high overhead on their way to bomb Germany, but on 3rd October 1944 the pattern was different. The bombers were flying lower and the throb of their engines did not fade as they would have done had they been proceeding on their way to Germany. When they were over the western tip of the island the bombers wheeled, vulture-like, over Westkapelle. Soon, from almost every part of the island, the crash of bombs could be heard in the distance.

Mr Lanthseer held the important appointment of 'dijkgraaf' in Walcheren, meaning that he was in charge of the island's defences against the sea. On that day his 18 year old son was on the flat roof of the family house in Middelburg. He heard the bombs falling in the direction of Westkapelle and recognised that this was an unusually heavy raid on the German defences, heavy enough for him to rush downstairs shouting,

The gap blown by the RAF in the Walcheren dyke at Westkapelle on 3rd October 1944.
(*Crown Copyright/MOD*)

'liberation has begun'. His father was more sceptical. That evening his
father was summoned to the German Commander of Walcheren to be told
that the dyke at Westkapelle had been breached and that the inflow of
water must be stopped. The Commander, however, soon had to accept that
the breach was irreversible, but he did express his admiration for the ability
of the RAF to hit such a small target.

The RAF bombers achieved the initial breach at Westkapelle. Flights
of Lancaster and Mosquito Bombers, 259 in all, in steady procession dropped
their bombs on the dyke. For a while the dyke held but as the remorseless
procession continued and bomb after bomb embedded itself and then exploded the dyke's height was steadily reduced and water at the critical
area of damage began to flow over it. The RAF now had an ally in the
old Dutch enemy, the sea. Before the day was out the dyke was crumbling

The destruction of Westkapelle. (*Crown Copyright*)

and the sea was beginning to flow with ever increasing force through a gap which during that day extended to 200 yards. Over the next few days further bombing and the tidal inrush enlarged the breach to over 300 yards.

A few days later the dyke north west of Flushing at Nolle (7th Oct.) and that north east of Veere (11th Oct.) were also breached by bombing. The saucer which was Walcheren filled with water. As the waters rose, streets became canals and people had to take to the upper floors of their houses. Ninety per cent of Westkapelle was destroyed. Successful as was the bombing of the dykes, the limited bombing of the coastal batteries which had taken place earlier and continued for a few days later and the artillery bombardment which was later directed at the coastal batteries from the Breskens area had only a minimal effect in reducing the highly protected batteries' fire power.

As the RAF bombs sank much of Walcheren into the sea and laid waste so much of its fertile land they also caused serious loss of life. In Westkapelle about 200 of its inhabitants died and many were wounded. Among those who died were 47 women and children who had taken refuge in a mill. They were trapped in the rubble of the mill when it was hit by one of the bombs and drowned when the waters released by the bombing flowed through the gap created in the dyke and flooded the mill. The bombing was not all as accurate as the German Commander had thought. A misplaced stick of bombs struck Biggekerke, some miles inland from Westkapelle and killed and injured some of its inhabitants.

The broad plan for the attack on Walcheren was that 4 Cdo followed by the 52nd Division would assault Flushing across the 4 miles of the Scheldt estuary from Breskens ('Infatuate I') while 41, 47 and 48 Cdos sailing from Ostend in a 40 mile seaward loop would land at the Westkapelle gap and clear the coastal defences between Domburg and Flushing ('Infatuate II'). 41 Cdo would move northward from the gap to Westkapelle village, Domburg and beyond. 47 and 48 Cdos would move southward from the gap to Flushing. The warship Warspite and the monitors Erebus and Roberts would bombard the Walcheren defences in advance of, and during, these landings.

The Westkapelle gap was virtually beyond the range of supportive Army artillery at Breskens. The landing of the three Royal Marine Commandos would be accompanied by a frontal assault on the coastal batteries which would be carried out by the Support Squadron of 'T' Force, a scratch flotilla of ships manned almost equally by Royal Navy personnel and Royal Marine gunners. 'T' Force would consist essentially of ships of the 'flat bottomed fleet'. Only shallow-draught (less than 7 feet − 213 cm.) vessels could get close to the Walcheren shore due to off-shore sand banks. The length of the sail, the possible roughness of the sea for very small ships like LCAs and the slowness of LCAs (about 4 knots per hour) made the latter unsuitable for this operation. The larger LCTs (Landing Craft Tank) 200 feet long, would be required predominantly. The LCTs of the Support Squadron had been adapted for a purpose for which they were not originally designed. They had been decked over, the deck forming a platform on which the guns were mounted. The ramp had been welded in the closed position. They had very little protective armour. These adapted LCTs consisted of 6 LCG(L) (landing craft gun) carrying 4.7 inch and other smaller calibre guns, 2 LCG(M) carrying 17 pounder guns, 6 LCFs (landing craft flak) carrying 20 mm Oerlikon and 2 pounder 'pom pom' guns and 5 LCT(R)s (landing craft rocket). In addition there were 6 LCS(L) (converted, partially armoured, wooden infantry landing ships) carrying 6 and 2 pounder guns. The Support Squadron was told that its mission would be a very dangerous one, worse than anything seen on D-Day.

As part of the 'T' Force there was also the Transport Group consisting of 35 standard LCTs with, in addition 3 LCI(S) (small infantry landing ships). The transport group would carry the commandos, their equipment and supplies ashore.

The idea of the Support Squadron had been developed after the Dieppe raid. There, when during the one hour gap between the time that aerial and naval bombardment of the coastal defences ceased – to let the assaulting troops get ashore – and the time that the troops were established ashore with their weaponry, the fire of the unmolested defenders had wrought havoc among the assaulting troops as they landed. Preliminary distal sea-borne and aerial bombardment alone cannot be relied upon to silence well-concealed, well-fortified coastal defences. The Support Squadron was to fill the 'one hour gap' by confronting the coastal batteries from close range while the commandos were going ashore.

On this occasion unlike the Port-en-Bessin operation where 47 RM Cdo was on its own and cut off from medical support services, Canadian medical support services in the form of Number 17 Field Ambulance, Number 10 Field Dressing Station (FDS), Numbers 8 and 9 Field Surgical Units (FSU) and Number 5 Field Transfusion Unit (FTU) would support the 4th Special Service (Commando) Brigade.

The Preparation

On 24th September 47 RM Commando had received word that it was to move to Wenduine on the Belgian coast. By 26th September the commando was established there. It was soon clear that a major opposed landing was in prospect and in due course the location was revealed as Walcheren Island. It was to be a frontal daylight assault landing. 47 RM Cdo and 48 Cdo were to attack the island's coastal defences extending from the West-kapelle gap to Flushing.

Planning for this operation had begun at the First Canadian Army headquarters in early September. The Naval Commander, Captain Pugsley, was not appointed until 16th September and the military commander Brigadier ('Jumbo') Leicester not until 1st October on which date Naval and Military Force Commanders' Headquarters were set up in Bruges. The time available for planning an operation of this sort was therefore very short.

In Wenduine the routine of intensive assault landing training was soon in full swing but a new dimension had been introduced in the form of two new military 'animals', the 'Buffalo' and the 'Weasel'. The correct name for the 'Buffalo' was Landing Vehicle Tracked (LVT). It looked like a small tank with an open top, was lightly armoured and was amphibious, with a maximum water speed of 5 knots and a maximum land speed of 25 miles per hour. It could carry about 24 marines. Buffaloes were under the charge of the Royal Engineers Amphibious Assault Regiment (80th Assault Squadron): they were essentially transport vehicles. 'Weasels' were also tracked amphibians but much smaller and driven by our own 47 RM Cdo drivers. Another new type of weapon with which the commando was provided was

The Landing Vehicle Tracked (LVT) or 'Buffalo'.

The 'Weasel'. (*Crown Copyright*)

a mobile flame-thrower. Sadly unforeseen circumstances resulted in it causing more harm to the marines than to their enemies. There would be no possibility of using offensive armour in the form of tanks on the steep shifting sands of the dunes in the section from the Westkapelle gap to Flushing. Small arms and mortars, together with fighting skill and courage, would have to be the commandos' main weapons.

In training, the buffaloes impressed as a valuable new addition to assault landing armamentaria. Before the actual operation there was only a very limited opportunity to test out the newly introduced weasel. This was at Blankenberghe harbour. There, the weasel, tested on the harbour surroundings and in its unruffled waters, performed satisfactorily in both media. Four stretchers could be fitted into it. Unfortunately, in due course, experience under the more rigorous conditions of the open sea, strong currents, soft sand, steep sand dunes and the actions of a hostile enemy were to demonstrate that the weasel's seaworthiness and reliability on both land and sea, under adverse conditions, left much to be desired.

A Warning from the Past

In 1809, with Europe under the grip of another tyrant Napoleon Bonaparte, Walcheren had been the graveyard of a calamitous British expedition involving the largest British expeditionary force, forty thousand strong, ever then assembled. The French Navy, based on Antwerp and operating off the Dutch coast at the mouth of the Scheldt, was considered to be 'a pistol held at the head of the English'. On this occasion, in reverse of the strategy of 1944, it was the French defenders who, as a defensive measure, sought to flood Walcheren by breaching the dykes. Their attempt to do so was not very successful, achieving only some partial flooding.

The British expedition, with the ultimate aim of ousting the French from the Scheldt, landed on Walcheren against little resistance and had some early success in reducing the siege under which Flushing was then suffering, but achieved no more. From that point onwards the campaign developed into a military disaster. Military incompetence was compounded by an outbreak of decimating disease among the troops which soon negated any prospect of success. Whereas approximately 100 men died in battle 60 officers and 3,900 other ranks died of 'Walcheren Fever' and during the campaign the number of those fit for duty was more than outnumbered by those afflicted with this incapacitating and persistent illness. The nature of 'Walcheren Fever' remains obscure but was probably a lethal combination of diseases which existed in the Netherlands at that time namely malaria, typhus, typhoid fever and dysentery.

Public consternation about this débâcle led to a parliamentary inquiry. There were serious criticisms and condemnation of the military leadership.

The expedition, under the joint military/naval command of the Earl of Chatham and Rear Admiral Sir Richard Strachan evoked a contemporary satirical ditty epitomising their command performance:

> Great Chatham with his sabre drawn,
> Stood waiting for Sir Richard Strachan:
> Sir Richard, longing to be at 'em,
> Stood waiting for the Earl of Chatham.

One redeeming feature of the 1809 expedition was that the Marines distinguished themselves and were alone congratulated on 'your excellent management and discipline, and the example set by your officers'. The severest criticism was directed at the medical service. Although individually some of the medical officers emerged with credit the performance of the service was considered to be incompetent, inadequate, complacent and uncaring, particularly in respect of the conduct of its higher ranks.

The 1809 expedition landed in oared barges carrying men, horses and turtles – incongruously, the pet turtles of the Earl of Chatham. The 1944 expedition was to land in motorised barges (LCTs) carrying men, buffaloes and weasels. It was hoped that it would fare better than its predecessor, and that the medical service would meet its responsibilities more adequately than did its counterpart of 135 years earlier.

Embarkation and Outward Voyage

Some of the preliminaries to a landing on the west coast of Walcheren were not encouraging. There was no possibility of maintaining the security which for the D-Day landings had been so successful. Preparations for the Walcheren landings had to go on under the noses of some who could make it their business to inform the German authorities of such matters. There was a fear that, with prior warning, German E boats known to be harboured in the Zeeland area, might attack 'T' Force after it had gone to sea – in the event this did not happen.

The weather before the landings and the unavailability of minesweepers was such that it was not possible to attempt to clear the outer reaches of the Scheldt of mines before the landings: the only hospital ship on the expedition would be lost as a result of this. Shortage of time prevented any rehearsal of the operation by all the units involved.

Attempts by a special unit (Keepforce) had been made to reconnoitre the Westkapelle gap from the sea on the nights of 15/16, 23/24 and 26/27 October. An MTB (motor torpedo boat) sailed from Ostend carrying a smaller powered boat (dory) which was then lowered into the water off the gap. From there the dory approached the gap as silently as possible and about 100 yards from it released a manned rubber dingy attached to

Lack of security. The preparations in Ostend harbour and the departure of the fleet of ships could not be concealed. (*Crown Copyright*)

it by a life-line. The rubber dingy was then allowed to drift, with an inflowing tide, into the gap and, if need be, could be rapidly pulled out again by the dory. On the first occasion the MTB and on the second the dory were caught by search-lights and had to withdraw under fire: on the third occasion, the dingy got near enough to enable it to be recognised that the gap was negotiable and that the tide flowed through it at 8 knots. It was evident from the immediate reaction of the coastal defences to the dory that there could be no surprise in the approach to the Walcheren coast.

On 29 October 1944 47 RM Commando marched the three miles to the marshalling area at de Haan and on 31st October travelled the 14 miles to Ostend where, on a cold frosty evening, it embarked on four Landing Craft Tank (LCT) in Ostend harbour. Under the command of Lieutenant Colonel C. F. Phillips the commando mustered 22 officers and 378 other ranks, with in addition the Dutch Troop (1 Officer and 12 other ranks) of No. 10 Inter Allied (I.A.) Cdo. The commando's fighting troops were 52 below strength (14 NCOs and 38 general duties marines); three of its most experienced officers had become casualties shortly before the operation and had had to be replaced. Each LCT carried 5 LVTs, and 19 weasels were distributed between the four LCTs. The marines travelled either in the

LVTs or weasels. Two of the weasels carried medical stores consisting largely of stretchers, field dressings, splints, antiseptics, morphia and a variety of surgical instruments such as could be used in emergency situations. Each of the five fighting troops designated A, B, Q, X and Y had one RAMC Lance Corporal medical-orderly/stretcher-bearer attached to it as did the Heavy Weapons (mortars and machine guns) Troop (HW). The Headquarters Troop (HQ) medical staff manning the Regimental Aid Post (RAP) consisted of one medical officer (Captain), one sergeant, and one private, all from the RAMC along with two marines trained in first aid, and the medical officer's MOA (marine officer's attendant), Cpl. Pymm. Although part of the HQ Troop the RAP staff operated at the discretion of the medical officer who was always fully briefed on battle plans. There was no padre on this operation.

Embarkation in Ostend harbour on the evening of 31st October was associated with the usual flurry of activity which precedes such operations. Bright harbour lighting was used in the loading for all to see what was afoot and with a token gesture towards security, which was as likely to indicate departure time to any interested watcher as to confer any secrecy, the lights were dimmed as the flotilla was ready to move out. By 0100 hours on 1st November 1944 the piers of the Ostend jetties were sliding past and soon the harbour with its subdued lighting was fading from sight as the LCTs headed for the open sea. At the off-shore rendezvous the whole armada, 150 ships in all, assembled. It was led by the frigate *Kingsmill* acting as Headquarters ship, with the naval commander, Captain Pugsley of the Royal Navy, and the Brigade Commander, Brigadier Leicester of the Royal Marines, aboard. Within the armada were the 25 'small ships' (or 'little ships') of the Support Squadron of 'T' Force under the command of Commander Sellar, and the LCTs and LCI(S) carrying the commandos. The four LCTs in which 47 RM Cdo was travelling were numbered 18, 19, 20 and 21. Most of the medical section were in LCT19.

As the armada headed northward the sea was fairly calm, without a swell – which can make the beaching of landing craft very difficult; and there was little wind. Within LCT19 the throb of its engines, the lapping of water against its sloping frontal ramp and vertical sides, and the periodic low-voiced commands among the naval personnel were the predominant sounds. There was a moon: it was largely cloud-covered but from time to time as the night sky temporarily brightened the shadowy, somewhat sinister shapes of accompanying LCTs loomed out of the darkness like creeping fellow conspirators, then faded from sight as if espied and anxious to withdraw into hiding. To those aboard it appeared that the die was cast, the operation was 'on'. By 0200 hrs most of those who had no specific duties, including the medical officer, were attempting to sleep wherever they could find a resting place, and a stretcher on the bottom of the LCT was as good as any.

What those sleepers did not know, however, was that the die was not cast and the operation not necessarily 'on'. Commander Pugsley and Brigadier Leicester had been informed on leaving Ostend that due to fog in England the heavy Lancaster bombers and fighter bombers, which it had now been agreed would cover the actual landing while the assaulting craft were moving in, were grounded. Some support from rocket-firing Typhoon aircraft might be available but not spotter aircraft to monitor the accuracy of the long range guns of the battleships or long range artillery firing from the Breskens pocket. The two commanders had been instructed to set sail and to use their discretion as to whether, in the light of the bombing situation, the artillery difficulties and the battle prospects as they saw them, they would or would not proceed with the operation. They carried a heavy responsibility. They knew that due to tidal conditions there would be only a few more days on which the operation could be mounted. As the little ships moved towards Walcheren the commanders made their decision, the operation would go on. The code word 'Nelson', indicating this, was passed to Canadian Army Headquarters.

By 0745 the commanders were aware that the conditions at Walcheren were suitable for close support naval operations – and may have hoped that this might encourage a supportive aerial response – but shortly afterwards they received a message that there would not be any aerial support. Without any air cover the support squadron ships would have to assault the shore batteries at closer range than had been planned. The support squadron were being asked not only to fill the 'one hour gap' but to take on as well the component of preliminary 'softening up' which would be expected to be carried out by bombers. The commandos for their part would meet defenders undistracted and unharmed by preliminary bombing. There was only one good piece of news although it is unlikely that it reached Commander Pugsley and Brigadier Leicester. A large German gun battery at Knocke capable of reaching Westkapelle was the last to hold out in the Breskens pocket and was captured on the morning of 1st November, one hour before the armada approaching Westkapelle came within its range.

As the night passed and darkness showed signs of lightening all were now alert. The day was cold and grey. By 0700 hrs the armada was turning toward the Walcheren coast through the mine-strewn waters of the outer Scheldt. As watching eyes turned landward, straining to penetrate the thin morning haze, the outline of the Walcheren coast now eleven miles distant gradually broke the line of sea and sky ahead. Then the prominent lighthouse tower at Westkapelle began to reveal itself, standing high like a signpost to the coming battle. Soon, more clearly, the jagged outline of the coastal dunes began to etch itself against a brightening sky. There was little sound of warlike activity in this lull before the storm but soon (0830) the first notes of battle were sounding and in the LCTs the marines were climbing into their buffaloes.

The big ships *Warspite* and *Erebus* 13 miles off-shore now opened fire – *Roberts* had a temporary delay due to a turret failure. The boom of their big guns was sounding across the water and the crash of their shells was echoing back from the Walcheren coast. Soon the lower half of the West-kapelle tower became obscured by a creeping pall of smoke from which the top half of the tower stood out proudly – the Germans were trying to put up a smoke screen but the wind was dispersing it.

Assault by the 'Little Ships'

The flotilla continued to move in with the 25 craft of the support squadron leading the way. In the absence of air support the latter were now carrying the full responsibility for protecting the commando landings. Their task was an extremely dangerous one. They would now have to sail right up to the coastal defences with all the advantages which the latter would have – more and bigger guns firmly based and protected by concrete, with supplementary support from smaller guns, mortars, machine guns and rifles fired from concrete pill-boxes, sand bagged protected positions and trenches; and no harassment from the air above.

As the support squadron sailed in the LCTs carrying 41 and 48 Cdos followed by those of 47 RM Cdo were behind. A remarkable scene now began to unfold. Thirteen of the 25 craft in the Support Squadron were to attack the defences north of the gap and 12 the defences south of it. The German coastal guns from Battery 15 north of the gap and Battery 13 south of the gap held their fire until the squadron was 3,000 to 4,000 yards from the shore then opened up. At 0815, with radar ranging, the 3 Landing Craft Gun Large [LCG(L)] positioned north of the gap and the 3 LCG(L) south of it replied with their guns – the biggest of those carried by the Support Squadron. The LCG(L)s then moved in closer, to within 800 yards of the beach, sailing back and forward parallel to it, engaging the two batteries and zig-zagging as they did so to try and avoid the shells which were being blasted at them from muzzles projecting from concrete embrasures menacingly close. One of these LCG(L)s was soon severely damaged and sinking and an LCT went to its assistance taking it in tow. Both struck mines and both sank. Another LCG(L) plastered with enemy shells was sinking and an LCS(L) went to its assistance, unavailingly – the LCG(L) slowly sank. Three others were hit, one set on fire, one severely damaged aft and one flooded. All kept firing to the last or until they were ordered to withdraw.

The Commando LCTs on course from Ostend to Walcheren. (*Crown Copyright*)

Looking keenly ahead: 47 RM Cdo approaching the Walcheren coast. Three 'buffaloes' (LVTs) are in line. (*Royal Marine Museum*)

One of the guns which opened the attack on Walcheren. Now sited outside the Imperial War Museum, the nearest gun is one of the 8-inch guns of the *Warspite*.

The shells of the *Warspite* land on the Walcheren defences as the LCTs move in. To the right of the main plume of smoke, the top of the Westkapelle Tower rises just above the ground smoke. (*Crown Copyright*)

Two Landing Craft Gun Medium [LCG(M)] were given the dangerous assignment of beaching one on each side of the Westkapelle gap with a view to engaging pill-boxes virtually on the landing areas which, unless destroyed, could seriously interfere with commandos as they landed. These LCG(M)s had been adapted with a ballast tank mechanism which gave them greater stability when firing and they carried 17 pounder guns designed for attack on fortified positions from very close range. LCG(M)102 on the south side of the gap moved in and beached under constant fire. She engaged her allotted pill-box but within minutes was engulfed in shell fire at point blank range. She was last seen ablaze on the beach. There was only one survivor out of the crew of 40 and he died of his wounds a few days later.

Captain Michael Peretz RM had been involved in training crews for these specialised ballasted craft and at his own volition was aboard LCG(M)101 to see how the craft performed in action. He had tossed a coin to see if he should join LCG(M)101 or LCG(102). LCG(M)101 on the north side of the gap opened fire on the north bank pill box from 2000 yards out and, firing as she went in, beached 40 yards from the pill-box which was found to have an anti-tank gun. One man ran from the pill box, seemingly in a panic, and was cut down. The forward half of LCG(M)(101) was below the lowest point of depression of the larger guns firing at her but the rear half was not and was repeatedly hit, and the whole craft was subject to small arms fire. The pill box was engaged with direct fire for 15 minutes, but most of the LCG(M)'s 17 pounder shells appeared to be bouncing off it. The craft's commanding officer Lieut Flamank, RNVR, then decided to pull away and then make a fresh attack. The craft unbeached but it soon became clear that it was sinking by the stern. It then keeled over and sank 800 yards from the shore. Before Capt Peretz abandoned ship he noted that there were bodies floating in the water and that survivors, many of them wounded, were bobbing up and down supported by their lifebelts while shells fell among them. From another ship, one of the few official photographers who would venture into operations of this sort took several photographs of the sinking LCG(M)101 one of which includes Capt Peretz swimming in the water.

Four of the 5 rocket firing LCT(R)s made successful shoots on battery W13 and on strongpoints near Westkapelle. Two of these craft were badly damaged and suffered casualties. The ranging of rockets fired from LCT(R)s was rather crude and depended on positioning the ship correctly, often a difficult thing to do. Unfortunately one of the LCT(R)s fired short hitting two of the Landing Ships Flak (LCFs). The magazine of one of the latter was hit, the LCF went on fire and had to be abandoned: there were many casualties. The forward part of the other LCF was hit repeatedly. The LCT(R)s were also employed to lay smoke screens.

The 'Little Ships'.

Above: The leading LCG on the left is on fire. (*Crown Copyright*)

Left: An LCG (Rocket) fires a salvo. (*Crown Copyright*)

LCG (M)101 has been hit several times and is sinking. (*Crown Copyright*)

LCG (M)101. The crew are having to abandon ship. (*Crown Copyright*)

LCG (M)101 has turned over and is sinking fast. Captain Perez is swimming away from the ship (right foreground). (*Crown Copyright*)

The 6 Landing Craft Flak (LCFs) had much lower fire power and had to go close to make this effective. Lieut Commander Lammert commanding the LCF Flotilla said that furious impotence was felt on board all LCFs at having insufficient fire power to smash the enemy batteries. They could only play one rôle, namely draw the enemy fire so that the German batteries would concentrate on them and not on the LCTs carrying the commandos. One LCF sailing very close to the northern shoulder of the gap and engaging the defences was hit on the water-line: the crew blocked the hole with hammocks. At 0945 she again came under increasingly accurate fire, put out a smoke screen and went full steam ahead towards the enemy – but the battery had her measure. She was hit astern and then a wave and scatter of water created by a near miss filled the bridge and upper deck with water. Two hits now blew off her bows and she lost her forward magazine. A direct hit at 0955 then struck her main magazine – 100,000 rounds of Oerlikon and 2 pounder gun ammunition exploded blowing most of the personnel into the sea, 43 of them perishing. As the survivors paddled away on rafts and floats the German gunners fired at them at 1,500 yards range. In another LCF the magazine was hit, she caught fire and had to be abandoned: another LCF took off her survivors but was herself hit, the bottom being holed without the ship sinking. This rescuing craft continued to engage the enemy defences at close range and under intense enemy fire. Of the three others one was the LCF less severely damaged by the errant LCR(R) rockets and it and the others continued firing although all were hit.

The 6 Landing Craft Support (LCS)L, small wooden fragile craft powered by petrol engines and lightly armed had to sail close to the shore to be effective. The three on the southern flank were all hit, blew up and sank with heavy casualties. One on the northern flank was hit and set on fire, its engines destroyed. Another (LCS)L towed the stricken vessel to safer waters then returned to the fight.

These actions lasted for 3 hours from 0900 hours and gradually as the 'little ships' sank, went on fire, were severely damaged or had exhausted their ammunition, the few which could still sail were withdrawn from the battle. They had more than fulfilled the dangerous task allotted to them. All told, as the support squadron was pounded by big guns, smaller guns, machine guns and rifles 9 of its 25 ships sank, blew up, or had to be abandoned when on fire, 7 others suffered severe damage and 4 minor damage. These are the statistics of a naval action which was conducted with the utmost gallantry.

As 47 Commando, the last commando to go ashore, lay off close by, it was a spectator of this unique naval action. It saw the 'little ships' of the support craft going right up to the shore, firing as they went, some closing with coastal batteries at point-blank range — they were fully matching Nelson's adage that, 'No captain can do wrong who lays his ship alongside the enemy'. The big enemy batteries were responding vigorously, the flashes and smoke from their gun barrels clearly visible. David in small, fragile, lightly-armed craft exposed on the open sea was taking on Goliath sheltering in concrete bunkers equipped with an overpowering array of weaponry. Soon the batteries from Westkapelle to Zoutelande had the range of the support craft and were exacting heavy toll. The support squadron was visibly shrinking. One was seen to be straddled by shells and appeared to disintegrate in a cloud of smoke. Some of the ships were sinking, at least one was floating bottom upwards, some were on fire, some exploding, some had smoke pouring from them. Men were in the water, guns were still flashing and the air still reverberating with explosions. A pall of smoke was drifting over the scene rendering it even more gloomy and forbidding on that sombre November day. As long as they remained afloat and their guns were capable of firing, the support craft continued to fulfil their task of drawing the fire of the enemy batteries while the commandos got ashore. Mercifully, as this uneven contest drew to a close, a few rocket-firing Typhoons of the RAF, which had at last been able to take to the air despite what had been said earlier, arrived to give the little ships some assistance by blasting the gun positions ashore.

There were also losses among the transporting LCTs and LCI(S). One LCT and one LCI(S) were lost by gunfire and the LCT converted as a hospital ship was lost when it hit a mine. We saw the latter floating upside down but from their LCT the members of the Canadian Field Dressing Station had seen its port bow hit the mine and lift out of the water: personnel were seen jumping into the sea and clinging to rafts: escort vessels were picking them up. As 47 RM Cdo waited, an LCT carrying Flail Tanks and Armoured Vehicles and a bulldozer of the Lothian and Border Horse was seen blazing from stem to stern (only 41 RM Cdo north of the gap was allocated armoured vehicles other than LVTs as the terrain south of the gap was not suitable for such vehicles).

Those who watched this fateful contest could not but conclude that casualties would be high, and they were. In the Support Squadron 19 officers and 151 other ranks were killed or missing and 15 officers and 110 other ranks wounded all within 4½ hours. The final casualty count for the total 'T' force of 1030 men, approximately half of them Royal Navy and half Royal Marines, showed that 172 had been killed and over 200 wounded. It is hardly surprising that General Eisenhower in his report on the Walcheren operation said,

Great credit for the success of the amphibious operations is due to the support craft of the British Navy, which unhesitatingly and in the highest tradition of the service attracted to themselves the point-blank fire of the land batteries, thus permitting the Commandos and assault troops to gain the shore with much lighter casualties than would have otherwise been the case.

The commandos owed the men of the Support Squadron an immense debt of gratitude.

THE LANDING

'In warfare do not be daunted by chaos, expect it'

These were the words of a distinguished Second World War Brigadier, Brigadier S J L Hill who, with the Parachute Regiment, was involved in some of the heaviest fighting in Europe.

As the support craft engaged the shore batteries the LCTs carrying 41 and 48 Cdos moved in towards the Westkapelle gap. From 47 RM Cdo's LCT19, carrying most of the medical section, their landing was obscured but just after 1000 hours one of the naval personnel, following radio contact, announced that both commandos had landed, 41 Cdo to the north of the gap and 48 to the south. The first wave of 48 RM Cdo's troop-carrying LCTs had a comparatively easy landing as the coastal batteries were so preoccupied by the terrier-like support craft snapping and snarling at their feet, but the second wave had a more difficult passage. The LCTs off shore, particularly those of 47 Cdo, were now attracting the fire of the coastal guns. That this scenario had been foreseen and accepted by Commander Sellar commanding the Support Squadron is evident from what he wrote:

> I considered that as long as the Germans made the mistake of concentrating their fire power on Support Squadron, close action was justified and casualties acceptable.

Now the support craft had been so depleted and disabled that the German batteries could concentrate on the later arriving commandos. There are those who think that the outcome of the battle for Walcheren might have been different had the coastal batteries concentrated on the troop-carrying LCTs from the start.

For over 2 hours 47 RM Cdo had waited off-shore for the order to land, alert and ready, spectators of a unique off-shore naval battle. Shells were falling around at periodic intervals. At 1230 hours, two hours beyond the planned landing time, a naval motor launch approached and shouted through its loud hailer, '47 Commando go in and land and good luck to you'. As the 47 RM Cdo LCTs moved closer to the shore the intensity of shelling increased. Each shell as it exploded raised a spreading column of spray, a spray concealing a lethal component of shrapnel. At times the sea seemed to be erupting. Standing inside an LVT there was a sense of security that, short of a direct hit, there were two layers of armour (the walls of the LCT and the LVT) between the bursting shells and the inside of the LVT. Amid this turmoil of gunfire, explosions and spray the Westkapelle tower and the smoking ruins from which it seemed to emerge was coming ever closer.

The two hour landing delay imposed on 47 RM Cdo not only increased the intensity of enemy fire and the length of time over which the commando was exposed to it on the open sea but it had other serious effects. A sandbank off Westkapelle could not be crossed within one and a half hours of low water and the debris of the dyke and underwater obstacles could only be seen before half-tide. Beyond half-tide, dyke debris and mine-tipped obstacles were just covered and constituted a hazard to incoming LCT. There was a one-and-a-half hour 'safe period' between the two tidal conditions but it was an hour past that before 47 RM Cdo sailed in. Access to the gap was now becoming partially obstructed by sunken craft and damaged or manoeuvring LCTs and LVTs. LCTs attempting to beach had to try and avoid other craft, rubble and large boulders, and the coastal cross current made exact navigation difficult. Bomb craters had created subsidiary channels and islands, making it difficult to determine where the main channel lay. Once in the water LVT's sank deeply and with the eye of a navigator only a little above sea level the main channel through the gap was difficult to find. A 6–8 knot current was flowing through the gap making the navigation within it of 'swimming' LVTs, with a speed of 5 knots, difficult.

The landing plan for 47 RM Cdo was that its LVTs and weasels would enter the water down the ramps of the LCTs in the mouth of the Westkapelle gap and that the LVTs and weasels would 'swim' to the southern edge of the gap where a Beach Maintenance Area had been established. It was thought that this arrangement would expose the troops less to hostile fire. The plan, compromised by the landing delay, encountered serious difficulties and in accordance with Brigadier Hill's opinion justified the comparable opinion of another senior officer of the Royal Marines who served throughout the war that there was no military action, not even the most successful, which did not have in it (in his words) a large element of complete 'cock up'. As far as 47 RM Cdo was concerned the landing had that element.

LCT 18 carrying the CO was leading in. Close to the southern edge of the gap it lowered its ramp but as it did so it received a direct hit. The shell passed through the driving compartment of one of the LVTs killing the driver and wireless operator, struck a weasel carrying the new flame-

The Landing. An LCT offshore discharges three LVTs which are 'swimming' to the beach.
(*Crown Copyright*)

Some LCTs discharge their LVTs directly on to the beach – one LVT ashore, one moving
down the ramp and four weasels following. (*Crown Copyright*)

Reconstructed aerial view of the landing at the Westkapelle gap in a model in the Imperial War Museum. (*Crown Copyright*)

throwing equipment and then passed through the ¼-inch armour on the far side of the LVT. The weasel 'brewed up' and set fire to another weasel. The port side of the LCT was now enveloped in flames and a number of marines suffered burns. The driver of the foremost LVT immediately drove down the ramp into the water. The next LVT, the one hit and now on fire, was blocking the exit of others. Corporal Malcolm of the Royal Engineers, realising that if it did not move none of the others could disembark, entered it and drove it, well alight, into the water. Its steering gear locked and it had to be abandoned. Those in it had to swim. One of the remaining LVTs had sustained a broken track and could not move. Its occupants, avoiding the spreading flames in the LCT, had to jump from the LVT into the water and swim ashore. The LVT containing the CO then moved down the ramp and as planned reached the south side of the gap successfully. The remaining LVT got into the water but its steering had locked. It picked up some marines from the water. Due to the steering difficulty it could only move in wide circles but it finally managed to beach, not within the gap but south of it on a seaward-facing beach.

Marine Battley was in LCT 18. He had been wounded at Port-en-Bessin and after hospitalisation in England had returned to the commando. When

Buffaloes and Weasels come ashore in a sea of mud and among beach obstacles, some of which are mined. (*Crown Copyright*)

A Buffalo moves up the beach under fire and will have to negotiate the obstacles ahead. (*Crown Copyright*)

the shell struck LCT18 he was in the LVT hit and on fire and with the flame-thrower fuel alight he found himself enveloped in flames from behind which seared the back of his head. He tried to climb on to the gunwale of the LVT but his left leg collapsed under him. He then found that the leg was shattered below the knee and that to lift it he had to support both halves. Achieving the gunwale he found that as he lay there his left foot promptly fell at right angles: when he righted it so that it pointed skyward it merely fell over again. As so often happens with the early shock of severe wounding he felt no pain, just numbness. As he lay there the LVT was driven off and settled in the water, extinguishing the flames. Lt Lloyd the platoon commander, who had already swum ashore, hearing of Battley's plight swam back to him and he and the platoon Corporal Albert Rutherford now rescued him, dragging him ashore on an inflatable raft. Battley did not feel particularly unwell and was even able to joke about being home for Christmas. On land, and in a crater, he was attended by Canadian medics who splinted his leg and gave him morphia. He remembers very little about the next three days but was one of those who, because of stormy conditions at sea, could not be evacuated for three days and lay in the very unsatisfactory conditions which I witnessed at the beach dressing station when I went back to visit it on 4th November. He was finally evacuated to Ostend in an open LCT crudely adapted to take casualties. Arriving at a tented field hospital he found himself among rows and rows of casualties on stretchers. As he entered the operating theatre he wondered whether he would come out with two legs or one. As he recovered from the anaesthetic he was presented with a piece of shrapnel the size of a match-box and some smaller pieces, but his main concern was to look down to the bottom of the bed: there to his intense relief he saw two feet sticking up!

Others from LCT 18 who were not wounded, having landed, swam back again to help those in difficulties. Marine Lanyon, no great swimmer, jumped into the sea to assist colleagues who had been wounded. With one of them he struggled to the beach, swallowed a lot of water and reached the beach exhausted. He removed his wet clothing at the beach dressing station and clad only in a blanket rejoined the commando, receiving more appropriate clothing at the RAP. Next day he was involved with his troop in the attack on the battery south-east of Zoutelande. His section had already lost four, including its NCO, but rallying it Lanyon rushed an enemy post killing three of them and wounding a fourth.

Marine Wildman was also in LCT18. To avoid the flames he had to climb on to the LCT's bridge and mindful of his experience on D-Day when his LCA struck a mine and sank he had undone his boot laces and webbing preparatory to jumping into the water. To his astonishment the LVT in which he was supposed to be travelling (the one whose steering had locked) suddenly drew up alongside the LCT and he was told to jump. He did so gladly but, falling from a height, had to endure some cursing as he landed on his comrades.

All told about 35 marines from this LCT, including some who had been burned, had to swim ashore – most of them had lost their weapons. Among them was Lt Hayward who then suffered a severe shrapnel wound to the head shortly after landing and was carried, along with Marine Thatcher who had received a similar wound, to the beach Dressing Station. Both died next day.

As LCT19, containing the LVT in which the second-in-command and most of the medical section were travelling, approached the gap its engines were revving up preparatory to disembarking. The LCT then found itself trapped between the sterns of two other LCTs and had to disengage, withdraw to the rear, and lower its ramp further out than intended, 60 yards off the north shoulder of the gap. The LVT then clanked down the ramp and churned into the water. The small amount of freeboard allowed little protection against swamping should a shell land nearby, but one felt a smaller less conspicuous target than in the LCT. The LVT, aiming for the south bank, twisted and turned in tortuous currents and muddy eddies which made navigation difficult but finally grounded apparently on the south bank. It waddled and splashed out of the water and moved inland through a vast sludge of water, mud and rocks and as it did the course of the main channel became clearer – we were on the wrong side. The area was under constant shell fire and the air was thick with the smell of cordite. One or two of the earlier LVTs had been blown up on mines or hit by shells and lay twisted, inert and silent. Two wounded marines (probably from 41 RM Cdo) suffering from shrapnel wounds were struggling through the mud. Jumping out, I examined them in what could be no more than a perfunctory way, bandaged them up and sent them off to the northern beach dressing station which, according to plan, should already have been established at Westkapelle. Two other LVTs which had struck mines further up the beach lay with their severed tracks draped about their sprockets. The main channel of the gap with current fast flowing, a mill-race of muddy water, had now to be crossed. Coils of barbed wire threatened to entangle the tracks of the LVT and wooden posts to obstruct it but, avoiding these, the LVT turned into the channel. The crossing seemed painfully slow as the LVT, behaving like a dodgem at a fair, was swept more sideways than forward. But the opposite bank was finally reached and by 1330 hours the LVT was successfully clawing its way on to the south bank. Another LVT from LCT19 had followed the same course but the other three had succeeded in reaching the south bank of the gap directly.

The next LCT, LCT20 was hit by a shell before it beached and a number of its occupants, including the Regimental Sergeant Major, RSM Wood, were wounded. Near the northern side of the gap it struck an abandoned LCT, delaying the lowering of the ramp. The LVTs then drove out landing on the north side of the gap. The occupants mistakenly thought – and Brigadier Leicester whom they met also thought this – that they could best cross the gap by making a detour on foot round the landward side. However, after floundering about up to their waists in water, beginning to get out of their depth and unable to stand against the inward rush of waters through the gap they realised that they could not get across on foot. Returning, they found that their LVTs had disappeared – someone else had found a use for them! The 'unhorsed' marines were later ferried across in other LVTs.

LCT21 received a direct hit while 300 yards from the beach, killing the Royal Engineer Captain in charge of the LVTs, wounding an LVT driver, the Y troop sergeant major TSM Tynan, and a marine. The five LVT's then landed correctly on the south side of the gap but, indicative of the difficulty of reading the ground, the leading troop commander thought he was on the wrong side and crossed the gap to the north side followed by the other four LVTs. Three of the five LVTs went on and halted near Westkapelle, disembarking with their weapons and equipment. They then realised that they had made a mistake, retraced their steps and after a detour re-crossed the gap to the south side. The other two LVTs recognised their mistake imediately and crossed back again As one of them did, it rescued four 47 RM Cdo marines who had been in a weasel which had sunk in the waters of the gap. The marines were clinging to the poles which the Germans had planted to obstruct invaders but which paradoxically were now serving as life-savers for these self-same invaders.

These difficult landings cost 30 casualties. In two weasels which had sunk the drivers had been drowned. A number of marines were missing. Three others were killed after landing, one by an air-burst shell. In November the water of the North Sea is cold. Some of the marines tossed into it, especially the wounded and burned, suffered from hypothermia. Two troops had lost a considerable amount of equipment. The casualties had to reach the Beach Dressing Stations, one on each side of the gap.

Thus of the four LCTs carrying 47 RM Cdo three had been hit before landing and two disgorged their LVTs on the wrong (north) side of the gap. Of the 20 LVTs, two were sunk and 12 ended up on the wrong side of the gap. The delay in the call in to the shore, the obstructions encountered, the intensity of the shelling, the currents and the navigational problems of LCTs and LVTs had caused a major disruption of 47 RM Cdo's landing.

The LVTs had proved their worth as amphibians but the weasels were not a success. Some had sunk in the open sea, swamped because of the very limited seaboard; others sank in the waters of the gap where they could not easily be controlled in the strong current. Only three of the 20 weasels reached the assembly area on the first day although at least two were recovered next day. Most of the equipment of the Heavy Weapons

Troop was in four weasels and the loss of one of these was a significant handicap to this troop. The heavier wireless sets (No 22 sets) were loaded in weasels and the loss of so many of these created communication difficulties later. The loss of one of the two medical weasels meant that half the medical equipment had gone. The loss of stretchers was to add greatly to the difficulty of evacuating wounded.

Driver 'Ginger' Liggins was in charge of the medical weasel which was lost. Deposited on the north bank of the gap he sought to reach the south bank but the current swept him inland and the weasel foundered 400 yards inland from the dunes. Up to his chest in water he managed to wade back to the landing area where there was a weasel which had just been salvaged but was driverless. Some time later a driver was called for and Liggins went forward but one of his friends Joe Muir, who had been on LCT18 and had escaped unharmed when the shell struck it and the flames engulfed it, was also there. Joe reached the Weasel before Liggins. He climbed in, the engine spluttered into activity and the tracks squelched into the mud as Muir drove off with a wave of his hand shouting to Liggins, 'Joe survived that lot Ginger, nothing can get me now'. Liggins watched as the weasel moved away. It had gone about 100 yards when an explosion enveloped it in a cloud of mud. It had run over a mine and Joe Muir was killed instantly. Seconds and chance separated life from death in this environment.

Badly disorganised 47 RM Cdo now sought to regroup. Some of the troops, many cold and wet, did not reach the assembly area 500 yards to the south of the gap until 2000 hours. A great deal of weaponry and ammunition and some of the wireless sets (including the equipment for making contact with the artillery at Breskens) had been lost in damaged and sunken LCTs, LVTs and weasels. The loss of weapons and ammunition and of the LVTs and weasels to carry them was potentially serious but the delay of itself was not of critical importance as 47 RM Cdo's main task was to pass through 48 Commando after that commando had reached Zoutelande. 47 RM Cdo's main task was to be on the morrow but it would be a morrow on which the commando was already seriously depleted of much of its equipment.

THE ASSAULT

Forming up

As the bedraggled marines of 47 RM Cdo gathered at the planned assembly area near a destroyed radar tower 500 yards south of the gap it was clear that 48 Cdo was making good progress. A number of German prisoners, cold, miserable and very docile, were huddled together in a bomb crater around which a single strand barbed wire fence had been hastily erected.

Number 10 Canadian Field Dressing Station (FDS) had already been established on the dunes south of the gap. Some of the members of the FDS had done excellent work in the shell-swept beaching area in rescuing naval personnel and marines who in the landing had been wounded, burned or near-drowned. One LVT carrying wounded to the FDS had struck a mine and went on fire. Six of the wounded could not be got out in time: the Canadian report said, 'their screams were terrible'.

Elements of 47 RM Cdo who had landed in good time were now being marshalled and moving forward on foot from the assembly area under the command of Major Donnell. At this stage all weaponry had to be man-handled including the three 3 inch mortars and 3 medium machine guns which were the only weapons of that sort which the commando now had. The remainder were 2 inch mortars, Bren guns, Tommy guns and rifles. I went with Major Donnell, the rest of the RAP staff following on. Air burst shells were proving a problem. As we stopped in a hollow in the dunes Major Donnell's MOA produced a bottle of beer. As he opened it an air-burst shell exploded above. A piece of shrapnel shattered the bottle, another small piece lodged in the MOA's buttock. The beer had gone and the MOA's forethought had been rewarded with inability to sit down for several weeks.

At this stage a section of 47 RM Cdo's Heavy Weapons (HW) Troop was sent ahead to be ready, if required, to give supporting fire to 48 Cdo's attack on battery W13, that commando's main target. 48 Cdo's first attack on the battery had failed and support from rocket firing Typhoons and artillery support from Breskens had been called in prior to a second attack. I decided that the RAP should be forward with the HW troop. Going forward we passed another collection of German prisoners in a wired-in compound. Outside the wire-netting was a young civilian woman with her arm thrust through a gap in the netting holding a German soldier by the hand and weeping profusely. The soldier sat impassively, eyes averted from his paramour towards his passing captors. Passing through Y troop we found that one of its marines had been wounded by an air burst shell and when we reached HW troop found that another, Marine Day, had been killed by an air burst shell exploding in his face.

The RAP was established in a captured German bunker on the inner side of the dunes not far from W13. Hardly had this been done than word reached me that 48 RM Cdo's medical officer, Captain David Winser, had been killed. He had been attending wounded in the form-up position for the second assault on W13 when the position was mortared killing Captain Winser and one of his RAMC stretcher-bearers, two other officers and two marines. I went ahead and contacted 48 Cdo now getting ready to move in for the second attack. This attack, now aided by aerial support and artillery bombardment of the battery, was successful and by 1830 hrs W13 had been taken. The forward move of 47 Cdo's RAP had placed it suitably to deal with 48 Cdo casualties at W13. Some were dealt with at the 47 RAP and then transferred to the 10th Canadian Field Dressing Station (FDS) near the Westkapelle gap, others were transferred directly to the FDS. The trail of casualties, walking, or stretcher-borne through the dunes had begun – although at this stage the evacuation route was relatively short and evacuation a much easier task than that which would soon confront 47 Cdo.

To Zoutelande and beyond

47 RM Cdo was due to move through 48 RM Cdo in the morning (2nd November) and Col Phillips would hold an 'O' (Officer) group at 0700 hours. After dealing with 48 Cdo casualties I spent the night in my RAP bunker: most of 47 RM Cdo spent it in the open, curled up on the cold sand, many very wet. Prior to that many of the marines had been involved in returning to the gap area to manhandle stores forward.

The early morning was cold and grey. Nearby the incoming tide was washing over the shell battered hulk of one of yesterday's 'little ships'. At the 'O' group it was arranged that the RAP would move with the commando HQ. The move began at 1000 hours along the seaward side of the dunes and then on to the higher part of the ridge. The ridge was being shelled and mortared from beyond Zoutelande and a few casualties were sustained and evacuated to the Field Dressing Station. Two Heavy Weapons Troop weasels which had now been rescued and were carrying mortars and machine guns broke down and the machine guns and mortars on board had to be carried forward manually. At this point the coastal dunes were narrow, about 250 yards, so that it was not difficult for the enemy to concentrate fire on the advancing troops. Groups of prisoners were being brought back by 48 Cdo. At 1230 hours 47 RM Cdo had covered the 2½ miles to the outskirts of Zoutelande, part of which was flooded. That morning, encountering little further resistance, 48 RM Cdo had occupied Battery 287 in front of Zoutelande and one of its troops had entered Zoutelande itself: there were no major defensive positions there – chiefly accommodation bunkers – and after a short exchange of fire 150 men surrendered.

Zoutelande was the point at which 47 RM Cdo was to take over, and from there clear the longer, more heavily defended, more distant, more difficult 5 miles sector extending southward to the outskirts of Flushing. For 47 Cdo there would be none of the 'little ships' of the previous day to distract the enemy gunners, nor as it turned out was there to be any of the aerial support which 48 RM Cdo had received in attacking Battery

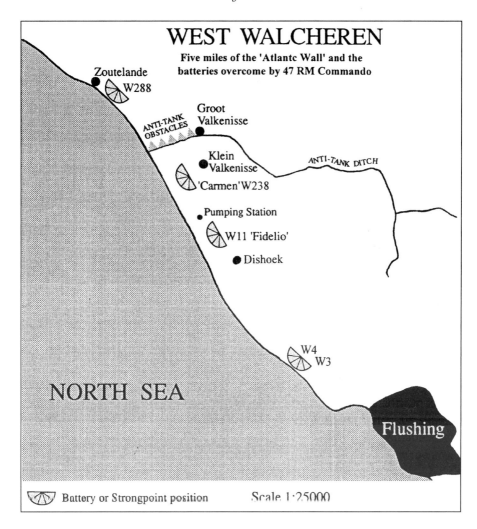

WEST WALCHEREN

**Five miles of the 'Atlantc Wall' and the
batteries overcome by 47 RM Commando**

Zoutelande

W288

ANTI-TANK
OBSTACLES

Groot
Valkenisse

Klein
Valkenisse

ANTI-TANK DITCH

'Carmen'W238

Pumping Station

W11 'Fidelio'

Dishoek

W4
W3

NORTH SEA

Flushing

Battery or Strongpoint position   Scale 1:25000

13. At Zoutelande the CO was asked if he had any targets for air attack but did not then wish to specify any. When later he did ask for air support for the attack on Battery W11 he was told that none was available.

There was continuing concern that the reserve ammunition which was to be brought forward had been delayed due to the loss of so many LVTs and the difficulty the latter were having in moving over the shifting sand of the steep dunes. They could not keep up with the advance.

As we passed through Zoutelande a Dutch flag was already flying. Many of the inhabitants were peering through their windows and as they gained confidence came out to the streets to express their delight, most dressed in their national costume. Perhaps, however, an incident earlier in the day had made them a little nervous and hesitant.

The Opposition: the terrain – steep dunes, shifting sands, no roads. German marines training on the dunes near Battery W11.

The planners. Vice Admiral Kleikamp and staff inspect the West Walcheren defences in the summer of 1944. (*Bundesarchiv–Bildarchiv, Koblenz*)

Above: The defenders were alert and ready. (*Bundesarchiv–Bildarchiv, Koblenz*)

Left: Lengths of railway line concreted into some parts of the dyke. (*Courtesy of 'After the Battle', no. 36*)

Barbed wire defences. (*Bundesarchiv–Bildarchiv, Koblenz*)

Above: An extensive trench system. (*Bundesarchiv–Bildarchiv, Koblenz*)

Machine gun (Hotchkiss) posts (*Bundesarchiv–Bildarchiv, Koblenz*)

Anti-aircraft guns. (*Bundesarchiv–Bildarchiv, Koblenz*)

When Captain Dan Flunder's troop of 48 RM Cdo entered Zoutelande, which had been subject to shelling from the British battleships, the village appeared empty until search of the concrete fortifications revealed the civilian population sheltering in a large bunker. Among them was a young lady who could act as interpreter and through her Flunder gave the message, proudly and somewhat dramatically as he admitted, 'Would you please tell the burgomaster you are now safe from the guns of the British Navy'. He had hardly uttered the words, however, when further talk was interrupted and his credibility was seriously compromised by a noise like a train approaching, everything shook and the air was filled with dust as another salvo from *Erebus* arrived and crashed through the roof of the local church, Zoutelande's most prominent building. It was the last shell to hit Zoutelande.

48 Cdo also encountered a little boy standing on top of the dyke wearing an orange sash, waving a Dutch flag and shouting in a shrill voice,' Good Morning, Good Morning'. When the marines responded with 'Good morning' he fairly leapt with joy waving his flag wildly.

Another incident in Zoutelande exemplified the villagers' response to those who were certainly in process of liberating them but at the same time had shattered their dykes, flooded their land, ruined their agriculture, bombed them, shelled them and killed many of their people. The village was under threat of snipers from adjacent dunes as Sergeant Hudson's section of 48 Cdo entered. Seeing movement among some wire at the base of the dunes and suspecting a sniper, Marine White fired and found that instead of a sniper he had shot a chicken. As bully beef and hard biscuits were the staple commando diet at that time White promptly grabbed the chicken. Along the street he met an 11 year old girl who spoke some English. Knowing of the local food shortages the marine promptly gave the chicken to the little girl to take home. The troops spent the night in a concrete bunker in Zoutelande but late in the evening there was a knock on the door. The door was opened cautiously and there was the little girl with the chicken on a platter now cooked and presented to the marines. This meeting had a sequel. While Sergeant Hudson – very good looking and with something of a heart-throb reputation – was thanking the little girl one of his colleagues said to her jocularly, 'don't talk to him he's a lady killer'. Returning to visit Zoutelande many years later Sergeant Hudson and his colleagues again met the little girl, now of course a grown woman, to learn that for years it had bothered her that a nice-looking, apparently kind man among those who had liberated her village made a practice of going about killing ladies!

Language did have its problems. Once a seriously wounded German soldier was lying on the ground muttering 'Ich Kaput'. Standing beside him was a marine nodding his head enthusiastically and saying, 'Yes mate, you'll be all right'.

Leaving Zoutelande about 1300 hours 47 RM Cdo continued along the dunes, now widening to at least 500 yards, with their dinosaur like ridge 200 feet above the sea. It was heavy going manhandling mortars and machine guns up and down loose sandy slopes and there was increasing concern that the inability of the LVTs to keep up might delay the arrival of necessary reserves of ammunition.

Through the Dragons' Teeth to the Tragedy of Carmen

Q troop was now leading. Just beyond Zoutelande it overcame a lightly defended battery, W288, without casualties but when it had advanced a mile and had reached a position west of Groot Valkenisse it encountered fire from gun positions and bunkers in advance of a line of concrete 'dragons' teeth'. In capturing one of the bunkers Sergeant Puddick was killed by a sniper and the officer leading, Lieut Thomson, was shot in the neck. A German rifleman in a trench had put his hands up to surrender, but as Thomson approached the trench the rifleman suddenly fired at him, fortunately without killing him. A marine immediately shot the German dead.

The concrete 'dragons' teeth' were part of a tank barrier which crossed a low point of the dunes and at its landward end became a deep water-filled tank ditch about 30 feet wide. Beyond the barrier the dunes widened out further to 600–800 yards from the sea to the flooded area inland so that the commando was now fighting on a wider front.

Establishing his command post at the tank barrier at about 1600 hours the CO gave out his orders for the attack on the increasingly ominous batteries ahead. Q Troop, with X following up, was to continue leading along the seaward side of the dunes. Y Troop, further back would advance along the crest of the dunes towards its landward side with A and B following up.

With oddly conceived analogy the Germans had attached the names of various operas to the different sectors of the coastal defences. About 600 yards beyond the tank barrier, west of Klein Valkenisse, was the next major defensive position – enjoying on German military maps the title of 'Carmen' (Battery W238). This battery consisted of a series of strong points manned by Grenadier Regiment 1019. As Q Troop advanced to about 600 yards beyond the tank barrier it came under fire from Carmen, diagonally ahead high on the dunes. Any exposure over the crest of a sand dune brought down rifle and machine gun fire and mortars were also being fired. Two of Q troop's sections under Lt Adam were ordered to 'right flank' with a view to capturing the positions. They moved forward reaching a point where they halted in a hollow while Major Vincent the troop

The 'dragons' teeth' – the mined tank barrier (1944).

commander went on alone to reconnoitre. At this stage the medical section was following up behind X Troop and heard machine gun fire and the explosion of mortar bombs ahead. Shortly Lt Adam came over the dunes urgently seeking help and saying that 'half of the troop has been wiped out' by a mortar attack which had accurately pin-pointed the position of the two sections in the hollow. Along with the Intelligence Officer, Lt Gower, I went forward and Gower went to collect stretcher-bearers from X Troop through whom we had to pass.

Reaching the Q troop location a tragic sight was revealed. There in a hollow were the remnants of the two Q troop sections. The waiting marines had been hit by an intense concentration of accurate mortar fire. Eleven marines including Troop Sergeant Major Spear lay dead and eleven had been wounded. The clothing of two of the dead was on fire, one with a phosphorus grenade burning at his belt looked as if he had been unable to release it when it caught fire. Another had been killed, apparently when one of his own grenades had been hit and exploded, the eye of another had been avulsed by a piece of shrapnel. Frothy blood surrounding the chest wound of another testified to the lethal effect of the shrapnel which had killed him. The sand was stained red with blood. The dazed survivors had mostly suffered shrapnel wounds of the limbs; they included the troop medical orderly. Some of the wounded had managed to move out of the hollow, most still lay there. The mortaring was continuing and as L/Cpl Sillett the X troop medical orderly and Captain McCormick the X troop commander arrived to help, both were wounded by shrapnel. Lt Gower then arrived with some stretcher bearers. The number of these was limited; only the most seriously wounded could be carried. Any who could walk at all had to do so. Any medical care was of a most perfunctory nature. The prime need was evacuation. The dead were left.

As the injured were being evacuated it was clear that Major Vincent was missing. We knew that he had gone ahead and might have been wounded. I went forward alone to look for him and as I did a strange thing happened. A solitary German soldier wearing a long greatcoat, flapping at his knees as he walked, suddenly came over a sand dune some distance in front of me. He made no attempt to take cover nor did he appear to have any obvious hostile intent. It was fortunate that he happened to meet only a medical officer, otherwise his strange foray into enemy territory would have been unlikely to have gone further than the crest of the sand dune. A medical officer in this position is in something of a dilemma. The hand gun I carried was for self-defence and I had to decide what constituted self-defence. I decided that if it was his intention to take me prisoner I would resist that, and that if he showed any hostile intent I would shoot. He showed no evidence of doing either of these things, however, and as he drew nearer I realised that there was something strange about this man. He was looking at the ground, he did not appear to be armed and he totally ignored my presence. As he drew level stooping slightly forward he was muttering to himself and he passed by a few feet away without letting his eyes rest on me. His mental state was clearly disturbed and he walked on into the captivity which he may have been seeking. He seemed to exemplify classically Siegfried Sassoon's description of those who suffered from the so-called 'shell shock' of the First World War:

> '... the shock and strain
> have caused their stammering and disconnected talk'.

The mortaring was still continuing. The mortars could be heard firing nearby from a position so close that the trajectory of the mortar bombs was very high. I could see the descending bombs coming. This was the only time I ever *saw* mortar bombs coming: as I looked up it seemed that one was coming straight at me. As I flattened myself against a low wooden barrier in front of me the mortar bomb screeched down just beyond the barrier which took the full force of the explosion. These wooden barriers ran across the dunes and were designed to prevent the sand shifting. I was showered with sand and was struck a blow on the chest by a piece of the barrier.

Crossing the barrier and moving some yards ahead I found Major Vincent. He was lying on the sand face downwards. He had been shot in the head. The bullet had struck the bridge of his nose, passed through his left eye and emerged above his left ear. Shortly, L/Cpl Thornton, one of the medical orderlies who was ever to the front when wounded required help, Marine Williams (killed later) and Cpl McKenna arrived with a stretcher. As Vincent was lifted on to the stretcher five German soldiers appeared over the ridge of a sand dune some distance away and opened fire. Sadly, with a single shot, they killed Sergeant Webb who had also come forward to assist with Vincent. The German soldiers did not advance but taking cover behind a dune ridge continued to fire on the stretcher party as we lifted Vincent, moved quickly to the lee of a dune, and began weaving our way among the dunes taking such avoiding action among them as we could. As we did so we were periodically exposed to further fire. Approaching and passing through the 'dragons' teeth' of the tank barrier (later found to be mined) our party was further targeted with mortars but finally reached the RAP through a smoke screen laid by a 47 RM Cdo mortar section to give us cover. It was about 1800 hours.

Major Vincent appeared wholly unconscious throughout these proceedings but when I visited him later in hospital as he recovered he surprised me by expressing satisfaction that I had been wrong. Mystified I enquired further. He remembered virtually nothing of his rescue except one thing, that as he lay on the ground he was vaguely conscious of me saying to someone (it was Thornton), 'It doesn't look as if Vince will last very long'. Happily, for a further 55 years, 'Nelson', as his former colleagues called him, continued to prove me wrong.

Among those in Q Troop injured, with shrapnel wounds of the leg and back, was Sergeant Esther. Despite his wounds he gathered a group of uninjured marines and charged the ridge from which the mortar fire had come gaining a foothold on the ridge and holding on until further marines arrived. There was little further resistance from Carmen. The Grenadiers appeared to have been withdrawn into the defences of Battery 11 (alias Fidelio) beyond.

The events at Carmen had temporarily held up the main advance which had been scheduled for 1700 hours. When the HW troop commander sought permission to test out the ranging of his mortars on Batttery 11 further ahead he was ordered to delay that because the medical staff were 'out in front of the foremost fighting troops' and there was a danger of hitting them.

The storming of Battery 11 – and the repulse

Battery W11, about a mile ahead from the tank barrier, represented 47 RM Cdo's major task. The battery included four lage calibre field guns in concrete casemates, at least one with a thick concrete 'umbrella' top, three anti-aircraft guns, 9 pill-boxes; weapon pits and trenches from which machine gun, rifle and mortar fire could be directed at attackers and grenades thrown. The machine gun, mortar and trench positions were spread out defensively to a depth extending to 300–400 yards from the main guns of the battery including from its landward (eastern) side. There were also German large calibre mortar positions along the inland side of the dunes which could harass the advancing commando but which, because of the width of the dunes in this sector, were far enough separated from the commando's main line of advance to preclude a diversion towards them. There were about 25 scattered bunkers providing protection and living accommodation for the troops manning the battery, administrative head-quarters, ammunition and equipment stores, etc.

The commando's planned line of advance to Battery W11 was close to

The major casemate in Battery W11 (Dishoek) with umbrella roof and mounting an 8.5-inch gun. (*Bundesarchiv–Bildarchiv, Koblenz*)

the crest of the ridge. The limited number of available troops meant that the attack had to be on a narrow front so that the enemy defensive positions extending out widely on the landward side of the main battery could not easily be contained. As troops Y, A and B fronting the attack moved off from the start line a 15 minute artillery barrage from the Breskens area was brought down on the enemy defences ahead, but the commando would have to advance without any motorised transport (LVTs could not go beyond the tank barrier), without air cover and with weapons no heavier than the mortars and machine guns carried by the HW Troop and the marines' personal weapons. Due to losses and delays the commando's personal weaponry and ammunition were below strength.

The attack would be a close contact engagement. The approach would be a 'down, up at the double, down' affair whose success depended on the field-craft, training, skill with small arms and grenades, and the dash and determination of the marines involved. One section had often to keep a position under fire while another crept round to take it by surprise. Advancing against enemy positions meant that the marines had to make use of dead ground skilfully, had to avoid raising their heads above the ridge in front of them in the same place twice, had to be good stalkers or, where necessary, be willing to dash across open ground under fire. The risks were high and the Battery 11 area was to be something of a killing field.

Soon, Y Troop leading was held up by enemy fire. As it moved down the forward slope of a sand dune an enemy shell caused seven casualties. At the same time HW Troop was having to respond to long distance mortaring from the direction of Koudekerke almost 1½ miles away on the left flank. This mortar fire, almost beyond the range of the commando's mortars, was threatening to cut off the forward troops and was making the carriage forward of ammunition, food and water difficult. There were also some machine guns and smaller calibre mortars on the landward side of the dunes which could fire from the flank on the advancing commandos. A and Y Troops succeeded in by-passing these flanking mortaring and machine gun positions but as B Troop behind came forward it was hit by this fire and the troop commander, Capt Moyes, was wounded, receiving a shrapnel wound of the arm.

Moving on, Y Troop now approached the outer defences on the W11 perimeter, reaching a platform which had apparently been the base of a searchlight about 400 yards short of the main part of W11. Half the troop was 'leap frogging' with the other, the advancing section being aided by covering fire and smoke (2 inch mortars) from the support section. Y troop pressed on, capturing the searchlight position and covered a further 100 yards. There it was held up but it was in a position where it could give

covering fire and A Troop passed through. As A advanced its Troop
Sergeant Major, TSM Plank, was killed by a sniper and as Marine Mac-
Gregor dashed forward to deal with the sniper he too was shot dead.
Sergeant Mansfield and Marine Lanyon of B Troop, which had moved up,
saw where this fire was coming from. They moved to the seaward side of
the dunes from where they could see the German gunner reloading and
firing as quickly as he could. Lanyon's Bren gun was loaded with T. I. T.
A. (tracer, incendiary, tracer, armour piercing) ammunition. As the German
gunner fell in a burst from the Bren his clothing was smoking as a result
of the incendiary bullets.

A Troop was now nearing the central 'umbrella' feature but at this point
Y troop had to detach a section to deal with fire from the defensive positions
well to the left (landward side) of the main battery which were holding
up the advance. The remainder of Y Troop and A Troop therefore joined
to form a composite troop. This troop then split into two groups, one
trying to advance towards the left of the main casemate and one towards
the right. Closing in on the casemate from the left, the left-hand group
ran into intensive fire and mortaring. Captain Flower, the Y Troop commander, was wounded in the chest, arm and leg by a German stick grenade.
Despite this, still under fire, he rushed a German weapon pit killing with
his Tommy gun the three men manning it; but he was again hit and fell,
shot in the chest (he was rescued and ultimately recovered). As the left-hand
group continued to press home the attack Captain Dobson the A troop
commander was also wounded as was Sergeant Ainsworth. Lieut Style
rushed an enemy position and was killed by a shower of stick grenades.
Further casualties were occurring all the time.

The right-hand group under Captain (promoted in the field) Winter and
Lt Wenham was trying to find a way to the right and made some progress.
Sergeant White asked Marine Delap, a Bren gunner, to try and deal with
a pill box whose fire was pinning the group down. Delap advanced with
his number 2 on the gun, Marine Turner, and took up position on the
crest of a sand hillock. While he did so Lt Wenham, Sergeant White and
a few marines took up position on their flank. While Turner was assisting
Delap to change the magazine of his Bren gun a burst of enemy machine
gun fire was directed at them. One bullet struck the magazine of Delap's
Bren, ricocheted off it, and hit Turner who rolled down the dune. Delap
ran down to him as the troop medical orderly behind came forward to
help. They found Turner, unconscious, with a head wound of his temple.
Leaving Turner, Delap returned to his firing position on the crest and
was then ordered to give covering fire while the rest of his group withdrew
so that they could assist the left-hand group – now so depleted and devoid
of officers and NCOs that it could advance no further. Realising that this

move was likely to leave Turner lying behind wounded, but ordered to retain his position, Delap shouted for the help of two other marines who, along with the medical orderly, put Turner on a piece of duck boarding and carried him back. (Turner died of his wounds two days later but this illustrates the kind of dilemma which Delap encountered, and other marines not infrequently experienced in actions of this sort – where duty on one hand and obligation to a wounded mate on the other are in conflict, often in situations of great danger. A soldier who feels that he has neglected his mate can for long experience guilt feelings). As Wenham now took up a defensive position with the A Troop component of the right hand group Winter with its Y Troop component moved left to join up with the composite A/Y troop.

Captain (promoted in the field) Lloyd now took over as B Troop commander and with TSM England, Sergeants Mansfield and Cumner and other members of the troop (which had been reduced to less than half strength due to losses at the landing) moved up to where the A/Y attack had been halted to be joined by Capt Winter and his few uninjured Y Troop marines. As the group came under heavy fire at close range from an enemy machine gun post above them, Troop Sergeant Major England charged alone up a soft sandy slope firing a Bren gun from the hip. He killed two of the machine gunners and the remainder fled. As he worked forward to another position thirty yards further ahead two of his troop joined him. They killed two more Germans and two surrendered. A German who had been taken prisoner was ordered to lead through an area which was possibly mined. As he did so he was shot in the leg by his own side. Following these attacks some of A Troop were close to a deep camouflaged trench covered with wire which was an outer defence of, and provided access to, the main casemate· and some of B Troop were on a bank above the casemate.

While A, B, and Y Troops were moving forward and by-passing some of the enemy machine gun and mortar positions there was still a danger that the forward troops might be cut off by by-passed enemy troops now behind them and that reserve ammunition etc. would not be able to reach the forward elements of the commando. The mortars and machine guns positioned widely on the landward side of W11 were also causing trouble. As Captain McCormick, the X Troop commander, had already been wounded Major Donnell took the troop over in order to clear up the area on the landward side of A, B and Y troops. In the face of this attack many of the enemy surrendered and X Troop was then moved forward to join the A and B Troops replacing Y which was now withdrawn. Reaching a forward position to the left of the main casemate X Troop came under fire from two separate machine gun positions and found themselves shown

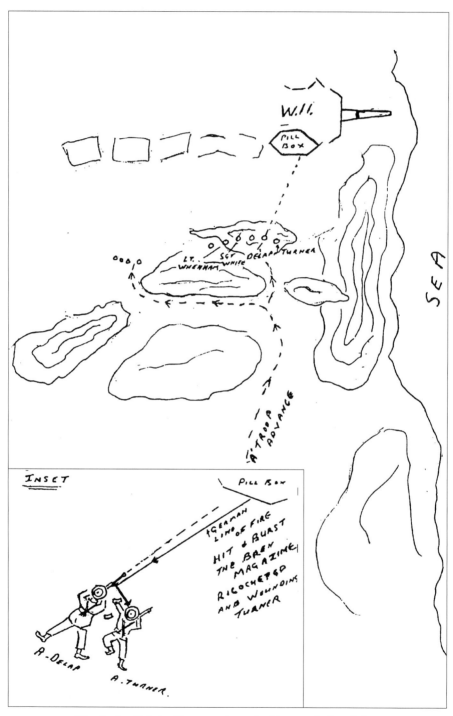

The death of Marine Turner – drawn by his mate Arthur Delap.

up against a patch of light. L/Cpl Buchanan was killed. Moving then to the right the troop was trapped by close-range mortar fire and had to withdraw throwing grenades.

Many of the events in this attack will not have been, and never will be recorded, but, against fierce opposition, the attack was probing, probing into the grim defences of W11 but suffering severely in the process.

After Q Troop had suffered so many losses in the Carmen area it was withdrawn to the tank barrier to regroup. It was then ordered to undertake the manual handling of ammunition, food, water and blankets from the tank barrier to the searchlight position. Some of the LVTs had now come forward from the Beach Maintenance Area at the Westkapelle gap. From the Westkapelle gap the only track running on the landward side of the dunes was impassable until it emerged as a cobbled track which led through Zoutelande to the tank barrier – which prevented the LVTs or any other form of motorised vehicle from going any further. Thus until they got to Zoutelande the LVTs had had great difficulty in advancing over the dunes and were correspondingly delayed.

Even yet, life near the tank barrier was not safe: Cpl Ripiner of Heavy Weapons Troop establishing a mortar position near there with a view to supporting the attack on W11 had been shot dead by a sniper.

It was now about 2100 hours and dark. Many of the outer enemy positions had been over-run in the persistent probing attacks and the commando was close to but had not captured the main casemates. The core of German defenders manning these casemates was well protected. The position was becoming very confused as the various troops had become somewhat disorganised and one group of marines was not too sure where another was. The commando was very depleted, all 5 fighting troop commanders, 2 other officers, 3 troop sergeant majors, 12 other NCOs and many of the marines had been killed or wounded. Many German prisoners had been taken and had to be guarded and removed from the fighting area. Wireless communication had failed. Wounded were lying on the ground in dispersed positions – they would have to be collected soon as some would otherwise be likely to die in the cold of that November night.

Col Phillips now decided that without reserves the attack could not go further that night and that he would make a limited withdrawal, regroup, replenish supplies of ammunition, water and food, reassess the position and plan for the morrow. He therefore sent forward the adjutant, Captain Spencer, with the Intelligence Officer Captain Gower to collect the troops and withdraw to a ridge 350 yards back, near the searchlight position. He planned that this would be the base from which the attack would be renewed next day.

Later that night, as Spencer was establishing his defensive position near the searchlight site, a German counter-attack on the position took place. A group of about 50 soldiers, more than Spencer had at his disposal at that stage, came over a shoulder of a nearby ridge and opened fire. In the confused situation in the dark Spencer thought that they might be members of 47 RM Cdo and called out, 'Cease fire. Is that 47?' Back came the reply in German calling on the commando to surrender. Fortunately Spencer was a fluent German speaker and his reply left the Germans in no doubt as to what he intended to do. With Spencer directing and coordinating the defence the attack was driven off. Later, the Germans attacked again and attempted to infiltrate the position. Again they were driven off. Had Spencer's group not driven the attackers off from the 'firm base' which he was defending any further attack on W11 next day would have been very difficult. The group spent the rest of a cold windy night 100 feet above the sea with very little water and a diet of hard biscuits and jam.

Clearing the casualty aftermath

The withdrawal of the troops meant that many casualties were lying forward of the position to which the commando had withdrawn. Those who could not walk had to be brought out from the W11 area and then carried to the rear RAP bunker, nearly a mile away, at the tank barrier. Casualties received, on the spot, such first aid as was possible – at that stage the forward RAP was a very mobile entity and was where the casualties, the medical officer and the medical orderlies were. The task of transporting them was performed by the withdrawing troops, the troop medical orderlies, RAP personnel and German prisoners. Among the latter were two captured German medical orderlies who proved very useful. No field ambulance support personnel were available. We ran out of stretchers and had to break down doors from some of the captured bunkers to use as stretchers. The shooting had mostly died down and darkness provided cover but at the same time made direction finding among the dunes difficult. Worst of all was the exhausting task of carrying stretchers, in the dark, up and down the shifting sands of the dunes back to the RAP at the tank barrier. Many of the wounded marines on the stretchers, particularly the 'door' stretchers, would groan with each jolt and tilt. One group of four men carrying a stretcher could only make one journey. Two of the medical orderlies had been wounded but even had they not been the medical staff would have been quite unable to cope with the transportation of the casualties without a great deal of help from the marines, tired as they were, and from the German prisoners. Thus odd caravans of mixed British marines and German soldiers carrying those whom the latter might have been instrumental in wounding threaded their way through the dunes. Among the British there was some talk; the Germans remained silent and submissive; none sought to escape, which in the dark would have been easy – but they would probably have been at greater risk if they had escaped. On reaching the RAP at the tank trap the casualties had then to be carried a further half mile to Zoutelande where the 17th Canadian Field Ambulance had been established in the school. Later that night it was possible to commandeer one of the few remaining LVTs along with a weasel to assist in transporting casualties from the RAP at the tank trap to Zoutelande, but the weasel broke down. Wounded Germans were also treated in the RAP and carried back to Zoutelande.

That night one of my medical orderlies had a somewhat similar experience to that which I had with Major Vincent. The medical orderly came upon Marine Griffin lying on the sand and thought that he was dead. He commented to the colleague with him, 'It's no use bothering with him'. Back came an angry growl from the 'corpse', a marine not known for the purity of his language, 'Isn't it f***'. Later that night Griffin's great friend Marine Burkinshaw heard in the dark the cursing and swearing to which he had long been accustomed as his mate, 'Griff', was carried off on an uncomfortable 'door' stretcher. The object of his expletives were the Germans carrying him who were being upbraided for lack of care. They may not have understood the language but they got the message. Griffin had the biggest hole in the chest that I have ever seen in a man who survived, yet on recovery he rejoined the commando.

Two strange forays

That night there was another of the day's strange occurrences. As the dunes were being combed for casualties one of the medical orderlies was standing outside a bunker with a group of German soldiers with their hands on their heads. It was not the function of medical orderlies to capture soldiers but what was more remarkable was that also with the orderly was a group of nurses in uniform. L/Cpl Cole RAMC had come across a bunker apparently deserted. As he approached it warily he espied what he thought was a female figure waving to him from the dark recess of the bunker's entrance. Never a man to refuse a lady, but suspicious of a possible trap, he approached the bunker cautiously and ascertained that the shadowy figure was indeed a female. When he beckoned to her to come out not only did one nurse emerge but three. Language difficulties prevented adequate communication but the nurses indicated that inside were some German soldiers who wished to surrender. Cole agreed and a group of soldiers came out with their hands up. A proud lance-corporal had achieved the distinction of 'capturing' an enemy bunker single handed and rescuing three rather frightened maidens. I went into the bunker and found a few wounded German soldiers but had no time to stay with them. One of them, apparently anxious to please, handed me a photograph which turned out to be that of the local area commander Korvetten Kapitan Hans Köll. The nurses were taken to the RAP and on the way passed the body of a dead marine – one of them became quite hysterical at the sight. At the RAP they were loaded into an LVT taking wounded to the Field Ambulance at Zoutelande. Tired as they were there was considerable enthusiasm among the marines for being detailed for 'protection duties' for the nurses. The arrival of a group of frightened somewhat sheepish nurses at the field ambulance in a situation where its staff were surrounded by seriously wounded men caused an initial ripple of surprise and then the determination that they would be put to work.

Well into the early hours of the morning when the last of the wounded had been transported to the Field Ambulance in Zoutelande and I had returned from Zoutelande to the RAP yet another strange event occurred. One of the medical orderlies was outside the RAP accompanied by a German officer who had arrived indicating that he wanted to see 'the British medical officer'. The German spoke some English, enough to indicate that he was the local medical officer and that he had a collection of wounded German soldiers in a nearby bunker. He went on to explain that he was not a fully qualified doctor but a medical student who had only partially completed his undergraduate training when, a short time previously, he had been called up for the army and posted as a medical officer. His concern was about a particular German soldier who had been seriously wounded and who in his view required an immediate amputation of his leg. The German 'doctor's' problem was that his medical training had been so limited that he did not consider that he was competent to amputate a leg. Would I come and amputate it? I had dealt with legs and feet blown off by mines but had had only limited experience of 'cold' amputation. There was something both sincere and rather pathetic about this medical student-cum doctor. He was out of his depth both in the army and in medicine, confused by conflicting loyalties towards his professional and military responsibilities and very conscious of his own inadequacies. He knew, of course, that the Germans were now trapped with no prospect of evacuating their wounded until the battle was resolved. He was willing however, at considerable risk – he had come alone, and a German officer in that particular area, even with a red cross arm-band, was hardly safe – to seek out the medical officer of the troops his combatant colleagues were doing their best to kill. He obviously knew his way about the trackless dunes, even in the dark, and I followed him.

The bunker we entered may well have been a different part of the one from which the nurses had come, or an adjacent bunker, but in the dark I did not recognise it. It seemed to be an accommodation bunker being used as a sick bay and had a number of wounded German soldiers in beds. One of these was the soldier with the damaged leg. He was shocked, semi-conscious, and had an open infected wound of the leg. It was adequate treatment of his general condition and the leg wound, not an amputation, which he should have had. He was fighting a losing battle with the last enemy and amputation would merely have precipitated his death. I explained this as best I could to my somewhat crestfallen colleague who, I noted, had already prepared a number of instruments, including an impressive amputation saw. Despite the inadequacies of the consultation I took my departure with a certain sense of satisfaction that medicine had transcended the enmities of war.

The Commanders confer and differ

Meanwhile other events of importance were taking place at the unit's command post. The Brigade commander, Brigadier Leicester, had come forward accompanied by Col Moulton of 48 Cdo, and was conferring with Col Phillips. Late as it was (0100 hours) both Brigadier Leicester and Col Moulton urged Col Phillips to put in a further attack on W11 that night but the Brigadier, recognising that Col Phillips was much more closely in touch with the situation than he was, did not order him to do so. Col Phillips considered his commando too disorganised to accept this advice. He considered that a new battle plan was called for and would take time to organise: he indicated that he would wait.

Again to the battle; Battery W11 finally vanquished

The plan to be put into action in the morning consisted of sending the two most depleted troops, Y plus the remainder of Q under Major Donnell to attack the defensive positions to the left of and wide of the main battery position from where much firing had emanated the previous evening. Col Moulton had offered help and one troop from 48 Cdo under Capt Flunder would come up to give covering fire from the direction of a water pumping station about 300 yards short of and landward of, the W11 casemate. The main assault would be made by A and B troops and the Dutch section of 10 I.A. Cdo. Under covering fire from X troop they would advance against the main battery position. Col Phillips again asked for a preliminary rocket-firing Typhoon air strike but none was forthcoming. A fifteen minute bombardment from the guns in the Breskens pocket was the best that could be provided before the attack went in.

Major Donnell's attack on the left was successful. As his marines advanced against the pill-boxes and strong points one after another of these surrendered. As a barrack-like building was approached a captured German volunteered to tell the occupants to surrender and was told to go into the building to do this. After four minutes nothing had happened so Donnell ordered bursts of Bren fire against the building. Within a few seconds about 40 Germans came tumbling out unarmed and with their hands up. In the meantime Flunder, operating beyond the limit of Donnell's advance, succeeded in advancing against spasmodic fire and occupied some cottages from which he could better give supporting fire against W11 as the assaulting troops moved in.

The attack on the main battery by A and B troops and the Dutch Troop, with our HW troop giving covering mortar fire, initially encountered more opposition. The troops advanced by a series of leap-frogging attacks in which one troop gave covering fire while the other attacked. The Germans were reacting with small arms, machine gun and mortar fire and lobbing grenades. A Troop reached a point close to the main casemate, somewhat below it on the seaward side: B Troop had worked round to the back of the casemate to a position above it. The Dutch Section was near the entrance of a trench leading into the casement. In the meantime X Troop, at first advancing along the beach, had moved up to assist A Troop by giving covering fire and cutting through wire defences – Marine Flannagan was killed doing this.

Captain Spencer, the adjutant, in the absence of so many wounded troop commanders, now took over the task of co-ordinating and leading A and X troops and the Dutch section in an assault into the centre of the battery. He ordered the troops to fix bayonets and finally led a bayonet charge up a soft sandy slope entering the casemate through an access trench which, strangely, did not seem to be manned. B Troop then followed up. The fighting was now close contact, at times almost hand-to-hand. Now, as had happened at Port-en-Bessin, the enemy morale began to crack. As the marines fanned out throughout the battery groups of Germans began to surrender and soon the whole battery was in the hands of 47 RM Cdo. It was 1130 hours. The commando's casualties were very light. One marine had been killed and nine wounded including Cpl. Luckman who lost his left arm and seven members of the Dutch Troop who had been caught by mortar fire. Col Phillips' judgement and Brigadier Leicester's trust in him had been vindicated.

Sergeant Gibson the 'I' Sergeant was ordered to accompany this final attack with his 'I' section – there would be intelligence issues if W11 was captured, prisoners, enemy operational orders, maps, etc. He described this final attack:

> At quarter to nine I went up to the crest by the searchlight position
> to look around. There was just an endless succession of giant sandhills
> along which we would have to attack. It was clear that we would be

safe enough while climbing up the reverse side of the hills but when leaping over the crests we would be in full view. We crept up looking grim and feeling blank. We still wore our green berets. Somehow all the ghastly experience and tiredness of yesterday seemed like a dream and neither discouraged nor dismayed us. Slowly, slowly we moved up the first hill, then – 9 a.m. on my watch – we went over the top, dashing like mad into the next trough. We were no sooner over than 'pizz', 'pizz' came enemy MG fire. I had never moved so rapidly before. But in this mass attempt to cheat the enemy there was a certain amount of exhilaration. I remember a distinct joy in life as I got past the danger point each time. Then slowly up again and over, dashing like bloody hell each time and halting to see if the section were all safe. We had to deploy to seaward in face of a minefield, stepping slowly among the barbed wire. A concrete pill box was ahead but before we got to it we kissed the ground as, with a fierce shriek and a thud, a mortar bomb whacked down just ahead. A position ahead was sending forth a hail of fire and like a vicious rattle snake casting grenades in all directions. As we went forward it was necessary to take up fire positions while others came up. Down behind a little bank we took pot shots at a pill box whose fire was almost parting our hair. Then for 10 minutes we were pinned down within the enemy's mortar range. Life appeared hectic and desperate – and then the enemy fire ceased. A Troop had broken into the position from the seaward side. Soon, prisoners were coming out, dozens of them: many lay dead and weltering in this gore: three 3 inch mortars, their barrels still hot lay abandoned. The rout had begun. Led by the Adjutant we rushed on as fast as the grinding sand would permit. Great concrete hulks, part of the battery, stuck out of the sand. Into one of these had crashed a 15 inch shell from the *Erebus*. The whole gun crew sat around as though still alive – a ghastly sight. We went to the great bunkers, some covered with grass, some with camouflage netting, and shouted to the occupants to surrender – they came tumbling out in tens and scores. Two ack-ack guns lay abandoned. The heavy coastal defence guns stood ready to fire. Sometimes we had to seek tortuous paths through minefields, sometimes we had to move down to seaward to enter another monstrous bunker now silent and deserted. By 1230 hours at the bottom of the dunes our men were already consolidating, getting ready to push on.

While the casualties among the troops taking part in the final assault were light they were less so among the battery defenders. The commando medical section had to deal with the German wounded and these were evacuated to the RAP and Zoutelande. Inside the main casemate was a large picture, 3ft × 2ft, of Winston Churchill on a door which bore no other designation. The door opened into a WC.

The Final Lap

Leaving mopping-up parties the main body of the commando, now down to about a third of its strength, moved south from the W11 position. Ahead was the last remaining major battery, W4, at Zwanenburg 1½ miles away and about ½ a mile north of the Flushing (Nolle) gap. It contained the command headquarters of the area. Beyond it and closely associated with it was Battery W3 consisting of defensive positions close to the northern edge of the Nolle gap.

It was a murky 3rd November afternoon: a gale was blowing, the cloud base was low and occasional swirls of rain were sweeping in from a grey and turbulent sea. The dunes of Walcheren were a gloomy, cold, wet and melancholy place.

The commando took with it three prisoners, one an officer, who were instructed to call upon the defenders of pillboxes and other defensive positions between W11 and W4 to surrender. With commandos bearing down on them there was little resistance.

As the commando neared W4 the troops were leap-frogging in the customary way when approaching a hostile position ahead. The leading elements were met periodically by bursts of fire. One of these killed Marine Patey. He was walking between Captain Spencer and Maj Donnell carrying the latter's map case and a pair of binoculars and it seems likely that the sniper who shot him thought that because Patey was carrying a map case and binoculars he was the officer. The commando returned such fire and shortly thereafter, as it drew close to W4 a white flag was seen on the enemy position. Aware that Flushing behind them was already occupied by British troops, that 47 RM Cdo in front of them was preparing to attack them, that there was no escape by sea or through the flood waters inland and that the over-all commander of Walcheren, Lieut General Daser, cut-off by water with about 1,000 men in Middelburg, could not help them, the occupants of W4 were trapped.

The Surrender

With the battery 150 yards ahead the CO sent Captain Spencer forward to investigate. There appeared to be some delay and the CO, suspicious of this and aware that he had only a very depleted exhausted commando around him, then sent Captain Winter (also a German speaker) forward to expedite the proceedings with the injunction, 'Get a surrender'. The Germans were to be given no time for parleying. Spencer and Winter

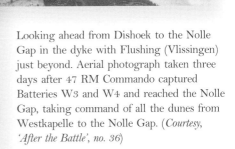

Above: Looking back from Dishoek to Zoutelande and Westkapelle. W11 is being built high on the dunes (1942).

Looking ahead from Dishoek to the Nolle Gap in the dyke with Flushing (Vlissingen) just beyond. Aerial photograph taken three days after 47 RM Commando captured Batteries W3 and W4 and reached the Nolle Gap, taking command of all the dunes from Westkapelle to the Nolle Gap. (*Courtesy, 'After the Battle', no. 36*)

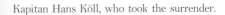

Kapitan Hans Köll, who took the surrender.

demanded to see the battery commanding officer and a message to that effect was sent in to the battery. Outside the battery was an SS Officer. As they waited they attempted to converse with him but he responded with, 'I do not speak with my enemies'.

After five minutes the battery CO who was also the Area Commandant – none other than Korvetten Kapitan Hans Köll – appeared. He was made aware that 47 Commando was in front of him and was informed, with a measure of hyperbole, that there was another commando behind (48 Cdo was certainly behind but too far away to be of any immediate help), that if necessary the RAF would be called in (there was little likelihood that such a call would be heeded) and that the off-shore naval guns would bombard the battery (which was quite possible). Kapitan Köll returned to the battery. Bursts of shooting then broke out from the battery, to which the commando replied. Spencer and Winter found themselves in the middle of this and as Winter put it 'had to assume the horizontal position, eating sand'. It looked as if the battery was having second thoughts on surrender, or perhaps that it wished to put up a token resistance before surrendering.

The firing then stopped and Kapitan Köll emerged in his best uniform and ordered a cease fire. He came forward to meet Col Phillips and indicated the surrender of both W4 and W3 by handing over his pistol to him saying, dramatically, as he did so, 'You will shoot me if you think I have not done my duty'. Afterwards, Col Phillips, not a man given to external displays of emotion, admitted that at that moment he felt more like embracing Kapitan Köll than shooting him, but instead he told him to call out his men there and then. The Germans, 192 of them, then emerged from the battery and under the direction of RSM Wood flung their weapons in a heap. It was 1430 hours. As far as 47 RM Cdo was concerned the battle for Walcheren was over.

Winter had returned to Col Phillips, rather pleased with the success of his negotiations. The response which he got was hardly what he had hoped for, 'Well Winter, they (the prisoners) are all yours, take them back to Westkapelle'. When Winter, now pretty exhausted, having been in the forefront of the fighting since landing, indicated that he had been on the go since Westkapelle the reply was, 'You will know the way back there then, won't you'. So, taking six men, Winter, accompanied by Kapitan Köll at the head of his disarmed troops departed for the six mile trek back over the dunes. At Westkapelle the prisoners were left in the usual temporary repository – a large shell hole – from which they would later be transferred to the German barracks, and Winter proceeded on his six mile trek back again, an even tireder and wiser man!

Within the battery complex there was a large medical bunker with a number of wounded German soldiers. Two doctors emerged and indicated

As prisoners were taken, they had to be gathered together in makeshift compounds.

that this was the main medical centre for the area north of Flushing. I let them remain to continue their work, along with their assistant staff, as their combatant colleagues were marched off.

It was subsequently learnt that at short notice on the previous night (2nd November) 4 Commando in Flushing had been ordered to mount an attack on Batteries W3 and W4 that night. For them this would have meant a night LVT crossing of the Flushing (Nolle) gap. It was expected that a current would be running and that in the gap there would be obstructions created by chunks of masonry from the bombing of the dyke. Unfortunately there were no photographs to assist in planning the best route across the gap. W3 and W4 were known to be well armed defensively. In the time available an artillery bombardment of W3 and W4 could not be laid on. After its exertions at Flushing over the previous two days 4 Commando was very tired but they duly concentrated. They were ready to move off and the LVTs were already being loaded when representations by the commando's CO that the operation was being too hastily conceived were heeded and the crossing was postponed for 24 hours.

Before the 24 hours were up 4 Commando was glad to receive the news that W3 and W4 had already been captured by 47 RM Cdo. 47 RM Cdo had cleared 5 miles of the vaunted Atlantic Wall from Zoutelande to the

Flushing gap in 26 hours. It had succeeded against daunting odds which at times seemed insuperable.

Mopping up

On 4th November I went back to the beachhead at the Westkapelle gap to see how the wounded were faring. They were faring badly. For the first two days after the landing the area round the gap had been under continuous shelling. On the evening of 1st November one of the LCTs which had brought in troops but was in no way equipped as a hospital ship – the original hospital ship had been lost on the run in – took off over 100 casualties. On 2nd November a storm blew up and continued until 5th November. Casualties occurring during this time, mostly in 47 RM Cdo had to be retained ashore. Crowded together, some in tented facilities, they lay in cold miserable conditions. Three of our wounded, Lt Hayward, L/Cpl Thatcher and Marine Turner, died during this period. On 6th November an LCT under Lieut David Dodson which had brought in supplies and had been unloaded by that day was loaded with 70 wounded, many on stretchers, and 250 German prisoners. The stretcher cases were subject to additional trauma as, to reach the 'hospital' LCT, they had to be carried over other beached craft. This was a difficult task as the intervening LCTs bumped and drew apart. Captain Scarrow RAMC was in charge of the wounded; his RAMC Sergeant had been drowned when he was trapped in a weasel which foundered while attempting to cross the Westkapelle gap. As the LCT set off the storm was still far from over. Of necessity the wounded lay in the open, soaked that day by driving rain and the spray from the 8 foot waves which were breaking over the ship's bows. The casualties were cold and wet and the heaving movement of the LCT aggravated the wounds of many. One of the wounded from 47 RM Cdo, Marine Fawcett, died during the journey. For a while the German prisoners were ordered to hold tarpaulins over the wounded to shelter them. Around midnight the German prisoners became restive and had to be 'quietened'. The journey to Ostend took ten hours, nearly twice the normal time. Captain Scarrow described the journey as 'horrendous'.

The storm which raged from 2nd to 5th November also threatened the operation's follow-up supply LCTs. The three supply LCTs which reached the waters off Walcheren on 1st November were expected to beach then, but the shell fire was such that they were ordered not to land but to wait off-shore out of range. As they withdrew one of them struck a mine and sank. The two remaining LCTs could not beach until 0030 hours on 3rd November. In the dark one of them, south of the gap, ran on to one of the wooden groynes which stretch out from the Walcheren coast as part of the breakwater protection against the sea. It stuck fast and its ramp

The supply LCT which was blown on to the rocks during the severe storm which raged
from 2nd to 5th November.

could not be fully lowered. It could be unloaded only partially and with
the sea breaking over it many of the stores were damaged. The other LCT
beached satisfactorily but the jumbled basalt blocks of the damaged dyke
which had to be crossed were very slippery and difficult for laden men.
But for the strenuous labours of the Pioneer Corps and the plentiful supply
of POWs, who proved very willing, unloading would have been very slow.
(It was this LCT which was used to evacuate wounded on 6th November.)
These losses meant that there were considerable shortages and delayed
delivery of reserve ammunition and other stores during the operation. The
shortage of food which the troops experienced was relieved by utilising
captured German food supplies – but the German black bread was far from
popular. On the 5th day an air drop was necessary to relieve shortages of
food and other commodities.

After W4 had been captured the commando was engaged in administrative tasks such as collecting the dead and burying them, sewn into
blankets, in temporary graves, checking equipment etc. It was made
responsible for all prisoners of war in the area. The prisoners were put to
work and did so with a will which seemed to be borne of relief that their
war was over. Captain Winter, with a working, but not perfect, knowledge
of German and a stentorian voice was put in charge of these operations.
One day he came upon a prisoner urinating where he should not. Sternly
reprimanding him he led him off to an area where there was need to dig

a latrine and instructed him to proceed with the digging. Returning later to inspect progress he found the man still digging but in a highly nervous state, visibly shaking and weeping. He had misunderstood Winter's order and thought that he had been ordered to dig his own grave prior to execution. Had he been a witness of what had happened on the dunes nearby six weeks previously? (Chapter 9).

'Valete'

Not long after he landed on 1st November Donald Gibson, already a writer of poetry, came upon the body of a young 19-year-old marine,

> pale and cold, lying on his back, his blue eyes open with the dullness that death imparts. I stood a while and looked at him; already the drift of the sand was covering him over. I could have said that he was still surprised, overtaken by events and now abandoned, with his cheek and forehead arched in a strange way, as if in protest. I moved on ...

Three days later, having 'staggered on leaden legs to the end of the dunes, now resting in a bunker muffled up against the cold and with pencil, pad and torch, a poem wrote itself down. My young marine was speaking through me':

> The battle stilled to dimness:
> No tracer more ripped through the ragged remnants of the brain,
> And even the parabolas of sound
> That herald mortars
> Grew dim and puny on the far dunes.
> Here I lie,
> While the wind blows round the corner of my house
> Silts up the sills with the drift,
> Drifting sand
> Fumbles feebly with the ashes
> On the cold hearth.
> Tomorrow no one will come
> Curiously peeping
> Through shutterless windows,
> Nor try the door.
> And I will be afraid
> That there is none to see
> No one to come,
> None to be cheerful in the silent rooms.
> I shall be eager to leave
> Quit my tenancy

Because my house has become no house.
On the day after
They will put it away,
Lifting with passionless hands,
Shaking off minute rivers
Of Sand.
For tenantless houses are horrors to living men.
I shall stand
Just near – beyond the gate
While they conceal the roof
And the walls
And the hearth and the rooms
And I will watch them go away
Back to the drift of the sand.
But I will know,
No more than now
What has really happened to me
Nor whom I am
Nor whither going.

On 11th November the commando crossed the Flushing (Nolle) gap in LVTs without difficulty and splashed its way into Flushing, now securely in the hands of 4 Cdo and the 52nd Division.

Casualties

Of the 400 officers and men of 47 RM Cdo (including 13 from the Dutch Troop of 10 I.A. Commando, who had set out from Ostend 118 (30%) had become casualties, 34 (8.5%) killed and 84 (21%) wounded, the latter including 9 who had suffered from severe hypothermia due to prolonged immersion in the sea. Several of the attached LVT drivers had also become casualties including at least one killed. Among the 22 47 RM Cdo Officers 8 (36%) were casualties (2 killed and 6 wounded) and among 378 other ranks 106 (28%) were casualties (32 killed and 74 wounded). Among the assault troops in closest contact with the enemy (A, B, Q, X, Y) numbering 288 (including medical personnel attached to them) as opposed to HW and HQ Troops (numbering 112) the casualty rate was 39% in the former compared with 9% in the latter. Among the officers in the assaulting troops the casualty rate was 57% (8 out of 14) and among the other ranks in these troops it was 37% (100 out of 274). Among the commando's medical personnel the casualty rate was 22% (2 out of 9) although, in addition, another member of the medical personnel was accidentally shot in the hand by one of our own troops.

The Beach Dressing area at the Westkapelle Gap where so many of the wounded lay for four days in cold, wet conditions. (*Courtesy of Westkapelle Museum*)

Casualties had to be evacuated by sea to the base hospital and had to be lifted across other LCTs to the improvised 'hospital' LCT which was to take them to Ostend. The only LCT equipped as a hospital ship had been sunk. (*Crown Copyright*)

Of the RM commandos taking part in the Walcheren operation 47 RM Cdo with 34 officers and men killed suffered most severely compared with 16 in 41 RM Cdo and 13 in 48 RM Cdo, although after the fighting was over the latter commando lost a further 19 when an LVT carrying 28 ran over a mine.

Antwerp Opens

With the coastal batteries on Walcheren silent, the mines could be cleared from the Scheldt and within a few days 100 mine-sweepers were engaged in this task. On 26th November three coasters reached Antwerp; two days later a liberty ship docked and by December 1st 10,000 tons of cargo had been unloaded. On 16th December the Germans attacked in the Ardennes. In containing that attack and making good the losses of equipment involved then, and the losses previously sustained at Arnhem, the port of Antwerp played a critical part. As those who understood the logistics of warfare faced the supply problems which these battles had created and contemplated the long haul ahead towards Berlin they blessed the capture of Walcheren and the speed with which this had been achieved, ten days instead of the expected thirty. The capture of Walcheren also released a great many Canadian, British and Polish troops for further deployment.

General Eisenhower had described the capture of Walcheren as 'one of the most gallant and aggressive actions of the war'. Twenty five years later, General Simonds, the wartime commander of the First Canadian Army and the over-all commander of the Walcheren operation, comparing that operation with the 'dramatic, much publicised but unsuccessful operation at Arnhem' which had preceded it, observed somewhat wistfully, 'If the assault on Walcheren had failed, it would have been as famous today as the gallant airborne landing at Arnhem'.

Fifty Years On

Fifty years later a large group of Walcheren citizens and members of the Dutch services stood by the dyke at Westkapelle to commemorate the liberation of their island. Among them, as honoured guests of their Dutch hosts, were members of the 4th Commando Brigade who had survived, assembled to pay tribute to their comrades who had not. Where there had been a torrent raging through the Westkapelle gap the sea had been restored to its rightful place and was gently lapping against the outer side of an enormous new dyke; where there had been mud and mines, barbed wire, mined obstacles and an all-pervading sense of hostility and apprehension, grassy slopes, trim wire fences and pedestrian paths led invitingly along the dunes; where explosions and anxious shouts had echoed among the dunes there was only the ripple of soft and friendly voices; where

They did not return. Temporary graves of Royal Marines at Walcheren.

unseen but hostile eyes and the barrels of guns, mortars and rifles had looked out from the dark recesses of concrete casemates, pill boxes and trenches, welcoming eyes surveyed the scene from the open windows and well tended gardens of trim houses; where the pervading smell of cordite filled the air there was a fresh morning breeze; where there had been a destructive inland sea covering 85% of the island, agriculture was booming and vegetation was lush. Close by, the Westkapelle Tower stood high, not above the acrid smoke of battle, but from a hazy ground mist, its upper reaches illuminated not by the intermittent flash of gunfire but by a fitful November sun.

Next day, on a still Sunday morning, six miles along the dunes, beyond the village of Zoutelande, beyond the concrete tank obstacles still in position, beyond the hollow where eleven marines of Q Troop had been killed and eleven wounded, beyond the cross erected high on the dunes above Klein Valkenisse, a solo pilgrim sought the site of battery W11. There a hundred feet above the shore at a site commanding a wide sweep of ground leading downwards to the beach and to an even wider sweep of sea beyond, a few strands of rusting barbed wire tangled among the vegetation and a few large slabs of cracking concrete, partially sand covered, were the insubstantial remnants of once mighty gun emplacements and of their surroundings where so many had died or lain wounded. But now the sea was calm, the high dunes were deserted and there was an air of Sunday morning tranquillity. On the beach below a jogger was running, children were playing with a dog and a mother was walking with a baby in a push

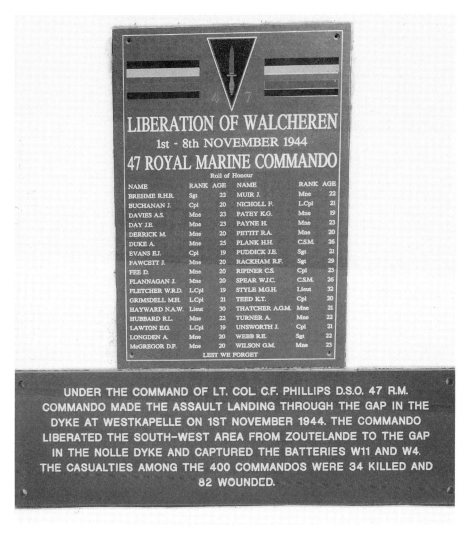

LIBERATION OF WALCHEREN
1st - 8th NOVEMBER 1944
47 ROYAL MARINE COMMANDO

Roll of Honour

NAME	RANK	AGE	NAME	RANK	AGE
BREHME R.H.R.	Sgt	22	MUIR J.	Mne	22
BUCHANAN J.	Cpl	20	NICHOLL F.	LCpl	21
DAVIES A.S.	Mne	23	PATEY K.G.	Mne	19
DAY J.B.	Mne	23	PAYNE H.	Mne	23
DERRICK M.	Mne	20	PETTIT R.A.	Mne	20
DUKE A.	Mne	25	PLANK H.H.	C.S.M.	26
EVANS E.J.	Cpl	19	PUDDICK J.E.	Sgt	21
FAWCETT J.	Mne	20	RACKHAM R.F.	Sgt	29
FEE D.	Mne	20	RIPINER C.S.	Cpl	23
FLANNAGAN J.	Mne	20	SPEAR W.J.C.	C.S.M.	26
FLETCHER W.R.D.	LCpl	19	STYLE M.G.H.	Lieut	32
GRIMSDELL M.H.	LCpl	21	TEED K.T.	Cpl	20
HAYWARD N.A.W.	Lieut	30	THATCHER A.G.M.	Mne	21
HUBBARD R.L.	Mne	22	TURNER A.	Mne	22
LAWTON E.G.	LCpl	19	UNSWORTH J.	Cpl	21
LONGDEN A.	Mne	20	WEBB R.E.	Sgt	22
McGREGOR D.F.	Mne	20	WILSON G.M.	Mne	23

LEST WE FORGET

UNDER THE COMMAND OF LT. COL. C.F. PHILLIPS D.S.O. 47 R.M. COMMANDO MADE THE ASSAULT LANDING THROUGH THE GAP IN THE DYKE AT WESTKAPELLE ON 1ST NOVEMBER 1944. THE COMMANDO LIBERATED THE SOUTH-WEST AREA FROM ZOUTELANDE TO THE GAP IN THE NOLLE DYKE AND CAPTURED THE BATTERIES W11 AND W4. THE CASUALTIES AMONG THE 400 COMMANDOS WERE 34 KILLED AND 82 WOUNDED.

Memorial at the church of Dishoek.

chair. As the pilgrim stood silent an old man appeared toiling up the steep path to the crest of the dunes. He passed along the path by the W11 site and as he did so he looked respectfully at the green beret and seemed as if he might stop, but he went on.

Chapter Nine

The Cross at Klein Valkenisse

Civil Rule in Occupied Europe, 1939–45

ALTHOUGH, in the War in Europe, there were individual examples of serious disregard of the Geneva Convention regarding the treatment of Allied prisoners of war the Convention was in the main observed. The majority of those in the Allied armed forces who were captured remained alive, were not subject to torture after capture and were incarcerated in prisoner of war camps which conformed to the rules of the Convention.

For civilians of the occupied countries the situation was very different: for them there was little concern with the Geneva Convention. Too often the norms of justice and humanity were replaced by arbitrary repression, prostituted justice, barbaric punishment, extortion, slavery and cynical disregard for human dignity. Jews were subjected to genocide, hostages innocent of any crime were executed merely because they happened to be at a certain place at a certain time; civilians were deported for slave labour. Those who were allowed to remain within their own communities were subject to the imposition of harsh, repressive laws and punishments. Community trust and loyalty could be put in jeopardy by the few who for personal motives of power and aggrandisement gave their services voluntarily to the oppressor, endorsing with him the abandonment of accepted standards of human behaviour and exploiting corrupt and intimidating practices. The brooding menace of the Gestapo hung over Europe and struck fear into the hearts of many as it conducted its evil affairs through the ritual of the secret informer, brutal interrogation, the torture chamber, the concentration camp, the gas chamber and the gallows.

On the other hand there were those, the great majority, who were prepared to resist the oppressor and to hinder and disrupt his activities in every way possible. These activities in themselves might carry only minor risk but could greatly increase the hardship to which all were subject, but which most were willing voluntarily to accept. There were those who accepted, or were forced into, positions of authority but used that authority, often at considerable risk, to protect those whom they represented from the worst excesses of the foreign overlords. There were others, men and women of great courage who, in the furtherance of freedom, willingly undertook tasks which, if discovered, meant for the individual not the provisions of the Geneva Convention but the concentration camp, torture and death and for his or her family a range of hardships which could only be contemplated with profound apprehension.

As volleys of shots from German riflemen straddled the prostrate form of Major Vincent on the dunes near Klein Valkenisse on 2nd November 1944, and killed Sergeant Webb who, with others, had come to his aid, little did Vincent's rescuers realise that six weeks previously another volley of shots had rung out, virtually over the same spot, in somewhat grimmer circumstances. Nor were they aware that the melancholy evidence of that earlier fusillade lay hidden only a few feet away. The events surrounding this have been recorded by Mr Hans Tuynman of the Documentatie Groep Walcheren 1939–1945.

'One of our bombers is missing'

On 30th March 1944 a group of Halifax bombers took off from Tempsford Airfield in Bedfordshire on a mission to bomb Nuremberg.* Taking off with them were five Halifaxes of another squadron, No 138, whose planes were not going to Nuremberg but would be better able to conceal their presence and purpose – the dropping of agents and arms, ammunition, medicines, pigeons, etc. to resistance groups – if they flew on a night when they could mingle, in the early stage of their journey at least, among a large group of bombers. One of the five Halifaxes, LL287 NF-S (for sugar) was to 'drop' over a wooded area near Antwerp. At the last minute, as it stood at the end of the runway in the dark waiting to take off, a crew member, known as the despatcher brought aboard two 'passengers'. They were Belgian agents. For security none of the crew other than the despatcher were allowed to meet the agents. About the same time the BBC was broadcasting a coded message which interpreted said that, 'the agents will be coming tonight'.

As the plane crossed the Dutch coast it had to abandon its concealment among the Nuremberg bombers as it made for the Antwerp area. All went well until the plane was near the dropping zone and had descended to an altitude of 1000 feet at which the drop was to be made. Unfortunately the night was clear and as the plane flew low over South Beveland, preparatory to dropping, it was hit by a burst of flak from a battery near Hansweert. It first went on fire and then some of the bombs exploded, killing three of the crew near the bomb compartment, Warrant Officer Anderson, Canadian Flying Officer Francis DFC, and Flight Sergeant Bates. The pilot struggled desperately to swing the plane towards the Western Scheldt

---

* This proved to be the costliest single attack by Bomber Command during the war. Of 795 aircraft taking part 94 were lost and 71 damaged, 12 beyond repair. 650 aircrew were missing.

to avoid the flak and put the fire out, and to return to England, but it was soon evident that that was not going to be possible: the plane was sinking lower and lower. The waters of the Scheldt below were now in sight and coming closer and closer. A wing tip touched the water and with a sudden twist and a splash the plane ditched and came to a standstill.

Unfortunately the two agents, one of whom was thought to be Lieut Robert Deprez from Deerlijk in Belgium, were getting ready to drop and were sitting near the edge of the hole through which they would leave the aircraft. Their parachute cords were attached to the interior of the adjacent wall of the fuselage. As the plane sank the water rose quickly through the hole and they were almost certainly drowned when the parachute packs with which they were encumbered, and the attached webbing, prevented them from getting out through the escape hatch. The five remaining crew, pilot Flight Lieutenant Mill and his fellow officer Denis Beale, and three NCOs, Canadian second pilot Godfrey, Australian rear gunner Weir and despatcher Kimpton managed to climb out and get into an escape dinghy. As those in the dinghy waited and watched the doomed plane remained afloat for only two minutes: there was no sign of other survivors. Now a vessel with a searchlight was seen approaching and those in the dinghy paddled away as quickly as possible. They reached the north shore of the Scheldt, deflated the dinghy and waded ashore on to South Beveland, burying the dinghy. The moon was now less bright. They crossed a sea dyke, took off their flying clothes and buried them in a culvert.

Deciding on their next course of action the survivors now split up into two parties, Mill and Beale in one and the three NCOs in another. Mill and Beale set off to the right along a road parallel to the sea dyke. The NCOs decided to take a road leading inland from the dyke. They had not gone far when they ran into a German patrol. Two were apprehended immediately. Godfrey managed to run away but, pursued by tracker dogs, was found early in the following morning hiding in a hen-house. The NCOs were taken to a Luftwaffe airfield at Woensdrecht where they were interrogated then transferred to a civilian prison in Amsterdam where they were put into solitary confinement for ten days and ultimately sent to a prison camp.

The two officers, travelling east, found themselves after some miles near 's-Gravenpolder and took a chance by knocking on the door of a farmhouse. Fortunately the owner Mr Vermus was 'reliable'. He informed the resistance and Mr de Putter led the two to the house of Mr den Dekker in Molenstraat in the village of Hoedenskerke. From there Mill was taken to the house of Dr Franssen van de Putte in Baarland and Beale transported by Policeman Hokke, on a bicycle, to the farm of Mr Acada at Kwadendamme. Beale had just arrived at the latter in the early hours of the morning when a

Wehrmacht motor cycle and side car drew up on the road outside. 'Treason' thought Mr Acada, as he was also sheltering some wanted Dutchmen and feared there might be a stool pigeon among them. To his relief the motor cyclists took out a torch, spent some time studying a map, remounted and departed.

After four weeks, during which false passports and identity cards were prepared by the minister of Hoedenskerke, Mill and Beale were taken to the ferry-boat which plied between Hoedenskerke and Terneuzen and smuggled aboard by Mr A. Koole, a member of the local resistance and the purser of the ferry. His predecessor Mr J. F. Meiboom had previously been arrested – he died in a concentration camp in December 1944. In pursuing resistance activities in such a suspect job Mr Koole took a considerable risk. During the crossing to Terneuzen Mill found himself sitting beside a member of the Luftwaffe who fortunately did not speak to him. The two RAF men were then taken separately to the Belgian town of Zelgate, Beale to the farmhouse of Mr de Colvenaer and Mill to the house of Mr Pierets, a blacksmith and a garage owner, who was a member of the Belgian resistance group 'Zero'.

It was hoped that Mill and Beale could be 'processed' through an established escape line through France and Spain but this was proving very difficult as, in preparation for the D-Day landings, the roads and railways were being continuously disrupted by Allied air raids. After four months the two were still billeted with Messrs de Colvenaer and Pierets and now there was further delay. The Normandy landings had taken place and the Allied break-out from the Normandy bridgehead had begun. The Wehrmacht was streaming northwards and Zelgate was bristling with German troops. Some of these were deserting and the German Feldgendarmerie were very active in searching for them, particularly in farmhouses.

Arrests in Zelgate, Belgium

On 7th September 1944 Mr van de Vijver of Zelgate, passing the Zelgate Grote Markt, encountered a commotion of German soldiers and found himself being herded into an adjacent farmyard. Identification papers were being examined and accusations of carrying arms made.

De Vijver and a Mr Alfons from Westdorpe were put under surveillance. Under guard in a separate penthouse de Vijer saw the entire de Colvenaer and Pierets families and others, including Beale.

It transpired that that morning, in a hunt for three German deserters, the Germans had found on the roof of a farmhouse a leather jacket containing a Belgian and Dutch identity card which belonged to Gilbert Belair who had been a trainee officer for the Dutch Army. He, with a British and an American airman, had fled via the roof of the farmhouse.

Moving then to de Colvenaer's house the German searchers first found ammunition in a farmyard hutch, some American and British flags and then, in the house, a revolver. Finally, hiding in a bedroom, they found Beale and arrested him. In civilian clothes Beale was brutally interrogated by a Feldwebel (Sergeant), not being recognised as British. Mr de Colvenaer and his 16 year old son were also arrested. Mill by this time was also staying in the de Colvenaer farm but escaped by jumping out of a window. He promptly encountered a German soldier who shot him in the foot but Mill still escaped. He believes that the German soldier thought he was a Wehrmacht deserter and aimed purposely at his foot. At great risk Mill was taken into the house of another Belgian. A fortnight later Zelgate was liberated by the advancing Allied armies and Mill was driven to Brussels and then flown back to England. The three Belgians, de Colvenaer and his son and Pierets faced a very different future.

At the Zelgate Grote Markt Albert de Colvenaer, Beale and de Vijver were found to be wearing the badge of the Zelgate swimming club and the Feldwebel thought that this must be the badge of some sort of terrorist group. He proposed to his lieutenant that all the men under his surveillance should be executed at once and de Colvenaer's house blown up, after being looted. All the men under suspicion, including Beale, were then put in front of a wall, their hands above their heads, guarded by five soldiers to await the arrival of a firing squad. After about an hour a platoon of 20–30 men arrived under Lieut Hoffman. Mr de Vijver then asked Hoffman if he could speak to him and explained that among those against the wall were some who had only happened to be passing by and had been randomly herded into the farmyard by German soldiers. Hoffman ordered any who were standing against the wall and were merely passers-by to step forward. The passers-by did so, but had to wait, and only de Colvenaer, his son Yvan, and Beale remained against the wall – in the meantime Pierets, the motor mechanic, had been despatched to undertake some repair work on a German vehicle. Hoffman then dismissed the platoon, the soldiers being ordered to loot de Colvenaer's farmhouse. Such an order involved the expropriation of money, gold and silver objects, clothing, blankets – anything which could be taken away. Leaving the primary suspects and arrested passers-by under guard Hoffman who had now discovered Beale's identity had him retained in a separate shed and departed (to take part in the looting?)

Four hours later Hoffman returned, re-examined the papers of those who had claimed to be passers-by and told them they could leave. Albert and Yvan de Colvenaer and André Pierets were handcuffed and with Beale taken for interrogation to the Town Hall in Zelgate where the German Feldgendarmerie was based. There they were interrogated for 2½ hours by Hoffman. He found the three civilians guilty of 'terrorist activities' and sentenced them to death.

After concluding his interrogation and pronouncing sentence of death Hoffman arranged that the prisoners should be transferred to the secure 'Bomb-proof Barracks' at Flushing across the Scheldt. A Dutch garage owner whose car had been confiscated by the Germans was now ordered to drive the four prisoners under guard to Flushing using his own, confiscated, car. Anxious to get his car back again the garage owner planned that it would break down on the way by loosening the nuts on one of the front wheels. The planned breakdown duly occurred. At the isolated village of Yzandijke the wheel came off, the damage being such that the German guards travelling with the prisoners recognised that there was no chance of the car being repaired on the spot. Swearing and shouting the guards demanded from the villagers rooms for themselves and their prisoners. One little old man answered their call but could not understand their loud harsh voices. The German guards pushed him aside and took possession of his house, imprisoning their prisoners in a back room, locking the door, and placing a guard outside. The prisoners, handcuffed except Beale, wondered if there might be a chance of escape but none could be found.

Next morning (8th September) a military truck appeared and took the four to Breskens. They waited there all day. Any attempted crossing of the Scheldt in daylight was dangerous at this time because the Allies knew that the Germans were moving men and equipment from the 15th Army northwards to strengthen their defences along the Maas. With their air superiority the Allies were patrolling the Scheldt by day to prevent such movement. When darkness fell the truck, embarked on the ferry, was landed at Flushing (Vlissingen) and in due course rumbled through Flushing's deserted streets to the 'Bomb-proof Barracks'. As it reached the barracks the gates swung open then closed behind it. In this secure prison the last chance of escape had gone. Albert and Yvan Colvenaer and André Pierets were locked in one cell and Denis Beale in another. Next morning Beale was taken via Middelburg to a prisoner-of-war camp in Germany.

An Arrest in Wissenkerke, North Beveland

In 1944, 5th September in Holland became known as 'Mad Tuesday' because on that date many rumours, which proved to be quite false, suddenly circulated. One of these rumours, to the effect that Breda had been liberated, reached North Beveland (to be occupied five months later by 47 RM Cdo). If Breda were free it would not be long until North Beveland would be liberated. Assuming this rumour to be true a number of German soldiers decided to 'disappear' and wait in hiding pending the arrival of the Allies, with the possibility that they might avoid involvement in any military action and/or incarceration as prisoners of war. They got in touch with the local resistance movement which agreed that, in exchange for the firearms which the resistance so needed, the resistance group would give the deserting Germans the food which they would need while they waited in hiding for North Beveland to be freed.

Unfortunately, next day it was not the Allies who arrived at North Beveland but the German police to investigate the loss of arms. The deserting German soldiers were apprehended and when interrogated defended themselves by saying that they had been disarmed by members of the resistance. In the light of these developments the members of the resistance decided that it would be wiser for them to move elsewhere.

The same rumour of impending liberation which led the German soldiers to plan desertion stimulated a young man, Andries Dieleman, of a somewhat naive disposition, who worked in his father's farm in Wissenkerke in North Beveland, to engage in premature celebration by driving around in a car to which anti-Nazi slogans had been fastened. Dieleman had nothing to do with the resistance and the arms deal.

North Beveland is a small island with a small population and secrets were difficult to keep. The German police heard that a 'car full of terrorists' had been seen the previous day and connected it with the loss of German arms. There were some 'ladies' who had friendly relations with the Germans and it was suspected that they dropped a hint as to where the police should look for the owner of the 'terrorists'' car. Dieleman was found working in one of the outbuildings on his father's farm, was arrested without even being given the chance to change out of his clogs, interrogated and then transferred to the so called 'Bomb-proof Barracks' at Flushing.

Arrests in Middelburg, Walcheren

In Middelburg at the time of 'Mad Tuesday' there was a considerable movement of the German soldiers of the 15th Army who were coming across the Scheldt to Flushing from where they travelled through Middelburg towards the causeway between Walcheren and South Beveland. The 15th Army was being redeployed to strengthen the Scheldt defences and the defence of Germany. In the same rather euphoric atmosphere of 'Mad Tuesday', two men, residents in Poelendaeleroad and Baarsstraat in Middelburg, went out after dark, at about 2100 hours on 6th September and pulled up some of the stone sets in Poelendaeleroad, making a yard wide gap, with a view to interrupting German road transport which passed along that street. Later that night a German truck drove into the gap and shortly afterwards a number of inhabitants of nearby houses were summoned from their beds, still in their night attire. They were ordered to put the stone sets back in place and having done so thought that this would be the end of the matter. Next evening, however, a German truck stopped in the Poelendaeleroad and took five male civilians, including Mr Gillissen-Verschage the Councillor for Education in Flushing, from their homes as hostages. They were taken to the residence of the German Commander-in-Chief of Walcheren, put in a barracks there and guarded closely. Among the five, unknown to the Germans, was W. Neisthoven, one of the two who had removed the stone sets. The five were interrogated repeatedly and intensively, 'not in a very polite or friendly manner' as one of them put it. The other perpetrator of the stone sets removal was not at home when the hostages were taken and disappeared for the next few months. The hostages knew that Niesthoven was one of the two responsible but none gave him away. Frustrated, the Germans then announced that if those who had committed this 'act of resistance' did not give themselves up all the male inhabitants of Poelendaeleroad along with the hostages would be shot. After a few days the hostages were told that as the 'terrorists' had not been found they would be shot next morning. In the state of fright and shock engendered by this news one of the hostages, a young man studying for the church, proposed praying with them. Niesthoven, who was an epileptic, joined in. Perhaps the emotion of the moment affected him but whatever the reason he took an epileptic fit and fell to the floor. As he lay there making a noise the German guards rushed in. They tried to quieten him and either from their action or as a result of the fit Niesthoven injured himself. In his injured, confused, post-epileptic state he admitted that he was one of the 'terrorists' for whom the Germans were looking. It is also considered just possible that one of the hostages' wives had mentioned his name at some stage. Niesthoven too was now removed to the 'Bomb-proof Barracks' at Flushing.

Execution

All five of those arrested at Zelgate, Wissenkerke and Middelburg were now in a cell in the 'Bomb-proof Barracks' at Flushing. Employed there was a young woman who was arrested after the liberation for being too friendly with German military personnel. She had sometimes watched the prisoners when they were allowed to exercise in the barrack yard under guard. She later provided some of the details of what happened.

On Saturday 9th September, Mr van de Velde, a printer in Flushing, was ordered by the German commander to print 370 copies of a poster in both Dutch and German which had to be ready by Monday 11th September. These posters were to be put up in every town and village in Walcheren, South Beveland and North Beveland and were to say that the Dutchmen Wilhelmus Niesthoven and Andries Dieleman and the Belgians Albert and Yvan de Colvenaer, and André Pierets had been sentenced to death because

The cross at Klein Valkenisse stands on the high dune ahead. (*Courtesy, 'After the Battle', no. 36*)

TER GEDACHTENIS AAN DE VERZETSSTRIJDERS

A. de Colvenaer   46 jaar   A.P. Dieleman   36 jaar
Y. de Colvenaer   17 jaar   uit Wissenkerke
A. Pierets   39 jaar   W. Niesthoven   28 jaar
uit Zelzate (België)   J. van der Wey   19 jaar
                                  uit Middelburg

Zij werden op 11 september 1944 in een duinpan.
bij het kruis dat van hieruit te zien is. door
een Duits vuurpeloton gefusilleerd.

A plaque at the foot of the dunes records the names of those executed by the Germans.

of various acts of terrorism against the German Authority and that the sentences had already been carried out.

On Sunday 10th October a military court of law with the infamous and dreaded Colonel Oberst Reinhardt, known as the 'King of Zeeland', as its President was held in the Flushing barracks. The five were found guilty and sentenced to death, the sentences to be carried out next morning. That day (Sunday) Mrs Niesthoven was allowed to visit her husband at the barracks for a very short time only. The two Niesthoven children who accompanied their mother to Flushing were not allowed to see their father nor was Mr Niesthoven's brother. Mrs Niesthoven saw that her husband had been beaten up and he told his wife that under such treatment he had signed a confession and that he and the other four were to be executed next morning. A Roman Catholic priest who wished to visit the prisoners that day was not allowed to do so.

Next morning, Monday 11th September, at about 0700 hours the five prisoners were put into a truck and taken to the sand dunes near Klein Valkenisse. Behind their truck was a second truck – it contained a firing squad.

A Polish soldier named Jan Rybicki, serving in the German Army, was on duty on the Walcheren dunes near Klein Valkenisse that morning. He watched the prisoners dismounting from the truck and being marched up the dunes by a roundabout route. It was a quiet morning. By the time that the five and their escort reached the top of a high dune the firing squad was already there. The wrists of the five were bound by leather straps and the prisoners were lined up with their backs to the sea facing the firing squad. At that point young Yvan de Colvenaer was released and taken from the row of men. 'If you confess you will be freed', he was told. Confronted by imminent execution and the opportunity of avoiding it, Yvan de Colvenaer stood silent. He was taken back to the vacant place in the row – without his wrist straps. Just as André Pierets shouted, 'Long live our country, long live Belgium', a rough German command was given and a volley of rifle shots rang out, reverberating over the silent dunes. It was 0805. A German military doctor examined all for death (was he the doctor I was to meet near the same site six weeks later?).

A hole was dug in the sand, the bodies were thrown into it in a careless, uncouth manner and the hole was refilled with sand.

Apocalypse

Some time before 47 RM Cdo's operation in Walcheren the Polish soldier Rybicki visited a Flushing photographer, Mr van Scherpenzeel, to tell the photographer about the executions and to hand him a sketch indicating

The tyrant humbled. Colonel Reinhardt in captivity. (*Crown Copyright*)

where the bodies were. After 47 RM Cdo had liberated the area the photographer lodged this sketch with the local authority.

Back in Zelgate, and the war in that part of the Low Countries over, Mr van de Vijver was anxious to find out what had happened to his friends the de Colvenaers and Pierets. Their wives and other relatives still did not know what had become of them. De Vijver discovered that the German Lieutenant Hoffman had been captured and was now in a POW Camp in Bruges. He visited the camp in November and was given the opportunity to question Hoffman. He learned first that under interrogation by Hoffman neither father nor son de Colvenaer nor Pierets had given anything away. De Vijver also realised that if he wished to pursue his investigations further he would have to make further enquiries at Walcheren. Going there he learnt of the execution of all five but apparently no one knew where the bodies were. In the following Spring, using Rybicki's sketch, the authorities decided to try and locate the bodies but a search was unavailing.

The cross.

Time passed, and then the authorities discovered that Rybicki had enlisted in the Free Polish Forces and was now serving with the occupation troops in Germany. He was traced and, guided by his interpretation of his sketch, another attempt was made to find the bodies. This time, on January 15th 1946, they were found and their identities confirmed by relatives. They were exhumed and reinterred elsewhere. An impressive service attended by hundreds of people took place at Zelgate on 21st January 1946. A cross was later erected at the crest of the dune where the five had been executed and at the foot of the dunes a plaque which bears their names was erected at the place where they commenced their last journey. It shows that another Dutchman, 19 year old J van der Wey, had been added to the other five.

Nemesis

After the execution on the dunes it was not long before Colonel Reinhardt's reign of terror came to an end. Nemesis was rapidly catching up with him and on 3rd November 1944 the dreaded 'King of Zeeland', without putting up any resistance, was captured by the Royal Scots Regiment which took part in the assault on, and capture of, Flushing. With him were captured a number of documents which showed that there was considerable disaffection among those he commanded and a great deal of confusion and incompetence in his administration. As the positions were reversed and he was interrogated in his own 'Bomb-proof Barracks' he was reduced to a pathetic cowering figure, humiliated by the total surrender of his troops, at times quite incoherent of speech, weeping frequently and unable to control his bladder. The qualities of courage, resolution and dignity shown by those whom he had condemned to death were singularly lacking in their executioner. Such is the stuff, and sometimes the end, of tyrants.

Chapter Ten

From Bondage to Freedom –
A Wartime Citizen of Walcheren
by Harry H. Schat

To a youth living in Walcheren throughout World War II that epoch brings back vivid memories; Stuka bombers destroying the heart of Middelburg, the historic capital of Zeeland, in May 1940; the sight of the first German soldiers, forerunners of rampaging German hordes from the East reminiscent of the Huns under Attila; the sound of groups of German soldiers marching and singing in Middelburg's historic streets; traitors belonging to the NSB (the Dutch Nazi party), few in numbers but nasty, aggressive and quite dangerous; and particularly, prominent and honest people in high places, politicians included, seeming to give up all hope and surrendering to the conviction that the victorious German hordes from the East were there to stay.

It is doubtful whether people living in Britain can imagine the unmitigated agonising fear for the future arising in the hearts and minds of people in a Europe controlled by Nazi Germany, fear of losing one's soul and identity personally and collectively in a social order which showed utter disregard for one's own and one's country's history.

Then as the years passed there was the hope and ultimately the fulfilment of salvation, the realisation that British resistance and endurance, British grit and courage could finally lead to the demise of these Eastern hordes and provide the alternative – spiritual and physical freedom instead of death or unwilling citizenship of the so-called Grossdeutsches Reich. Living in Walcheren, this longed for alternative finally expressed itself dramatically on 2nd November 1944 in the exhilarating experience of catching the first sight of a British soldier, the khaki clad figure of a 47 Royal Marine Commando, moving along the dunes where for so long only the field grey of the Wehrmacht had been evident. The 47 RM Cdo liberators spoke a language then new to me but one which sounded like music in my ears; freedom in its deepest sense had finally arrived and a future which for long had seemed so dark and foreboding was now bright.

I did not stem from a native Walcheren family but from a more internationally rooted clan whose *pater familias* headed a company supplying life-saving equipment for lifeboats on ocean-going vessels all over the world.

This contributed to a more international outlook in my family: journeys throughout Europe provided opportunities to evaluate feelings among the various people visited. With the company's headquarters in Utrecht and an office in London, Walcheren, with a ferry connection between Vlissingen (Flushing) and Harwich had been chosen as the family home.

HISTORICAL RELATIONSHIPS IN EUROPE BEFORE THE SECOND WORLD WAR

Pre-Hitler

The culture and feelings of a people and their reactions are conditioned by their history; by immobility or mobility in a geographical sense including the availability of transport facilities; and by communication facilities and technologies. The first half of the 20th century did not experience the uniformity of to-day which results from untrammelled communication and travel opportunities. Continental Europe was a multifaceted mosaic of distinct and different societies characterised by their own languages, arts and literature but with one common aspect, proximity.

The smaller countries in Europe such as the Low Countries, Finland and Scandinavia reacted in various and different ways to the presence and domin-ance of much larger societies such as those of France and Germany. The Dutch Republic came into existence in the Sixteenth Century as a haven for religious freedom and trade. The Germans, not united until 1870 under Bismarck, were perceived as akin to the Dutch by language and culture. Although Holland was more open to the world and much less continental than Germany there was an affinity between these two countries which played a rôle in the attitude of the population of Walcheren to the Germans.

Even after unification in 1870, Germany had posed no apparent threat to Holland, not even during World War I in which Holland had been neutral. After World War I there was no outcry when Queen Wilhelmina granted Kaiser Wilhelm asylum in Holland. Thereafter the rather relaxed attitude towards Germany was further encouraged by a strong, religiously conditioned fear of, and antipathy towards, Russian communism as it had developed after the 1917 revolution. It was a 'safe' feeling to have big Germany between Russia and Holland.

Language, too, contributed greatly to the sentiments and feelings of people in various continental nations towards each other. Before the Second World War French was the dominant language and English was so un-familiar in Holland that although I had had a thorough classical education in the Gymnasium of Middelburg and was fluent in French, German and Italian at an early age I could not communicate at all with the 47 RM Cdo liberators when they arrived in November 1944.

Post-Hitler

The scene in Europe changed in 1934 when Hitler seized power. The relaxed attitude of the Dutch towards Germany was replaced by apprehension about the future. There was some rationalisation – perhaps Germany had been treated somewhat unfairly in the Treaty of Versailles and could be excused for its belligerence; anti-communism feelings may have led to German violence against minorities, particularly anything Slavonic, and could be excused: but despite these rationalisations an overall feeling of insecurity prevailed in Holland from 1934 onwards.

It was when it became clear that the Germans were persecuting and murdering Jews that the feelings of the Dutch population finally turned to disgust with all that Germany stood for. Concomitantly with these changes Dutch feeling towards Britain became much more friendly.

THE ONSET OF WORLD WAR II

The Invasion of Poland

It was against an overall background of apprehension and nagging fear that Germany finally attacked Poland on 1st September 1939, an event followed by a declaration of war by Britain two days later. The Germans at that time, for the first time in modern history, broke all agreed war conventions by attacking civilian populations in order to break the resistance of their enemies.

In the eerie and ominous silence that followed the overpowering of Poland there was plenty of scope for nurturing feelings of insecurity and helplessness and for pipe-dreaming about the possibility of refuge or escape from the ugly menace presented by Germany. Nowhere was the latter more evident than in the Western parts of Holland particularly Zeeland and Walcheren. There was a feeling that, as in World War I, the Dutch could stay out of trouble. Beyond that, if they prepared for resistance to attack and combined this with their expertise in strategies of water manipulation, such as artificial inundation, perhaps they could conceivably make the Germans think twice about attacking or possibly prevail against them if they did. Much of this thinking centred round the so-called 'Waterlinie' which gave the Dutch the ability to inundate a swathe of land which could cut Holland in two – hadn't this strategy worked in the past against the French? It was admitted that there was not much chance of preventing the Germans from overrunning the eastern half of Holland but in the minds of many it seemed possible that inundation of Central Holland, cutting of the dykes plus the rough seas round the islands of Zeeland, including Walcheren, could possibly stop a German advance into that area?

The people of Zeeland and Walcheren considered that they, particularly, had a reasonable chance of keeping the Germans at bay.

The Attacks on Denmark and Norway: 9 April 1940

The attacks on these two countries came like a bolt out of the blue, a total surprise for the people of Holland. The attacks increased the feeling of apprehension and prompted further speculation on how to avoid a similar fate or successfully resist an attack if the Germans came.

At first strict neutrality was the watchword and such it was when a British bomber was shot down by Dutch flak in the Rotterdam area early in 1940. Hopes mounted when it was learnt that the British had sent an expeditionary force to Narvik in an endeavour to stop the German advance. It proved to be a vain hope and increasingly an over-all feeling of imminent disaster prevailed throughout the country.

The Attack on Holland, Belgium and Luxembourg: 10 May 1940

It was a beautiful spring day on which the announcement came over Hilversum Radio that the Germans had crossed the Dutch border and were invading the country. Queen Wilhelmina ordered Commander in Chief Winkelman to resist the German advance and fight. It was war! Would inundation of Central Holland, cutting of the dykes between some of the Zeeland islands and German fear of water stop the invaders? The Royal Navy would help. Would the French Army come up from the south? Rumours spread and there was a general atmosphere of excitement. The stiff resistance of the Dutch Army at De Peel in Eastern Holland and at Grebbeberg in Central Holland, constantly broadcast by Radio Nederland, caused a glimmer of hope that the advancing Wehrmacht might be slowed down or even stopped. The people of Walcheren at the extreme western end of the country, furthest from the enemy, felt some sort of safety and their hopes were bolstered with news that the Wehrmacht had been stopped in its tracks at Afsluitdijk in the North.

In Poland the invading Germans had not shrunk from attacking the civilian population and now likewise they turned on the Dutch civilians. The defenceless city of Rotterdam was subject to a devastating bombardment which broke the Dutch resistance. The Queen ordered the Army to surrender with the exception of Zeeland, which it was thought might be able to hold out. It had apparently never occurred to the Army that the barbarians from the East would not hesitate to repeat in Walcheren what they had done to Rotterdam. A few days later they did when the Wehrmacht had been stopped from crossing the Sloedam, a natural water barrier which ran across the eastern part of Walcheren. Rotterdam would be repeated by attacking the civilian population.

As a 12 year old I watched the Stukas of the Luftwaffe circle undisturbed over the historic city of Middelburg as they bombarded it mercilessly until the centre of the town was reduced to rubble and its one thousand year old City Hall severely damaged. Large clouds of dense smoke were billowing high into the sky like smoke from a furnace.

The local population now made sure that no German aircraft could land on the island's only airfield at Vlissingen (Flushing) by covering it with hundreds of farm wagons and other vehicles. Ironically, Dutch flak shot down one of its own G–1 Fokker aeroplanes which had managed to get into the air in a heroic effort to create havoc among the swarms of Luftwaffe warplanes. At this point the Queen ordered the surrender of the Army in Zeeland and soon German troops were moving into and all over Walcheren.

Our home, beside the sand dunes, was at Groot-Valkenisse. Near there, on a biking path at the foot of the high dunes I saw my first German, a solitary soldier on a motor bicycle.

Strangely, from almost the same spot but with very different emotions, 4½ years later, I was to see the first British soldiers, men of 47 RM Cdo moving along the top of those same sand dunes as they proceeded towards the German gun batteries and entrenchments.

The Defeat of the Allied Armies: May/June 1940

When the French finally surrendered and the British had been evacuated from France an atmosphere of deep pessimism and despair set in and spread throughout Western Europe. Ominous booming of cannon far to the south-east had continued for several days and nights as the Wehrmacht endeavoured to block the British Army evacuation from Dunkirk. As this eerie sound finally became weaker we knew that the Allied Armies had been beaten and that now we had to face the naked power of Germany alone. It is difficult to describe the all-pervading atmosphere of hopelessness which that engendered in the population of now occupied Holland. This atmosphere was mitigated to some extent by the experience of my parents who had lived in the UK and even in the USA and entertained the hope that ultimately the invading hordes from the East would have to face the full force of the Anglo-Saxon world. In a peculiar way despair in our family was further mitigated in that we were still fairly regularly visited by my father's German business friends from Bremen and Hamburg who were strongly opposed to the German war effort. I remember specific phrases which would crop up in conversation such as, 'the British usually lose all the battles except the last one' and 'the Americans easily outproduce any military losses in battle theatres'. These lifted the spirits within my family with its special contacts but the situation was different among the population

The bondage begins. The first of the invading German soldiers enter Westkapelle in 1940. (*Courtesy Westkapelle Museum*)

... and ends. In 1944 the defeated Westkapelle invaders are rounded up for despatch to prisoner-of-war camps. (*Crown Copyright*)

at large. They were deprived of any outside contact because English was virtually unknown in continental Europe.

LIFE IN WALCHEREN UNDER GERMAN OCCUPATION

First Impressions

In the early days of the occupation the limited interference by the German-controlled civilian administration of Walcheren and its initial efforts to befriend the local population allowed some retention of the rhythm and seasonal characteristics of agricultural life in Walcheren and an unspoken and unadmitted endeavour for compromise. It was admitted that it would be a long time, if ever, before the Germans could be dislodged from power in Europe. A 'live and let live' attitude prevailed. Thus, during the summer of 1940, life in Walcheren was little different from the quiet life which had existed before. The main disturbance to a pastoral way of life was the loss of the regular Thursday Farmers' Market in front of the City Hall as a result of the destruction of the centre of Middelburg, and the ubiquitous presence of German soldiers, mostly with motorised equipment. The German authorities were trying to win over the Dutch population including Walcheren's predominantly farmer community. These overtures were not immediately rebuffed by a people who largely stood in awe as the Wehrmacht displayed its power and splendour, its military equipment and its disciplined ranks.

Developing Resistance

Gradually, however, there was a progressive development of resistance to the occupying forces aggravated by a pervasive restriction of freedom. Those who have not suffered occupation do not know what it means to be unable to make decisions on simple national, provincial, local government and even personal matters and to have democratically elected leaders gradually eased out from all their positions and replaced by the lackeys of an oppressor. The citizens of Walcheren whose farming population was set in its ways and religious began to resist Nazi doctrines and to resent increasingly the influence and power of German-supported traitors of their own kin, and the sickening propaganda, Dutch and German, continuously promoted by a German civilian administration.

Unlike the Belgians who had surrendered to German advance in the Spring of 1940, and whose King remained in Belgium, the Dutch at a national level were carrying on the fight from London to which their Queen and legal government had moved. The Dutch were therefore progressively punished by the imposition of a German civil administration in which each region had its own German 'Orstskommandant' possessing all final civilian power. The Orstskommandant for Zeeland was located in Middelburg. Civilian government, under control of the Wehrmacht, was gradually infiltrated by local traitors, members of the Dutch affiliate of the Nazi Party the NSB, whose prime aim was to appoint, or to be appointed as mayors in all important towns and villages. These became saddled with such people in the top positions in administration including universities and colleges.

As it became clearer to the German military administration that the Dutch population had no intention of being Germanised in any way and resented the crude German ideologies and indoctrination, new sets of restrictions were imposed, some voluntary others obligatory. The national and provincial press accommodated the new situation by avoiding the printing of news and commentary that could be singled out by traitors and offend the German military administration. The church press, which was large and influential, initially resisted all forms of censure but gradually it too had to accommodate or be forbidden to publish. As the screw tightened, day-to-day conversation in public places and in public transport had to be toned down, to avoid anything which might be heard by traitors, interpreted as anti-German and reported – with arrest as the likely consequence. Any anti-German demonstration in public was strictly proscribed and dangerous. Periodically there would be a rash of propaganda banners with texts like 'Duitsland wint voor Europa op alle fronten!' (Germany wins for Europe on all fronts) spread across main streets and avenues and accompanied by showers of leaflets carrying the same propaganda humbug. Teenagers like myself on leaving church after morning service would spit on these leaflets and then escape quickly among the crowd lest they would be reported and arrested.

As time passed and doubts about a German victory began to arise restrictions became more repressive. One which was particularly resented was the forced carrying of a so-called Persoonsbewijs (identity cards) at all times. This turned the Dutch underground into experts in the manufacture of false identity cards. As a pupil at the Gymnasium College in Middelburg I had to carry such a card. Dutch feelings towards Germany gradually became outright hatred so heartfelt and so deep that for many Dutchmen it has coloured evaluations and attitudes towards Germany for decades since World War II.

Communication and the BBC

Among the multiplicity of new communication technologies the radio broadcast has stood the test of time. During World War II radio played an important rôle in providing information and maintaining morale. To begin with unfamiliarity with English among the population of Holland, especially the predominantly static farmer population of Walcheren, left them more exposed to German propaganda. The best that they could do was to listen to the Swiss radio broadcasts in German (which was considered bad Dutch) from Beromünster. When 47 RM Cdo landed on Walcheren I could not even say 'Hello' to our liberators! Gradually, however, the British Broadcasting Corporation (BBC) counteracted continental unfamiliarity with English by broadcasting in the languages of continental Europe. The influence which this exerted was enormous. Living in Walcheren I remember vividly the Dutch and French broadcasts emanating from the BBC including the satirical songs which did much to keep up the courage of the Dutch population. The BBC became synonymous with truthful news reporting unencumbered with distorted nationalism. It also did much to dispel a pervasive sense of isolation. Its vitally important rôle during the war cannot easily be overestimated. Such was its influence that even today, living in the USA, I am a life-time supporter and paying subscriber to the BBC at Bush House, London.

It did not take long for the German military-civilian administration and their Dutch underlings to appreciate that radio was a serious threat to their power and administrative control. The possession of a receiver was prohibited under threat of arrest and deportation. Knowing that there was extensive hiding of radios the Germans also jammed British broadcasts but in an internationally orientated family such as mine in which English (by my parents) and French were understood there could be no complete radio news blackout. From such sources, within an old-fashioned work-place-centred community, a great deal of information was spread by word of mouth.

Signs of Hope

The mood of depression throughout Europe in 1940–41 was mitigated by the determination of the British not to surrender in any shape or form. It is easy now to underestimate the ray of hope that British resistance to the Germanic hordes instilled into the population of Holland. Walcheren and all Holland experienced the depths of despair as victory after victory was trumpeted for the German Army; but always behind that was the knowledge that Britain had not surrendered and was actively engaged in fighting the Germans, that behind Britain were the English-speaking nations including, last but not least, the United States of America. As long as the sound of English-speaking voices and the chimes of Big Ben were on the air there was hope. My family took the chance of not surrendering radio sets and with its pre-war connections in the ship-building industry in Germany were occasionally visited by pre-war friends. In some measure they constituted a form of protection for our family. Most were quite disturbed by the Nazi onslaught and crimes, others less so, and this sometimes led to highly emotional outbursts and hotly debated arguments to which we children listened intently. Such conversations in German could be interrupted by English voices coming straight from the BBC in London. On one occasion a high ranking Kriegsmarine (German Navy) officer in blue uniform with a half golden sleeve entered the living room in our family home at Groot-Valkenisse as a clear voice sounded out from the radio, 'This is the BBC Home Service and here is the news, Frank Gillard reading it'. The German was clearly annoyed but my younger brother inadvertently, but conveniently, diverted the conversation into other less sensitive channels when he was told to ask the visiting German if he would stay to dinner. With limited knowledge of German he addressed the visitor, 'Herr Roscher, fressen Sie mit?', confusing 'essen' (how humans eat) with 'fressen' (how animals eat). Herr Roscher laughed. We took this as a sign of hope.

During the Battle of Britain the sight and sound of swarms of Luftwaffe planes on their way to England was an extremely depressing experience for the population of Holland. Walcheren Island was exactly located on the route from Germany to England. The younger generation, who had learnt to identify and count the Heinkel bombers and Messerschmit hunters as they were called, realised that these were on their way to try to subdue Britain, the only country still resisting, to destroy its airforce and attack its civilian population as they had done in Poland and Holland. Fresh in the minds of these young Walcheren citizens was the memory of the bombardment of the age-old defenceless capital of Zeeland a few months earlier. 'Would the Germans succeed', they asked themselves? The swarms of Luftwaffe planes continued to fly over Walcheren for only a relatively short period. Was this because they had won another victory; or could this be a defeat? Gradually the absence of these German warplanes in the sky, the continuing sound of English voices on the air and other information which seeped through began to alert the population to the reality. The Germans had failed to subdue Britain and for the first time in the war had met defeat: the German propaganda news was mere humbug. There was hope! The result of the Battle of Britain in September 1940 was of enormous significance and an important contributory factor to the efforts which many young Dutch people made to escape to England.

The evidence of British aerial retaliation against Germany despite the depressing news of German military victories, including their successes in North Africa, was also a source of hope and comfort. The lonely night flights of Blenheim bombers passing over Walcheren confirmed the defeat of the Luftwaffe and as these flights increased in frequency the oppressed and depressed people of Holland, particularly in Walcheren over which the Blenheims flew, gained further encouragement. The sound of the engines of these warplanes, easily differentiated from that of German planes, was music in the ears. When an RAF plane was heard many would turn out to watch as the German anti-aircraft guns opened up. Then the plane from England would usually make a sudden stark dive and disappear from the German searchlight beam. When this happened there was a 'Hurrah' from the watchers. Although a frequent watcher, I never saw any German successes. These routine nightly flights in terms of hope and comfort for the local population were of inestimable value and had a lasting unforgettable effect.

The grossest manifestation of Nazi doctrines was the persecution of the Jews and their gradual elimination from all positions in the civilian administration and educational institutions. The College which I attended in Middelberg had a Dutch language teacher called Cohen. It was not widely appreciated that he was Jewish until he suddenly disappeared from the classroom and the College rector gave a rather crooked 'explanation' as to why he could no longer teach. Mr Cohen was now overwhelmed with requests from pupils for 'bijlessen' (additional private tuition) that gave him a higher income than he had enjoyed in his official position! The response was a further worsening of relationships on Walcheren Island.

The Turning Tide

In 1941 Hitler attacked the Soviet Union. Reaction among the predominantly conservative Dutch population was mixed. Many considered the attack criminal and further evidence of the character of the Germans, but there was no general outcry because communist Russia was considered a major threat to established law and social order in Western Europe. Queen Wilhelmina had refused to recognise the Soviet Union diplomatically until 1934, more than 16 years after the October 1917 revolution in Russia. There was also among some a vague feeling that the attack on Russia might result in the two nations finishing each other off.

My father employed three Russian engineers who had escaped from the Bolshevik Revolution. They would listen to Radio Moscow so that my family had a better idea than most of what was going on in Russia and later of the successes of the Russian Army. First reactions, fostered by apparent invincibility of the Wehrmacht and the feeling that the Slav people were inferior, were that the Red Army would quickly be defeated, but when General Montgomery triumphed at El Alamein and General von Paulus surrendered at Stalingrad it was shown that the Wehrmacht could be beaten. Now the people began to look at the singing German troops differently and with greater contempt. They realised that the British and behind them the Americans were now in a dominant position and that Russia could turn out to be a German graveyard. At the same time they recognised that but for the heroic refusal of the British to settle with Germany in the first place there would have been no hope and the population of Holland would have been incorporated into Germany.

The Final War Years

During the first half of 1943 quiet despair had begun to change to hope and by the end of 1943, in Walcheren as elsewhere, these hopes and expectations were expressed in one word – Invasie! Invasion now dominated the hearts and minds of friend and foe. The portent of this, the never ending processions of Allied warplanes on their way to Germany, galvanised the population of Walcheren. As the drone of incoming planes increased gradually to a deafening roar as they passed overhead, youngsters tried to distinguish the silvery birds and shouted excitedly for joy – toning down quickly in the presence of any Germans – as the planes disappeared to the East and the noise died away. For the islanders this was one of the unforgettable sights of the war.

By 1944, with increasing Allied success on so many fronts, invasion had become a near certainty but the formidable nature of that task was becoming clearer. Massive defensive constructions constituted the so-called 'Atlantic Wall'. On Walcheren the range of concrete bunkers and gun positions occupying so much of the high sand dunes which constituted the island's rim spoke clearly of what might come. Most heavily defended were the dunes from Westkapelle through the villages of Zoutelande and Groot Valkenisse to Vlissingen (Flushing). All civilian access to the dunes was forbidden.

As the feverish construction of large fortified positions continued, there was an atmosphere of tension among both the local population and the occupying forces. There was much questioning as to how an Allied landing could ever be effected against the enormous odds presented by the huge German fortifications, the mined obstacles and the ubiquitous trenches.

Invasion and Freedom

Great relief followed the news that the Allies had landed in Normandy. The invasion was now 'for real' and had taken place far from Walcheren. Perhaps the Allies would sweep northwards in a massive defeat of the German Army which would obviate the necessity for a landing on the coast of Walcheren.

It was soon realised, however, that there would be no quick sweep and routing of the enemy. The Wehrmacht was putting up a stiff resistance. These doubts were powerfully reinforced by the débâcle at Arnhem in September 1944 when the Allies failed to break through the German defences in an effort to move quickly into Northern Germany. The Germans were clearly determined to fight and to defend Walcheren, now of major importance in depriving the Allies the use of Antwerp.

It was in this atmosphere of tension and expectation that the RAF early in October 1944 at Westkapelle struck the first blow by bombing and breaking the main dyke that prevented the sea from flooding the whole island. A few days later the protective dykes at Vlissingen and at Veere were also bombed and broken, flooding the island further.

Despite the damage done to the island, to the farms, to the very structure and beauty of Walcheren previously known as the 'Garden of Zeeland', in spite of the casualties, and some mistaken bombing of civilian dwellings, there was not the slightest resentment against the Allies. On the contrary there was a general feeling among the population that these disasters were part and parcel of the necessary struggle for freedom and the eviction of the despised Germans. On 17 September 1944 the small rustic road from Groot Valkenisse to Biggekerke was erroneously bombed by the RAF. There were many civilian casualties, a number of well known local people lost their lives and I nearly lost two sisters. The Germans did not suffer in any way yet among the population affected there was no complaint or ill-feeling.

As the island filled with water a few German defences inland were rendered useless. Many of the island's population had to flee to safety in higher places in towns and at the rim of the island.

On 1st November, against a background of gunfire from the sea, shells began falling all along the fortified positions on the sand dunes on the rim of the island. Later we learnt that these came from the Royal Navy's *Warspite*. The sound of exploding shells, either smothered in sand or exploding in the water that covered the whole of the centre of the island was an unforgettable experience whose danger was not clear to the young sters of Zoutelande and Groot Valkenisse. The feeling among the beleaguered civilian population was that at long last 'they are going to get rid of them' strengthened by the fact that most of the shells did not reach the civilian population safely protected from shelling by the high dunes. The shelling continued throughout the day and following night. There was an atmosphere of intense excitement: the great moment anxiously awaited since May 1940 had come! There was little sense of danger among the youngsters and teenagers in the area under attack or of realisation that they could be killed in the fighting between the two armies. The elderly people may have felt differently but I do not recall that this was so.

When on the same day the Royal Marine Commandos landed on both sides of the Westkapelle gap the people of Zoutelande and Groot Valkinesse a few miles further south soon knew of this as a result of the BBC Dutch language broadcast. As the British advanced along the dunes word of the advance got through from Zoutelande to Groot-Valkenisse by biking youths who knew the paths through the woods at the foot of the sand dunes on the inner side. Thus the youngsters at Groot Valkenisse were ready on 2nd November and waiting for the arrival of the advancing British troops. The first dramatic sign of them was of khaki-clad figures moving along the top of the high sand dunes and taking German prisoners – the ones we saw without a shot being fired. It was a moving experience to see known Germans lift their arms high above their heads in surrender as they walked slowly towards the advancing British. The youths looking up from the foot of the high dunes had no sense of danger and somehow no sense that this was real war and not play. The only form of English which many of the youngsters knew came from pre-war gramophone records so we started singing loudly, 'It's a long way to Tipperary, a long way to go'. We never knew what impression this made on the advancing British soldiers or indeed whether the singing carried the distance!

The liberation of Groot Valkenisse itself was rather peaceful, very different from the fierce struggle which we now know was taking place on the other side of the dunes and beyond, towards Vlissingen. Unaware of this we were celebrating the impending victory of the British and the enormous relief that the Germans were going to disappear. On the following day (3rd November), however, we youngsters did venture further and were now confronted with the horrors of war – dead German soldiers lying on the dunes. I saw my first dead German soldier at virtually the same spot where I had seen my first living German soldier more than four years earlier.

THE AFTERMATH

In our home one of the paradoxes of war was working itself out. Three Italian deserters, who had switched sides in 1943 and left the army barracks in Middelburg in search of shelter had been taken into our family home, clearly at a substantial risk if this had been found out. Fortunately, among several German soldiers located in the immediate surroundings of Groot Valkinesse there were some who were opposed to the German war effort. Some of these were also welcomed to our dinner table. They never betrayed our family despite these Italian deserters in uniform and other 'illegals'. The local commander of a nearby bunker position, who in civilian life was the minister of a Lutheran Church in Germany, had indicated that he and his men would surrender on arrival of the British. This he did on 2nd November 1944. On the previous evening he visited us praying the 'Vater unser' ('Our Father') at the start of the family dinner, with the three Italian deserters and other 'illegals' and children round the table. Two days later this dinner was repeated with the same family, the same three Italian deserters and the 'illegals' but on this occasion 'Our Father' was said, not by the German pastor, not in German, but in English by a Lieutenant of 47 RM Cdo. To the children present the German version had sounded very familiar but this English version sounded very strange.

With the resistance of the defenders broken, the Wehrmacht soldiers had been despatched to prisoner of war camps away from the Island and the British soldiers had gone off to other duties. An eerie silence now settled over the liberated strip of sand dunes, the village of Zoutelande and the sparsely populated area around Groot Valkenisse. It was, however, a time of great fun for the younger generation, living on that isolated strip of dry land, as they went exploring into the deserted German bunkers and emptied them of any edible or otherwise worthwhile goods or 'goodies'. We became adept at handling guns, rifles and especially German hand grenades. Whereas the guns were too big or too complicated to be fired there was no such problem with rifles and hand grenades. The latter were effectively used for fishing purposes. The procedure was quite simple; pick up a hand grenade, unscrew the top and pull out the small rope – you had exactly seven seconds to duck down and watch, and hear a huge and exciting explosion. If you threw the grenade into the sea it took only a very short time before all the fish in the area came floating to the surface, dead and ready to be collected. It was a miracle that none of the youths who for months were playing such games ever got killed. There was little chance of the few police who had been quickly appointed after liberation being able to control the area effectively.

For some time after liberation communication with and transportation to Middelburg, which was liberated on 8 November, was possible only by rowing boat. There was now no food problem anywhere on the island inasmuch as the inundation had forced all farmers to slaughter their cattle and chickens: in fact an overabundance of food was available on the dry areas of the island.

There were few other war activities. A few very low flying German aircraft attacked the Allied shipping convoys, now able to go into Antwerp. Standing on the dry sand dune strip, youths were very tempted to use, and sometimes did use, German rifles to shoot at the planes – without any result. The only other military activity registered during the early months of 1945 consisted of a few landings by German one-man submarines coming from Schouwen in the northern part of Zeeland. These sorties were largely ineffective. One day a heavily armed, shivering German sub-mariner knocked at the door of our house. He was promptly disarmed, then fed, and sent to bed. Next day he was arrested by the only policeman in the one-man local police force and put into a rowing boat bound for Middelburg and a POW camp.

It is with deep and heartfelt thanks that I remember the valiant men of 47 Royal Marine Commando and in general the British who refused to surrender or compromise in 1939–40. Their heroic stand saved civilisation and the future of this contributor and of all the people of Europe.

Chapter Eleven

Holding the Thin Line on the Maas

O<small>N</small> 25th November, now very much below strength, the commando moved to Bergen-op-Zoom. It had been hoped that after Walcheren it would be given time to make good its losses.

South Beveland Patrols

The commando was given the responsibility for mobile defence at two sites. The first involved patrolling the road junctions around Woensdrecht at the narrow neck of the isthmus connecting the east end of South Beveland with mainland Holland. There was a fear that there might be an attempt to cut this isthmus and gain access to the Scheldt, now the Allies' main supply route to Antwerp. Lieut Brent described the duties as, 'two hours on and four hours off for 14 days with lots of false alarms, sleepless nights and endless rain'.

The other responsibility was at the Kraaijert area at the west end of South Beveland where the only land connection across the Sloedam to Walcheren was a Bailey Bridge, the Germans having blown up the original bridge. It was reported by the local civilians that the Germans had left behind saboteurs in this area who might attempt to blow up the Bailey Bridge and there was also the fear that attempts might be made to infiltrate from the sea. These responsibilities were met by standing patrols operating in conjunction with mobile patrols.

The Maas patrols

On Christmas Eve the commando moved to Oosterhout as its HQ, with troops stationed in Geertruidenberg, Raamsdonksveer and Raamsdonk, close to the River Maas which was now the dividing line between the British and German Forces in that section of the front. Oosterhout was 6 miles, Geertruidenberg 1 mile, Raamsdonksveer 1½ miles and Raamsdonk 2 miles south of the river.

Earlier in December there had been rumours that the Germans might attempt to recapture Antwerp which was of such strategic importance to the Allies. On the northern front there had been a small German landing on North Beveland, a small naval engagement off Walcheren and several sightings of German midget submarines. Concentrations of motor boats had been seen east and south of the island of Schouwen. When the German counter attack did materialise on 16th December – it was at the Ardennes – British units including the 3rd Division were diverted from the northern front to the south leaving the First Canadian Army with a very long, very thinly held, Maas frontage of approximately 150 miles. Serving with the First Canadian Army 47 RM Cdo was now defending a section of that front with elements of the Polish Armoured Division on its right.

The intelligence now available was that although the German counter-attack in the Ardennes had been contained there was still a large concentration of enemy troops consisting of elements of the German 30th Corps and the 5th Parachute Division in the area opposite the 47 RM Cdo sector which was on the main approach line from North Holland to Antwerp – the most likely direction of any German attack. If the Germans did try to cross, 47 RM Cdo would be in the forefront of the troops which would have the responsibility of repelling them. The commando's task was to mount river patrols to give warning of any threatened crossing while the main body of the commando in the villages further back provided defence in depth. Because of the length of its frontage – approximately three miles – three troops of 48 RM Cdo had been placed under 47 RM Cdo's command along with the Norwegian troop of 10 I.A. Commando. Of particular concern to the patrols was the damaged Keizersveer Bridge which was a possible crossing point. In keeping with the intelligence reports of the concentration of German troops opposite 47 RM Cdo's position there was a good deal of German activity in the form of patrols which crossed the river.

The weather was cold and the days short, winter had Holland in its grip. The situation at this time was described by Sergeant Gibson:

Day by day as the frost grew in intensity the ground hardened until spade and pick had to be rejected as of no further use. There was no furious blizzard of snow, only a slow steady freezing which relented for a few hours daily under a wan and watery sun and about four in the afternoon renewed its grip for the night. There was no escaping it. In a treeless land of open polders and dead straight roads the frost found its way to within a yard of the fireside.

To the north the polders presented an expanse of white intersected by a gridwork of ditches and canals, now frozen over so as to make night patrol work hazardous and uncomfortable. The townships of Geertruidenberg and Raamsdonk bore a cheerless aspect. The neat steep-sloping-roofed Dutch houses stood out defiantly before the warring enemies, but life in them was poor, with scanty rations and an absence of coal. Beyond Geertruidenberg, running north, was the road to the river, which, as it reached the river's edge, rose up a ramp on to the Keizersveer Bridge whose three great spans lay in twisted contortion among the turbid waters of the Maas – but we could only come this far by night. The dark of night, the stars above, and below the terrifying swirl of the black waters – this was all we ever saw of the bridge, for on the other side, three hundred yards across, the enemy had his slit trenches and fixed lines.

Standing patrols, day and night, at various points along the river were the main strategy with occasional offensive forays across the river. Lieut Brent – he had only recently joined the unit and been in action for the first time – led one of the early patrols consisting of one lance-corporal and four marines. In addition to their own personal weapons the patrol carried a Bren gun and a radio.

It was a bitterly cold night and the patrol's orders were to gather information, to 'look and listen'. Transported to the Canadian manned checkpoint near Geertruidenberg the patrol moved off along the 1½ miles of road leading to the Keizersveer Bridge. There had been a lot of heavy artillery shelling in the area and large craters pitted both sides of the road. These required careful watching – bomb craters provided good ambush possibilities – but without incident the patrol reached its 'headquarters', a small transformer hut about 100 yards from the river and the bridge.

A 'look and listen' patrol had to use all its senses, sight, sound and smell. A German patrol could be heard a long way off in the still of the night, their heavy leather hobnailed boots making a crunching noise on roads and even more noise over frozen undergrowth off roads – and the ground frozen hard. In contrast the commandos could move more silently with their rubber soled boots. When they patrolled in strength the Germans could also be heard because of their continuous chattering, apparently doing this to frighten off small standing patrols or to give the impression that they were very secure. Most German patrols could also be smelt up to 25 yards to windward because of their ever-present aroma of tobacco.

The transformer hut had to be approached with caution to ensure that there were no Germans lying in wait there. The patrol moved slowly toward it: peering to right and left and across the river, waiting and listening then concentrating on the hut and cautiously entering it after one man had done so while covered by the others.

Having taken up position Brent decided to explore the area; to reconnoitre a small, as yet unexplored, disused shipyard half a mile up stream, surrounded by four or five dilapidated houses. The patrol set out and approached the position with great caution, moving slowly and as silently as possible in this unfamiliar territory. Its caution was justified. While still in the open but approaching the dilapidated houses German voices were heard ahead. They seemed very close. There was another house on the right from which no voices emanated and the patrol crept over to it and into it. They were lucky, there was nobody in it and they huddled down in one room on the ground floor ready for any intrusion.

It was now clear that the Germans were in considerable strength and unlike Brent's patrol they seemed to know the area. Brent and his patrol settled down to sit and wait, watch and listen. It was anticipated that the Germans would withdraw before morning but as dawn broke they had not moved and showed no sign of doing so. Brent could not move. Now in daylight he decided to explore the house his patrol was occupying. He crept upstairs and, as he reached the top, found himself facing a sinister object lying on the floor – an unexploded panzerfaust (a German explosive anti-tank projectile used by infantry). It had been fired but had not gone off and in that state could go off at any moment blowing up the house and its occupants. It was clear why the Germans were not using this house. Brent decided to get rid of the panzerfaust and with a care, such as he later averred he had never given to any other object in his life, he carried it downstairs and, out of sight of the Germans and holding his breath, deposited it ever so gently on the ground outside. The patrol spent a long and anxious day waiting, hoping that the Germans would continue to avoid their house because of the unexploded panzerfaust.

As soon as it became dark again Brent decided to return to base, armed with some useful information. He hoped that he could depart without being observed or heard by his unwelcome neighbours. The patrol was in luck: a snowstorm had blown up. This provided some cover and enabled the patrol to leave more silently, but it also compounded the darkness by covering and obliterating roads which, even before the storm, were ill-defined among the craters. Unable to see much in front but knowing that dykes tend to follow the line of roads, the patrol, hand on the shoulder of the man in front, stumbled its way back to the transformer hut and then the check point. They had been due to report back on the previous day and were a day overdue. That created a problem. They did not know today's password, only yesterday's. Unidentifiable, snow-covered figures, emerging from a snowstorm from the direction of the enemy on a dark winter's night would be very close to the sentry before they could be seen and they would not be able to give the password. A nervous, light-fingered sentry might shoot. Fortunately the check-point sentry was not of a trigger happy disposition and responded favourably to the earnest disembodied English voices explaining from a distance their inability to give the password. Cold and frozen, the patrol entered the checkpoint. There they found the Canadian duty officer sitting in front of a roaring fire with his feet up. Their reception was almost as frosty as the weather outside, the patrol apparently unwelcome, the duty officer unfriendly. Gradually Brent realised what the duty officer's problem was. When the patrol had failed to check back, as expected on the previous day, it had been officially reported as 'missing'. That involved paperwork but the return of a missing patrol involved even more. Brent thought that he and his patrol had done quite a good 'see and listen' job and had displayed initiative in spying out the disused shipyard. His interrogator made him feel more like an officer being charged with AWOL (absence without leave).

Billeted with a Dutch farmer Gerry Brent was impressed with the anti-German feeling which the farmer and his family exhibited, a feeling also demonstrated by the farmer's dog, a little Bitser terrier which sported a black patch round his right eye. The patch, together with a permanent snarl resulting from a facial accident in earlier life had given the terrier a 'Fuhrer' image. This, however, belied his true heart. Starved as the poor dog was, like everyone else at that time, the most delicious bone offered to him with the words, 'This is from Hitler' would immediately be met with a growling snarl and there was no way he would touch the morsel offered. If, however, the offer was accompanied with the words, 'This is from Gerry' – or anyone else – the bone would be accepted with great haste and appreciation.

All patrols did not escape as lightly as Brent's. One night a standing patrol in a factory by the river just north of Geertruidenburg, led by Lt Gardener, was ambushed and Lt Gardener was killed. On another night a patrol on a different part of the river led by Capt Hoskins of the attached 48 Cdo group was likewise ambushed and Capt Hoskins and a marine were wounded. Germans on the other side of the river were active in their cross-river patrols.

47 RM Cdo also undertook patrols across the river to the German side. The Norwegian troop, on one of these, shot and killed a German. On another occasion, on a night when the river was blanketed in fog a 47 RM Cdo patrol found that after negotiating a twist in the river and the swift current in almost zero visibility they were having difficulty in reaching the other bank. Finally, after considerable delay they did so. As they crept up the bank they heard German voices ahead. Preparing to attack they stopped and listened. 'Wait', was there something strange, even familiar about these German voices? 'Wait. Wait'. 'Good Lord, these are Norwegians, we are on our own side of the river!'

There was also an unusual 'cloak and dagger' operation during this spell on the Maas engendered by the very thin defence line on the river and the need to identify the German units on the other side, particularly to find out if there were any parachute units, as there had been reports suggesting an impending parachute attack. Capt Winter was detached from the commando and told to report to the village of Made some three miles away. There were no Allied troops in the area and the local 'underground' had been authorised to undertake a raid with a view to capturing prisoners. Capt Winter was to liaise with them on the raid. The crossing was to be made from Drimmelin, a village which had been raided frequently by German troops. On the other side of the river the ground consisted of a large area of swamp, bog and high reeds. Entrance was not difficult but for the return the nature of the ground was such that it put a high premium on local knowledge. Several preparatory trips were made and on these Capt Winter was accompanied by the 16 year old daughter of the Drimmelin schoolmaster. The schoolmaster had been given the initial briefing for the task. Only first names were used by those participating in the raid, the leader being a Dutchman known as Ben.

On the night in question the 'underground' patrol crossed the river and took up position. Near a route likely to be used by German patrols it set up a machine gun manned by a Dutch café owner and his wife thirty yards from a wire fence which would hinder any German patrol. In due course a German patrol was seen approaching and the ambush plan put into action. As the patrol reached the fence the machine gun opened up. Three of the patrol were killed and two who were wounded were captured and taken back over the river with a view to delivery to Breda by Captain Winter.

Years later Winter was at the 50th anniversary of these events. An old man in a black cloak emerged from the crowd and approached him but Winter did not recognise him. 'Drimmelin' was all the old man said – then all the old memories flooded back. It was Ben.

Chapter Twelve

The Battle for Kapelsche Veer –
Death on the Dyke

In the Course of Duty

I N the reading room of St Christopher's College, Blackheath, London, on the morning of 17th December 1944, a solitary khaki-clad figure surrounded as it seemed by the higher echelons of His Majesty's Senior Service – a group of distinguished Captains RN – sat in the comfort of a home-based Royal Navy establishment. As the morning papers arrived a buzz went round the assembled company – the Germans had launched a counter-attack in the Ardennes and appeared to have broken through. A quick look at the wall map showed that this offensive was in the American sector well removed from 47 RM Cdo's current sector in Holland. 'Is your unit near the Ardennes' the khaki figure was asked? 'No' was the answer. There was nothing to suggest that 47 RM Cdo would be likely to be involved and its medical officer could relax. The Americans would deal with the Ardennes problem. They did, but the Ardennes offensive was not to be without its 47 RM Cdo repercussions.

The *raison d'être* for this sojourn in London was the fortuitous outcome, or so it seemed, of one of the muddles, accidental or exploited, which the complexities of administering wars render inevitable from time to time. The wording of the signal (naval messages are signals) which had reached 47 RM Cdo was not revealed but Col Phillips informed me early in December that he was sending me on 'a course in London' apparently not for any good military reason but rather for what seemed to me to be the very good reason that I was one of the few officers of the unit who had served with it since D-Day – most of the original officers had been killed, wounded or drowned. I had been on duty continuously and had not seen my wife for nearly a year, and my one-year-old daughter for only the first few days of her existence. I suspect that, Nelson-like, Col Phillips had read the signal with an intentionally sightless eye. I had little clue as to what the the course would be about and who would be on it and certainly did not strive to look this gift horse too closely in the mouth. I arrived in London on 15th December,. On the morrow I would learn about the course.

The morrow proved a little disconcerting. Looking to the future the Admiralty had arranged a course on current affairs and likely developments in post-war civil administration in Britain which would benefit officers who might be called upon to advise naval personnel returning to civil life. The course was for captains but for captains of the Royal Navy, not for an *Army* captain whose rank in equivalent terms was two grades below that stipulated, whose dress unlike the immaculate naval blue service dress and gold braid of all the other course members consisted of a battle-dress which did not belie its name, and whose terminological jargon despite some re-educative experience with the Royal Marines smacked more of the regimental officers' mess than of the battleship's wardroom. But the captains of the Senior Service (at least two of whom went on to Admiral Rank) accepted their under-ranked, immigrant colleague with immaculate courtesy and good humour, according recognition more to the rankless status of a doctor than to any three-pip shoulder grading. I learnt something of current affairs, but perhaps as much about the intelligence, dedication and enviable personal qualities of senior naval officers.

During an otherwise peaceful fortnight the only acute sign of warfare was that of the periodic V-1 rockets ('doodle bugs') with their explosive warheads. It was salutary to be reminded that civilians too were fighting the war. By day we could watch the course of a doodle-bug, apparently moving slowly but actually at 300 miles per hour, with some anxiety as it advanced to reach the critical overhead position and continue watching with some selfish relief, as it passed on. By night the sound of the motor was critical. If the crescendo of sound from the approaching V1 slowly changed to diminuendo it was proceeding safely on its way, at least as far as the listener was concerned: if the throb of the motor suddenly ceased there was an ominous expectant silence – the rocket with its ton of high explosive was descending from the heavens above and was about to explode, precisely where? For most the blast revealed that, for some it did not.

The course over, the return journey began on New Year's Day. Unlike the two-day inward journey the return journey was fraught with delay and took 12 days. First there was a five-day delay in the transit camp at Petworth due to shortage of sea transport. This gave me the chance to visit my brother, a medical officer in the Parachute Regiment, who was stationed nearby and about to depart to India. It was the last time I saw him – he was killed some months later. After a further day's delay at Tilbury we set sail in a Liberty ship. During the first day the boat slowly rolled and lurched through heavy seas until it was off Ostend but it had to anchor outside the harbour as a vessel had sunk, or been sunk, in the harbour mouth, effectively blocking it. Anchoring off Ostend was not considered the safest place to wait and next day our Liberty ship sailed back again, anchoring near Folkestone where it lay off for another two days before returning across the Channel to berth at Ostend five days after it had set out. They were five days of the misery from the sea sickness which invariably afflicted me on large unstable boats like Liberty ships – but not on small boats like landing craft or on aircraft. A consolation was that being an unattached army passenger with no duties I could un-ashamedly ameliorate the symptoms by lying flat while similarly affected naval officers and ratings on duty had to go about their allotted tasks, their pale anxious expressions and absence from meals revealing the malady which pride and a sense of duty prompted them to try to conceal.

It was now 10th of January 1945 and with further transport delays Oosterhout was not reached until the evening of the 12th. On the way there I met a 47 RM Cdo Marine from the quartermaster's department who informed me that '47' was about to be involved in another 'do' adding, 'we will be crossing the Maas tomorrow'. This was very surprising news considering the military significance of the Maas and the kind of major operation which would be required to cross it. Reaching Oosterhout, the information was found to be true in respect of timing but not wholly accurate in respect of the action planned. Twenty-four hours on, the commando was to attack a hitherto little known German occupied island called Kapelsche Veer, lying not across the Maas, but in the middle of it. I had some catching up to do.

What sort of island?

A hurried perusal of maps revealed that Kapelsche Veer, about six miles north-east of Oosterhout, lay on a stretch of the Maas which ran east to west up river from 47 RM Cdo's current sector. The island took its name from the small harbour of Kapelsche Veer on its northern side towards the eastern end. In peace-time a ferry plied between this harbour and a corresponding harbour on the northern side of the Maas. The island was elongated, east and west, five miles long tapering to a point at each end, and one mile wide at its centre. The mainstream of the Maas, the Bergsche Maas, flowed along the northern side and a smaller branch, the Oude Maas, along the southern side, the two branches rejoining downstream. There was a bridge across the Oude Maas (the Oude Maas Bridge) towards the eastern end of the island but this had been blown by the Germans. Near to the Kapelsche Veer ferry terminal on the German side of the Maas was the town of Dussen. Like a large football pitch, Kapelsche Veer island stretched flat and featureless from the Oude Maas on its southern side to the northern side where, resembling an elongated spectator stand over-looking a pitch, there was a 30 feet dyke, designated a 'winter-dyke' in view of its rôle in holding back the Bergsche Maas if it overflowed its

Aerial view of Kapelsche Veer Harbour (26 December 1944), showing the Oudemaas and the broken bridge over it, the road leading north from the bridge, the wide polder bordering the Bergsche Maas with the harbour leading through it to the main Bergsche Maas Dyke, the diagonal dyke between the main dyke and the Oudemaas, and the large tree (largest blurred mark – which includes under it the 'dykewatchover' house). (*Crown Copyright/MOD*)

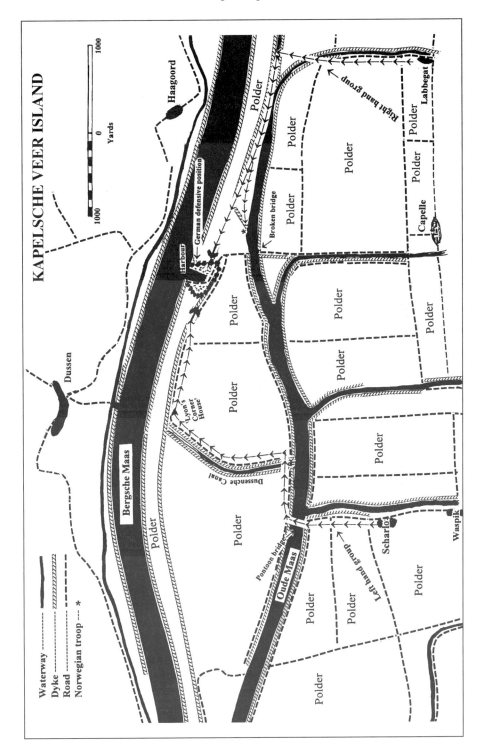

KAPELSCHE VEER ISLAND

Waterway
Dyke
Road
Norwegian troop — *

Yards
1000　0　1000

Haagoord

Polder

Right hand group

Labbegat

Polder

Polder

Polder

Polder

Capelle

German defensive position

Broken bridge

Harbour

Polder

Polder

Polder

Polder

Dussen

'Lyon's Corner House'

Dussensche Canal

Polder

Polder

Polder

Bergsche Maas

Polder

Polder

Scharlo

Waspik

Pontoon bridge

Oude Maas

Left hand group

Polder

Polder

Polder

Polder

Polder

Polder

banks in the winter, which it was prone to do. Beyond the dyke was a 200 yard wide strip of polder and then the southern bank of the Bergsche Maas. The polder was indented by the elongated harbour at right angles to the river, stretching from the bank of the Bergsche Maas to the base of the dyke. From the Oude Maas Bridge a road led northwards to the dyke turning left there and traversing westward at the base of the dyke until, opposite the harbour, it turned right to lead over the dyke and down into the harbour. On the dyke, above the point where the road from the Oudemaas bridge turned left at the base of the dyke (i.e. at the east end of the German defensive position) was the 'dykewatchover house' (the dyke house). Close by stood a large 40 foot high willow tree, the commanding feature on the dyke. The road over the dyke to the harbour divided the defensive position into two. The German garrison was well dug in, in trenches and fox-holes in an area about 400 yards long and 150 yards in depth tapering back towards the harbour. Thus the defensive positions were sited on the top of, and down the north side of, the dyke, The siting of strong defensive positions in depth behind the crest of the dyke was such that these defensive positions could not easily be hit by artillery fire, or by the fire of attacking troops until the latter advanced over the crest of the dyke and were close to the defensive positions; but that meant that the attacking troops were very exposed and could be swept by defensive fire as they came over the crest of the dyke and when advancing along it. The dyke also shielded the German positions on the north bank of the river from sight from the south so that the Kapelsche Veer garrison could be supplied and reinforced without this being seen. The inhabitants of the villages on the north bank of the Bergsche Maas had been evacuated from their homes. Both banks of the Oude Maas in the region of the Oude Maas bridge were visible from German positions.

Personnel changes

In my absence Col Phillips had been promoted to Brigadier and was now no longer with 47 RM Cdo. The second-in-command, Major P M (Paddy) Donnell, had just taken over as CO. His place as Second-in-Command was taken by a regular Marine officer, Major Martin Price who had just joined the unit.

Col Donnell was now in charge of a commando which because of preceding losses, particularly at Walcheren – where 30 per cent including 60% of the fighting troop officers had become casualties – was depleted both of numbers and of soldiers of experience. With the need to retain some of the commando to fulfil patrolling duties in the Oosterhout area its operational strength for Kapelsche Veer was only about 250. It was evident that the number of Royal Marine reserves available was now limited. Most of the commando's new fighting troop officers and marines were young, recently-joined replacements. A certain amount of 'posting' for all ranks was now required. In addition, because of shortage of Marines an increasing number of Army personnel, particularly officers, were being used to make good deficiencies. Irrespective of the origins of the new intakes Col Phillips had communicated with Brigade Headquarters at the end of November questioning the 'capability' of some of the new arrivals and complaining about 'lower category men' and their apparent lack of training. A final blow was that two days before the battle two of the remaining senior troop commanders, Captains James and O'Connell, were involved in a motor accident requiring evacuation to hospital. Because of these deficiences a Norwegian Troop of 10 Inter Allied Commando, and a small company of Polish troops – to be held in reserve to act as occupying troops if Kapelsche Veer was captured – were attached. The commando had now become a somewhat scratch polyglot unit which had had no chance to train together for the operation.

The Battle Scene

This part of the Maas was the responsibility of the First Polish Armoured Division, commanded by General Maczek, one of Poland's most distinguished and respected soldiers. When Poland was overrun by the German Army in 1939 Colonel Maczek, as he then was, had, under orders, conducted a withdrawal of what remained of the Polish army into Hungary so that, from Britain, it could continue the fight against Germany. The First Polish Armoured Division at this time, like 47 RM Cdo, was part of the First Canadian Army which had played such a notable part in clearing the Breskens Pocket. The Poles had made two unsuccessful attempts to eliminate the Kapelsche Veer garrison and 47 RM Cdo, operating under the First Polish Armoured Division, was now to be given that task … There appeared to have been a certain irritation at Canadian high command, possibly ill-informed and almost certainly unjustified as later events were to show, that the Poles had failed to overcome the Kapelsche Veer garrison.

During November the retreating German army had withdrawn to the north of the Maas but, at the beginning of December, prior to the Ardennes offensive, had crossed back over the Bergsche Maas and established a bridgehead at Kapelsche Veer. This bridgehead was concentrated round the harbour but manned outposts had been established at a few strategic points at other parts of the island so that the island was effectively in German hands.

At the start of the Ardennes offensive, Canadian intelligence obtained evidence suggesting a likely complementary German offensive on the Maas front. Enemy forces were known to be concentrated north of the Bergsche

Maas opposite Kapelsche Veer and with a bridgehead established at Kapelsche Veer that seemed to be the point at which any supportive, pincer
mevement, crossing would be attempted. After the war it was found that
these assumptions were correct because on the first day of the Ardennes
attack (16/12/44) von Rundstedt the German Commander-in-Chief West
had ordered,

> … that if the operations of Army Group B (i.e. in the Ardennes)
> continue to develop as successfully as they seem to promise up to
> now and headway is quickly made in the direction of Antwerp, an
> advance by strong elements of 25th Army (German) across the lower
> Maas can contribute materially to success by completing the large
> envelopment of enemy forces in the area north of the area currently
> under attack.

On 18th December von Rundstedt had ordered his northern Army Group
to be ready to cross the Maas when ordered and to advance to the
Wilhelmina Canal 8 miles to the south of that.

The crossing point was to be at Kapelsche Veer. The Germans knew
that if they could recapture Antwerp the Allied armies, who were so
dependent on that port, would be brought to a standstill.

By 26 December the Ardennes offensive had been halted but, despite
that, there were indications that the garrison at Kapelsche Veer was being
strengthened and the concentration of German troops opposite Kapelsche
Veer maintained. A continuing threat of further offensive action from that
quarter was deemed to exist.

47 RM Cdo, patrolling on the Maas further west, knew little if anything
of these High Command matters. Its prior understanding of the operation
which it was ordered to undertake at short notice was very limited. It
knew little more than that the First Canadian Army had decided that a
German bridgehead at Kapelsche Veer should be eliminated and that,
operating under command of the First Polish Armoured Division, it was
to undertake that task.

The Polish Preamble

Near the end of December 1944, in preparation for an attack on Kapelsche
Veer, a Polish patrol had crossed the Oude Maas by boat at night. Approaching the German defensive positions along the dyke from the west (left)
the patrol was fired on. Three of its members were wounded. The Germans
were alert and active.

A full scale Polish attack was then mounted on the night of 30/31
December. The Poles were aware that the garrison had recently been
strengthened as reinforcements had been seen being ferried across to the

harbour from the northern side of the Bergsche Maas. The importance attached to the attack seemed to be indicated when, before it, Lieut General Crocker, Commander of the First (British) Corps of the Canadian Army, visited the troops involved.

The attack was preceded by a two hour bombardment by the divisional artillery. As tanks could not get across the Oude Maas Cromwell tanks were positioned south of the river near the Oude Maas bridge from where they could shell the German garrison from as close a range as possible: the corollary was that the Germans could fire back at the tanks. A Polish section armed with machine guns and mortars and using planks got across the Oude Maas bridge which although blown had been only partially destroyed. Gaining lodgement on the island the section established a bridgehead from which it could provide supporting mortar and machine gun fire for two groups of infantrymen who would attack the garrison. When the tanks opened fire after the artillery bombardment this produced an immediate response from the Germans. One tank received a direct hit from a panzerfaust and exploded. Other tank crews were wounded. The bridgehead party also came under fire and suffered casualties. In the meantime the assaulting groups advanced towards the eastern and western ends of the German position on the dyke in a pincer movement. The left-hand party reached the dyke and advanced along it towards the outer German trenches and fox-holes, killing or capturing some of the occupants. Now, however, as they advanced further they came under intense machine-gun and sub-machine-gun fire. The leading elements got within 100 yards of the main defensive position but could go no further and their ammunition was running low.

The right-hand party meanwhile reached within 50 yards of the main enemy position, near enough for grenades to be thrown. They too could not advance further and casualties were mounting. In this situation both groups were ordered to withdraw bringing their wounded with them. Forty nine casualties had been sustained, 11 killed and 38 wounded.

Stung by this reverse the Division mounted a second attack on the night of 6/7th January. This attack was preceded by a more intensive artillery bombardment from south of the Oude Maas augmented by multiple (32 barrel) mortars in a concentrated barrage. Again a bridgehead group crossed the Oude Maas and gave supporting fire to the forward troops with 3 and 4 inch mortars and heavy machine-guns firing tracer bullets. Two groups of assaulting troops attacked from east and west. The left hand group again over-ran forward German fox-holes and trenches killing some of the occupants and capturing at least nine prisoners. As it approached the core of the defence position the group, like its predecessors, came under intense fire from the well protected enemy positions. They had virtually no cover from this fire and were suffering many casualties. The attack was halted and the order given to withdraw. Some of the Polish soldiers were in a position where, lying flat on the ground they could not easily be hit but if they attempted to move could be mown down by machine-gun fire. As dawn was breaking their predicament was getting worse. The January winter day may have been short but for them it was very long as they lay all day, almost frozen to the ground. Throughout the day, with a view to restricting enemy activity which might threaten the prostrate Polish soldiers, the enemy position was kept under observation from the tanks which had provided the covering fire the previous night. Any movement apparent in the German position resulted in a fusillade of shots from the tanks. When dusk fell another company was sent out to help the trapped men who managed to inch their way out, bringing their wounded with them.

On the other flank the right-hand group had advanced to the road running below the ridge of the dyke. They ran into a minefield and a machine gunner lost his foot. As they turned upwards towards the top of the dyke they were held up by a deep ditch full of water and came under Spandau fire. Some Germans ahead of them ran back from the forward fox-holes. As the Poles approached the main defensive position a Very light was fired from the garrison position, apparently a signal, and in response to this mortar bombs, Spandau fire and grenades rained down on them. Their position too became untenable and they had to withdraw. Casualties in this assault were high, 34 killed and 89 wounded out of a force of less than 300 men. Kapelsche Veer was beginning to extract a heavy toll and the serious difficulties in attacking it were becoming clear. Disappointingly, in these two attacks, the artillery and mortar bombardments which had preceded them seemed to have had little effect on the German garrison's capacity to defend its main position.

In the latest attack, compared with the earlier attack, some of the German prisoners captured were found to be members of a German Parachute Regiment indicating that the garrison had been strengthened by troops of the highest quality.

47 RM Cdo, thrown in with little opportunity for adequate preparation, had little knowledge of these preceding attacks. The perception was that KapelscheVeer was manned by troops of poor quality but the reality, as is now known, was that the garrison had been further reinforced on the day before 47 RM Cdo's attack with a further tranche of 60 additional troops from the Parachute Regiment and the 745 Grenadier Regiment, bringing its complement to 160.

After this second Polish attack, the Germans had flooded the low-lying polders south of the dyke by blowing a retaining dyke near the Oude Maas

Bridge thus creating a further serious barrier to attack. The furrows and ditches running north of the Oude Maas up to the dyke then filled with water making large parts of the polder water-soaked, ice-covered and impassable. Any attack across the island had now to be confined to a one mile long track beside the Dussensche canal which reached the dyke at a point a mile west of the German positions. The Germans were able to site defensive positions commanding the route along which the commando would have to attack. From the bridgehead at the eastern end of the island the distance along the dyke to the German defensive position was also a mile. Thus from east and west the commandos would have to advance along very narrowly restricted routes much of which could be covered by machine guns firing on fixed lines. There was no possibility of 'going wide' and 'taking out' a defensive position by attacking it from the flank, nor of going round the back – the strip of polder between the north side of the dyke and the southern bank of the Bergsche Mass was flooded.

The Operational Plan: by the Left and by the Right

Commanding his first major operation Col Donnell had very limited time to prepare his plans. Brief consultation with the Canadians, whose own troops had not so far been involved at Kapelsche Veer, suggested that this would be a straightforward operation and it was only just before embarking on it that Col Donnell became aware of the Polish experience and the heavy casualties which they had suffered. Among the rank and file of 47 RM Cdo the prevalent notion was that after a 'terrifying bombardment' a low grade garrison would be 'happy to surrender' and to 'spend the rest of the war in the safety of prisoner of war camps'.

The tactics planned for 'Operation Horse', as 47 RM Cdo's attack was codenamed, were similar to those adopted for the Polish attacks. There would be no air support and no tank support. The attack would be prefaced by an intense gun and mortar bombardment from south of the Oudemaas provided by Corps artillery. This bombardment would be released when the assaulting troops were in their assault positions close to the German positions. This time the duration of the artillery bombardment would be shorter, 15 minutes, followed by the laying down of a smoke screen on the road running north from the Oude Maas bridge, then a further 5 minutes bombardment. As previously, two assaulting commando groups would attack along the dykes from left and right making the Germans defend in two directions.

The left-hand group consisting of A, B, X, and Y troops would form up at Scharlo and march half a mile north from there to cross the Oude Maas by a pontoon bridge which would be built by engineers of the Polish Division. They would then cross the island via the Dussensche canal path led by A Troop acting as a fighting patrol. At the dyke the commando would turn right along its base and A Troop in front would clear the ground and establish a strongpoint 400 yards from the enemy position. Y troop supported by X troop would then lead the assault along the dyke from the left. HQ with Col Donnell would be with this left-hand group.

The right hand assault group, under Major Price, would consist of Q troop and the Norwegian troop – the attached 'occupying' Polish Section would wait in reserve at the Polish bridgehead. The right-hand troop would form up at the Labbegat (factory), near Capelle, march north one mile to the Oude Maas, crossing it to the Polish bridgehead at the eastern tip of the island. The group would then advance along the dyke sending a fighting patrol in front to deal with any opposition en route and establish a secure strong point on the dyke short of the main German defensive position. Q troop's objective would be the dyke house at the east end of the defensive position. Capture of the dyke house position would enable Q troop to give covering fire to the left-hand group in its assault. As Q Troop advanced along the dyke the Norwegian troop would veer left to seize a subsidiary diagonal dyke ½ mile from the start point running between the main dyke and the Oude Maas, cross that and, with the benefit of the smokescreen provided by the artillery, advance to an enemy post on the road running north from the Oude Maas bridge. The main attacks from right and left would go in simultaneously. Withdrawal would be completed by daylight and one troop would be left to hold the position until relieving forces arrived.

In my absence the Polish ADMS (Assistant Director of Medical Services) and the 11th Polish Field Ambulance undertook the medical planning for the operation and laid down the plan. It was that a Polish Field Ambulance would be located at the Polish bridgehead and would be responsible for onward evacuation of seriously wounded casualties. I would operate with the left-hand group establishing an RAP for that Group. Two of my already under-strength complement of stretcher-bearers had been wounded at Walcheren and not yet replaced and one had to be left behind at Oosterhout. As the Heavy Weapons Troop would not be used in this operation – the Corps artillery bombardment included mortaring – it was called upon to provide troop stretcher-bearers. On the morning of the day of the operation, however, I was informed that due to the need for effective linkage with the Polish Field Ambulance unit the Polish ADMS had allocated six additional Polish stretcher-bearers who would report to me at Oosterhout that morning. The new Chaplain, the Rev A. R. Thornley, would be with the RAP.

By midday (13/1/45) the Polish stretcher-bearers had not arrived. Unable to contact them I decided to go and collect them from the Field Ambulance which was to supply them. It was a cold day with snow and ice on the roads. I set off on my motor-cycle but at a certain point found myself travelling through a wood. My route should not have traversed a wood and I realised that I was on the wrong road. I stopped to turn round and as I did there was a stentorian shout from nearby and a Polish soldier emerged from the wood advancing menacingly, rifle pointed at me. He spoke no English and I no Polish but he signed to me to leave my motor cycle and go with him. He then marched me at rifle point into the wood until we reached a command post occupied by a number of Polish soldiers and an officer who fortunately spoke some English. After I had explained the reason for my presence I had a frustrating wait while he used the field telephone. He also wanted to see the fibre identity discs (the 'dog tags') which I carried round my neck. (I was later told that German spies in American uniforms had been captured in the Ardennes but that their 'dog tags' were in German and he presumably wished to ensure that mine were in English). After some more questioning I was able to disabuse him of the idea that I was some sort of spy in British uniform. He then undertook to convey a message to the Field Ambulance re the stretcher-bearers. I impressed on him the urgent necessity for me to return to my unit as H-Hour was fast approaching. Now suitably impressed with the urgency of the situation and anxious to ensure that I should not again lose my way he instructed my erstwhile Polish soldier captor to take me back to Oosterhout on the pillion of my own motor-cycle. I was not too happy with this arrangement but dare not demur. My captor was clearly seized with the importance and urgency of his task. He was no stranger to riding a motor-cycle but I was something of a stranger to the speed and the angled cornering with which, on icy roads, he demonstrated his skill. I arrived back at Oosterhout just before the transport departed, not too sure about the medical arrangements and how they would work. At the last minute the six Polish stretcher-bearers arrived. In view of language difficulties and their unfamiliarity with the commando they would act as back-up stretcher bearers mostly on the long haul from the left.

THE ASSAULT

The Left-Hand Party

On the day before the attack a patrol led by Lieut. Brent carried out a reconnaissance of the left hand route, getting close enough to see the outline of the dyke house. A Polish patrol was also despatched that day to ensure that a house on the northern bank of the Oude Maas which was known to be used by the Germans as an outpost and was near the point where the left-hand group would cross the Oudemaas, was not occupied.

From this house fire could have been directed at the left-hand group as it collected on the north side of the Oude Maas.

Saturday 13th January 1945 was a cold, frosty day. The sky was clear but there was some ground fog spreading over the river. Debussing from transport at Scharlo at 1700 hrs, A and B troops marched north half a mile to join up with the Polish engineering boat and bridge party at the Oude Maas. X, Y and HQ moved off at 1900 hours. The bridging of the Oude Maas was delayed because only two boats (to be used in construction of the pontoon bridge) were available. The others (the boats were heavy) had been dropped by the Polish carrying-parties when being unloaded, had been damaged, and could not be used. Thus the pontoon Oude Maas bridge was not completed until 2145 hrs rather than the 2000 hrs planned. The narrow wooden bridge floated on its pontoons over the 150 yard wide Oude Maas. The five troops then prepared to cross it. It was dark and the bridge was wet, icy and very slippery: it bobbed up and down and twisted sideways in both directions as the shadowy figures of the marines crossed in single file, spaced out to reduce weight on the bridge. The water surface, very black and speckled here and there by floating ice, was a foot or so below the bridge's deck. The river's edge was just delineated by the frozen, and in parts snow-covered, banks.

Sergeant Gibson has described the bridge:

> It was 18 inches wide over that black deep stretch of water, covered with a coating of ice which made going treacherous indeed. I cursed the (Polish) engineers for making a noise and smoking in the darkness. I took a look at the bridge and instinctively felt sick. Just the beginning was possible, a few floating duckboards extending out into the inky blackness. Turning aside I asked for strength to conquer my apprehension. We went forward, not daring to think as the duck boards rolled and slithered underneath our feet. How endless it was. I don't imagine I thought, or dared to think, a single complete thought in all that 150 yards till with relief we reached the enemy bank.

The bridge made crossing and carriage of equipment across the river a slow business and added to the delay. Fortunately, the fog provided some screening from enemy observation. Seeing and experiencing the bridge for the first time it was obvious that it would be extremely difficult to carry stretcher cases across it. A stretcher-borne casualty and his stretcher-bearers on this narrow, twisting and turning slippery ribbon of wood would run a serious risk of ending up in the freezing Oude Maas.

After assembly and weapon priming the left-hand group set off, A Troop leading. Sergeant Gibson was with the group as it advanced:

The Oudemaas where the left-hand group crossed it.

It was incredibly eerie to be marching in enemy territory. Soon we turned northwards along a dyke by whose side ran a narrow deep canal of icy water, the Dussensche canal. A Bren rattled in the darkness. It was 2225 hours. Our hearts turned over: the column halted. What could this be? We lay down on the frosty snow; just lay there for 20 minutes while A troop ahead was presumably dealing with this incident.

A Troop ahead had almost reached the angle between the track running north along the Dussensche canal and the Bergsche Maas dyke when it encountered a German defensive outpost. It over-ran the position killing three and wounding a fourth, who was taken prisoner. It then advanced along the base of the dyke, setting up a strong point about 400 yards from the enemy positions. Gibson again:

Then we got up as the file began to move again. A single Jerry had been captured but was suffering from shock and exposure and couldn't talk. I left him with Minckley with instructions to follow me up as soon as he could hand him over to the rear troop. Then we came to an isolated barn which we labelled Lyon's Corner House. The Doctor set up shop there but we did not pause. We reached the main Maas dyke, halted again, and then moved along the base of the dyke. X troop was now forward (at the 400 yard strong point), supported by A. We climbed the bank ahead and found slit trenches at its top; into these we climbed. I raised my head very cautiously to look over and there for the first time saw the Maas broad and gleaming in the natural luminosity of the stars.

At 0049 hrs I heard the code word 'Whisky' (for commencement of the bombardment) go out spoken clearly across the air. Q troop on the east and X troop on the west were in position, gone to ground. There were 5 of minutes prearranged silence, then suddenly the whole horizon from end to end sparkled with light, flickering and flashing. It took a whole half minute before they reached us; the crash!, crump! An incessant bombardment pounding down on Kapelsche Veer, 8000 shells and 1300 4.2 inch mortars bombs, rent the night. We looked on, our eyes transfixed with the horror of the sight – until whizz!, bmph!, crash! and a shell burst just behind us. We disappeared into the trenches. Soon another came and another nearer and nearer to the top of the bank. Had the enemy got wind of it? Was this counter fire? I guessed at the truth. It was one of our own bloody guns trying to fire over the bank to silence the enemy across the river. It was hitting us every time. Meantime the thunder of the shells continued and the flash of their detonations made the night garish. A couple of tanks from the far side of the Oude Maas were stabbing the target with white tracer which frequently overfired and hit the river only to ricochet in flashes of light.

Close by was Lieut. Brent. He considered that the bombardment must have been similar to the massive bombardments of the First World War: 'The earth began to quake and groan under the impact of exploding shells: it appeared to move with each shell that landed'.

As the shells rained down it seemed to Brent that among the enemy ahead there would not be much chance of survival in this inferno. Then, as suddenly as it had begun the bombardment stopped. 'A' troop was now in reserve and B Troop took over the manning of the strongpoint at the base of the Dyke. X and Y went ahead along and up the dyke for about 100 yards. Forewarned, the Germans were ready. As X and Y troops moved towards the enemy positions over the top of the dyke they met a hail of machine-gun and rifle fire, and mortaring, from the German positions on the Dyke and other German positions on the north side of the Bergsche Maas. The only way that they could advance was to keep to the south side of the dyke a little below its crest where they were partially sheltered from the fire, but as they got closer to the enemy positions they had to

The exposed approach along the Western dyke as it reaches the harbour (at this end). The ground on each side of the dyke was flooded.

advance over the crest of the dyke. There was little sign that the Germans had been subdued by the preliminary bombardment. X and Y advanced a further 150 yards but were sustaining casualties and had to pause. As the Poles had found they were now in an increasingly exposed position and as they advanced further towards the enemy position the firing intensified. On the top of the dyke there was virtually no cover. In seeking this the advancing troops became somewhat scattered and again had to pause.

Gibson, behind the advancing troops, was waiting in his trench and describes the scene:

> I had stopped to look and listen. It was one of these moments of intense consciousness when the individual seemed to be his own little island in time, and all the vexatious world but a swirling distant murmur all around him. The shelling of our position (by the support artillery) had ceased and even the flickering fire at the forward position had died down. Minckley had come up and I suggested we go forward; anything was better than inactivity, and my better judgement was better suspended lest it should begin to ask questions. I felt that

things were not going too well. We shouldered our rifles and picked up a stretcher – might as well make maximum use of ourselves. We met the I.O. (Lt Gower, returned after recovering from his earlier wounds) standing up defiant and leaning on his stick with his Tommy gun at the ready. I knew that here was the stuff of real courage. A single telephone wire lying on the hard frozen ground kept becoming entangled in our feet. Suddenly I thought of the Jerry who had been captured earlier. 'What happened to him, George?', I asked. 'Well it was a bit sad' he said. 'In the darkness I kept hold of him but he wouldn't keep quiet. He wanted to shout out. Then he fell into the canal. It was his own fault. He was pretty stiff when I left him'. 'Floating?' 'Yes, floating'.

For several hundred yards we plodded on meeting a few parties of wounded on the way back and almost stepping on the bodies of two Poles who had been lying frozen stiff on the ground for a full fortnight. How abstract their faces seemed. The air was now distinctly dangerous but we did not realise how dangerous till someone from A troop called out from a foxhole for us to get down. X troop had just attacked and been beaten back; they came streaming back in the darkness, a huddle of sub-human figures. I contacted the troop commander whose wireless had broken down: he gave me a message for the CO imperatively requiring more ammunition – his troop would have another attempt when they collected themselves he said. As we went back to relay this message we encountered a fellow of Heavy Weapons troop (Kitson) on a stretcher, shot through the head. What a weight to carry under these conditions. Again I nearly stepped on these Poles and recoiled at the thought of it.

'A' troop in reserve were now preparing to make an attack. In the darkness we joined them. I tried my Tommy gun and felt the fins of the three grenades strapped to my belt. Now we were moving forward, George and I with two flame-thrower fellows. I watched open-eyed like a lynx in the darkness. Yet another yard, continuously, cautiously, and nothing happened. How long would it last – and then tat – tat – tat – machine gun fire zipped a few yards to the left. We dropped to take cover instinctively, crushing ourselves into the frost bound earth. The MG suddenly spattered over our heads, a few inches above. We shut our eyes until it stopped. With a madding determination we were up rushing forward towards it.

All around in the flickering light there was movement, dark convulsive figures moving up and down while tracer from the enemy whistled past us. Why were we not hit? I called up the first flame thrower: he went ahead of me to where the (enemy) MG was firing to the left – only a few yards away now – and we watched fascinated. Then he let it go, a searing stream of flame that made me turn my eyes away. With a shriek the enemy gunner toppled backwards as we reached the trench.

Another two MGs now opened up, dangerously near, as we dropped into the trench that had just been torched. There the smell of burning and decay hung heavy on the air, the grass was singed: the barrel of the MG red hot. I called up the other flame-thrower manned by a young marine and we ran forward to wipe out the particularly aggressive MG on the right. It turned on us viciously and we dropped to the ground. The young marine hung back momentarily; I knew he was having a terrible battle with his own courage. I felt terribly for him, wanted to help him with his lonely battle – so I went ahead and slung in two grenades, first one, drawing the pin slowly and throwing it desperately, the explosion ringing in my ears: then the other; throwing the pin away like a spent match then, one – two – three, I threw it in. Still the gun fired and the world was filled with deafening noise and intermittent light. The young marine took courage suddenly and ran up beside me. He pulled the trigger and the spurt of flame shot forward, but he was shot as he ran, the flame searing across his chest and over his face (Gibson thought he was dead but he survived and ultimately recovered). I fell to the ground wondering vaguely if I had been struck and not he. Blindly, frantically I found myself crawling back to the trench I had left. The troop had been beaten back. I too had to go back and joined the remnants of A troop huddled together in the darkness. I wondered what time it was but at that moment a shell shrieked to earth – I saw it burst 5 yards away but miraculously I was not hit. Cpl. Tucker was. We helped him to his feet and George went with him to the RAP at 'Lyons Corner House'.

While these events were unfolding Lieut Brent took his section forward. He took a very different view of the flame-throwers. They were 'burning up sticks and stalks on the ground and illuminating our men against the black of the night for any German gunner to shoot at'.

A marine with a flame-thrower shouted to Brent that there was a machine-gun nest on the top of the dyke ahead. With a dash up the dyke Brent saw the machine-gun nest right in front of him and fired a burst with his Tommy gun. The man did not move or utter any sound. He then saw a second occupant, apparently crouching in the trench, but before he fired again Brent realised that the man was already dead. He thought that the second man, and possibly the first also, had probably been killed by the bombardment. This led him to think that the bombardment might after all have had some effect in subduing the defenders. At the same time he was encouraged to hear shouting and firing coming from Q troop on the other side of the enemy position. He felt that they must be making good progress.

Re-grouping with a fellow officer, two corporals and a group of marines, Brent then led a further assault over the ridge. As they went over, bracing themselves with a wild shout, they found that they were again being illuminated by a flame-thrower and the burning ground debris. Brent felt that they must be appearing to the German machine gunners like puppets in a shooting gallery. And so it seemed they were. Corporal Dyke was killed immediately, the other officer, Lieut. Brooker was wounded and the other corporal fell shot in the head. They had no time to open fire or throw grenades and had to withdraw dragging the wounded corporal along the ground on his back with them.

The left-hand attackers were now low in ammunition and were having to obtain it from those who became casualties. The attack had stalled and the attackers had to withdraw to a defensive position, waiting for further ammunition and further orders, huddled and dejected in the darkness. Withdrawn from the crest pending a possible further attempt on the ridge they were sheltered from machine-gun fire but were still under mortar fire and shelling. It was about 0330 hrs. A section of the Polish reserve platoon at the right hand base was now ordered to carry ammunition across to the left hand group but with so much of the intervening polder flooded that circuitous journey would take two hours.

The Right-Hand Party

The right-hand party crossed the river and advanced to the dyke reaching it at 2345 hrs. Their route was partly screened by the smoke laid down by the tanks. They encountered some resistance at a bank along the dyke but overcame that and reached their waiting position near the 'dykewatch-over' house, lying there as the supporting artillery bombardment rained down. When the bombardment ceased Q troop advanced further along the dyke reaching the proximity of the house. The house had been damaged by previous shelling but could still be used for defence and was further defended by an extensive network of trenches and fox-holes in the garden, all protected positions. For the marines any approach to these positions was now very exposed. Again they were in a position where machine guns firing on fixed lines in the dark were likely to hit them. They had to advance over an area where the only cover in front of the German position consisted of a bomb crater and a dead horse. As they went forward they were suffering casualties. They temporarily halted then resumed their attack. In the dark, despite the noise, the voices of the Germans could

The exposed approach along the Eastern dyke where, close to the left-hand end above, it reaches the harbour. The ground on each side of the dyke was flooded.

be heard easily. The marines were now near enough to throw grenades. When he had used all of his, Marine McLennan in desperation primed and threw a can of flaring self-heating soup (the can has a central tube containing magnesium and when activated the magnesium flared and heated the soup). The attack was taking its toll in casualties and soon this reached a crisis. Closing in on the house, Q Troop's commander, Captain Stickings, a man of great courage and determination, led the troop into a wall of fire accompanied by Corporal Tye and the troop second-in-command Lieut. Adam. First Tye, about twenty yards from the enemy, was hit, a bullet shattering his left arm; then Stickings was hit and fell mortally wounded. As Adam took Stickings' place he too was hit and killed. Marine Greenhalgh and Marine Williams were also killed. Further progress was not possible and the remnant of the troop had to withdraw. Their ammunition was now very low and they too were forced to take ammunition from casualties.

The Norwegians had also encountered serious resistance at their objective on the road from the Oude Maas and had suffered casualties.

Withdrawing to a more defensive position Q Troop continued to exchange fire with the German defenders while Major Price sought to regroup for a further attack in which he planned to involve some of the attached Polish company, although part of that company had already been earmarked for carrying ammunition to the left-hand section.

The Decision

Each of the assaulting troops was now in a defensive position waiting for further orders from Col Donnell. By 0530 hrs he had concluded that it was not going to be possible to mount a further meaningful attack that night and that the troops would need to be withdrawn. Tired, dispirited and disillusioned men now made their way down to the base of the dyke and back to the Oude Maas. Sgt. Gibson has described his withdrawal:

> The shells were coming over, belting down on either side of us: concussion terrific: cordite smoke stifling. Said Tim, 'Funny, before these 'dos' you feel you want to be in it, and when you are you wish to bloody hell you were out of it'. From below I heard the IO calling me down. Our withdrawal route was under fire from across the river. We passed Lyon's Corner House (RAP) and then along the ditch. The 'Jerry' was still floating there. I scarcely looked at him for I had been struck with the thought of the young flame-thrower lying alone in the wasteland.
>
> There was a little more light for the crossing of that plank bridge and somehow the crossing did not have half the terror. On the other side of the river I breathed a sigh of relief and looked up at the paling stars: and backwards at the island, at the luckless Kapelsche Veer where a few small spurts of flame and crackling told that all was not quite spent.

The walking wounded stumbled along assisted by their colleagues. Due to the dangerous nature of the floating Oude Maas bridge, stretcher cases and most of the other wounded were routed to the Polish Field Ambulance at the eastern end of the island. For casualties from the western side this involved a long and difficult carry. The additional Polish stretcher-bearers proved a valuable asset. Marine Wildman, a member of the Heavy Weapons Troop, was acting as a stretcher-bearer that night.

> ... there were many casualties lying around and in serious trouble because of the freezing conditions. Tommy and I picked up one casualty who had a bullet through his jaw and it turned out to be a fellow HW troop stretcher-bearer, Ken Kitson. We began the long haul back to the first aid post. It became obvious this task wasn't physically possible for two men and we picked up a couple of volunteers to help. Even so, carrying a casualty along the narrow top of a frozen dyke

under fire proved immensely difficult and I'm afraid the poor chap was dropped a few times.

After the war Wildman said that he would remember this journey as long as he lived: Kitson, the man on the stretcher, remembered nothing whatsoever about it! This is what wound shock will do. As Wildman moved off the dyke he passed another HW troop stretcher-bearer, Marine Benny Pry, who had also been seriously wounded. Benny Pry said to him, 'mind where you're treading Fred, I think I've lost my feet'. Mne. Pry was rescued but died from his wounds two days later.

Conclusions

All told there were 53 casualties, nearly a quarter of the force: 11 killed and 42 wounded (including 3 Norwegians killed and 8 wounded, and 4 Poles wounded).

47 RM Cdo's attack on Kapelsche Veer was carried out at short notice and there were liaison difficulties in operating under Canadian direction, part-delegated to a Polish-speaking Division. There was probably little chance of this attack succeeding with the forces used, as subsequent events demonstrated. While the artillery bombardment may have eliminated a few of the outer defensive posts it had little effect on the main defences. They were mostly sited behind the top of the dyke. The artillery shells either thudded into the southern face of the dyke or, because of their trajectory, carried over the defensive position on its northern side and landed on the far side of the Bergsche Maas. As the First World War had so often demonstrated, a massive bombardment which looked as if it might destroy the defences and the defenders against which it was directed often did not have the effect anticipated. Far from being 'base troops' the German troops in the latter stages of the battle for Kapelsche Veer were of the highest quality.

The lie of the land and the flooding of the polders forced the attackers on to the dyke and because of the siting of the defences the marines could only fire on the enemy when they reached the crest of the dyke. There, in the dark, machine guns on fixed lines could command the ground over which they had to advance. The defenders were in entrenched positions, the marines were in the open. Also, with the frosty ground, even in the dark, the marines could be silhouetted as they came over the dyke's crest to advance to their objective. On the crest they were confined to a narrow approach which gave no room for wider deployment. They were in a position somewhat similar to that which so often defeated Scottish clansmen of a bygone era when they had to attack the castle stronghold of a rival clan situated in the middle of a loch and approachable only along a narrow causeway. At closer range the marines could be reached by hand-thrown grenades – the Germans' long-handled 'stick grenade' – which could be thrown further than the British type. The final and critical factor was that the assaulting troops were running out of ammunition.

The mixing of Polish, Norwegian and British soldiers created difficulties. The differences in language, training and understanding, and lack of any opportunity to prepare together, made co-ordination difficult. Orders tended to be mistranslated or wrongly interpreted. There was another risk. Confronted in the dark by a shadowy figure speaking a language which he thought was German Cpl. Tye was about to shoot and only at the last second realised that he might be mistaken. The man was a Pole or a Norwegian.

Col Donnell who had been with the commando since D-Day was in a very difficult position. Anxious to succeed in his first operation as CO he might have tried to press on regardless with a further assault. In discussion with him afterwards it was clear that he had concluded in as objective a way as possible that he was not going to succeed and that to press on would be likely to result only in the unnecessary sacrifice of men. The steps which were finally necessary to subdue the garrison at Kapelsche Veer would tend to support that judgement.

The Final Elimination of the Kapelsche Veer Bridgehead

Kapelsche Veer remained a thorn in the flesh of the First Canadian Army which decided that it had to be removed. It was now recognised that, based on the knowledge gained from the earlier attacks, a very much larger force would be necessary to subdue it and would probably have to be supported by tanks. For the latter, Canadian engineers commenced building a tank bridge across the Oudemaas. Thus a much bigger operation code-named 'Elephant' (in contrast to 47 RM Cdo's operation 'Horse') was planned. The task was allotted to an armoured division, the 4th Canadian Armoured Division under Major General Vokes, and an infantry brigade, the 10th Canadian Infantry Brigade under Brigadier Jefferson.

On 26th January, before the tank bridge was ready an infantry attack supported by artillery was launched by the Lincoln and Welland Regiment. There were many casualties and like its predecessors the regiment had to withdraw. This was followed by another infantry attack by the Argyll and Sutherland Highlanders, which too was repulsed with heavy casualties. Meantime, artillery bombardment against the north bank of the Bergsche Maas was making it difficult for the Germans to reinforce and supply the Kapelsche Veer garrison or to evacuate its wounded.

The tank bridge was completed on 27th January and on that day and the next the tanks gained lodgement on the island. On the night of 29/30

January a full-scale attack was mounted by the combined forces of the South Alberta Tank Regiment, the Argyll and Sutherland Highlanders and the Lincoln and Welland Regiment. The tanks played an important part in this attack and at its conclusion the battlefield was littered with spent shell cases. The battle lasted all night. Gradually one emplacement, one trench, one fox-hole was overcome until all had been subdued. The German paratroopers fought to the last.

The Canadians paid very heavily for this success. Over the five days of the battle they suffered 234 casualties of whom 65, including 9 officers, were killed. Some of the elderly citizens of Waalwyk and Waspik still remember vividly Canadian soldiers returning in white snow suits covered in blood. All told there were 472 Allied casualties at Kapelsche Veer of whom 118 were killed.

When the Kapelsche Veer garrison was finally overrun 149 Germans lay dead and 65, some wounded, were taken prisoner. After the war the commander of the German 6th Parachute Regiment estimated that his losses were 300 to 400 'serious casualties' plus 100 more men frost-bitten. On the captured German commander of the 10th Parachute Company was found a note to his superiors which revealed the state to which the defenders had been reduced as a result of the constant attacks and the action taken latterly by the Canadian artillery to prevent reinforcement and maintenance of the garrison by bombardment of the opposite bank of the Bergsche Maas: 'The physical condition of the men is giving rise to anxiety. The food and drink are ice cold. Their feet are soaked and they are suffering from severe frostbite ...'

The defenders on Kapelsche Veer saw themselves as defending their homeland. One could not but admire the courage with which they did this during 'this struggle by the frost-bound Maas'.

German and Allied Strategies at Kapelsche Veer

After the Ardennes offensive had been brought to a halt on 26th December the Germans must have known that there was little chance of mounting a meaningful attack across the Maas. They would have had to bridge the river so that tanks, heavy equipment and troops in large numbers could cross. In the face of the Allied air supremacy that would have been very difficult and unlikely to succeed. Why then did they continue to make such strenuous efforts to maintain and increase the garrison at Kapelsche Veer and also retain, on the north side of the Maas, some of the concentration of forces which had been built up for complementing the Ardennes offensive had it succeeded?

General Student commanding these forces was an outstanding German general and would be unlikely to waste his resources. He is said to have been frustrated when the Ardennes offensive failed and the opportunity to lead a matching counter-offensive across the Maas was denied him. After 26th December Lieut. General Plocher was apparently against the retention of a garrison at Kapelsche Veer and the forces opposite it on the north bank of the Maas but was overruled by Student, his superior. It seems that Student had decided that the retention of forces there would be an advantage because, although there was now no prospect of them being used offensively across the Maas, they would be seen as a continuing threat which would tie up large numbers of Allied forces. He therefore practised a deception. His concentration of troops north of the Maas opposite Kapelsche Veer would not now be trained soldiers but trainee soldiers who could as well train opposite Kapelsche Veer as anywhere else. Retention of the garrison at Kapelsche Veer would be an essential component of this plan and have the additional advantage that in such a defendable position a small garrison would be likely to inflict more casualties on the Allies than they would inflict on it. If this was his plan it would be difficult to say that it did not have a fair measure of success.

Questions have also been raised regarding the necessity to attack Kapelsche Veer after the Ardennes offensive had failed. General Crocker has been criticised for persisting with attacks on Kapelsche Veer and for underestimating the difficulty of assaulting it even when these difficulties had been revealed by the experiences of the Polish troops. Given the extent of Allied air supremacy and nature of the position an aerial attack would have been more likely to eliminate it and at greatly lessened cost. Even if it had just been contained it would soon have been of little relevance.

The Last Act

The bodies of those who were killed at Kapelsche Veer were buried on the spot, mostly by the Germans, and after the war many graves were found in dykes and fields on Kapelsche Veer island. When 47 RM Cdo withdrew, the bodies of Captain Stickings, Lieut. Adam and Marines Greenhalgh and Williams had to be left behind. The bodies were later dug up for reinterment – in the case of British troops in British War Cemeteries. In 1989 Lieut. Brent, now living in Australia, visited these cemeteries. and found the graves of all the members of 47 RM Cdo who had been killed at Kapelsche Veer with the exception of his friend Lieut. Adam whose grave he particularly wanted to visit. To further his search he enlisted the help of the former Burgomaster of Sprang-Capelle, Mr van Prooijen, who found that in Sprang-Capelle General Cemetery there was the grave of 'An Unknown British Soldier' who had been buried there in 1946. It was ascertained that the body had been found on Kapelsche Veer island among a group of four who were all at first thought to be Germans until it was recognised that one was a British soldier. There was no identity disc, normally worn round the neck, and no other means of identification. Those who had dug up the body and those who had reburied it were contacted. They had recorded the features. The help of Mrs Rijckevorsel of Oosterhout, now aged 81, was sought because she had billeted a number of members of 47 RM Cdo. One of these was Lieut. Adam whom she liked to refer to as 'my officer'. She was able to describe Lieut. Adam's features, colour of hair, uniform, etc and this tallied with the features which had been noted by the grave-diggers. Adams' relatives wished him to remain at Sprange-Capelle and in conjunction with the British War Graves Commission a formal head-stone with appropriate inscription was erected. These investigations and the redesignation of the gravestone had been completed by May 1992. The local people involved then held a commemoration ceremony for Lieut. Adam in Sprange-Capelle Cemetery in which Mrs Rijckevorsel and Burgomaster Octrels laid wreaths. In Waalwijk, near to Kapelsche Veer the 'Friends of the Allied War Graves' is another Dutch organisation which very generously seeks to honour Allied soldiers killed in that area.

Below the large willow tree still standing on the Kapelsche Veer dyke is a plaque which, translated into English, says:

Sprange-Capelle was liberated from the Nazi occupation
by the Allied Forces during the autumn of 1944. During the following winter the Germans tried to return
over the River Bergsche Maas, close to this old willow-tree.
The inhabitants of this village were saved from new
suffering thanks to the courage of British, Polish and
Canadian troops. Living now so many years in freedom,
their memory of those brave men, who defended freedom in this area, gets stronger with the passage of time.

Chapter Thirteen

Return to Walcheren

Following Kapelsche Veer a very depleted commando was sent back to Walcheren to garrison it along with the Dutch Princess Irene Brigade, elements of the Royal Engineers (manning LVTs) and a Norwegian troop. A number of enemy agents had been captured and the continuing concern of the Army command was that there might be infiltration and sabotage aimed at disrupting the use of Antwerp. The possibility that an attempt in greater force might be made to achieve that aim had not been ruled out.

The Sacrificed Island

During the assault on Walcheren, when the troops taking part were so heavily engaged in battle, there was very little opportunity for them to see much of the island. Now they had the opportunity to do so. Mostly what the eye saw was a large expanse of seawater which covered 80 per cent of the island. It was sometimes calm, sometimes choppy, dotted with houses, here and there church spires, poplar trees, telegraph poles with a few forlorn strands of wire hanging from them, water lapping against all of them. Floating in the water were often the odds and ends of human living, household rubbish, drifting timber, brushwood – sometimes draped on fences or the lower branches of trees. Civilians who tried to retain contact with their waterlogged homes had usually to reach them by boat and boats were at a premium. With the water nearly up to the window-sills of ground floor rooms, and doors shut to try to limit the destructive effect of waves and tide, entry was usually through these ground floor windows. From them, inside, a causeway of furniture, usually tables, often led to the stairs and access to the only rooms intact, those upstairs. Looking into such a house, water-soaked carpets and moquette-covered furniture presented a sorry spectacle, wallpaper was peeling from the walls, flotsam moved back and forward in dreary rhythm with every surge of water. There was often a pervading smell. Attempts had sometimes been made to accommodate farm animals in the upper storeys – otherwise the animals would have drowned – but lack of animal foodstuffs meant that most of the animals had to be slaughtered. There was a serious shortage of drinking water. Crops had been ruined. The trees rising out of the water were not obviously affected as yet but the salt water which now permeated to their

Walcheren under water.

A lower floor. (*Crown Copyright*)

An upper floor.
(*Crown Copyright*)

A street. (*Crown Copyright*)

roots would in due course kill them. Many habitations had been destroyed by bombing and shelling. While most of Middelburg was above the flooding, and life there could go ahead with some normality, travel outside it in anything which would float was the order of the day, with some very ramshackle boats in evidence. The whole economy of the island had been gravely damaged and its administrative and social services severely disrupted.

On 12th of May, Queen Wilhelmina, who had been rescued from Holland by the Royal Marines in 1940 to seek refuge in England along with her government, left England to return, after over five years. Three days later she visited Walcheren, formerly the 'Garden of Zeeland', and was shocked at what she saw. She later described,

> how tragic was the aspect offered by the Island of Walcheren, once so picturesque: a sheet of water as far as the eye could reach, with church spires and roofs rising out of it, and trees which would never put forth leaves again.

Garrisoning the Island

The commando acted as a mobile reserve based on Middelburg and had troops in Veere and Zoutelande. The Cdo's defensive system consisted essentially of mobile patrols ranging round the island using LVTs and boats. A few hundred troops were now spread over an area which had previously been defended by several thousand German troops.

The Germans made no attempt to recapture the island but artillery based in Schouwen periodically shelled it and sporadic attempts were made by midget submarines to sink Allied supply ships making for Antwerp along the Scheldt. On one occasion three midget submarines were sunk off Flushing, on another three German motor launches which had come from Schouwen ran on to a sandbank off Walcheren and were shelled. Off Domburg a midget submarine broke down and sank: the submariner swam ashore and was captured. On the same day another midget submarine was found stranded with the submariner unconscious – probably due to defective breathing apparatus. He recovered and was interrogated. On land on one occasion a cable to one of the artillery units was cut.

One night I was called to Middelburg prison to see a German midget-submarine officer. He had been captured when his submarine was rammed and in escaping from it he had injured his hand. Middelburg prison was a dark, gloomy place, in appearance sinister and in reputation feared – used by the Gestapo to imprison, interrogate and torture those who opposed the Nazi–imposed régime. The room where the submarine officer was being interrogated carried the same aura. Sitting on a chair he was immediately visible as the only light in the room was concentrated on him. The rest of a very large stone-walled room consisted of shadowy emptiness with the exception of a trestle table almost outside the concentrated pool of light. At the table sat two rather fearsome, casually dressed naval officer interrogators, one British and one American. The German submariner was very young, quite boyish in appearance. He was rather dishevelled but his clothing was dry. He looked apprehensive but almost relieved to see me. He was not badly wounded and required only cleaning and dressing of his wound. While I carried this out the two interrogators sat back silent in the brooding shadows and showed no inclination to engage in conversation with me or with the German.

The only other 'enemy' visible in Middelburg were those who had been the hated and despised collaborators. Roped together in labour gangs they were being put to community tasks, particularly clearing of snow from the streets during the severe winter of 1944/45. A few years of spurious authority were to be followed by a life-time of shame.

The Civilians of Walcheren

After the breakout from the Normandy bridgehead 47 RM Cdo swept through France and into Belgium. They were the first troops into a number of towns and villages which had largely escaped damage. They were liberators, and nearly everywhere they went in that summer of hope and redemption the civilians rejoiced and the troops were received with thankfulness and joy, generous hospitality, gratitude and congratulation. With the prospect of life returning soon to the freedom of a previous era most of the French and Belgian people in these liberated towns and villages saw a happy future ahead.

As the autumn and winter of 1944 closed in on the citizens of Walcheren liberation proved to be a very different experience, more akin to that which had been experienced by the citizens of Caen when that town was destroyed, and one which, likewise, they had no power to control or influence. For Walcheren the price of liberation, ardently as that was desired, had had to be paid in human lives and in a devastation which would last for years. Those who had held the island in bondage for many years had certainly been evicted but at what enormous cost to the people whose home and heritage the island was. What would the citizens of Walcheren think of the destroyers of their cherished island who, although they came as friends and liberators, had killed so many of its people and laid so much to waste?

That question was answered in 1944/45 and in the years which have followed. There was no complaint, no recrimination, no argument that different tactics should have been used, only gratitude, welcome and friendship. Those whose lives had always been a struggle with a hostile sea, who over four years had endured a brutal oppressor, were stoical in character and willing, without demur, to pay the high price which liberation had demanded. They faced the future with fortitude.

Very strong links have been established and maintained between Walcheren and the Allied Units which liberated it. The citizens of the island have been very generous in establishing Memorials to members of these units who lost their lives there – in the case of 47 RM Cdo a Memorial at Dishoek close to the site of Battery W11, promoted and largely planned by Mr Jacob van Winkelen of Serooskerke in conjunction with the 'Foundation to Support the Liberators of Walcheren'. The 'Foundation' has been very active in promoting ceremonial and friendship return visits to Walcheren of the units who participated in its liberation.

Chapter Fourteen

On the Beveland Bus –
The Storm Blows Out on the Roompot

North Beveland and Schouwen

47 RM Commando was first in action when its Timberforce was part of the Shetland bus service to Norway. It was last in action when it was involved at the island of North Beveland in journeys across the Roompot (Ooster-Scheldt) to Schouwen, in what might be called the Beveland bus service.

To reach North Beveland, transport from Walcheren across the Zandkreek was by a catamaran-like ferry-boat constructed from two individual ferry-boats joined together, side to side like a pair of Siamese twins. A wooden platform large enough to take a 15 cwt truck stretched across the joined boats. With a truck aboard, the ferry looked ominously top heavy. With such limited transport it took four days to get the commando and its equipment across to North Beveland, a move finally completed on 16th March.

In North Beveland the commando's rôle in the guardianship of the Scheldt estuary was continued. North Beveland, approximately 10 miles long and 4 miles wide, was just north of Walcheren, separated from it by the Zandkreek. The German-occupied island of Schouwen was to the north of North Beveland across the stretch of water – 4 miles wide at its narrowest point – called the Roompot ('the Bedpan' to the medical section). The intelligence estimate was that there were 1600 enemy troops on Schouwen: the commando strength was just over 300.

The German Headquarters on Schouwen were at Haamstede at the western end of the 20 miles long, 6 miles wide, island. Zierikzee 8 miles east of Haamstede was the main town. For defensive purposes the Germans had flooded the island by blowing sluice gates through which seawater could flow. The level of the inundation rose and fell with the tide. Only the rim of the island, its west end, the town of Zierikzee and the main road between Haamstede and Zierikzee were high and dry. This main road along which most of the island's military traffic had to travel touched the southern coast of Schouwen, opposite Colijnsplaat on North Beveland, over a one mile stretch three miles west of Zierikzee. This was the obvious

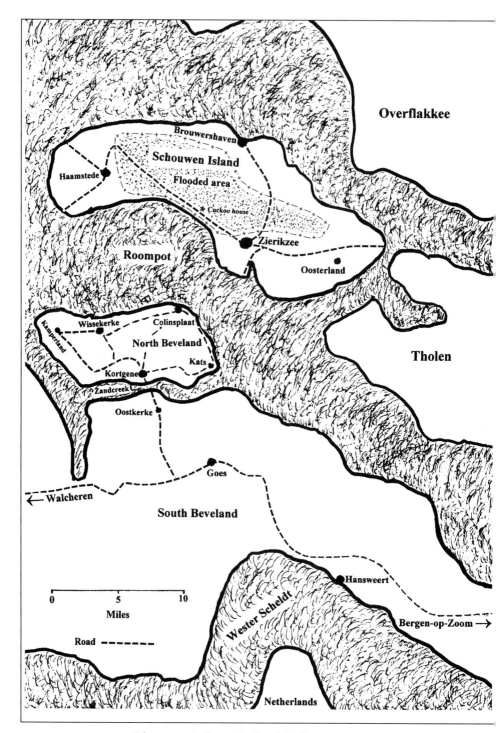

Schouwen, North Beveland and the Roompot.

place where observation of military activities, an ambush or a snatch operation could be carried out. There was an E Boat base at Brouwershaven on the north coast of the island.

In November a very unimpressive attempt had been made by a so-called German commando (two platoons of 4 Company Marine Einsatz Commando) to gather information and to destroy Colijnsplaat harbour. The attack was repelled and it was thought that most of those who took part became casualties. In December collections of outboard motor boats and rubber craft observed at the east end of Schouwen and along its south coast suggested the possibility of some sort of landing operation. In February a German naval force had attempted to attack Colijnsplaat but had been repelled. The artillery on Schouwen frequently shelled Walcheren and North Beveland; and Schouwen was the nearest point from which enemy naval vessels such as midget submarines, based at Brouwershaven, could attack Allied supply ships entering the Scheldt on their way to Antwerp.

The inadequacy of the ferry meant that the commando would be virtually cut off operationally from Walcheren should it be called upon to repel any enemy raid in force. Its rôle was to repel any attack from Schouwen, contain that island and gather intelligence information regarding what was going on there. The 47 RM Cdo troops were distributed defensively around North Beveland with one fighting troop and the Heavy Weapons troop in Wissekerke and a fighting troop in each of Kamperland, Colijnsplaat and Kats. The main body of the commando was in Kortgene. Coastal observation posts manned day and night, and communicating patrols between them at night, were the system of defence.

Also on North Beveland, attached to the commando, was an artillery group with a collection of guns ranging from 40 mm Bofors anti-aircraft guns to 5.5 in. medium guns. Their task was to counter-attack artillery positions on Schouwen and to harass any enemy naval craft seen off the island. To achieve better identification of targets, particularly artillery positions which could be moved from place to place, the artillery group had a two-seater Auster spotter aircraft.

Operation 'Swipe'

On the day, or rather night, of the commando's final installation on North Beveland the commando carried out a so-called 'Swipe' operation with the aim of capturing and interrogating a prisoner. A section under Lt Lloyd crossed by landing craft and mounted an ambush on the main road. No military traffic came along the road and the patrol returned empty handed

The 'Cuckoo' Patrols

In view of the limited time – night only – during which a 'Swipe' patrol could remain on Schouwen it was decided that a 24 hour survey would be likely to yield more information. The first of three 'Cuckoo' operations in late March was therefore planned and put into action. The plan was that a patrol, led by Lt Biagi, would be put ashore at night for 24 hours. The patrol, carrying with it an inflatable rubber dinghy, would be landed on Schouwen by LCA. In the dinghy the patrol would sail to a suitable house tentatively identified beforehand from a large-scale map. The house chosen would allow the patrol to keep the main road under observation. The patrol would carry a radio. Nobody quite knew what the position would be if the 'Cuckoo' patrol was captured. Would they be treated as spies? Would such activities invoke Hitler's order for the execution of commandos?

The first 'Cuckoo' patrol was landed on the night of 19/20 March and was to be picked up on the following night. The outward LCA journey was completed satisfactorily. LCAs, however, were not very suitable for rough seas and storms on the Roompot could very quickly whip its waters into a frenzy which precluded the sailing of LCAs. Unfortunately, by the second night the weather had deteriorated so badly that it was not possible for the LCA to sail and pick up the patrol as planned. To make matters worse the radio link with the patrol had broken down: the patrol could not be warned that it could not be picked up. When the darkness descended on the night of 20/21 March the patrol, now incommunicado, set out on the return journey in their rubber dinghy and finally reached the pick-up point to await the flashed signal from the dark and stormy waters of the Roompot. They waited: the appointed trysting hour was reached and passed, but no light shone from the murky void into which they were collectively gazing. They waited with mounting anxiety but still the unrelieved impenetrable seaward darkness remained. If they were not to be picked up they must give themselves time to return to their house of concealment before daylight. And so it was: up and over the dyke beside the Haamstede/Zierikzee road to face a return journey in their flimsy craft over that inland lake now experiencing the same weather as the angry Roompot.

Back at their observation house they waited throughout the next day, plagued with unanswered questions and faced with the decision that they must venture forth again that night on the assumption that an attempt would be made to rescue them. Fortunately, as darkness fell the intense efforts of their radio-operator resulted in the crackles and the communication linkage which he had been struggling to achieve. Again they crossed their Rubicon to the highway, then up and over it to the beach. This time the signal light did not fail them. This patrol was able to identify military personnel moving along the road and civilians during daylight but there was little activity at night.

The 'Cuckoo' operation proved a valuable information-gathering exercise and another was planned for a fortnight later. This would be a four-man patrol without radio under the command of Intelligence Sergeant Donald Gibson. Gibson wrote a detailed account of 'Cuckoo II'.

The hour is that when sea and sky rush together, when colour flies and leaves only black shapes to people the world. Our adventure is under way. We clamber off a truck in the little street of Colijnsplaat, sheltered by a 15 ft sea-dyke to northward from a roaring inshore North-Easter. A few lights flicker here and there: it is still winter in North Beveland and the leafless trees round the band-stand bend before occasional buffets of wind. Black figures emerge and recede into the darkness.

Timo goes off to report to the troop office while Bruin, David and I zip up our camouflage jerkins tight about our necks. I am full of times and map references: Bruin mocks our hopes with talk of sea-sickness tablets. I listen to the wind and the faint sound of the high tide on the seaward dyke. Shortly after, Timo returns and we walk along two by two. Our berets are pulled down close over our ears, our web belts are tight around us but we carry no arms, no Tommy guns, no grenades as we usually do, only haversacks, compasses, maps and two blankets among us. As we reach the top of the dyke we clutch our berets: the full blast of the wind smites us in the face. In the greying darkness nothing can be seen of Schouwen on the horizon. Dave mutters 'Himmelreich' ('Good God') – he uses German in preference to military exclamations – and I wonder as I look at the angry lapping water whether it will be possible to sail. An LCA rocks at her moorings just below us, and we learn that a lull is forecast, – – – and well it might be because the Roompot is a fickle water, now calm as a millpond, now squally to shipwreck. We go back to the Troop office and wait for four hours.

Now with the turn of the tide the wind has dropped. The sea, still restless after a day of turmoil, sports with our LCA as we move out and makes the cox take frequent bearings to check our course. For half an hour after we set sail we have hardly said a word. Beneath and behind us is the angry lapping of the water on our plywood sides and the small chug-chugging of the exhaust, scarcely heard above the wind. Over our heads from horizon to horizon a rush and swirl of rain-clouds courses like the chariots of Hell. Cox says something to the engineer: we slow down to walking pace: he peers forward with his night binoculars and returns to check his compass. Impelled by curiosity I too step up and peer over the gunwale to where my eyes, now dark adapted, seem to discern the low line of a sea dyke. Based on patrol sightings of the previous 'Cuckoo' we reckon to expect a possible enemy patrol about 2 a.m. The luminous hand of my watch says ten minutes to midnight. Cox calls me over and together we check the spot on the map, illuminated by a tiny spot of light from the engine house, the shape of the dyke ——, its angle ——, there is little enough to go by. We decide to cruise along for 200 yards: and there, sure enough, is what we want, an obtuse angled fold in the dyke. With throttle almost closed we drift along to the bank, turning slowly round to meet it, till with a shudder we grate on the stonework.

The others had been standing athwart the beam to keep us balanced and now gently scrambled on to the gunwale. This is ticklish as the craft rocks crazily, and stubbornly tries to drift away from the bank. Timo springs ashore and holds the rope. Then Bruin and I go overboard, but oh!; my heart aches at the thought of our clattering hooves on the stone dyke. With some whispering in the dark Dave manhandles over to us a large floppy bundle with which we struggle, trying hard to keep our footing: we take a chance and heave it to the grass on the top. Cox beckons me, and cupping his hands against my ear, promises to lie out to sea for half an hour, then, if no signal is given, will go back to Colijnsplaat, returning the next night at 3.30 a.m. Timo casts off throwing the rope deftly inboard and a small huddle of figures waves good luck to the LCA as it is whirled away by tide and wind out to sea. Turning, we retrace our steps to the dyke top.

The manoeuvring of that rubber dinghy gives no small trouble. In the endeavour to keep it from grazing the ground or the sea wall we must first take off haversacks: then with the utmost of exertion and prodigies of gymnastic skill heave it over the parapet wall at the top on to the eight foot metalled road on the other side. I doubt whether we stop to realise that we are standing on the main enemy road between the garrison commander at Haamstede and the town of Zierikzee: but we are, and to our infinite curiosity the interior of the island, previously only known from air photographs, opens out before us. We stare bemused at the salty waves lapping darkly against the landward side of the road and at the few odd lights which spring into our vision – careless black-out at Zierikzee, a car towards Haamstede and a searchlight beam raking among jumbled clouds above Brouwershaven on the north coast of the island.

Bruin and Timo are adept at inflating rubber boats so Dave and I move, one to the east and the other to the west, along the road to keep watch. Then for the first time it occurs to me that loneliness, man's inheritance and greatest dread, is upon me. Our enterprise is co-operative: we have taken thought against the loss of one, even two, of our four but one alone can do nothing. It is twenty minutes past twelve: we will still be on time: we return and don our haversacks. Our unstable craft has already been launched on the inland sea: I set my compass at 73°, its luminous paint glowing eerily. Timo steps into the boat and, losing his footing on the wet rubber, coggles it violently. I was thankful that there is no one within half a mile to hear the volley of rage and fear, for the wind carries that. Then Bruin, extending a leg like a ballerina, edges his way in and equipoise is restored. Dave and I check to make sure that no tell-tale equipment is left behind and take up our positions in the overladen vessel, its inside already ankle deep in water. A jolt, an uneasy slither, a gurgle as the paddles hit the water and we move away on 73°.

This is a nightmare island. We stop abruptly, the paddles holding water, as black shapes loom up out of the waves; twice the dead and menacing fingers of a noble tree drowned, once the long low roof of a barn with water lapping against the eaves and lowest gutters. Bruin talks facetiously of swimming round and round as we once did in the English Channel: I silence him with a curt word. David nudges me, pointing to the compass: we are two degrees off course and it takes infinite patience to persuade the round craft to go the way we want. A pile of driftwood comes floating by and is eyed suspiciously. We should be at our destination by now. Timo first draws my attention to it and there it is, the gable of a two storey house looming up against the lurid skyline, the first floor windows about a foot and a half above water level. Through one of them we go in.

Our tell-tale boat had to be hidden and we might all speedily have been detected and hastened to perdition had not Timo in a desperate circumnavigation of the house found a re-entrant part of the building facing away from the dyke where he stowed the boat. This required entry through the upstairs and this proved a far more formidable task than we had bargained for, our estimates of the water levels being too low. He had to land on a slippery roof crawling up to a little balcony from which he reached an upper window. Inside the house we were beginning to be alarmed for his safety when we heard a hammering at an upstairs window. Somebody yelled out, 'For heaven's sake Timo be quiet !' and indeed in that forlorn waste of water the sound seemed gigantic. Bruin scrambled upstairs and together he and Timo reappeared, Bruin laughing over some quiddity of speech which sent echoes like bats flitting to all the darkest corners of the house. It would not be till daylight that we would be able to discover what the inside of that house was like. We then made dispositions, enforcing

silence, the least possible movement, no smoking and a two hourly
watch until 6 a.m. when light would break and reveal our surroundings
more precisely. I took the first watch, it was then 1.45 a.m. and the
others made what comfort they could upstairs, three together with
two blankets on the wooden boarding of a bedstead. Silence had fallen
and I was left to myself staring through a first floor window in the
direction of the dyke. What was to be done in the darkness? Nothing
but stare and stare into the black of the night. I felt that nothing
could be done but partly from military habit, partly from a sort of
ascetic desire, I felt that there had to be a watch. By 2.15 I was uneasy
for I knew that any enemy night patrol would pass along the dyke
about 300 to 400 yards from us; but the hour was untroubled for no
flares went up through the darkness as had happened previously.

At times, standing or sitting among the debris of that uncharted
room I tried to think of similar night watches during the past year,
of the nights at la Grande Ferme du Buisson near Sallenelles, of the
barn at Goustranville close to Dozulé, of the acrid smell of mud on
the Somme, of night after night of uncertainty at Dunkirk – and at
times my mind, freed by the darkness from its earthly tenement, would
wander forth fantastically connecting up loose ends of thought. Once
I caught myself laughing at an incongruous situation my brain had
conjured up – then returning to reality I was convinced that I saw
movement out there in the black, but I knew the tricks which nervous
strain could work. The night was black and empty and I had nothing
to record save the tireless play of the searchlights over Brouwershaven
and once a bright flash over Zierikzee.

Bruin wakened us at 6 a.m. and with some reluctance we left the
warmth of our sardine tin bed. But the day was before us, and our
main task. The ground floor of our house was under water and the
staircase leading from the depths emerged in the centre of our first
floor and continued in narrower form to the two bedrooms above.
The first floor had been denuded of most of its useful furnishings –
it seemed to have consisted of two public rooms and two bedrooms
but one of the public rooms which we did not reach until we had
spanned a sunken bit of the floor with planking caused us to gasp.
Inside in incredible confusion lay all the amenities of an elegant
drawing room – oval-backed, tapestry-seated chairs, hand-worked
draught screens, china and glass, some smashed on the floor, a clock
and, wonder of all, a drawing-room grand piano. For a while we
simply stood and gaped. I bent down; the carpet, strewn with little
family treasures, greetings and birthday cards, was damp; a cold wind
blew through a broken window. It was Bruin who did it – – – but

his action was the unvoiced wish of us all: he stepped forward and solemnly touched the F sharp – – – a dull chug betokened the piano's dumbness, a year of damp had done its work.

During that long day we kept watch, two of us facing towards the dyke east and west, one upstairs commanding a view over the inland sea, while I went between collecting reports and logging events. Timo was our Acting Temporary Cook – he had once attended an utterly futile cookery course – and when he was so engaged I replaced him at his window. The day had dawned grey and cold but light and visibility improved during the morning. From Bruin's window upstairs there extended a spacious panorama of the island from the bleak white scrub-covered sand dunes of Haamstede to the west across an untidy waste of water which eddied and swirled aimlessly as the tide came and went, over to the massive silhouette of Zierikzee in the south-east, the steep pointed gateways, the four square hulk of the bell-tower and a huddle of red roofs among leafless trees. Here and there in the waters stood out the forky branches of dead trees and the red roof of a house and barns, while on the shifting luminous floor of the waters there moved hither and thither the flotsam of happier days, a stool, a mattress half unstuffed, empty bottles, straw, a lady's shoe – a melancholy sight so full of imaginative implications. Bruin, a dedicated sketcher, constructed a panorama of his view.

Our main objective was the dyke road. We desired a full day's loggings of the comings and goings along it with special reference to the presence of an Infantry Division. We were all aghast that morning to discover how near we really were to the dyke: the 400 yards had seemed quite a voyage in the dark; indeed we were so near that on David's suggestion we plastered on some green paint to break the outline of our faces should they be noticed at a window. We made ourselves as comfortable as possible but that was meagre comfort as the water level only a foot or so beneath our floor had reduced everything to a clammy dampness.

The world was slow to wake up that morning: a sort of Sunday calm prevailed with all its overtones of melancholy and bleakness and undertones of inactivity and rest. Some of the entries on our log that day were:

0850:   Two dyke workers clad in ragged clothes pass along East to West carrying spades and talking voluble Dutch which comes over to us quite clearly.

0917:   A fast staff-car cruises past W to E at 20 miles per hour and stops suddenly when about 400 yards past us. An officer dismounts – we are seized with apprehension – stands talking to another and pointing out to sea, then turning towards the flood surveys it with his field glasses, swinging round in a broad sweep and finishing with our house. I have an intense impression of being observed. Then he turns towards Zierikzee. Dave and I have a go at him with our glasses – he is undoubtedly a staff officer – but the head of the other prevents us from seeing him clearly.

0926:   All mount and depart.

1001:   Horse and cart loaded with tables, W to E.

1025:   Two soldiers in service green approaching W to E apparently examining wire and other defences on the seaward side. They stop almost opposite us pointing – so it seems to us – and argue.

1031:   They sit down on a stone banking facing us – uniform of a German Infantry division. They compare notebooks or photographs – laughter.

1040:   They throw stones at driftwood between us and the dyke. Their insignia are quite clear; they belong to a signals section.

1044:   They compete in throwing stones toward our house.

1049:   They move away to the east.

1053:   W to E a small military van, driver in same uniform.

1134:   A woman and a man in peasant clothes come along W to E, stop about 500 yards from us; remove some loose slabs of stone, place a bundle on the ground and gently replace the stone on top.

1151:   They go away.

1212:   Noise heard from E, perhaps motor engines.

1216:   Convoy of vehicles approaching E to W, 4 trucks emblazoned with a small Seahorse emblem. The large truck is laden with ?105 mm ammunition, the van with wooden equipment of some kind.

1310:   NCO on bicycle E to W.

1323:   Two young women on bicycles E to W.

1352:   Sounds of horse transport.

1402:   Three open carts full of soldiers in marching order, possibly 23 of them altogether with cooking utensils, E to W; there seems to be a unit moving in. The soldiers point to objects as if they were novelties.

1435:   Staff car returns E to W, again stops almost opposite us. Staff officers and three others dismount. The three wear a Seahorse on their insignia.

1439:   They fire revolver shots at floating driftwood: one junior officer is a good shot.

1446:   Pointing to our house they all fire at the upstairs window. All miss and try again. The young officer puts a shot through it – crash of glass above us, laughter from the dyke.

1450:   They climb in and drive on W.

1512:   NCO and two soldiers on bicycles W to E – no seahorses.

1520:   Covered truck ? ammunition E to W.

1525:   Woman on bicycle W to E.

1549:   Puffs of smoke from Zierikzee – sounds of shell-fire.

1618:   Horse truck laden with sacks E to W.

1629:   The two gossiping soldiers return E to W, this time without stopping.

The dark hours were upon us again and the log became a record of sounds with long periods of silence. After tea we separated, two and two, facing each direction as the nervous strain of being alone upstairs was too heavy. We were all cold, mostly silent; the waiting seemed interminable. The only event that we could remember was that about 9.15 p.m. sounds of a largish motor vessel could be heard out to sea. At about 10 p.m. Bruin and David were told to go to bed upstairs, now somewhat less comfortable since the window was broken. The night drove on, Timo and I sitting close together, silently staring at the luminous air, listening to the modulations of the wind or the occasional swirls of the watery domain beneath us.

Said Timo suddenly, 'I'm worried about that rubber dinghy'.
I shivered; his voice was the very telepathy of my own thoughts.
After a moment he said, 'I think she's leaking a bit'.
'Yes' said I, 'I had a look at her this afternoon'.
A long pause followed.
'Maybe its just splashes over the side' he said.
I: 'I don't think so'.
He: 'in that case she won't carry four of us'.

I, sounding his thoughts; 'Need to make two journeys then?'.

He, after a pause, 'Difficult to time that; what if we miss the boat? we've no more food'.

I:'Then we'll set out earlier and two can lie up on the bank while the second journey is made'.

But it wasn't easy. We were all up at 1 a.m. but partly through the darkness of the night and partly through the wind we could not get the boat manoeuvred out of that quiet harbour. At 2 a.m. we were suddenly illuminated by a flare sent from some 200 yards along the dyke. By good fortune we were still behind the house as the world suddenly burst into an eerie glow of greenish light, dropping slowly over our statuesque forms till it went out with a soft phut. But the patrol was not satisfied: up went another flare: we cowered against the walls, listening to the crunch of feet on the dyke – for the wind was still. After a time the danger had passed and the rubber dingy was brought round to the 'landing stage'.

I said to Timo, 'Take this torch; if the LCA returns before second return of the rubber boat, show it green once then push off to Colijnsplaat'.

Timo replied, 'It won't be necessary', then somewhat inconsistently, 'We could come back next night at the same time'.

Turning to Dave, I put my hand on his shoulder, 'You stay Dave: if necessary you and I can — '. There was no need to complete the sentence.

'Right' he said quietly, knowing that he was forechosen.

The voyage was completed with three of us and continuous baling out. Timo and Bruin, together with a copy of the log which Bruin had made before night fell, as well as his panoramas, sketches and other informative articles were put ashore at 2.40 a.m.

I set out on the return at 73° but soon found that it was an awful task to move single handed on a fixed bearing. Perhaps the mind had already admitted the fixity of the about-to-be but I knew as I once more sailed up under the shadow of our house that it was going to be too late. Paddling up to the landing stage I called up to David. 'You'll need to paddle round to the back' he whispered hoarsely, 'tide's too low now'.

When I got round to the quiet harbour he was waiting for me. 'Too late' he said, 'The green light's just gone'.

It was 8.30 by my watch when we awoke. There was no particular trouble about food: we had two bars of chocolate and ten cigarettes but as the latter were of no use to us we wrapped them up and put them in a dry spot for some unimaginable future use.

We had no grease paint left and therefore kept well back from the windows. We maintained a watch upstairs in the two rooms, but at times sat together facing the dyke. The day was bright, almost attractive, but towards evening rain clouds came up from the West. The day's log, patiently recorded, resembled that of the previous day. Ample confirmation of the 'Seahorse' Division was given: more truck loads of 105mm ammunition passed E to W: the peasants who had so mysteriously buried an object returned, dug it up and continued on past us to Zierikzee. Then darkness fell once more about 5 p.m. and once more we abandoned the watch to wait.

We watched the blackness fall, and almost the last record in our log was of a German NCO on a bicycle W to E who dismounted and gazed through binoculars, first to the right of us over the flood, then at us most intently. I don't suppose he really could see us, but he fixed his glasses, now on the room below, now at our window, then stowed them away and rode off. I suppose it was chiefly the lack of food – we had eaten nothing all day – possibly the chill and damp confinement of our quarters, but from that moment we did not leave one another. At times there were short conversations: sometimes half an hour passed without a word being uttered. Then it began to rain out of the blackness, reverberating the moving waters which hissed angrily.

At the appropriate hour Donald and Dave set out in their leaky rubber dinghy. Baling out throughout the journey they duly reached the dyke, managed to heave the sodden dinghy over it, and were picked up at 3.30 a.m. A few days later a third 'Cuckoo' operation was successfully mounted

The 'Postal Bomber'

The spotter Auster aircraft had an official and an unofficial purpose. As it circled to gain height preparatory to attempting to spot enemy artillery positions or other targets on Schouwen it flew over the various positions occupied by 47 RM Cdo troops. On the days when it was flying, an exercise depentent on the weather, this was a wonderfully easy way to distribute the mail and the pilot was happy to oblige. But his job was made much easier if he had someone in the second seat beside him to throw the mail out of the window. When the opportunity was offered I couldn't resist it. Off we went with the bundles of mail well tied up, separately identified on my knee with the Auster's sliding, plastic window beside me open, ready for action. The pilot knew his 'bombing' runs well and at the appropriate moment gave the order to 'post'. Down dropped the bundle of mail to the 'landing zone' where khaki-clad figures were poised ready to dash to receive it as it bumped along on the landing place. The high point of their day had arrived.

The pilot assured me that there was no risk in flying with him as he was the last person any enemy anti-aircraft guns would fire at – he would promptly identify the enemy artillery position and bring down the fire of the North Beveland artillery on it. And so it was. We flew over the Roompot unmolested and looked down on Zierikzee and the Haamstede-Zierikzee road and beyond over the hinterland of a pathetic water-filled island dotted with water-destroyed dwellings stretching away to Brouwe-shaven in the north and Haamstede in the west. Only a few wisps of smoke from some of the unflooded houses suggested human habitation. A solitary German soldier was walking along the critical section of the Haamstede/Zierikzee road at the point where it passed close to the sea.

A Booby Trap

One day I received a message that a soldier in another unit had been seriously wounded by a booby trap which had gone off when he opened a door in a cupboard under a stair in a house near Kortgene. He was trapped in the building. Arriving there I found that not only had the explosion injured the soldier but that it had also demolished the lower part of the stone stair which formed the roof of the cupboard, and that that had fallen on him. His left leg was trapped under a mass of heavy stone steps and bricks. Some of the higher steps of the staircase, attached only at one end to a tottering, leaning wall, hung menacingly above him like a series of Damoclean swords.

The man at first appeared to be dead with a corpse-like facial pallor resulting from the layer of fine dust generated by the explosion covering everything around, but examination revealed that he was not dead although barely conscious. His left leg had been virtually severed: the femur (thigh bone) had been broken and much of the tissue of the lower two-thirds of his leg seriously damaged. The loss of his left leg was inevitable but he could not be extracted from the masonry which trapped him unless the damaged part of his leg was cut off: it would have taken time to remove the masonry which anchored his leg and any attempt to do so might have brought down the unstable stone-work and brick-work hanging threaten-ingly over the proceedings.

The only solution was to do an urgent *in situ* operation and detach him from the crushed, trapped part of his leg. There was no time or call for surgical finesse. Kneeling beside him, and without anaesthetic or sedation, I cut away the frayed remains of his battle-dress trouser leg and, with a pair of scissors, severed the leg at mid thigh below the upper end of the fractured femur. As the scissor blades closed there was good deal of sandy grinding due to the mortar which the explosion had blasted into his wounds. He seemed to feel little but when I cut his sciatic nerve he let out a loud scream and then lapsed back into semi-consciousness. I was back to the pre-anaesthesia era of surgery. As so often happens in such circumstances there was little bleeding; shock lowers the blood pressure, and the tearing of blood vessels – his main femoral artery had been torn by the explosion – is associated with better contraction and more rapid blood clot formation than cutting with surgical instruments. Urgency demanded minimum clean-up and bandaging and, beginning to show some signs of recovery, he was taken by the 'Sallenelles jeep' across the Zandkreek by the top-heavy ferry and thence to Bergen-op-Zoom.

The Ambush

Armed now with greater knowledge of the enemy but frustrated by the inability to interrogate a prisoner it was decided to lure a German patrol on to the Haamstede-Zierikzee road at night. The operation would be codenamed 'Magnet'. The date was 11th April 1945. The enticement had to be such that it would be unlikely to be ignored. The night was dark and a dory would be sent out to a point, just offshore, somewhat west of the place where the ambush party, travelling by LCA, would land and position itself on the critical stretch of the road close to the shore. At the agreed time the dory, by firing off flares and a rocket, would create a disturbance which, it was hoped, the enemy would feel bound to investigate. The dory would then depart. Meanwhile the LCA which had landed the ambush party would withdraw into the off-shore darkness to await a signal from the ambush party to come in to take them off, hopefully with a prisoner.

On Schouwen the Germans had very little motor transport and relied largely on horses and carts. The dory had hardly done its work than the ambush party, just landed and grouped below the sea wall and the road beyond, heard in the distance the sound of a horse and cart approaching from the Haamstede direction. Captain Carey in charge recognised that the time interval since the dory had created a disturbance was so short that the near presence of the horse and cart must be fortuitous: in any case an investigative patrol would not use a noisy horse and cart as its means of transport. As the patrol waited and the horse and cart drew nearer it was soon evident that the sound being heard was not that of one set of cart wheels grinding on the road but of many carts and as they approached there was added to the noise of the grinding wheels the sound of voices, soldiers' voices – the carts were full of German soldiers. Carey realised that his small group could not attack a large body of troops and fulfil his orders to bring back a prisoner. Even if they succeeded in taking a prisoner without themselves being captured or killed in the process there would be no chance of the landing craft being able to come in and take them off in the face of a large body of German troops overlooking the point at which the landing craft would have to touch down.

Confident that a patrol would be sent out to investigate the disturbance caused by the dory Carey waited, his group flattening themselves against the seaward side of the sea wall knowing that the horses and carts would pass along the road just above their heads. As they waited the column of carts creaked and groaned towards them and was soon clattering above them. To Carey it seemed that 'the whole of the Wehrmacht was out on a night exercise in horses and carts'. The column was passing, however, and soon would be on its way ——. But no! – one cart was stopping. It ground to a halt just above the patrol, still flattened like a row of tailors' dummies against the sea wall, collectively holding breath, critically alert to the need not to allow any bit of equipment to clank or scrape. Was it that they had been spotted and that grenades were about to be thrown down on them or enfilade fire rip into them? A certain amount of movement of feet could be heard in the road above. There was a moment's silence and then the patrol's second-in-command heard an ominous shuffling noise, right above him – someone was approaching the seaward edge of the road. He tensed, there was nothing more that he could do but wait for whatever was now inevitable ——. Then it happened. Something was dropping from above. There was a barely discernible swishing noise. But no, it could not be the feared grenade: it was too slow for that. And then it hit him with a splash. It was fluid, it was warm, and it smelt a little. It did not take him many seconds to identify its source, the bladder of a German soldier standing above him. He stoically maintained immobility and silence until the last drop of the pernicious fluid had soaked into his beret and his battle-dress. His patience was rewarded. A further shuffle from above, a guttural voice and a jerk prefaced the resumption of a cartwheel grind, as one member of the Wehrmacht proceeded more comfortably on his way.

Confident still that a German patrol would appear, Carey waited, the patrol positioned at the roadside at the ready. His confidence was rewarded. Footsteps were heard approaching, the steps not of one man but of several. Weapons were pointed at the as yet unseen patrol. As the sound of the footsteps drew closer waiting eyes strained into the darkness. Yes – the shadowy outlines of soldiers in single file carrying rifles were approaching. Nearer they came and then, crack!, a shot rang out – crack!, crack!, crack! Three Germans lay dead on the road and one, apparently injured, was seized. The alarm would now have been sounded and a large body of the cart-travelling troops was nearby: it was time to withdraw quickly. At the pre-arranged signal the LCA closed the shore and the patrol, now lifting their prisoner, scrambled aboard – and from the German point of view disappeared into the darkness which shrouded the Roompot.

The prisoner was delivered to the RAP in the early hours of the morning: he was said to have 'refused to speak'. The reason for that was soon very evident. He had been shot in the head, was now unconscious and exhibiting the evidence of brain damage which left little doubt that he would shortly be included in the German lists of 'killed in action'. He died a few hours later, one of the last passengers on the 'Beveland Bus' – and carrying the posthumous distinction, if it can be called that, of being the last of the 400 or so battle casualties to be dealt with at 47 Royal Marine Commando's RAP since 6th June 1944.

The End

It was now evident that the war was drawing to an end and although there was no official relaxation of the duties which the commando was ordered to fulfil this undoubtedly affected the rigour with which Col Donnell sought to apply the orders he had received. He had no desire that one of his marines should be among the last, in Europe, to be killed in the Second World War.

On 7/8th May, the war was over, and 47 RM Cdo was given a final operational rôle, acceptance of the surrender of the Schouwen garrison. Crossing the Roompot it was difficult to dissociate the coastline of Schouwen ahead from the sinister significance it had held for the past few weeks. First stop was the German Headquarters at Haamstede where the local Commander formally surrendered. The assembled company of officers and men was disarmed and paraded outside. They were to be marched from Haamstede along the main road to Zierikzee passing along, on the way, that strip of the road bordering the sea which had been the object of so much attention by the 'Cuckoo' patrols and the site of the recent bloody killing of the type which war demands. Standing at the roadside as the column marched off to a captivity which would be short-lived I studied the reactions of these defeated troops. The remnants of a once all-powerful army, for long the ruthless masters of this peaceful island were now impotent. The tall bespectacled officer in charge, holding the lead of a dog which was walking in front of him, held his head high, carried himself arrogantly and looked steadfastly to the front. He marched his men correctly but looked uncomfortable to be under the command of the four attendant marines who were now his masters. He did not let his eyes rest on the one or two Dutch peasants who appeared rather nervously, as yet apparently unable to throw off their fear of those who for so long had subjected them

The Schouwen garrison surrenders.

The commander now led by his dog.

The first of those who had had to flee Schouwen during the occupation set off from Colijnsplaat to return to Schouwen.

to draconian administrative regulations and, should they fail to implement these, persecution or death.

Among the bystanders, however, there was one young Dutchman who was very conscious of the persecution and death which these departing remnants of the 'master race' had brought to the island. His interest amounted to much more than curiosity. He was not motivated by fear but, on the contrary, by a much more positive emotion – revenge. As he was taken across the Roompot in the 'Beveland Bus' which was now made available to returning Schouwen citizens he indicated what his mission was. Along with his brother he had been involved in resistance activities on the island. He had escaped to North Beveland but his brother had been arrested and executed. The young man knew the identity of the German officer involved and was bent on retribution. If the officer concerned was in that column it was as well that the marines were there because the young man was armed and the officers in the column were not. Paradoxically the marines were now protecting the 'enemy' whose members they had shot dead a few days previously. Was it that the arrogance of some of these officers was a mask for fear, the fear of summary execution by civilians? The German other ranks were much more relaxed. They looked about them, some smiled, some were surreptitiously communicating with each other: the war was over and they had survived.

Chapter Fifteen

The Dishoek Affair

K ILLING and wounding are the business of the armed forces but most civilised nations accept that indiscriminate killing in warfare is not justified and that the practice of war despite its basic aim of overcoming an enemy should be regulated by agreed rules as prescribed in the Geneva Convention. Not all civilised countries have observed these rules and Germany, at times, did not do so in World War II. Hitler flouted the Geneva Convention with his order of 1942 that captured commando soldiers should be interrogated and then shot. At the Nuremberg trials Keitel, Hitler's Chief of Staff, had to confess to the illegality of Hitler's order, but many German military commanders in the field ignored it – at some risk, as Hitler demanded 'returns' of such executions – and Rommel is said to have torn up the order.

An accusation that the Commanding Officer of a British commando shot unarmed German officer prisoners in cold blood after they had been captured and disarmed would be a very serious charge. One such, made against 47 Royal Marine Commando 50 years after the war was over, had to be formally investigated.

The Bodies at the Searchlight Position

As indicated in Chapter 8, 47 RM Cdo had to withdraw from Battery W11 on the dunes near Dishoek on the night of 2nd November 1944 and moved back 400 yards close to what was designated 'the searchlight position', a circular platform with a metal stand built into its centre which looked as if it had been used as the mounting for a searchlight. The commando had lost five out of six of its troop commanders and required to reorganise before resuming the assault. Major Donnell, the Second-in-Command and the Adjutant Captain Spencer went forward to reorganise the withdrawn commando. While the commando was in that position, during the night of 2/3 November, a German counter-attack was launched against it. The attack was beaten off, as was a later attempt that night to infiltrate the position. No German prisoners were taken during these encounters. Donnell and Spencer remained with the troops near the searchlight position during the night with a view to leading the resumption of the assault on Battery W11 next day. Next morning (3 November) before the renewed assault began they found the bodies of two German officers close to the searchlight position. Maj. Donnell, a man of great honesty and objectivity 'had every reason to surmise that they were shot by their own men' and he confirmed this in a letter which he sent to Major General Moulton on 3 June 1974. The bodies of the two German officers were later revealed as those of Oberleutnant Helmut Lange and Leutnant Dr Bernhard Eschershausen.

When 47 Cdo had completed its task of overcoming the German defences between Zoutelande and Flushing on 3rd November it had a 'clearing up' task to perform described in the official report written at the time:

> The rest of the days at Walcheren were spent recovering and burying the dead, tending the wounded, guarding the POWs of whom a certain number were formed into a fatigue party under a very competent Feldwebel (i.e. a German army sergeant, not a German marine).

This fatigue party was responsible for the temporary burial of the German dead.

The Buried Thirteen

In 1981 a local historian, W. P. Roose, from Koudekerke near Dishoek, investigated a photograph taken at Vijgeeter by a photographer named as van Wolferen. The photograph was of the graves of 13 German soldiers. Over each grave was a wooden cross and a German helmet. Over the graves a crude wooden board headed with, 'FONDEN HIER DEN HELDENTOD' ('They Found Here a Hero's Death') had a single date on it, 3 November 1944, and gave the names of those buried. Among the names were those of Oberleutnant Lange and Leutnant Eschershausen.

Roose tracked down two Dutch brothers, Local Council Workers of Koudekerke (names and addresses given), who had been involved in the reburial of these bodies. The brothers had been ordered on Sunday 5th November to go to a point on the dunes at Kaapduin, below Battery W11, where a number of partially buried bodies of German soldiers were lying. They lifted the bodies and reburied them at Vijgeeter. One feature that surprised the two grave-diggers was that all 13 of the bodies appeared to have been shot in the neck and showed no other injuries. Among the bodies the grave-diggers recognised two as those of Kapt. Terlinden and Ob. Lt Lange, two Marine Officers particularly noted for their harsh discipline.

Roose then tracked down five other local citizens (all specified by name and address) who lived in the area and had had some contact with German soldiers serving at W11. Four of these five local citizens had also seen the German bodies as they lay at Kaapduin.

There were two groups of German servicemen at W11, namely the marines who comprised over 80 per cent of the personnel, and the soldiers. The soldiers were infantrymen and it would appear that they were of a lower calibre than the marines. They had complained about the fanaticism of the Marine Officers at Battery W11 and had expressed their dislike, even hate, of them. Two of the infantrymen who expressed this animosity had indicated that when the time came the marine officers would be 'removed' or 'killed'.

One of those among the 13 in the grave was recognised by a husband and wife (names and address given) as Heinrich Höfel a 19 year old German marine Lance-Corporal whom they had befriended. He spoke good Dutch and may have had a Dutch mother. He would listen to Radio Oranje at his hosts' home. He had told them, without giving specific reasons, that his German comrades did not trust him and that he was very afraid of what they might do to him. He tried to make arrangements that when the time came he could borrow a civilian suit and mix with local farm-workers. It would appear that there were those among the German soldiers who represented an ominous threat to those whom they did not like.

In 1990 two young Dutch historians H Sakkers and J H Houterman published a book entitled 'Atlantikwall in Zeeland en Vlaanderen' ('Atlantic Wall in Zeeland and Flanders'). In this they put forward their interpretation of the circumstances surrounding the deaths of Lange and Eschershausen (English translation by J H Houterman):

> Not until October 1981 did Mr W. P. Roose make known in an article in the journal of the Haemkundige Kring Walcheren, 'De Wete', the remarkable story that in battery Dishoek the Germans were presumed to have liquidated their own officers. Something that would have been possible because 30 infantrymen had been added to the battery, possibly in addition to the soldiers who were withdrawing. These infantrymen had practically no wish to continue fighting, certainly not in comparison with their comrades in the Marines. These men were supposedly forced to fight by their Marine officers. This could have been a motive for getting rid of their superiors to obtain a quicker surrender. Thus saving their own skin. The only thing not clear about this way of reasoning was the question how the infantrymen were able to kill the 'cadre'(?)[1] without any resistance, after all the total naval crew must have amounted to 150 men. If, however, one reads the report about the experiences of 47 RM Commando, written by Lt Col Phillips and the K.T.B.[2] of the Adm. Ndl.[3] the arguments become somewhat doubtful. Phillips writes about fierce fighting in which on the side of the Allies one officer died and six were wounded. In the other ranks the proportion of dead to wounded is 25–45. It is

---

[1] Controlling officers   [2] Action Report   [3] German Admiral of the Netherlands

easily possible that these high losses caused a lust for revenge among
the Commandos which led to the execution of the two officers of the
battery, namely Ob. Helmut Lange and Lt Dr. Bernard Eschershausen.
A defence that offers so obstinate a resistance, and with this (is)
capable of bringing about so many heavy losses of the enemy, finally
does not decide to murder its own officers. The intensity of the fighting
compelled the respect of the German Marine Command so greatly
that they mentioned the battery because of their fighting spirit
especially in a war diary report dated 9th January 1945. Phillips'
reports make no mention at all of the dead officers. This is surprising
because these people would have negotiated the surrender of the
battery. If the Germans would have killed their own officers, the
commanders no doubt would have realised the fact as the bodies of
the two officers showed that they were killed by a neck shot. Probably
they would have tried to find out if this was a mutiny or not, as there
were plenty of eye witnesses.

Although on the British side the death of the two officers was never
mentioned, on the German side something was known. Kapt. Robert
Opalka, commander of M.A.A. 202,* was made a prisoner of war in
Oostkapelle. During his POW time, he wrote a letter, on 24th February
1948, to Marinepersonal-Dokumentenzentrale in Hamburg. From
correspondence with the widow Frau Eschershausen, he learned that
she had a photograph of the grave near Vijgeeter where, among others,
the officers were buried. It surprised him that the 'cadre' (?) of the
battery had died and he requested an explanation from the 4
Commando Brigade. Also he would try and obtain details from the
NCOs of the battery. Unfortunately a later report could not be found.
Also a search for Opalka led to nothing.

An alternative, suicide, is most doubtful owing to the shots in the
neck. At any rate it is sure that two officers in the battery Dishoek
died because of this. Whether either the Germans or the British
Commandos were responsible is very hard to say for sure with the
documents available. Considering the documents, the author of this
publication is inclined to put the suspicion on the disadvantage of the
British.

It was some time before the 'suspicion' being voiced by Sakkers and
Houterman became known to former members of 47 RM Cdo ('Atlantikwall
in Zeeland en Vlaanderen' was published in Walcheren, in Dutch). The
suspicion expressed by Houterman and Sakkers was considered by ex-
members of 47 RM Cdo to be quite false and, lacking any justifiable factual

* Marine Artillery

basis, to be little more than capricious speculation and biassed innuendo by writers who had a very distorted and naive understanding of the realities of the battlefield. In the light of this, of the disapprobation expressed by other commentators in Walcheren about the views of Sakkers and Houterman and because of the friendship, goodwill and mutual respect between British servicemen who had served in Walcheren and the citizens of Walcheren – as expressed in the organisation generously established by the Dutch, the 'Foundation to Support the Liberators of Walcheren' – no action was taken.

It was later learnt that previously (1st February 1989) a Dutch journal (re the forthcoming publication of 'Atlantikwall in Zeeland en Vlaanderen') had published a photograph of Sakkers along with a statement by him to the effect that, in contravention of the Geneva Convention, German prisoners of War had been murdered by Allied soldiers at Walcheren. When 'Atlantikwall in Zeeland en Vlaanderen', was published a year later it was evident that it was 47 RM Cdo which had been referred to although this statement had been toned down to a 'suspicion' of murder.

A Mysterious Story

In 1994 a letter was sent by Houterman – not to any former member of 47 RM Cdo but to a former officer of another commando – which purported to provide further evidence in support of his and Sakkers' views and now contained a serious and specific allegation. This letter was one which could not be ignored and was the subject of formal investigation by the relevant authorities. It referred to information said to have been obtained a year or so after the publication of 'Atlantikwall in Zeeland en Vlaanderen' and included:

> A year or so after publication of our book we were informed that there had been a Dutch eyewitness to the Dishoek incident. He did not want to have direct contact with us nor would lay down anything in writing for he did not want to discredit our liberators in any way. His observations were, however, passed to us in some detail. From the dunes the Dutchman had seen a vehicle arriving at the battery, from which an officer got off. This officer approached the gathered POWs, took out the two officers, let them kneel, and cool bloodedly shot them in the neck. The Dutchman later met that same officer, and learned it was Lt Col Phillips. This 'eyewitness account' has no legitimacy whatever but it is a confirmation of our suspicions.
>
> We have never elaborated any further on the Dishoek incident although we are still very keen to know what happened. —— I have no new evidence and cannot prove a thing. It is certainly no zest in

pointing a finger at the 'guilty one', but merely historical interest to know what happened ... We all know that atrocities take place in war, on both sides. Stating that 'liberators' were such fine men who did nothing wrong and saying that 'occupying forces' were all bastards, would be sticking your head in the sand. I think it is the task of us historians of a post-war generation to put things into some perspective, only not forgetting for which cause one fought.

My coming study will not be just a 'blind' tribute to our liberators; certainly some points of criticism will be uttered about mistakes, things that went wrong etc. I hope though that there will be no doubt as to my gratitude to those men of foreign nationalities who fought and sometimes gave their lives, for a cause, even not directly theirs, that, however, enables me to live today in a free and democratic West European society.

The Refutation

- Col Phillips could not confront the charge of murdering two German officer POWs in contravention of the Geneva Convention. It was brought fifty years after the capture of Battery W11, when he was dead.
- The bodies of the two German officers thought to have been murdered by their own men were seen by Major Donnell and Captain Spencer on the morning of 3rd November before the final attack on the W11 battery. These two German offices could not therefore have been present at the surrender of Battery W11 and could not have been executed after that by Col Phillips.
- There was no vehicular access to W11 on 3rd November 1944. This was prevented by the anti-tank wall (the anti-tank obstacles and ditch). The late Major Flunder of 48 RM Commando who was also present at the surrender of W11 confirmed in writing, 'that there were no vehicles of any description there'. It was due to the anti-tank wall preventing vehicles going beyond it that 47 Cdo's mortars, machine guns and ammunition had all to be manhandled forward from the anti-tank wall. For the same reason all the casualties from W11 had to be carried by stretcher-bearers over the long carry to the far (northern) side of the anti-tank wall before they could be loaded into any sort of vehicle.
- During the occupation of Walcheren the Germans banned local residents from the dunes. No member of 47 Cdo saw a civilian there and Major Flunder also confirmed this in writing – 'there were no Dutch civilians present at W11 when it was captured'. Mr Schat who lived beside the dunes near Dishoek throughout the German occupation of Walcheren confirmed that civilians were not allowed on to them.
- The means by which the unidentified informant – who would not put

anything in writing or make any contact – transmitted the story to Houterman must have been known. Why was this not revealed?

- There is no proof that the mysterious informant was a Dutchman, or existed.
- The implication that there was any negotiation about the surrender of W11 reveals ignorance of warfare and the realities of the battle for W11. There was no negotiation about the surrender of W11. Its defenders raised no white flag. They had only two choices, to fight to the last man or surrender unconditionally. No one negotiated with them. As the commandos overcame the machine-gun, mortar and rifle fire and the throwing of grenades from the outer defences of W11 and gained entrance to the main battery casemates, the defenders, faced with imminent slaughter put their hands up, laid down their arms, submitted to the orders they were given and were marched off as POWs.
- Front-line troops in action take little notice of ranks or regiments of prisoners. The priority is to disarm them and get them out of the battle zone. It is naively absurd to imagine that commanding officers in the middle of life and death battles go poking around examining corpses on the battle-field to ascertain the nature of their wounds. The capture of W11 on 3rd November was only the start of that day's battles. The commando immediately proceeded southward along the dunes and during the rest of the day captured all the positions down to the Flushing gap including Battery W4, the German Headquarters battery. Col Phillips' aim was to complete the task which he had been set (i.e. to clear the dunes down to the Flushing gap) as quickly as possible. He could not, and did not, hang around dealing with prisoners who were left behind when the commando advanced to Battery W4 immediately after capturing battery W11. He was on his feet, not in a vehicle. It is equally nonsensical to suggest that in such circumstances he would be mounting an enquiry into a matter which had nothing to do with him, namely a possible mutiny among elements of the German forces.
- When W11 was captured there were not only many German prisoners at the battery site but also many 47 RM Cdo officers, and marines who were guarding them. It was daylight. If Col Phillips had executed anyone, there is no way in which such an action would be unknown throughout 47 RM Cdo. If German soldiers had witnessed such an action, knowledge of it would be widely available in Germany.
- Col Phillips was a highly professional regular officer of the Royal Marines, a Corps with very high disciplinary and ethical standards. The suggestion that he would flout the Geneva Convention and carry out an illegal execution which would be observed by so many, both of the

enemy and of his own commando, and inevitably lead to his being court-martialled and disgraced is ridiculous.

- As Col Phillips had arrived on the island only 24 hours before and had been constantly engaged in running a battle on dunes to which access by Dutch civilians was forbidden, it is highly unlikely that any Dutch civilian was in a position to meet and recognise him.

- It is implied that the two German officers found by Donnell and Spencer could not have been shot on the night of the German counter-attack on 2/3 November by 30 disgruntled infantrymen, because the latter were out-numbered by 150 fanatical naval personnel. This may not be true. If, as would be logical, the German infantrymen (as opposed to the German marines), led by the two naval officers, were called upon to carry out the counter-attack on the night of 2/3 November, the setting was one – with the disgruntled infantrymen now separated from the 150 fanatical marine personnel at W11 – which would provide disaffected troops with the chance to liquidate their officers and pretend that they had been killed in the counter-attack.

- On 14 November 1986 the Deutsche Dienststelle für die Benachrichtigung der nächesten Angehörigen von Gefallen der ehemaligen deutschen Wehrmacht (German Department for informing the next-of-kin of persons of the former German army killed in action) replied to a letter it had received from Mr Hans Sakker, dated 17 July 1986, with the following statement:

> We can merely confirm that according to the declarations (in particular of the Commander of the Marine Artillery Unit 202) all officers of the 8 Battery (Coastal Battery Dishoek) were killed in action.

Major Opalka was that Commander. In 1948, after correspondence with Frau Echerhausen he had indicated that he would contact the NCOs of Battery W11 and also 4 Commando Brigade regarding the death of her husband. It would have been very easy for him to contact the NCOs of Battery 11 who would be well known to him. These NCOs would have been well aware of any execution, carried out by a British officer, which had taken place at W11. They would hardly have remained silent about such a crime but might well have done so had their own men been involved. There is no evidence that Opalka did contact 4 Commando Brigade. If he had already discovered that his own men had been involved he would have had good reason for not doing so.

- Sakers' accusatory 1989 statement, and that in 'Atlantikwall in Zeeland en Vlaanderen' which he made along with Houterman, were made after

Sakkers had received the official 1986 letter from the German military
authorities. In the light of Opalka's declaration and the circumstances
surrounding it, it seems inconceivable that the interpretation which
Sakkers and Houterman sought to put on the dubious uncorroborated
information available to them from an unidentified Dutchman about
whose story they had merely been 'informed' could be considered to
have any validity.

- Thus over a period of 42 years, despite the enquiries which had been
carried out during that time, nothing had been discovered by the relevant
agencies in Germany which gave any credence to the so-called Dutchman's story. If Lange and Eschershausen had been executed by Col
Phillips as described, in front of so many German eye-witnesses who
would have returned to Germany after the war, knowledge of such an
event would have been widely known and testified in Germany. Troops
who have seen their fellow soldiers murdered illegally by their enemies
talk about it; those who have been involved in murdering their own
fellow soldiers do not. The original German burial party under the
charge of the German army sergeant would also return home and,
significantly, had not raised any issue of 'neck shots' and their possible
significance. They may well have had reasons for not doing so.

- The implication of the so-called 'neck shots' which are mentioned is
presumably that they were a method of execution – the Gestapo method
of a shot into the nape of the neck. All thirteen of the German corpses
reburied, including those of Lange and Eschershausen, were said to have
neck wounds and to show no other wounds. Also among these corpses
was that of another officer, Kapt. Terlinden, who was particularly fanatical and feared and who was stated by Houterman to have been killed
in action. This adds another strand of confusion and contradiction to
Houterman's analysis of the story. Neck shots in the case of Lange and
Eschershausen were interpreted as an indication of 'execution' yet in
the case of Terlinden and the others were compatible with being 'killed
in action'. Without better understanding of 'neck shots' and of their
exact nature any interpretation of their significance can be only speculative and arbitrary. The other 11 buried Germans, all with 'neck shots',
are ignored.

- The German POW working party which buried the thirteen could well
have been responsible for the board about 'hero's death' which was found
at Vijgeeter. If the thirteen had been murdered the epitaph could have
been designed to direct suspicion away from a matter into which they
did not wish any inquiry.

- The informant's reasons for seeking anonymity, that he 'did not want
to discredit our liberators in any way', are cynically hypocritical when

he was doing just that. To accuse a British Commanding Officer of murdering captured prisoners in cold blood in the manner described would inevitably bring the most serious discredit on that officer, on the Commando which he led and on the British Liberation Forces in general. If the story were an invention, anonymity would be the cloak behind which its perpetrator would seek to hide his deceit.

- All the evidence suggests that the uncorroborated, hearsay anecdote attributed to a mysterious, unidentified, uncontactable story-teller, whose existence or nationality has not even been proved or vouched for, was a complete fabrication.

- What is more surprising, and difficult to reconcile, is that self-styled 'historians of a post-war generation', while so overtly – but unconvincingly – expressing gratitude for what the liberating forces did, should seek to give any credence to such an apocryphal story and engage in so much biassed innuendo. It appears that while they pursued sources of information from 'the German side' (which provided no support for their story) they ignored the sources from the British side, namely the members of 47 RM Commando who were present at these events and from whom they could have obtained so much of the factual information which they required if they were to write responsibly. What, it might be asked, was the objective in purveying such a damaging story when there is no evidence to support it and so much to disprove it? What are we to think of historians who, in respect of this story admit that they 'cannot prove a thing' yet use the same completely unproved story as 'confirmation' of the grave accusation they make. Had not some of those who could refute the story still been alive to do so, the name of a distinguished British officer who was not alive to defend himself, and the unit he commanded, would have been disgraced. Presumptuously, Houterman makes the somewhat vainglorious statement that 'the task of us historians of a post-war generation is to put things into some perspective'. It is to be hoped that the perspective of those who claim the right to undertake such a task will be based on responsible and scholarly analysis of established facts, otherwise such 'historians' are going to distort and falsify history, not clarify it, and in the process shamefully discredit the part which individuals and regiments played in it when the opposite is their due.

- The Dishoek affair, and the story about it, leaves many unanswered questions but the conduct of Lt Col Phillips is not one of them.

Chapter Sixteen

Counting the Cost

W AR may alter the standing of nations, enforce the re-drawing of boundaries, cripple or benefit economies, transform relationships between countries and races and result in profound political, social and cultural change. Politicians may see war in terms of the broad strategies required for its conduct and the planning which will be necessary for the new order which it will create; lawyers may see it in terms of its legal basis and the courts and councils which will determine national and individual guilt and retribution; historians may see it in terms of its causation and the rich source of historical material which it will provide.

For those involved in war at the level of a fighting unit in close contact with the enemy, grandiose political, legal or historical concepts are likely to take a very secondary place, if they take any place at all. As the front-line soldier endures the day-to-day hardships and dangers to which war exposes him the 'bottom line' for most is the hope that he will do his duty, survive intact, return to an ordered and settled civilian life, protect and develop the emotional ties which bind him to others, obtain meaningful employment and enjoy the restoration of the right to order his own affairs. Overshadowing these prospects, however, while war continues, there is always the gloomy possibility that war, through injury, will remove or blight such hopes.

For military pedagogues in the classroom the realities of war are often encapsulated in phrases such as, 'death, disability and destruction are the currency of war'. This, of course, is true but fortunately, when the need came, there were plenty of young men in 1939–45 whose courage, loyalty, purpose, self respect, and sense of duty were such that they would discount the logic of such aphorisms, even if they heard them. They did so either voluntarily or on the basis that when the vagaries of military conscription consigned them to tasks which in the order of things carried high risks they would accept that without demur, complaint or attempt at evasion.

Casualty Philosophy

In purely military terms there are commanders who will order that in an attack no fit man must deviate from his attacking duties to help a wounded colleague lest that prejudice the chance of success of the attack. There is, of course, logic in this but the counter argument is that if a man feels that he will not be left unattended if wounded, his morale and his will to fight will be greater and his chance of survival, possibly to fight another day, increased. Also a man who leaves a wounded 'mate' can suffer severe guilt feelings. In practice there has to be a balance of judgement between these two philosophies often dictated by circumstances. There never was an order in 47 RM Cdo that wounded were to be left until an attack was over, and its medical officer was allowed to exercise a good deal of discretion as to how marines might be used as stretcher-bearers when the number of casualties swamped the established stretcher-bearer resources.

Casualties: Number, Nature and Risk

If death and disability are the currency of war a regimental medical officer might by analogy be considered the book-keeper of this currency as well as the medical executive. Each element of the fighting forces has its own task and the amount of risk attached to that task inevitably varies according to the nature of the task and the circumstances in which it has to be performed. The history of 47 RM Cdo, numbering 420 all ranks at full strength, provides some quantitative and qualitative measure of the risk of service in a commando in North West Europe in 1944.

CASUALTIES   47 RM COMMANDO, D-DAY (6TH JUNE 1944) TO
VE DAY (9TH MAY 1945)

Killed	*Wounded – evacuated*	*Wounded – not evacuated*	*Total wounded*	*Total casualties*
112* (26%)	284 (65%)	38 (9%)	322† (74%)	434† (100%)

* Excluding 4 personnel killed while attached to 47 RM Cdo, but including 8 members of 47 RM Cdo who were wounded but died later.

† Excluding three commandos wounded off the Norwegian coast by enemy air attack during pre-D-Day attachment of a section of 47 RM Cdo to the Shetlands: and excluding 7 personnel wounded while attached to 47 RM Cdo.

Including the numbers of wounded from other units treated at the 47 RM Cdo RAP the total treated for wounds (taking no account of the number of sick treated) would be approx. 400.

Casualties less severely wounded were dealt with at the RAP. Those severely wounded were first dealt with there then evacuated. Eight of those evacuated died subsequently 1, 1, 2, 3, 3, 7, 10 days and 6 months later: the evacuation of 4 of these was delayed, in one case for 36 hours when the commando was cut off in Port-en-Bessin and in the other 3 cases because they lay in cold wet conditions at the Westkapelle gap and died there, or at sea, during a belated evacuation when a storm prevented any evacuation of casualties for a period of 5 days. Thus 97% of the more seriously wounded casualties (i.e. evacuated) who were not killed outright survived, a result which can be attributed to early use of the first field dressing (every marine was trained in the use of the first field dressing), to the rescue from the battlefield as soon as possible of wounded who could not walk, to further care at the RAP and to rapid evacuation to Field Surgical Units or Hospitals. The casualty rate among those attached to 47 RM Cdo from other units, usually volunteers for such attachments, was high.

There are two obvious elements in a sea-borne landing, (a) the sea-borne period when the assaulting troops are approaching the landing beach and disembarking there and (b) the period when, now ashore, they are fighting on land. As far as 47 RM Cdo was concerned the relative sea-borne periods were at Port-en-Bessin and Walcheren on 6th June 1944 and 1st November 1944 and the corresponding land fighting days, 7th June 1944 and 2nd November 1944.

RATIOS OF KILLED TO WOUNDED IN THE SEA-BORNE PHASE AND THE LANDED PHASE, OF SEA-BORNE LANDINGS

6/6/44 + 1/11/44 (Sea-borne)		Ratio K/W	7/6/44 + 2/11/44 (Landed)		Ratio K/W
Killed (K)	28		Killed (K)	43	
Wounded (W)	23	1.2	Wounded (W)	122	0.35

Thus, while most casualties occurred in the land phase of these assaults the proportion of troops killed compared with that wounded was nearly four times as high during the sea-borne phases of assault landings – the chances of being hit were less but if hit, usually in a confined space, the chances of being killed or drowned were greater.

The majority of wounds from which the marines suffered were caused by shrapnel (from shells, mortar bombs, mines and grenades) and bullets. Other casualties resulted from drowning, immersion followed by hypothermia, burns, blast injuries and so-called 'battle shock'.

BATTLE INJURIES IN 263 SURVIVORS ATTENDING THE RAP OVER A 7-MONTH PERIOD*

Shrapnel wounds	62%	* The detailed medical records of those wounded but not the names were lost for the period following 12th January 1945. The records of all those killed were complete.
Bullet wounds	20%	
Near drowning/hypothermia	8%	
Blast injuries	4%	
Burns	3%	
Combat stress disorder ('battle shock')	3%	
	100%	

It is evident that many wounds are caused by the 'invisible enemy', the artilleryman, the mortarman out of sight, the mine-layer. The smaller number of bullet wounds in view of the array of machine guns and rifles with which the marines were confronted and which they overcame is a tribute to their fieldwork.

The sites of wounding among 247 wounded but surviving marines who sustained 293 wounds and in whom the location of wounds was clearly recorded, were as follows:

SITES OF WOUNDING   293 WOUNDS AMONG 247 WOUNDED

Leg and/or Foot (L)	85	35.0%
Trunk (T)	68	28.0%
Arm and/or Hand (A)	29	12.0%
Head and/or Neck (H)	27	11.0%
L+ T	8	3.0%
L + H	8	3.0%
T + A	6	2.0%
H + A	6	2.0%
L + A	3	1.0%
H + T	1	0.4%
H + A + L	2	0.8%
T + A + L	2	0.8%
L + T + A + H	2	0.8%
(293 individual wounds)	247	100%

The incidence among the 293 wounds – leg/foot region (38%), trunk (30%), arm/hand (17%) and head/neck (16%) – is in keeping with ground level explosion of most of the shells, mortar bombs, mines and grenades which infantrymen encounter.

The commandos attacked with fixed bayonets at close quarters on at least two occasions but did not themselves suffer from bayonet wounds: nor was there any evidence that the Germans did either although the imminence of a bayonet probably had a psychological effect on a defender.

Relative Risk of Different Commando Duties

Risk is an important consideration in military activities. Throughout the whole of World War Two (WWII) there were many in the Armed Forces who, not necessarily of their own volition, never heard a shot fired in anger or only heard one from a long way off. In contrast there were those who could serve for a short time and hear and experience many such shots. The danger of the duties performed and the duration of exposure to these determine an individual's position on the risk spectrum. An American involved in front-line soldiering recognised the striking distinction between those who 'did the fighting' and 'the world of the rear'; another commented,

Shrapnel: a large piece which just missed 47 RM Cdo's Medical Staff outside the Sallenelles RAP.

'we existed in an environment totally incomprehensible to men behind the lines'.

When a man becomes a casualty and is evacuated he has, of course, to be replaced and during the campaign in Europe 47 RM Cdo received about 330 replacements (in addition to those who later returned to their posts after recovering from their wounds) to try and keep its establishment up to strength – but often the commando was under strength for considerable periods. Risk has to be calculated in terms of the risk of serving in a particular *post.* Thus, over the eleven months of the commando's active service, in respect of the number of posts (417) many posts were occupied by 1, 2, or more individuals due to death or wounding and replacement. On a hypothetical model in which every man in the commando (i.e. in a commando post) had become a casualty once during the 11 month period, and had been replaced, the casualty rate would have been 100% (417/417 × 100). If, however, in one half of the commando two of the occupants of each post in that half had become casualties (208 × 2) and in the other half no occupant of a post had become a casualty there would still have been 416 (say 417) casualties within the over-all commando establishment i.e. again 100%: but this figure would conceal the marked difference in risk between the two halves. In 47 RM Cdo the element of risk varied considerably between different posts.

Casualty risk can be subdivided into risk of being killed or of being wounded and surviving. The table below shows the percentage risks to officers and other ranks occurring in different posts (i.e. 5 fighting troops, the heavy weapons troop [HW], the headquarters troop [HQ] and the medical section).

		Troop strength (posts)	Killed (K)	Wounded (W)	Casualties (K+W)
All Troops	Officers	24	10 (42%)	15 (63%)	25 (104%)
	Other ranks	393	102 (26%)	307 (78%)	409 (104%)
	All	417	112 (27%)	322 (77%)	434 (104%)
Fighting Troops (A, B, Q, X, Y)*	Officers	16	10 (63%)	12 (75%)	22 (138%)
	Other ranks	290	87 (30%)	250 (86%)	337 (116%)
	All	306	97 (32%)	262 (86%)	359 (117%)
Heavy Weapons Troop*	Officers	2	0 (0%)	1 (50%)	1 (50%)
	Other ranks	35	6[†] (17%)	12[‡](34%)	18 (51%)
	All	37	6 (16%)	13 (35%)	19 (51%)
HQ Troop*	Officers	6	0 (0%)	3 (50%)	3 (50%)
	Other ranks	60	8 (13%)	40 (67%)	48 (80%)
	All	66	8 (12%)	43 (65%)	51 (77%)
Medical Section[§]	All	16½	3[¶] (18%)	13[#](79%)	16 (97%)

* including troop RAMC medical orderly/stretcher-bearers.

† excluding 1 who was killed when acting as a replacement stretcher bearer with the medical section.

‡ excluding 5 wounded when acting as replacement stretcher-bearers with the medical section.

§ including padre (½ the time), medical officer, sergeant and 8 troop medical-orderly/stretcher-bearers RAMC, 2 RM stretcher-bearers, 2 medical-Jeep drivers and 2 MOAs.

¶ including 1 HW Troop other rank acting as a replacement stretcher-bearer with the medical section.

\# including 5 HW Troop other ranks acting as replacement stretcher-bearers with medical section.

Thus, for the commando as a whole, throughout its 11-month period of active service the average risk of becoming a casualty was 104% but the risk associated with service in different troops varied widely from 138% in officers in fighting troops to 50% among officers in the HW and HQ troops. Fighting troop officers experienced the highest risk of being killed (63%); they were twice as likely to be killed as other ranks in these troops; but the latter experienced a higher risk of non-fatal wounding (86%). The risks to medical personnel were higher than those to HW and HQ Troops and over-all came close to those of fighting troops. All these figures considerably underestimate risk, because there were unrecorded periods when the commando was considerably under strength and posts were not filled. The denominator in the calculations should therefore have been lower than that used.

Over the same period in the war in Europe the casualty figures reported for the 50th Division (with which 47 RM Cdo landed on the morning of

D-Day) were 16.5% for officers and 8.7% for other ranks killed, and 66% for officers and 50% for other ranks 'hit'.

Combat Stress Disorder (Battle Shock): Nature and Incidence

Marie-Louise Osmont (page 128) has given a graphic description of severe combat stress disorder. This revealed itself in 47 RM Cdo on D-Day + 1, in a marine who 'could not carry on'. He was an uninjured member of a group who came under fire, one being killed and 11 wounded; he lay trembling when he reached cover, spoke only in irrational terms and was reluctant to move again seeking only the asylum of the RAP.

Officers of 47 Royal Marine Commando – photograph taken a few days before D-Day.

Back row: Lt Wilson (FT) (wounded), Lt Whittaker (FT) (killed), Lt O'Brien (FT) (wounded), Capt Vincent (FT) (wounded), Lt O'Hare (HQ), Lt Leigh (HW), Capt Spencer (HQ), Lt Borne (FT) (killed), Lt Goldstein (FT) (wounded).

Middle row: Capt O'Connell (HW), Major Walton (FT) (killed), Capt Isherwood (FT), Capt Winter (FT) (wounded), Capt McCormick (FT) (wounded), Capt Stickings (FT) (killed), Capt Hughes (HQ) (wounded), Capt Lloyd (FT) (wounded), Capt Cousins (FT) (killed), Capt Tunnicliffe (Admin.)

Front row: Padre Haw (FT), Major Faecey (FT) (killed), Major Donnell (HQ), Col Phillips (HQ), Capt Wood (HQ) (wounded), Capt Wray (FT), Capt Forfar (HQ).

Inset: Lt Bennett (FT) (wounded).

Key: FT = Fighting Troop; HW = Heavy Weapons Troop; HQ = Headquarters Troop; Admin. = Administration.

At Sallenelles, during a heavy mortar attack a mortar bomb landed close to a marine but did not injure him. He lay on the ground, trembling all over, his eyes rolled up and he did not respond to being spoken to or being shaken. He remained in this state for two hours and then recovered but remained for days thereafter in an anxious, withdrawn state. The reality of battle was revealing in him a gross reaction from which none of his colleagues were suffering.

A regular sergeant, older than the rest, exhibited continuing hysterical symptoms expressed as physical weakness, difficulty in handling his Bren gun and inability to deal with his responsibilities.

Another sergeant developed persistent symptoms of acute anxiety, agitation, impaired concentration and withdrawal. All of the above were evacuated.

A junior fighting troop officer who had suffered severe battle stress, with several members of his section being killed and more wounded around him twice in one day while he himself, unwounded, was in grave danger, exhibited a preoccupying nervous anxiety, lack of conversation, a change in mood, and reluctance to take charge of his men, for a few days. His symptoms were discussed with him and he succeeded in overcoming them. Two and a half months later in another battle situation he again exhibited the same symptoms and it was considered that he should not continue in frontline duties. For years this officer suffered, not from the symptoms which are attributable to combat stress but from a feeling of failure, of inadequacy, which the psychiatric 'label' which had been attached to him induced in him. He did not blame anyone. He was reluctant to meet his ex-colleagues. In the light of what he had actually achieved his self-despising was quite unjustified. Perhaps he should have been retained in the unit with less onerous responsibilities. Any counselling should have concentrated on what he had achieved.

One other marine who had been in action continuously for a month was becoming nervous, anxious, preoccupied and withdrawn and it was thought appropriate to send him to a Battle Exhaustion Centre. He did not return.

All of these marines had volunteered, or been picked, for commando service and had gone through and passed the training and assessments necessary to ensure that they were physically fit and had the willpower to endure the physical and psychological stresses imposed in training. The different order of stress encountered in actual battle when the enemy was trying to kill and wound them, and obviously succeeding in respect of some of their colleagues, could not be replicated in training: it remained a largely untested dimension and there were apparently a few who could not endure such a challenge and remain effective fighting soldiers, at least without further rehabilitation. All had complained to the medical officer of their symptoms and all were evacuated.

A seventh marine reacted differently. He screamed whenever a mortar bomb landed near him. He did not complain at all and declared that he did not wish to be evacuated. As he could not control this symptom his presence was too disruptive for those around him to allow him to continue. His symptomatology seemed hysterical and may have been contrived, although his colleagues did not make this charge.

PROPORTIONS AMONG 47 RM CDO CASUALTIES: Over the seven-month period these were the only cases considered to be suffering from combat stress disorder requiring evacuation, giving, for all battle casualties who survived, an incidence of nearly 3 per cent (7/263) and for all battle casualties, including killed, and wounded, an incidence of 2 per cent (7/353)

PROPORTIONS AMONG ALL TROOPS IN 47 RM CDO: Over the seven-month period the incidence of combat stress disorder among all troops who served in 47 RM Cdo was 1.25% (7/560 − 560 is the number of original troops plus replacements who served over the 7 month period) or 1 in 80.

What of Combat Stress Disorder? Comments from the Battlefield

- At the war-time RAMC training depot in Leeds in 1942, Dr John Ryle, a distinguished physician and Professor of Medicine who had served for five years in the RAMC in the First World War addressed the most recent batch of embryonic military medical officers gathered before him on, 'Clinical Opportunities in Military Service'. He emphasised that it was nearly always 'general duties' doctors, not psychiatrists, who were the medical officers of front line battalions and that it was these, in the field, who had a special opportunity to observe at first hand, and try to understand, the psychological reactions of soldiers to the stresses of battle.

- The number of psychiatric casualties (so called 'battle shock') in the British Armies in WWII in North West Europe was 13,000 and one of the Army's Director's of Medical Services commenting in 1978 on the need to prevent such casualties commented, 'obviously the system is not a roaring success'. The RAMC's Professor of Psychiatry at a 'Realities of War' symposium in 1997 stated that 70 per cent of battle casualties and 70 per cent of psychiatric casualties occur in infantry; and that in land battles (in which infantrymen are primarily involved) psychiatric casualties comprise 20 per cent of the casualties. The military historian, Professor Richard Holmes, has recorded medical estimates of psychiatric casualties in the British Army in Europe as 10 per cent of all battle casualties on and after D-Day, rising to 20 per cent in the period July to September 1944 and then declining steadily to 14 per cent in October to December 1944, 10 per cent in January to March and 8 per cent in April to May. Clearly there is a significant difference between such figures and the 3 per cent of all of 47 RM Cdo's casualties who were psychiatric casualties. This difference is unlikely to be wholly accounted for by the selective recruitment of 47 RM Cdo or its high proportion of wounded and is worthy of further examination, particularly so as the British Army today, as a professional volunteer army, would be expected to have an incidence of combat stress no greater than that of a war-time commando. The question arises as to whether military psychiatry is over-diagnosing psychiatric disturbance in servicemen.

- 'Post-traumatic stress', 'post disaster stress trauma' and 'combat stress' are fashionable labels for something which has always been a part of life and of man's proclivity for fighting, being involved in accidents and having to endure experiences which cause emotional upset. Post trau-matic stress can manifest itself as psychiatric disturbance in someone who has suffered physical injury – *post physical*, or as psychiatric dis-turbance associated with profound personal emotion, such as the loss of a near relative – *post emotional*. Another relatively new sub-category of emotional stress is that claimed to result from the mere witnessing of a disaster (*post witness*) in which the complainant is usually seeking financial recompense.

- The terms 'combat stress' or 'battle shock' refer particularly to the emotional stresses of the battlefield. By any standard front-line fighting on the battlefield constitutes a stressful environment. For 47 RM Cdo, as with other front-line units the commonplace stresses were apprehen-sion, fear, pain, sounds and sights of a particularly threatening character, 'near misses', sleep deprivation, physical exhaustion, cold, wet, isolation, men in anguish – not infrequently the torn shattered bodies of comrades, continuity of exposure to risk, strict discipline, the threat of death. If in civilian life, under the heading of post traumatic stress disorder, many commonplace stresses formerly accepted as no more than part of life's vicissitudes such as work-related stresses, the witnessing of accidents, subjection to verbal stringency, and the hearing of bad news can be adduced as the justification for claiming compensation on the basis that they have caused psychological symptoms categorised as post traumatic stress disorder, the serving front line soldier who has been engaged in battle will, by such standards, have a much stronger case than most for claiming the military counterpart of post traumatic stress disorder, namely battle shock. If policemen with a professional responsibility for crisis management can successfully claim substantial compensation for post-witness traumatic stress, what effect will this have on the serviceman who has been stressed on the more threatening field of battle? Today's compensation culture, and largesse in civilian redress for those who successfully plead post-traumatic stress disorder, could be in danger of having an adverse effect on the attitude of serving soldiers to their profession and to their duties. Perhaps, however, the more recent realistic appreciation that the symptomatology of civilian post-traumatic stress disorder may well owe more to invention and to the creation of a socially useful psychiatric category rather than to genuine psychiatric illness[*] will remedy some of the civilian misconceptions regarding the effect of stress which, if applied in the military field could affect the fighting soldier's concept of his duties, and military morale in general. Perhaps the conclusion, in recent reviews of the outcome of treatment programmes for post traumatic stress disorders in Vietnam veterans,[†] that treatment had failed and had bred a population of veterans with a professional investment of being chronic cases and little else will provide a more realistic appreciation of the significance and value of a diagnosis of 'battle shock'.

- The expression of fighting qualities in a soldier is influenced by many factors including the degree of risk to which he is exposed; the depth, the duration and the frequency of his traumatic experiences; his sense of commitment to his 'mates', to the task in which he is engaged, to his unit; the number of casualties which his unit is sustaining; his understanding and appreciation of why he is fighting; his sense of duty and obligation to the community of which he is a part; his physical fitness and state of health; his self respect and desire to avoid any loss of respect in the eyes of his colleagues or family; his desire for recognition; his qualities of optimism or pessimism, of selfishness or unselfishness; his will power; and, of prime importance, that substrate so necessary in any good military formation, difficult to define but not difficult to recognise, the morale in his unit – possibly best equated to team spirit. Lack of commitment, reluctance to 'do his bit' in sharing a community burden, unwillingness to accept the risks which others are carrying, selfishness, laziness, lack of will power are not qualities which an 'opting out' soldier is likely to declare and, when these are the real motivating factors, psychiatric symptoms are more likely to be the vehicle, through which he chooses to declare himself. There are some in whom psychiatric disturbance renders them unsuitable for front-line soldiering but it is all too easy to accept on false premises, and to attach a pathological significance too readily to the psychiatric symptoms commonly experienced

---

[*] Summerfield, D., 'The invention of post-traumatic stress disorder and the social usefulness of a psychiatric category'. *British Medical Journal*, 2001; 322:95–98.

[†] Shephard, Ben, *A War of Nerves: Soldiers and Psychiatrists, 1914–94.* Jonathan Cape, London, 2001.

by soldiers and to label the complainant as a 'casualty', particularly if he wishes, for his own reasons, to be so labelled.

- Combat stress symptoms are not an 'all or nothing' phenomenon: there is a battlefield normality about many of the symptoms encompassed within terms such as 'combat stress disorder' and 'battle shock'. If every man in 47 RM Cdo had been questioned about fear, apprehension, periodic reluctance to fight, a feeling that he 'had had enough', a desire to withdraw, muted speech, excited loquacity or unusual irascibility, there are those who would have admitted that at times they had temporarily suffered from such symptoms, and the incidence of 'combat stress disorder' or 'battle shock' symptoms would have risen. But the marines did not go about talking about such things, preferring to leave to the media the absolutism of the 'fearless fighter' image so commonly accorded them. One of 47 RM Cdo's Sergeants, Roy Mansfield, who served with distinction as a troop sergeant continuously from D-Day until the end of the war in Europe recognised such symptoms and, where they occurred after battle, the need to recover from them as a normal process of 'limbering down': he understood their nature and their control. Sergeant Donald Gibson was a sensitive introspective man of great courage, seen as such in 47 RM Commando and formally honoured as such, but when, post-war, he described the inner feelings which he experienced in battle these revealed the anxiety, the nervousness and the reluctance to fight which he had to overcome. Such symptoms usually occurred after, not during, a battle. The majority of marines who experienced them came to terms with them, controlled them and continued to be effective, often better, soldiers experiencing a sense of satisfaction that they had 'coped'. A few who experienced these symptoms, particularly if they were of an introspective nature, could feel that they had a unique problem. In these, inappropriate psychiatric labelling could contribute to a misplaced sense of illness. If the frequency and, in battle terms, the normality of such symptoms is discussed with them, and indeed with all soldiers, particularly by an officer whom they trust, or by a medical officer who knows them and shares some of their stresses on the battlefield, many will come to terms with them, but if ill-considered pathological significance rather than explanation and understanding is too readily attached to such symptoms by civilian-orientated military psychiatrists who have never lived with troops on the battlefield, soldiers may be wrongly convinced that they have a psychiatric problem. In the interest of military effectiveness military morale and the serviceman himself the dividing line between normal stress symptoms of combat on the one hand and states, on the other hand where these symptoms have reached a point at which it is appropriate to consider them pathological, should be drawn with the greatest care and understanding.

- One of 47 RM Cdo's most dedicated fighting troop officers – severely wounded on D-Day, returned to serve at the forefront of two of 47 RM Cdo's most stressful battles, witnessed many of his comrades killed and wounded – was prompted post-war by presumptions of 'battle shock' to consider that as a result of the experiences he had come through he *ought* to have some psychiatric disturbance. He went to a civilian psychiatrist to find out. Fortunately, the psychiatrist, in uncompromising terms, told him that there was nothing wrong with him! So assured the officer went on to pursue a very successful career in civilian life.

- Men who have developed psychological symptoms and because of these are discharged from their unit or service can suffer in civilian life due to feeling loss of their own self respect and assumed loss of the respect of their erstwhile colleagues from whom they can feel ostracised. It is in their own interest and in the interest of the service that such men are given every opportunity to recover and return to duty, and are given supportive help quickly. A period of rest without labelling, or a diagnosis of 'battle exhaustion' without any derogatory implications, with a period of rehabilitation and return to duty is the most satisfactory solution if that can be achieved. The injudicious labelling of a soldier as 'a case of battle shock' with irreversible connotations can be a disservice to a man who may have done his best.

- Misleading pseudo-psychiatric terminology which is so readily taken up by some doctors, lawyers and the media can do harm to those about whom such terms are used. 'Mental scarring', vicariously implying irreversible physical damage to the brain where none exists, or 'burn out' implying irredeemable finality to processes that may be temporary, even 'flash back' ('cash back' as one cynic called it) to give mere recollection a more dramatic character, may be the emotive catchwords of the courtroom where the highest possible damages are being sought: but such fanciful terms are irresponsible and can stigmatise an individual in his own mind and in that of others quite inappropriately. As far as the military are concerned terms which only carry the implication of a temporary and recoverable disorder such as 'battle exhaustion', 'battle fatigue' and 'temporary combat stress' are much more suitable for the majority of cases where psychological symptoms following battle are involved. The currently prevalent term of 'battle shock' with its exaggerated overtones of inexorability and persistence should be defined much more strictly than it is and used very carefully.

- The long history of medicine is littered with confounded fallacious reasoning in which diagnosis based on the classical adage of *post hoc ergo propter hoc* has had to be abandoned when assumptions, based on the idea that because an event precedes an illness it must be the cause of it, have been proved to be quite unjustified. Two hundred years ago Samuel Johnson, Britain's greatest lexicographer, recognised this fallacy when he wrote, 'it is given to physicians above all men to mistake subsequence for consequence': in other words when the doctor applied a treatment to his patient and the patient got better, the getting better was certainly a subsequence (something which comes after) but not necessarily a consequence (something which comes after as a result of), as the patient might well have recovered, and often did, without the treatment. It is all too easy to invoke *post hoc ergo propter hoc* in those who exhibit symptoms of a psychiatric nature after military service and today's excessive indulgence in this practice is in danger of undermining the morale of serving personnel. Disorders of a psychiatric nature are very common. Often their true causation is not understood although factors such as genetic inheritance, childhood abuse, childhood neglect, parental divorce, a seriously disturbed social background, bullying at school, poverty and earlier childhood illness are among likely causative factors. Factors such as these exist in the life-history of many, including soldiers. Given an uncritical desire for proclaiming 'causes' it is all too easy to pick on a preceding 'stress', such as the stress of battle, when other factors may well have been far more significant and the real cause. Further, the constant uncritical acceptance of *post hoc ergo propter hoc* in relation to the possible effects of stress can be a form of auto-suggestion which can in itself contribute to psychiatric disturbance.

- One senior naval psychiatrist[*] who served in the Falklands campaign has written of the limitations of military psychiatry and of the overriding importance of morale and, by implication, of the factors which contribute to it – in dealing with battle stress.

> Without adequate leadership morale is defective. Where there is defective morale the incidence of psychiatric casualties goes through the roof. Trying to manage the problem by pumping in more psychiatrists and psychiatric nurses is like trying to manage a haemorrhage by pumping in blood as opposed to tying off the bleeding vessel. It is therefore crucial at all times that the military are reminded of the importance of addressing the issue of morale. Morale is a management problem not a medical problem

The climate of morale and interdependent trust among men created by military leaders at all levels is of primary importance in preventing

---

[*] Surgeon Captain M. R. O'Connell, Comment on Post Traumatic Stress Disorder in the Falklands War. *Scottish Home and Health Dept. Health Bulletin,* 53(6) November 1995.

combat stress disorder. Given that basis, it is for doctors at the regimental level to assist the military as far as they can in promoting morale and in ensuring that those who command men in the field of battle are closely involved in *medical* policy and decisions concerning the diagnosis and management of combat stress disorder in the men they command. The current run-down of the medical services of the armed forces makes such a joint responsibility in the field almost unachievable.

- There is a certain wantonness in proclaiming high incidences of 'battle shock' in front line soldiers and at the same time in exemplifying 'battle shock' as a cause of violence, murder and serious psycho-social crimes – as the media prompted by some psychiatrists, even military psychiatrists, does with the implication that soldiers who have served in the front line may be proleptic criminals. The notion that the 'combat stress' of the battlefield influences men towards violence dies hard. In the House of Lords on 1st June 1948 Viscount Stansgate in discussion of the Criminal Justice Bill then going through Parliament said: 'You cannot have commandos, people smearing themselves with blood and dancing about with bayonets without degrading the moral sense and reducing respect for human life'.

Replying next day to this apparent slur on commandos, the Lord Chief Justice said:

> In justice to the commandos, I want to say that in the 2½ years that I have held my present office – which involves my being President of the Court of Criminal Appeal – I suppose that at a low estimate I have had at least 500 or 600 cases before me. Naturally, many of these have seen service in the Army during the last war: but until last Monday week not a single case of a commando had ever come before my court. That is not only my own experience. I was told the same thing by one of His Majesty's Inspectors of Constabulary.

If a soldier or ex-soldier does commit a crime it is all too easy to blame his military training and/or experience as the cause.

- Those of 47 RM Cdo who suffered wounds were very anxious to have *medical* counselling at all stages about their wounds and about the possible outcome They sometimes found such a service lacking in adequacy and sensitivity. Few, if any, feel that they would have looked with any favour on today's enthusiasm for psychological debriefing programmes conducted by non-specific 'counsellors'. As the reactivation of the memory of traumatic events can be distressing the common practice of 'talking through' such events – psychological debriefing – on the assumption that this is beneficial needs more careful evaluation. There is increasing evidence that it may do harm and delay recovery.* Almost anyone can claim to be a so-called 'counsellor'. There is continuing need for critical evidence-based analysis of the risk/benefit effect of counselling and of the training, qualification and personality of those who practise it.

- Former members of 47 RM Cdo who were wounded have revealed no evidence of continuing *post-physical* stress injury. Few suffered subsequently from post-traumatic psychological symptoms and in no case were such effects considered to have *added* to the effect which physical post-traumatic disability had on their ability to work.

- To the individual soldier the 'cost' in war is not necessarily negative. The great majority of the members of 47 RM Cdo did not suffer from psychological symptomatology to any significant degree. Front-line battle is a test which can prove the courage of those who did not realise they had it, and demonstrate qualities of loyalty and dedication which civil life will not reveal: it can provide the opportunity for the quiet man to demonstrate initiatives and decisiveness which his demeanour and occupation might otherwise conceal and for the 'born fighter' to channel his aggression into activities which bring him renown, not censure. It can give a man a self-confidence, a capacity for self-reliance, a maturity which can serve him well in civil life. One wrote, 'This sharing in action and doing one's best remains a precious experience'.

---

* Justin Kenardy, Associate Professor of Clinical Psychology, 'The current status of psychological debriefing. It may do more harm than good'. *British Medical Journal*, 2000; 321:1032–1033.

Chapter Seventeen

Human Dimensions

COMMAND IN 47 ROYAL MARINE COMMANDO

Lt Col C. F. Phillips (later Major General Sir Farndale Phillips)

THE commanding officer is the most important member of a military formation. 'CF', as he was always known, was selected, straight from school aged 18, for entry into the Royal Marines in 1923 when the number of applicants greatly exceeded the number of places. Early in the war he served in ships and was on the aircraft carrier *HMS Glorious* when she was torpedoed off Ireland. He spent a year at the Staff College – that institution to which posting points to higher military command – from 1940, and after a number of training appointments was appointed commanding officer of 47 RM Commando as from 1st August 1943. 10th Battalion had reached a low ebb militarily and in morale and the arrival of CF had an immediate galvanising effect as he exerted his dynamic personality and gave the new commando a sense of purpose in training, in discipline, in self-respect and in charting its future.

When 47 RM Cdo landed in France on D-Day it was a well trained, well disciplined unit imbued with confidence in itself, largely thanks to CF. To mould a commando which had never been in action before and to succeed at Port-en-Bessin and at Walcheren as 47 RM Cdo did in the face of so many difficulties and set-backs was an achievement of command of a high order. CF remained commanding officer until after Walcheren when he left on promotion to Brigadier commanding 115 Infantry Brigade RM. As he pursued his military career he served in the Pacific as Fleet Royal Marine Officer, in Malaya, and as Chief of Combined Operations. He was promoted to Major-General and was knighted in 1957. On leaving the Royal Marines he became President of the British Trawlers Federation and as such plunged into another war – the Cod War with Iceland.

Planning for action and conduct in action reveal the qualities of a commanding officer. When CF was given the choice of a frontal assault on Port-en-Bessin or of a landing followed by a 12 mile cross-country march behind enemy lines he chose the latter and there are few who would doubt that his judgement was correct. He would study a problem, listen and consult, but once his mind was made up his decision was firm. At Battery W11 on Walcheren when the initial attack had not succeeded he was brought under considerable pressure by his superior officer the Brigade Commander, Brigadier Leicester, and the CO of 48 RM Cdo, Lt Col Moulton, to change his plan and remount an attack that night. Moulton considered that, given the circumstances, failure to do this would be a contravention of an accepted command tactic, but Phillips, with a more flexible, less stereotyped, concept of command adhered to his plan and captured W11 with minimum casualties in the morning. At critical moments his judgements both of what his commando could achieve and how it would achieve it were correct, realistic and fully vindicated.

The descriptive adjective frequently applied to CF was 'formidable'. He was tall, had a powerful, dynamic, commanding personality, was a strict disciplinarian and was decisive. He had a sharp voice, an inclination to an abrasive manner in speech, a demeanour which was austere and could be roused to anger. He could be, and often was, rude. In the mess he had a well developed sense of humour related often to the amusing occurrences within his own unit. He was intelligent and believed that it was his primary task to train his unit to the highest possible level, to plan, to maintain discipline, to give orders and to see that they were carried out. In dealing with

Lt Col C. F. Phillips (later Major General Sir Farndale Phillips).

his superior officers he could show moral courage in questioning orders. He also occasionally revealed a 'soft' side to his character, probably only when he was alone with one other: I believe that otherwise he felt that he should suppress this in the interest of maintaining the appearance of a man of inflexible will. Travelling with him in a Jeep on one occasion, we passed one of my medical orderlies carrying a basket of washing for a frail old Frenchwoman. CF expressed his appreciation warmly and gave me instructions to convey his commendation to the L/Cpl for what he had done. When I accompanied him to le Havre on the day after it was captured he was clearly very upset when he saw two women fighting in the street and trying to tear out each other's hair.

In the field, CF considered that, as commanding officer, it would not be in the interest of the commando for him to become a casualty and he avoided unnecessary risks. As the CO of a commando he was, of course, often at considerable risk but his philosophy regarding his rôle meant that he was primarily planner, director, manager, instigator and promoter. Such a rôle had to be complemented by devolved leadership of a high order at troop level. Fortunately with troop commanders such as Walton, Cousins, Flower, Vincent, Stickings, Spencer, Winter, O'Connell, O'Brien, Wood, Lloyd, Isherwood, McCormick, Moyes and Dobson, and splendid NCOs, 47 RM Cdo had that quality of leadership. In the harsh discipline of battle CF generated a drive which along with the many dedicated officers and men who served with him and were subject to his orders created a momentum which carried the commando to success.

CFs main criterion in dealing with his officers was, 'I judge by results' and by that criterion he himself was undoubtedly a successful commander. The unyielding application of such a yardstick of performance, however, could be unfair. Few of the battles of the type in which 47 RM Cdo was involved were, or could be, without elements of failure in the inevitable ebb and flow, the confusion and the chaos of battle. Yet any officer who did not achieve his objective, who made a judgement which although probably valid and conscientiously taken did not result in success could be harshly criticised. The criticism could include charges of lack of leadership and lack of resolution. Some of those criticised later performed outstanding acts of courage and leadership for which they were decorated but such harsh criticisms left their mark and could continue to disturb those who received them long afterwards.

It is one thing to make dispassionate objective judgements of those whose responsibilities you never carried and another to recognise subjective experiences. With his medical officer CF was entirely fair and straight and I had great respect for him and his ability as a commander. His task was not an easy one. He involved his 'surgeon' in all his planning but allowed me to run my own affairs and always gave me the support I wanted. Short on praise as he was he did on one occasion commend generously the performance which the medical section was putting up and the confidence which the marines had that, if wounded, the medical section would rescue them.

When last I saw CF, not long before he developed a fatal illness, he was full of enthusiasm for his Presidency of the British Trawlers Federation. As my wife and I sat with him at dinner in the North British (now the Balmoral) Hotel in Edinburgh he was obviously anxious to give us a short lecture on the assessment of quality in fish! Much of the old authority was there and we listened intently, but the unyielding autocracy which he had exhibited as a commanding officer had mellowed as he declared with some warmth that among trawlermen he had found that many were natural leaders and admitted that he had difficulty in keeping up with them let alone leading them. But the stern facade, the acerbity of speech and the stentorian reproof soon returned when the waiter served ice-cream on a warm plate!

CF died in 1961. Aware that the illness from which he suffered was terminal, he re-enacted his commanding officer rôle to the end, planning his funeral with military precision.

Lt Col P. M. (Paddy) Donnell

Paddy Donnell became second-in-command of 47 RM Cdo prior to D-Day and succeeded Lt Col Phillips as CO in January 1945. He had been commissioned in the Royal Marines in 1935 but while serving aboard *HMS Revenge* had changed his mind and bought himself out in January 1939. In a Corps priding itself in the tenet, 'Once a Marine always a Marine' his departure created quite a stir at the time. In the Royal Marine Reserve he was, of course, called back to the colours when war broke out. His style of command, exercised with quiet authority, was in contrast to that of CF, and complemented it. He played an important part in training 47 RM Cdo.

Paddy took part in all of 47 RM Cdo's actions. As second-in-command on D-Day he showed his capacity for decision when, with the CO, many men and much equipment missing, he took the decision to lead the commando off on its march to its objective, Port-en-Bessin.

Throughout the European campaign Paddy was a competent 2 i/c who combined quiet leadership with integrity and a strong sense of justice. His abiding interest in human nature and the problems of others made him a popular officer.

Major (later Lt Col) P. M. Donnell. Behind is Capt P. Spencer (Adjutant).

As CO at Kapelsche Veer the odds were stacked against him when his depleted commando, with many new recruits, short of ammunition, and at short notice found itself pitched against a fanatical enemy in well entrenched positions. Again he had to make a critical decision, which some criticised, but most commended.

Paddy was interested in dramatics. On demobilisation he was travelling to London by train when he noticed a lady sitting opposite him watching enviously as he munched his sandwiches. There was no restaurant car and, characteristically, he offered to share his sandwiches with her. She turned out to be the lady who ran the Shakespeare Memorial Theatre Company and by the time he reached London he was in line for an appointment there, eventually becoming General Manager. Later he became Chief Administrative Director of the National Theatre.

Regimental Sergeant Major Eric Wood

Eric Wood joined the Royal Marines in 1935. His competence as a sergeant in charge of training was recognised and when he volunteered to join the RM Commandos when they were formed his application was turned down for that reason. His chance came one morning in the first week of July 1944, however, when he was told to report to Col Phillips (back from France to select a new RSM after the capture of RSM Dollery) at 11 a.m. outside the Officers' Mess at Chatham. There CF asked him if he remained a commando volunteer. Assured that he did CF then ordered him to report back at 3 p.m. that afternoon to depart immediately for a two week spell of duty as RSM of 47 RM Cdo. Eric dashed back on his bicycle to tell his wife and obtain his new badges of rank. The two weeks proved to be nine months. During this time his wife was informed – on 4th November – that he was missing, presumed killed and received a follow-up letter confirming his death. He had in fact been wounded and dealt with at the RAP from which he duly returned to duty. There were several Lazarus-like cases of that sort. Somebody somewhere seemed to be taking the uncharitable view of the performance of 47 RM Cdo's RAP that if anyone who was wounded and reached it did not then appear among the names of those evacuated to medical units further down the line he must have died!

RSM Wood proved to be a man of high intelligence with a competence in man management derived from the high standard of his military professionalism, a quiet air of authority and fair dealing. As a regular NCO of the Royal Marines he was held in high respect not only by his fellow regulars but also by the 80% or so of the unit who were civilians serving on a 'hostilities only' basis.

Troop Sergeant Major Tynan

'Tiny' Tynan was the boxing champion of the Royal Marine Corps in his weight group and immensely popular. One morning he reported to his Troop officer Lt O'Brien who noticed that one side of Tynan's face was rather bruised. 'What have you been up to Sergeant Major?' asked O'Brien. 'Disciplining Marine Griffin Sir', answered Tynan (Griffin was a known 'bull terrier' type). 'And what about Griffin?' asked O'Brien. 'Unmarked Sir' was the low key answer. To the strait-laced officer – and O'Brien was anything but that – such 'goings on' would have been severely frowned upon but TSM Tynan was one of the most effective NCO's in the commando and had a special quality of leadership and command. Griffin would follow him anywhere and carry out his orders, if not to the letter, at least to completion, à la Marine Griffin.

Sergeants Ray Esther and Donald Gibson

Sergeant Esther volunteered whenever volunteers were called for. He epitomised fearlessness, the will to fight, leadership and aggressiveness in the face of the enemy. He was wounded three times, returning to duty in the minimum of time. At Walcheren, he was quite severely wounded and was evacuated to the military hospital at Ostend. After some time it was decided by the doctors there that he should be evacuated to England for convalescence. Next day he walked into the unit, having escaped from hospital and hitch-hiked his way back, to avoid being sent to England. His explanation of his conduct, strictly speaking a breach of discipline, left me in a dilemma when he explained with disarming charm, 'I would rather be looked after by my own MO than by a bunch of hospital doctors!'

In contrast Sergeant Gibson of the 'I' Section was a quiet, contemplative, highly intelligent, highly educated man. Destined for the church he could have escaped military service altogether. His physique put him on the borderline for meeting the criteria for commando service. Wounded on D-Day he was, on recovery, given the opportunity of continuing in less exacting duties but returned to the commando. During the war he rejected all suggestions that he should become an officer, but post-war accepted a commission as an education officer and in civilian life became a headmaster. He admitted that he was plagued with fear and spoke of 'the gay laugh which often concealed mortal fear'. But he controlled his fear to the extent that he never sought to shirk any duty, never complained, never failed to carry out any task allotted to him and did all well.

Both Esther and Gibson were decorated for their courage: the majority of the members of 47 RM Cdo lay between the extremes of successful commando personality which they exemplified.

The Front-Line Soldier

Of his first experience of battle as an infantryman in the front line D. C. Simpson* wrote:

> It was that morning that I had, for the very first time, a perception that the shelling and mortaring were not happening as an incident in my ordinary life, but that I had somehow gone through a door out of the real world I knew, where that sort of thing couldn't happen, into a separate world where it could.

Different forms of war-time military service involved different patterns of decision-taking. The member of a bomber crew, in flight over hostile territory, had to endure a short time of very acute anxiety over the target, possibly the sight of a plane containing his friends being shot down; and then a return to his home base. The sailor on a Murmansk convoy had to endure severe cold week after week and the prospect of ending in water at a temperature in which survival time would be measured only in minutes. The submariner might have to wait in claustrophobic silence on the bottom of the sea, threatened by the episodic boom of depth charges dropped from above with the object of splitting open the steel casing which was all that could now protect him. These operations varied widely but had one feature in common: it was the decision taken by one man, the bomber pilot or the ship or submarine captain which would determine communally the actions and the fate of all aboard whatever their rank or duty.

The nature of front-line soldiering is different. Decision-taking has to be a much more devolved process. The commanding officer can make plans and give orders but in the carrying out of these orders a great deal of decision-taking rests with his officers individually and this element of individual decision-taking has to devolve downwards through non-commissioned ranks to the individual soldier, who is not necessarily immune from decision-taking involving interpretation of orders. As Sir Arthur Bryant has put it:

> On the day of the battle everything turns, not as in a ship on the captain, but on the individual private.

The NCO could find himself in a position where, although operating within an over-all framework of command, he yet had to interpret his orders and make an individual discretionary decision – when encountering an unexpected enemy position ahead, on patrol when a change of planned route was necessary, encountering an unplanned opportunity for action,

---

* *Interesting Times: a Foot Soldier's Verses.* The Ramsay Press, Edinburgh, 2001.

deciding how long he would stay when left behind to give covering fire. But Sir Arthur Bryant's dictum did not apply equally to all in the Army. The higher ranks in the artillery made tactical decisions but the task of the individual artilleryman beside his gun was usually a technical, not a tactical one. The front-line infantryman on the other hand often had to combine the technical use of his weapons with tactical responsibility on how he should use and deploy them in a variety of different situations. This devolved decision-taking, implicit in the mobile nature of front-line infantry soldiering, must be based on understanding, trust, and mutual reliance among those who have to operate in this way. It has to be under-scored by disciplined conduct moulded by training to a high level of military competence supplemented by initiative and 'spirit' such as is recognised in commando medical standards.

Personality Traits

The members of 47 RM Commando were committed soldiers. The great majority had volunteered for commando service (at the end of the war there was a certain amount of posting) or had not taken advantage of the opportunity to leave 10th Battalion RM when it was converted into a commando. They wanted to be good soldiers. Many were quiet men whose outward bearing in civilian life prior to D-Day had demonstrated little or nothing of the determination, will power and courage which they would exhibit in battle: but there were a few 'wild men' among them. Amongst all, their motivation was too complex to be easily defined and they seldom discussed it: they disliked any attempt to uncover their inner emotions and seldom sought to analyse them, at least openly. If asked for their reasons for being in a commando they usually grunted rather embarrassingly that they weren't very sure or gave some trivial, or overtly facetious, reason. An objective observer might judge their motivation and actions in terms which would embarrass the marines as being sanctimoniously praiseworthy but such judgements would have been well justified. Many had a spirit of adventure and possibly a desire to take advantage of an opportunity to play a part in history as expressed by Shakespeare:

> And gentlemen in England now abed
> Shall think themselves accursed they were not here,
> And hold their manhood cheap whiles any speaks
> That fought with us (Henry V):

or would echo the words of the soldier, James Graham, Marquis of Montrose, spoken three hundred years earlier:

He either fears his fate too much,
Or his deserts are small.

The front-line soldier takes pride and satisfaction in the fact that he is the man who is actually fighting the enemy – coping with 'the terror of close combat' as it has been described. He knows that behind him there is a long train of services whose task is to support him and he recognises the essential rôle which they play but he does see a difference. One of our marines, who had been wounded and had just returned from what he considered the safety of a field hospital had been surprised to hear the staff there talking about being 'in the front line' because they could hear the guns well ahead of them. With astonishment he exclaimed on return, 'They are the same guns that we can hear far behind us'.

Various communal qualities provide the supportive substrate within which front-line soldiers are enabled better to carry out their duties. Two of the most important are comradeship and humour.

Comradeship in war develops to a depth probably greater than is seen in any other walk of life. In the heat of battle even the most diffident of men can become outgoing and establish relationships with fellow soldiers which otherwise would not occur and it is these relationships which so often sustain and embolden. Often men formed individual relationships in which they became very dependent, one on another, and would do anything for each other. This was often a uniquely bonding relationship and in the stresses and fears of the battlefield was of the greatest value. When, unfortunately, a 'mate' of this sort was killed outright, died of wounds or lay with gravely mutilating wounds the remaining member of the duo could be disturbed and saddened to a depth akin to the loss of a close relative. Sometimes a man would have irrational feelings of guilt that his 'mate' had been taken and he had been spared.

War can bring out the worst in men, it can also bring out the best. One of the best features of the British soldier is his capacity for humour and his ability to use it to raise morale in trying situations, whether from the boredom of living in slit trenches during a period of inaction or at the height of a battle with shot and shell flying in all directions. In helping men to make light of dangerous situations the Marines' humour was never offensive but could have a subtly helpful contrivance about it. In the Sallenelles area, for instance, there was a great deal of mortar bombing and shell fire on troops who were living in trenches. On many occasions during a mortar attack a man would be caught out of his trench in the open. As a mortar bomb screeched over he would flatten himself on the ground, ground which was often wet and muddy. When the bomb exploded – and if its shrapnel did not hit him – it added to his misery by spattering him with more mud and often adding grubby dishevelment to his woes. As the mud and debris settled and the mud-drenched and somewhat shaken victim dragged himself to his feet from a somewhat undignified horizontal face down posture his colleagues in the meantime had kept their heads down in the safety of their trenches. One or other of these safely entrenched colleagues would then raise his head and shout to the victim in somewhat disparaging tones, 'What's the matter with you?'. The victim was jolted from any sense of shock at his narrow escape as he cursed his colleagues for their lack of concern and their cowardly crouching in their trenches: but he knew what they really meant and so did they, and all felt better for it.

Marine Delap liked to draw, to produce cartoons of day-to-day events with which he amused his colleagues and sought to reassure his mother back home. A few of his cartoons have survived.

Marine George Wood, captured at Port-en-Bessin, was one of those who in his prison camp promoted the idea of pinning up anonymously on a notice-board headed 'Mail Bag Howlers', amusing extracts from letters written from home with every good intention. His 'Prisoners log' contained some of these:

From one of George's relatives:

'I was so thrilled when I received the telegram from your mother to say that you were a prisoner'

From a mother to her pilot son:

'I'm so glad you were shot down before flying became dangerous'.

From a grandmother:

'I am glad you have met some nice boys. I hope the Germans keep you there'.

From a father:

'Well son you have done something I did not do in the last war and live'.

From a friend:

'The first lot of 'repats' arrived home today, terribly maimed, I hope you are with the next lot.

From a girl friend:

'I hope you haven't transferred you affections'.

From another girl friend:

'Don't lose heart darling, you're nearly round the bend now'.

And yet another:

'I was out when the letter came saying you were missing which you will agree was a blessing.

Marine Delap's Cartoons.

Civilians Again

For six months, after the European war finished, 47 RM Cdo was engaged in civil administration in Germany, involved with the large number of displaced persons of many nationalities who were scattered across that country: many engaging in marauding activities at night and requiring policing.

During that time, as 1945 moved to its conclusion, drafts of those who had served longest were leaving the commando for demobilisation. For them, duty done, the civilian suit was now the important vestment. Finally in November the whole commando was posted back to England for disbandment and on 31st January 1946, at Haywards Heath, 47 Royal Marine Commando as an entity passed into history.

For some, handicap and determination in adversity were the sequels of war

At about 1 o'clock in the morning on 14th October 1939 a 21 year old Lieutenant in the Royal Marines J. T. E. VINCENT had just completed his spell as officer of the watch on board the battleship *HMS Royal Oak* lying at anchor in one of the Royal Navy's safest anchorages, Scapa Flow in the Orkney Islands. He had had nothing untoward to report. As he prepared to go below little did he think that, less than a mile away, among the surrounding shipping there was one ship that he had not seen because it was not on, but below, the surface of the dark waters of the Flow: nor was it of the British Navy, but of the German Navy, submarine *U47* commanded by Lt Gunther Prien. The latter had his eyes glued to the submarine's periscope. The view which was concentrating his gaze was the huge bulk of the *Royal Oak* and on her he was lining up the *U47*s torpedo tubes. Aerial intelligence had suggested that entry to the Flow might be possible through the narrow Kirk Sound and despite treacherous tides, and going aground once, Prien had navigated *U47* past the two sunken ships which blocked the Sound. Shortly, he gave the command 'Los' ('fire') and waited. A minute or so later there was a muffled explosion in the bow of the battleship, only one of the several torpedoes fired had found its mark. The Admiral and Captain aboard the *Royal Oak* were so confident of the security of Scapa Flow that they did not consider the possibility of a submarine attack, concluding that the explosion must be an internal one. Twenty minutes passed: aboard the *Royal Oak* there was still no thought that a German submarine close by might be reloading her torpedo tubes, but that is what *U47* was doing, astonished that there had been no destroyer depth charge response to the first attack. Again, in the submarine, 'Los' rang out. A few minutes passed and this time 3 or 4

Years later: Major 'Nelson' Vincent with L/Cpl Eric Thornton and Capt Forfar.

Marine Norman Fussell.

Peter Spear at his father's grave in Bergen-op-Zoom Military Cemetery.

Marine Ted Battley.

torpedoes ripped into the battleship. There was now no doubt about what was really happening.

In less than two minutes *Royal Oak* capsized trapping virtually everyone below deck. She sank in 13 minutes. From the deck where, fortunately, he was standing Lt Vincent was flung into the water. He was one of the lucky ones: 834 of the officers and men, including the remainder of the Royal Marine detachment, perished.

Lt Prien, now sure of success, had to move fast. The ships in the Flow had been stirred into action. At full 'steam' ahead he avoided an oncoming British destroyer and again *U47* crept silently, and successfully back through the Sound. Among its crew was a young submariner, decorated later with the Iron Cross like all members of the *U47*'s crew for that night's action. This would not be the last time that he visited British shores.

Before D-Day Vincent, now a captain, joined 47 RM Cdo and his activities as a troop commander have already been recorded. He was a professional Royal Marine officer and might well have reached the highest ranks in that Corps; but about 1700 hours on 2nd November 1944 at the moment when a German bullet struck him on the bridge of his nose, destroyed his left eye and emerged above his left ear the prospect of that achievement died. He lay at the Westkapelle gap under the influence of morphia awaiting evacuation, then for some days in hospital in Ostend before reaching England. For the next two years he was in and out of hospital for a series of plastic surgery operations. Lacking one eye, partially deaf, suffering from frequent 'black outs' and precluded from such activities as driving a motor car, his career in the Royal Marines was over. He was a man dedicated to service life, however, and he accepted a commission in the Royal Army Catering Corps, remaining there for fifteen years.

Returning to civilian life, still in his early forties, he remained proudly independent. With a patch over his left eye, a service background and no loss of the commanding personality he exhibited in 47 RM Cdo he was often addressed as 'Nelson'. As much for the interest of pursuing an occupation within the community as for augmenting his limited pension, he tried to keep himself busy with such tasks as his physical condition would allow, pursuing these and the eccentricities of his inevitably altered life-style with an admirable sense of humour.

Resident in Bognor Regis he joined Sainsbury's to serve in what he admits was at a low level in its hierarchy, responsibility for trolley arrangements. Trolleys were going missing and being found abandoned all over Bognor Regis, so he sought to introduce a scheme whereby shoppers would buy a refundable ticket for taking possession of, then returning, a trolley. The idea, attractive to the disciplined mind of a serviceman, was apparently too advanced for its time, even when Nelson added rather loftily that as a shareholder in Sainsbury's he was 'anxious to ensure the capital of the Company was not being wasted'. He lost the job. He was more successful with another form of employment. One summer he responded to an advertisement for someone to take an elderly lady confined to a wheel-chair for walks in the afternoon. Chair-pushing on a hot summer afternoon in Bognor is thirsty work but to his chagrin Nelson found that his charge was a committed teetotaller. Before the summer was out, however, the old lady on a hot day, and latterly also on not so hot days, was happily repairing with him to the 'local' for a shandy!

Years later when Major Vincent, ex 47 RM Commando, was enjoying a visit to the 'local' he got into conversation with a man who was a farmer and revealed that he had been a German POW who had been incarcerated in Britain and put to work on a farm. There he had formed a liaison with the farmer's daughter and, the war over, had married her and stayed on in Britain. 'What Service were you in?' asked Vincent? 'The Navy' was the reply. 'What branch? said Vincent. 'I was a submariner' was the answer. Vincent was mildly curious and then revealed that as a Royal Marine officer he had been on a British battleship the *Royal Oak*, which had been sunk by a German submarine with the loss of over 800 lives. The German stilled, an anxious frown crossed his face as he looked at the floor. After a pause he looked up and declared dramatically, 'I was a member of the crew of that submarine when she sank the *Royal Oak*'. I asked Vincent how he reacted to this remarkable coincidence. With characteristic nonchalance and lack of enmity towards another serviceman whom he saw as merely doing his duty he had merely said, 'Well Hun you can buy me a drink now'.

Marine NORMAN FUSSELL remembered advancing along a hedge on D-Day en route for Port-en-Bessin. He heard a shot and a cry and as he turned his legs gave way under him. He was aware that he was still being shot at and lay still but soon found that he could not move his legs and get up. He felt no pain yet a German bullet had smashed his femur, tracked round inside his pelvis, damaged his spinal column and emerged from his mid-lumbar region. He caused us worry because he had to be left near to where he had fallen along with the two others who had been wounded with him but were able to walk. He was probably among the wounded British soldiers seen by Mr Phillipe de Bourgoing at la Rosiére.

Fussell remembered nothing more until he found himself lying inside an LCT where someone was cutting off his trousers causing him great pain, and then in hospital in Ascot. His life thereafter was characterised by chronic, often severe, pain and a series of major operations: he required constant medication to try to control his pain and was largely confined to a wheel chair. As a man who had given so much, perhaps what he resented more than anything was the insensitive, insulting remark by a civilian doctor in an orthopaedic hospital who, looking at the wound in his back, asked somewhat cynically in what direction he was running when he was wounded. Fussell could no longer pursue his pre-war career in engineering and had difficulty in getting any job beyond clerking. Despite his severe handicap he was initially awarded only a 30% pension although this was later raised to 70%. He married in 1945 and his devoted wife looked after him with great care until he died a few years ago. He had accepted the lifelong disability which the war had imposed on him with equanimity and without rancour.

Marine TED BATTLEY, 20 years old, was wounded at Port-en-Bessin on 7th June 1944. While his section was engaging the defences of the Eastern Feature with Bren and rifle fire a mortar bomb exploded a few feet away. Battley felt a high pitched buzz in his ears and as he had been told that if he opened his mouth and let out a high pitched scream an explosion of this type would be less likely to damage his hearing he proceeded to do this. A fellow marine looked at him anxiously and, not realising that he had been wounded, Battley assured his friend that he was all right. He then looked down and saw that his trousers were stained with blood and torn and realised that he had sustained multiple shrapnel wounds of the legs. He was evacuated to England and made a satisfactory recovery. In August although offered the opportunity of not returning to the front line with 47 RM Cdo he elected to do so.

After the burns and severe compound fracture of his leg which he sustained at Walcheren on 1st November (Chapter 8) Battley was in hospital for eighteen months, for twelve of them bedridden. He endured eleven operations. He appreciates the kindness, accompanied often with a sense of gratitude, which he received in all the medical establishments he had passed through until that time and is still 'forever indebted to the military medics whose prompt action and thorough professionalism saved my leg and probably my life, and to the care of those at the London Hospital Annexe, Brentwood, who nursed me back to near normality'. While still on crutches he was transferred to the Royal Naval Hospital at Chatham where the beneficent character of his previous medical care was replaced by discourtesy, petty and senseless discipline, even hostility by male nurses who treated him as if he was a malingerer and gave him menial tasks to perform which were almost impossible to do on crutches. His War Pension Assessment 'was conducted by a naval officer whose prime rôle appeared to be to recommend the lowest sum possible, short of making a farce of the whole humiliating procedure'. During the 19 months he was under treatment he received no pay. These experiences led him to leave the service a 'rather embittered young man'.

Battley's fifty years and more post-war as a civilian have been characterised by frequent episodes of pain in his leg, 'it only takes a step too far, or a bag too heavy or a cold wet day to set off excruciating pain in the lower joints'. When his daughter was young he never felt that he could let her see his deformed wasted leg. A year after his discharge from hospital he began to experience disturbing nightmares in which he was being bombarded by shellfire; walking on water or floating in the air looking down on the battle. The nightmares were terrifying and it was a relief to wake up. At their worst, they would make him afraid to go to bed and to sleep. They never affected him during waking hours and he did not suffer from any of the other symptoms which have been attributed to post-traumatic stress injury (physical). As the years passed the intensity and frequency of the nightmares diminished and by the age of forty-five they had disappeared. Battley considers that, 'counselling or compensation would have made no difference, only a common sense acceptance and time were the healers'.

Ted Battley came from a family which was one in the mass of poor people living in the slums of London's East End. At school he did well and showed particular aptitude for art having his work shown at the Schools Exhibition at Whitechapel Art Gallery. There was talk of sending him to grammar school with a view to eventually going to Art College but this came to naught as his parents could not afford the cost. He left school at 14 undertaking a number of low paid jobs, but he was a frequent visitor to London's art galleries and museums, often walking a considerable distance there and back to visit them. Post-war, because of his injuries, he had to have a sedentary occupation. A turning point came when he joined the General Post Office (GPO) as a night telephonist at a large exchange which boasted a drama company. Utilised for scene painting, his work was seen by a lecturer from the local College of Art which offered him a job as a studio assistant with occasional responsibilities for teaching. A provincial theatre director then asked Ted to work for him: the stage manager of that company was Lannah who became his devoted wife. He retired early to pursue life as a full-time professional artist. Although entirely self-taught, he has achieved great success: his paintings now go all over the world. He set up a studio in Newcastle Emlyn in Wales and has given something additional to art by stimulating local interest in it by establishing the Emlyn Art Society.

Before Lance Corporal JOSEPH McGUIRE, RAMC, had his left leg blown off when he entered a minefield to rescue a marine who lay there wounded it had been his intention to return to his trade as a butcher, but when he was finally invalided out his lack of mobility proved too much of a handicap to continue. Instead he became a sedentary caretaker. Thirty-

The re-walk of the 47 RM Cdo approach march 53 years later. Local citizens, young and not so young, RM recruits and a few of those who had marched 53 years previously took part.

Captain Winter enjoying horse-drawn travel pleads with the 'doc' for 'excuse marching' on account of a sore foot.

three years later when I wrote to ask him how life had treated him he made no reference to the loss of his leg and uttered no complaints or regrets. His letter seemed to contain a note of undeclared satisfaction that he had done his duty and ended, 'I am content'. He died shortly afterwards.

PETER SPEAR, a successful oil-rig operative, stood with his mother among the invited visitors who attended the fiftieth anniversary of the Royal Marine landings at Westkapelle. The mortar bomb which had so quickly robbed Troop Sergeant Major WILLIAM SPEAR of 47 RM Cdo of his life had done more than that. It had robbed his wife and son of much of the happiness, the security and the ordered family life which might otherwise have been theirs. Peter Spear was seven months old when the 26-year-old father whom he had never seen died with his 10 Q Troop companions in the hollow on the Walcheren dunes. A bereft wife, then 22 years old, had later, but unsuccessfully, sought companionship and support by re-marrying. The adoptive stepson status acquired by her son led to a stressful, disrupted, penurious childhood. Four years of this childhood were spent in a charitable home, when his mother, again on her own, and against her wishes, was prohibited by the local authority from allowing her eight-year-old son to share with herself and her daughter the single room of council accommodation which had been allocated to them. As soon as he could Peter Spear changed his adoptive name back to that of his father. Fortunately, despite a peripatetic occupation, he achieved in marriage at the age of seventeen the stable and ordered family life which he had so long desired. As he stood many years later with his mother for the first time at his father's grave at the British Military Cemetery at Bergen-op-Zoom, there was no recrimination but only sadness and pride regarding the man whom the war had taken from them, and a feeling of final family reunion.

A New Generation Remembers

On the 53rd anniversary of the D-Day landings the pupils of College Hemingway, the senior school in Port-en-Bessin, under the guidance and inspiration of English Master Michel Désérable assisted by Mathematics Master Michel Laulier undertook a project of remembrance and thanks for what 47 RM Commando had done.

The theme name given to the project was '6–8 JUIN 1944 LA MARCHE D'APPROCHE DU 47È ROYAL MARINE COMMANDO POUR LA LIBÉRATION DE PORT-EN-BESSIN', a re-run of 47 RM Cdo's D-Day 12 mile march from the beach near les Roquettes to Port-en-Bessin.

The march was waved off from the commando's landing beach near Les Roquettes area by Monsieur Philip de Bourgoing the French Government Senator for the Calvados region and President of the Group of French

Senators dedicated to promoting Franco-British relations. The marchers included members of the local population from all over Calvados, a detachment of RM Commando recruits from the RM Commando Training Depot in England and a muster of as many of the original marchers as was possible – for whom it has to be admitted horse-drawn transport was available if required and proved not to be entirely redundant!

Six miles along the route the marchers reached a point where, fifty-three years earlier, 47 RM Cdo passed stealthily by the big guns of the Longues Battery which were hurling shells at the invading forces with booming defiance. The column on this occasion did not pass by. At the magnificent and historic Abbaye Saint Marie at Longues, owned and restored by Dr Georges d'Anglejan and his wife Marie Jeanne – daughter of a distinguished Frenchman who lost his life fighting with the Allies – the column turned into the beautiful Abbaye grounds to be entertained there in beautiful surroundings by the Anglejans. A sumptuous lunch included unlimited supplies of Calvados cider – consumed with abandon by the thirsty dehydrated marchers and with equal abandon by their quite adequately hydrated horse-drawn counterparts!

Proceeding onwards to Mont Cavalier (Point 72) the column then travelled by transport, including WWII Jeeps, to a welcome and reception by the Mayor of the Port, Dr Camille Huet.

For the College Hemingway students the project was not just a march and a historical re-enactment: it had a human purpose: to find out who these veteran commandos were when they landed fifty-three years ago; what part they had played individually in the capture of Port-en-Bessin; and what they had done since they returned to civilian life. The questions involved in achieving these objectives were asked on a one to one basis using tape recorders during the march and previous exchanges of letters on a student/veteran 'twinning' basis.

The answer to the first question was that most of those who had landed fifty three years ago were young men in their early twenties, some 19 years old and not much older than some of the students. Few had had much experience of life then, many had never been out of Britain or travelled far from where they had been brought up. They had been members of a generation swept up early in life on a tide of war and they had responded by addressing themselves to, and willingly accepting, the rôle of front-line sea-soldiers.

An attempt has already been made in Chapter 4 to answer the second question but this will have been be a very incomplete account of all that happened over the three-day period involved. There would have been many deeds worthy of record and of recognition which had been lost to posterity – those who carried them out had struggled, wounded and dying, in the

To the Everlasting Memory of the men of 47 Royal Marine Commando
who gave their lives in the Liberation of Europe 1944-1945
Port-en-Bessin, Sallenelles, Sannerville/Dozulé, Walcheren, Kapelsche Veer

Lt	Adam I.W.	14/1/45	Mne	Flannaghan J.	3/11/44	Cpl	Ripiner C.S.	2/11/44
L/Cpl	Andrews H. (10I.A.Cdo)	6/6/44	Mne	Fleet A.	7/6/44	Cpl	Robertson G.	14/6/44
Mne	Ansel R.E.	17/7/44	Sgt	Fletcher T.P.	7/6/44	Mne	Rowlinson C.	27/7/44
Mne	Ashcroft V.	28/10/44	L/Cpl	Fletcher W.R.D.	2/11/44	Mne	Sambrook W.D.	6/6/44
Mne	Bainbridge C.	6/6/44	Sgt	Fuller E. (10I.A.Cdo)	16/6/44	Mne	Scott F.L.	6/6/44
Mne	Baxter G.H.	7/6/44	Lt	Gardener M.C.	6/1/45	Mne	Smith B.G.	6/6/44
Mne	Bedworth H.W.	6/6/44	Mne	Goude M.H.	7/6/44	Mne	Smith J.	6/6/44
Sgt	Bee E.E.	6/6/44	Mne	Greenhalgh S.	14/1/45	Mne	Smith T.W.C.	17/7/44
Lt	Borne F.	11/8/44	Mne	Griffiths J.H.	8/8/45	CSM	Spear W.J.C.	2/11/44
Sgt	Bradley A.J.	7/6/44	L/Cpl	Grimsdell M.H.	2/11/44	Capt	Stickings B.J.	14/1/45
Mne	Breach E.T.L.	7/6/44	Mne	Guymer A.W.	16/12/44	Mne	Stovell W.C.	14/1/45
Sgt	Brehme R.H.R.	2/11/44	Lt	Hayward N.A.W.	2/11/44	Lieut	Style M.G.H. (Suffolks)	2/11/44
Cpl	Buchanan J.	2/11/44	Mne	Hubbard R.L.	1/11/44	Mne	Sweeney E.J.	6/6/44
Mne	Bunyan K.C.	6/6/44	Sgt	Hughes D.	6/6/44	Mne	Talton N.Y.	14/6/44
Mne	Cable A.V.	23/7/44	Cpl	Jenkins A.A.	7/6/44	Cpl	Teed K.T.	1/11/44
Mne	Carter A.	7/6/44	Cpl	Jones N.	7/6/44	Mne	Thatcher A.G.M.	2/11/44
L/Cpl	Catts J.H.	7/6/44	Mne	Kemp J.	21/8/44	L/Cpl	Towle W.H.	7/6/44
L/Cpl	Chatfield A.J. (RAMC)	6/6/44	Mne	Kinloch W.C.G.	6/6/44	Mne	Tull A.F.P.	7/6/44
Mne	Clark D.J.	7/6/44	L/Cpl	Lawton E.G.	2/11/44	Mne	Tullett D.A.R.	16/6/44
Mne	Collins J.W.	7/6/44	Mne	Longden A.	2/11/44	Mne	Turner A.	4/11/44
Capt	Cousins T.F.	7/6/44	Mne	Lumsden J.	6/6/44	Mne	Turner S.H.R.	6/6/44
L/Cpl	David E.N.	7/6/44	Mne	McGregor D.F.	2/11/44	Major	Tyndale-Biscoe W.J.	21/1/44
Mne	Davies A.S.	2/11/44	Mne	Maud N.S.	15/6/44	Cpl	Unsworth J.	2/11/44
Mne	Davies W.N.	18/6/44	Mne	Mills G.W.F.	7/6/44	Mne	Walker J.C.	14/6/44
Mne	Day J.E.	1/11/44	C/Sgt	Morley C.N.	20/8/44	Mne	Walker R.	7/6/44
Mne	Derrick M.	2/11/44	Mne	Muir J.	3/11/44	Major	Walton D.H. MC	4/9/44
Mne	Duke A.	2/11/44	L/Cpl	Nicholl F.	2/11/44	Mne	Waygood L.T.	6/6/44
Mne	Dutton C.	7/6/44	Mne	Norie G.	6/6/44	Sgt	Webb R.E.	2/11/44
Cpl	Dyke F.J.	14/1/45	Mne	Oates B.	7/6/44	Mne	Webb R.H.	1/7/44
Mne	Evans C.	14/1/45	Mne	Patey K.G.	3/11/44	Cpl	Webster E.G. (10I.A.Cdo)	6/6/44
Cpl	Evans E.J.	2/11/44	Mne	Payne H.	2/11/44	Lt	Whittaker G.B.	28/6/44
Mne	Evans J.E.M.	7/6/44	Mne	Pettit R.A.	2/11/44	Mne	Wilkinson R.M.	6/6/44
Mne	Fawcett J.	7/11/44	CSM	Plank H.H.	2/11/44	Mne	Williams R.	14/1/45
Major	Feacey J.R.	6/6/44	Mne	Pry B.C.H.	15/1/45	Mne	Wilson G.M.	2/11/44
Mne	Fee D.	2/11/44	Sgt	Puddick J.E.	2/11/44	Mne	Withington J.V.	7/6/44
Mne	Fellowes P.B.	7/6/44	Sgt	Rackham R.F.	2/11/44	L/Cpl	Young R.	17/7/44
Mne	Fewtrell C.J.	6/6/44	Mne	Redman W.	6/6/44	Mne	Zammit R.	31/12/44
Mne	Flaherty J.	6/6/44	Mne	Reynolds B.C.V.W.	25/8/44			

Opposite. 47 Royal Marine Commando Memorial stone in the Garden of Remembrance in the
Royal Marine Museum

To the Everlasting Memory of the Men of 47 Royal Marine Commando who gave their lives
in the Liberation of Europe 1944–1945

Port-en-Bessin, Sallenelles, Sannerville, Dozulé. Walcheren, The Maas, Kapelsche Veer.

Lieut Adam I.W.	14/1/45	Sgt Fletcher T.P.	7/6/44	Cpl Robertson G.	14/6/44
L/Cpl Andrews H.		L/Cpl Fletcher		Mne Rowlinson C.	27/7/44
(10 I.A.Cdo)	17/8/44	W.R.D.	2/11/44	Mne Sambrook W.D.	6/6/44
Mne Ansel R.E.	17/7/74	Sgt Fuller E.		Mne Scott F.L.	6/6/44
Mne Ashcroft V.	28/10/44	(10 I.A. Cdo)	16/6/44	Mne Smith B.G.	6/6/44
Mne Bainbridge C.	6/6/44	Lient Gardener M.C.	6/1/45	Mne Smith J.	6/6/44
Mne Baxter G.H.	7/6/44	Mne Goude M.H.	7/6/44	Mne Smith T.W.C.	17/7/44
Mne Bedworth H.W.	6/6/44	Mne Greenhalgh S.	14/1/45	CSM Spear W.J.C.	2/11/44
Sgt Bee E.E.	6/6/44	Mne Griffiths J.H.	8/8/45	Capt Stickings B.J.	14/1/45
Lieut Borne F.	11/8/44	L/Cpl Grimsdell		Mne Stovell W.C.	14/1/45
Sgt Bradley A.J.	7/6/44	M.H.	2/11/44	Lieut Style M.G.H.	
Mne Breach E.T.L.	7/6/44	Mne Guymer A.W.	16/12/44	(Suffolks)	2/11/44
Sgt Brehme R.H.R.	2/11/44	Lieut Hayward		Mne Sweeney E.J.	6/6/44
Cpl Buchanan J.	2/11/44	N.A.W.	2/11/44	Mne Tatton N.Y.	14/6/44
Mne Bunyan K.C.	6/6/44	Mne Hubbard R.L.	1/11/44	Cpl Teed K.T.	1/11/44
Mne Cable A.V.	23/7/44	Sgt Hughes D.	6/6/44	Mne Thatcher	
Mne Carter A.	7/6/44	Cpl Jenkins A.A.	7/6/44	A.G.M.	2/11/44
L/Cpl Catts J.H.	7/6/44	Cpl Jones N.	7/6/44	L/CplTowle W.H.	7/6/44
L/Cpl Chatfield A.J.		Mne Kemp J.	21/8/44	Mne Tull A.F.P.	7/6/44
(RAMC)	6/6/44	Mne Kinloch W.C.G.	6/6/44	Mne Tullettt D.A.R.	16/6/44
Mne Clark D.J.	7/6/44	L/Cp Lawton E.G.	2/11/44	Mne Turner A.	4/11/44
Mne Collins J.W.	7/6/44	Mne Longden A.	2/11/44	Mne Turner S.H.R.	6/6/44
Capt Cousins T.F.	7/6/44	Mne Lumsden J.	6/6/44	Major Tyndale-Biscoe	
L/Cpl David E.N.	7/6/44	Mne McGregor D.F.	2/11/44	W.J.	21/1/44
Mne Davies A.S.	2/11/44	Mne Maud N.S.	15/6/44	Cpl Unsworth J.	2/11/44
Mne Davies W.N.	18/6/44	Mne Mills G.W.F.	7/6/44	Mne Walker J.C.	14/6/44
Mne Day J.E.	1/11/44	C/Sgt Morley C.N.	20/8/44	Mne Walker R.	7/6/44
Mne Derrick M.	2/11/44	Mne Muir J.	3/11/44	Major Walton D.H.	4/9/44
Mne Duke A.	2/11/44	L/Cpl Nicholl F.	2/11/44	Mne Waygood L.T.	6/6/44
Mne Dutton C.	7/6/44	Mne Norie G.	6/6/44	Sgt Webb R.E.	2/11/44
Cpl Dyke F.J.	14/1/45	Mne Oates B.	7/6/44	Mne Webb R.H.	1/7/44
Mne Evans C.	14/1/45	Mne Patey K.G.	3/11/44	Cpl Webster E.G.	6/6/44
Cpl Evans E.J.	2/11/44	Mne Payne H.	2/11/44	Lieut Whittaker G.B.	28/6/44
Mne Evans J.E.M.	7/6/44	Mne Pettit R.A.	2/11/44	Mne Wilkinson R.M.	6/6/44
Mne Fawcett J.	7/11/44	CSM Plank H.H.	2/11/44	Mne Williams R.	14/1/45
Major Feacey J.R.	6/6/44	Mne Pry B.C.H.	15/1/45	Mne Wilson G.M.	2/11/44
Mne Fee D.	2/11/44	Sgt Puddick J.E.	2/11/44	Mne Withington J.V.	7/6/44
Mne Fellowes P.B.	7/6/44	Sgt Rackham R.F.	2/11/44	L/Cpl Young R.	17/7/44
Mne Fewtrell C.J.	6/6/44	Mne Redman W.	6/6/44	Mne Zammit R.	31/12/44
Mne Flaherty J.	6/6/44	Mne Reynolds			
Mne Flannaghan J.	3/11/44	B.C.V.W.	25/8/44		
Mne Fleet A.	7/6/44	Cpl Ripley G.O.	2/11/44		

Queen Elizabeth (the Queen Mother) unveiling the Commando Memorial near Spean Bridge on 27th September 1952. Beside her (in kilt) is Lord Lovat. (*The Scotsman*)

sea or fought and died in obscure corners or by-ways of the battlefield. The recollections of many no longer alive would have died with them. The accounts given by those present were likely to have been characterised by understatement of their own achievements; avoidance of disturbing discussion on for instance the loss of a 'mate'; a preference for recalling the humorous rather than the sad; difficulty in communicating to a generation brought up in relative peace many of the extremes of human feeling aroused in the maelstrom of war.

The liberators were seen by the College Hemingway students as a unique group of historically significant men and they were so treated, but what the students did find out was that these same liberators, whatever their special significance might be, were no supermen but a group of very ordinary Britons. Over five decades of post-war civilian life they had pursued occupations and life-styles which did no more than represent an average cross section of the community from which they came. As the veteran 47 RM Commando marchers approached Port-en-Bessin it was not only that march but most of their march of life which was now over. Ordinary citizens they were but they had happened to be part of a generation which was called upon to carry a particularly heavy responsibility at a time of national crisis. Perhaps they felt that the values of their generation had been too lightly brushed aside as succeeding generations rushed to modernity and to lifestyles in which insubstantial trappings, 'the quick fix' and 'spin', seemed to be assuming increasing importance and in which so much emphasis was on rights and recompense rather than responsibilities. They found it greatly encouraging that a group of the youngest generation, from Port-en-Bessin, was anxious to look back to the act of liberation from which it had benefited, to interest themselves in how that had been achieved and to seek out and understand the values of those who had achieved it. War may divide generations but the College Hemingway Project bridged at least one divide.

Bibliography

After the Battle, Number 36, Walcheren. 1982; Battle of Britain International Ltd, Church House, London.

Bruce Lockhart, R. H. *The Marines Were There.* 1950; Putnam, London.

Butcher, H. C. *Three Years with Eisenhower.* 1946; William Heineman, London and Toronto.

Churchill, Winston. *The Second World War, Vols I–IV.* 1948–1954; Cassell & Co. Ltd, London.

Cowles, Virginia. *The Rothschilds, a Family of Fortune.* 1973; Weidenfeld & Nicolson, London.

Crew, F. A. E. *The Army Medical Services. Vol 10.* 1962; Her Majesty's Stationery Office, London.

D'Este, Carlo. *Decision in Normandy.* 1984; Pan Books Ltd, London.

Dear, I. *Ten Commando 1942–45.* 1985; St Martin's Press, London.

Ellis, L. F. *Victory in the West. Volume I, The Battle of Normandy.* 1962; Her Majesty's Stationery Office, London.

Ellis, L. F. *Victory in the West. Volume II, The Defeat of Germany.* 1968; Her Majesty's Stationery Office, London.

Forfar, J. O. 'The Battle for Port-en-Bessin'. *Proc. R. Coll. Physicians Edinb.* 1994; 24:218–246.

——, '"… But Our Patrols are Out": Medical and Military Brinkmanship at the Normandy Bridgehead and a Royal Rescue'. *Proc. R. Coll. Physicians Edinb.* 1998; 28:229–245.

——, 'The Battle for Walcheren'. *Proc. R. Coll. Physicians Edinb.* 1995; 25: 451–475.

48 Royal Marine Commando: The Story 1944–46. Published privately.

Giorgano, G. N. *World War Two Military Vehicles.* 1994; The Book Package Co. Ltd.

Hamilton, Nigel. *Monty, Master of the Battlefield, Vols I, II, & III.* 1983; Hamish Hamilton, London: 1987; Sceptre Books, London.

Hastings, M. *Overlord.* 1984; Michael Joseph, London.

Hibbert, C. *The Recollections of Rifleman Harris.* 1998; The Windrush Press, Moreton-in-Marsh.

Hillsman, John B. *Eleven Men and a Scalpel.* 1948; Columbia Press, Winnipeg.

Holmes, Richard. *Firing Line.* 1985; Cape, London.

Horrocks, Sir Brian. *Corps Commander.* 1977; Sidgwick and Jackson, London.

Howard, M. R. 'Walcheren 1809: a medical catastrophe'. 1999; *British Medical Journal;* 319: 1642–1645.

Howarth, David. *The Shetland Bus.* 1955; Collins, Fontana Books, London.

Imperial War Museum Archives. London.

Joint Services Command and Staff College Reports.

Keegan, John. *A History of Warfare.* 1994; Pimlico, London.

Keegan, John. *Six Armies in Normandy.* 1994; Pimlico, London.

Ladd, James. *The Royal Marines 1919–1980: an Authorised History.* 1980; Jane's Publishing Company, London.

Mitchell, R. *They did what was asked of them.* 1996; Firebird Books, Poole, Dorset.

Montgomery of Alamein, Viscount. *The Memoirs of Field-Marshal Montgomery.* 1958; Collins, London.

Moulton, J. L. *The Battle for Antwerp.* 1978; Ian Allan Ltd, London.

——, *Haste to the Battle.* 1963; Cassell, London.

Persico, Joseph E. *Nuremberg, Infamy on Trial.* 1994; Allison and Busby, London.

Public Record Office Archives. London.

Rawling, Gerald. *Cinderella Operation.* 1980; Cassell, London.

Roitero, D. L. *Fall Braun/De stridom Kapelsche Veer 1944–45.*1991; H Gianotten, Tilburg.

Saunders, H. StG. *The Green Beret.* 1949; Michael Joseph, London.

Snyder, L. S. *Encyclopedia of the Third Reich.* 1998; Wordsworth Editions Ltd, Ware, Hertfordshire.

Taylor, Telford. *The Anatomy of the Nuremberg Trials.* 1993; Bloomsbury Publishing Ltd, London.

Thomson, R. W. *The Eighty Five Days.* 1957; Hutchinson, London.

Van der Zee, Henri. *The Hunger Winter – Occupied Holland 1944–45.* 1982; Jill Norman & Hobhouse Ltd, London.

Warner, Philip. *Horrocks – The General Who Led From the Front.* 1985; Sphere Books, London.

Whitaker, W. D. and S. *The Battle of the Scheldt.* 1984; Souvenir Press, London.

Wilmot, Chester. *The Struggle for Europe.* 1952; Collins, London.

Index

Where appropriate, page references are chapter-grouped with a semi-colon
and enlarged spaces between groups
Mne = Marine